The
Road
to
ROMANIAN
INDEPENDENCE

The
Road
to
ROMANIAN
INDEPENDENCE

Frederick Kellogg

Purdue University Press
West Lafayette, Indiana

99   98   97   96   95   5   4   3   2   1

The paper used in this book meets the minimum requirements of American National
Standard for Information Sciences—Permanence of Paper for Printed Library
Materials, ANSI Z39.48-1984.

Printed in the United States of America
Design by Anita Noble

Library of Congress Cataloging-in-Publication Data
Kellogg, Frederick.
       The road to Romanian independence / Frederick Kellogg.
           p.   cm.
       Includes bibliographical references and index.
       ISBN 1-55753-065-3 (alk. paper)
           1. Romania—Politics and government—1866–1914. 2. Romania—Foreign
       relations—1821–1914. 3. Nationalism—Romania. I. Title.
       DR246.K45 1995
       327.498—dc20   94-38654
                                                                              CIP

For
PATRICIA

Contents

Illustrations

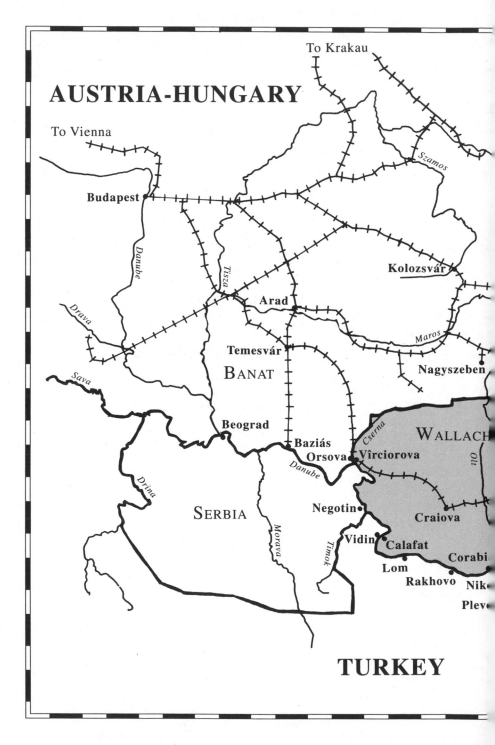

AUSTRIA-HUNGARY

To Krakau

To Vienna

Budapest

Danube

Drava

Szamos

Tisza

Kolozsvár

Arad

Maros

Temesvár

BANAT

Nagyszeben

Sava

Beograd

Drina

Baziás

Orsova

Cserna

Vîrciorova

WALLACH

Oltu

Danube

SERBIA

Morava

Negotin

Craiova

Timok

Vidin

Calafat

Corabi

Lom

Rakhovo

Nik

Plev

TURKEY

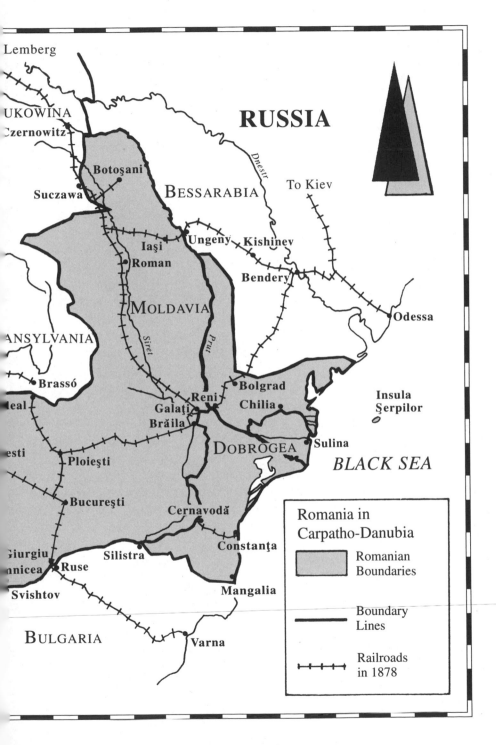

Lemberg

UKOWINA

Czernowitz

RUSSIA

Botoşani

Suczawa

BESSARABIA

To Kiev

Dnestr

Iaşi

Roman

Ungeny

Kishinev

Bendery

MOLDAVIA

ANSYLVANIA

Siret

Prut

Odessa

Brassó

Reni

Bolgrad

Chilia

Insula
Şerpilor

eal

Galaţi

Brăila

esti

Ploieşti

DOBROGEA

Sulina

BLACK SEA

Bucureşti

Cernavodă

Giurgiu

nicea

Ruse

Silistra

Constanţa

Svishtov

Mangalia

BULGARIA

Varna

Romania in
Carpatho-Danubia

Romanian
Boundaries

Boundary
Lines

Railroads
in 1878

Preface

My thoughts first turned to Southeast-
ern Europe in the wake of World War II and the dramatic changes it unleashed.
Grasping the complex situation there with the societal transformations and
shifting frontiers required more information than I could glean from newspapers. I looked to scholarly and travel accounts for help and became enthralled
by the fashioning of new states after World War I. I felt an investigation of
yet more remote ages might assist in gaining more understanding.

Thus began my intellectual odyssey back to antiquity and then forward to modern times. Romania stood out initially due to its name—suggesting the Roman Empire—its location, and its culture. I unearthed rather
little about this country in local libraries, antiquarian book shops, and pres-
tigious halls of learning. The Cold War kept me from visiting Carpatho-
Danubia, but I managed to pursue my studies abroad. I encountered
fascinating materials about Romania's economic and political affairs in London and Paris. Vienna offered even more valuable data, and a sojourn in
Sigmaringen provided additional insights. After starting to write up my dis-
coveries, I participated in the first United States-Romania cultural exchange.
In Bucharest, I came upon rich collections of correspondence. Subsequent
stays in Romania, Russia, and Moldova also proved highly rewarding.

The following chapters reflect my findings on Romania's quest for
independence from 1866 to 1880. I selected themes illustrating the Danubian
Romanians' aspirations and concerns regarding their principality, surrounded
as it was by three empires. But I eschewed examining the roles of peasants
and industrial workers as being tangential to my focus on Romania's place
in the international milieu. The reader may nevertheless sample in my pages
some challenges and triumphs that many Romanians experienced in winning a sovereign state.

Transliteration note. Cyrillic and Modern Greek letters have been transliterated to the Roman alphabet according to modified versions of systems used
by the Library of Congress. Names of Bulgarian persons, places, and publications in the text and footnotes—as well as locations on the map—are in
the orthographic style adopted in 1916; Russian words are in the post-1918
orthography.

Geography note. On the map of Romania in Carpatho-Danubia, some names are in conventional English—such as Moldavia (Moldova), Wallachia (Ţara Românească), Transylvania (Erdély), Bucharest (Bucureşti), and the Danube River. Other rivers and towns on the map are in the official languages of the times: Magyar in Transylvania and the Banat, German in Bukowina, transliterated Russian in northern Bessarabia, and Romanian in Romania—including Southern Bessarabia and Dobrogea. In the text and footnotes, Carpatho-Danubian names are in official languages with Romanian appelations sometimes in parentheses, such as Bukowina (Bucovina). Toponyms outside this region are in official languages, or in conventional English with official languages occasionally in parentheses—such as Constantinople (İstanbul).

Currency note. In the mid-1860s, the Danubian Romanians' piastru was worth 0.4386 French franc, that is, 4.18 British pence (£.02) or 8.50 American cents ($.09). In 1867 Romania adopted principles of the Latin Monetary Union and set its new leu on a par with the French franc. One Romanian leu or one French franc was then equal to 9.54 British pence (£.04), or 19.38 American cents ($.19). Other currencies used in this book include: the Austrian ducat—12 lei/francs, 9 shillings 4 pence (£.47), $2.28; the Russian ruble—4 lei/francs, 2 shillings 1.5 pence (£.11), $.51; and the German mark—1.25 lei/francs, 11.75 pence (£.05), $.24. These conversions do not, of course, reflect the dynamics of international exchange rates during the 1870s.

Calendar note. Danubian Romanians used the Julian calendar (until 1919), as did Bulgarians, Serbs, Russians, and Greeks. During the nineteenth century, it was twelve days behind the Gregorian, or New Style, calendar used in Austria-Hungary, France, Germany, Italy, and Great Britain. A solidus (/) separates Julian from Gregorian dates in my text and footnotes. Single dates for Romania and the Balkans are ordinarily in the Julian calendar, and in the Gregorian for the West.

Acknowledgments

Financial support was indispensable for my research in Romania and elsewhere. Aid came from the American Council of Learned Societies; the International Research and Exchanges Board; the U.S. Department of Education: Fulbright-Hays; and the University of Arizona Graduate College and Faculty of Social and Behavioral Sciences. My father-in-law, Kent Hanbery, helped fund my earliest studies abroad. Ross N. Berkes at the University of Southern California was a brace upon my return.

Librarians and archivists in Romania were extraordinarily cooperative. Especially so in Bucharest were Fila Mihai in the manuscript and correspondence section of the Biblioteca Academiei Române, and Viorica Secarescu in the manuscript collection at the Biblioteca Naţională României. Useful as well were deposits in the Arhiva Statului and Arhiva Ministerului Afacerilor Externe. No less vital were my stimulating discussions with fellow historians—Cornelia Bodea, Andrei Oţetea, and many others.

Robert Stropp and his colleagues in Vienna furnished assistance at the Haus- Hof- und Staatsarchiv, while Johannes Maier in Sigmaringen did likewise at the Fürstliches Hohenzollernsches Haus Archiv. I found important materials in Paris at the Archives du Ministère des Affaires Étrangères, the Bibliothèque de l'Alliance Israélite Universelle, and the Bibliothèque Nationale. Liudmila A. Mandrykina showed me manuscripts at the Russkaia natsional'naia biblioteka in St. Petersburg; librarians were obliging in Moscow at the Russkaia gosudarstvennaia biblioteka, and in Kishinev for publications on Bessarabia at the Institut de istorie of Moldova. In London, the Public Record Office and British Library afforded much of value. Credit is due to William N. Medlicott at the Institute of Historical Research and Reginald R. Betts at the School of Slavonic and East European Studies for pointing the way. Later, Charles and Barbara Jelavich at Indiana University extended a capital hand. Highly significant also were files of Germany's Hauptarchiv des Auswärtigen Amtes on microfilm at the University of California in Berkeley, as were books and periodicals in a myriad of American libraries.

A bevy of resourceful librarians at the University of Arizona, such as Andrew L. Makuch, facilitated my investigations by locating and acquiring essential volumes. Another librarian and friend, Rebecca Watson-Boone, provided tools for my writing. The map of Romania in Carpatho-Danubia was drafted by Michael W. Longan—aided by David K. Adams and supervised by Stephen R. Yool. A visiting scholar from Iaşi, Laura Cuţitaru, carefully checked some bibliographic entries. Patricia A. Foreman skillfully converted my manuscript's format to one that was fit for the publisher. My daughter, Kristine Marie Calvert, cheerfully and graciously abetted my endeavors. My deceased wife patiently and accurately turned my scribbles into a coherent form that could be easily revised. To these individuals, and many more too, I am deeply indebted. All infelicities and errors in the text are, of course, my own.

Chapter One
INTRODUCTION

In the nineteenth century, after more than four centuries of Turkish suzerainty, Romanians seized opportunities afforded by the diplomatic milieu and military campaigns in Europe to create their own fully sovereign state. The Romanians' quest for independence deeply immersed their affairs in those of the European great powers. What drew the powers' attention to Southeastern Europe? And what was the nature of Romanian patriotism? The interplay of Romanian national ambitions and endeavors in modern times, on the one hand, and the powers' designs and policies regarding Romanian-inhabited areas, on the other, deserve comment.

Romanian patriotic sentiments stemmed primarily from romantic and liberal concepts that formed the core of Western thinking during the nineteenth century.[1] Romantic musings upon the past led Romanians in the Habsburg Empire, especially the Uniate scholar-priests of Transylvania, to recognize the common provenance and fundamental Latinity of the Romanian-speaking people. Uniate Christians, who had turned to Rome for ecclesiastical guidance by the late seventeenth century, were the first to emphasize the Romanians' Roman origin, citing classical sources as evidence to confirm their Latin genesis. One sign of this current in the nineteenth century was the substitution of Latin letters for the Old Church Slavonic alphabet, which had been the Romanians' transmission line for the Gospels and writings of the church fathers from the medieval era to the modern.

Eddies of romantic national convictions coursed from Transylvanian Romanians through Carpathian mountain passes to fellow Romanians in the Danubian principalities of Moldavia and Wallachia, where they blended with liberal rivulets. Those landed aristocrats who had been educated in Western Europe during the middle of the nineteenth century understood liberalism to encompass freedom of association based on equality of rights as well as self-government in accordance with the secular rule of law. Such Romanians readily adopted the notions of their Transylvanian brothers and sisters about the Latinity and continuity of their nationality. They also sought to control their own destiny, free from the suzerainty of the Ottoman Empire and the meddling of neighboring Austria and Russia. They wished moreover to retain their Orthodox Christianity, rejecting a religious union with

Catholic Rome, unlike some Romanians in Transylvania. Hence, Danubian Romanians dreamed of an independent nation-state in which their traditions would be preserved and strengthened.

The road to Romanian independence began in Moldavia and Wallachia rather than in Transylvania. Romanians in Transylvania would remain in Austria until that empire's collapse in World War I, notwithstanding their initiation of Romanian patriotic stirrings. Transylvanian Romanians indeed failed to make common cause with Danubian Romanians; Austria's military might, comparatively secure economic position, and advanced cultural level made them less anxious to change the status quo, despite the divisive effect of the Magyarization policy upon the ethnic minorities of Transleithania after the Austro-Hungarian Ausgleich of 1867. Danubian Romanians, however, lacked vested interests in the relatively backward economy and culture of the Ottoman Empire, and they disparaged the conventionalism of Turkish society, which they reckoned to be the antithesis of progress. So it was in Moldavia and Wallachia that Romanians first consciously started to break with the past so as to achieve national goals, and their efforts commenced the building of a Romanian state.

The Romanian state-making process embraced five major stages: first, the growth of national awareness, sprouting in the abortive 1848 rebellions; second, the joining of Moldavia and Wallachia in 1859; third, the accession of a foreign prince in 1866; fourth, the winning of sovereignty in 1880; and fifth, the completion of ethnic unity following World War I. During the third and fourth stages, which constitute the focus of our study, the powers of Europe repeatedly intervened in Danubian Romania's internal affairs and, by so doing, unintentionally inspired patriotic visions, encouraging Romanians in their pursuit of independence.

The European powers—Austria, Russia, France, Great Britain, Sardinia/Italy, and Prussia/Germany—which collectively guaranteed the existence of Danubian Romania from 1856 to 1878, together with the suzerain Ottoman Empire, had their own discrete political, economic, military, religious, and humanitarian concerns in Southeastern Europe. To identify these concerns and to locate Romania's place in the international arena, I shall now briefly delineate the origin and course of each power's association with Danubian Romania.

For the Ottoman Empire, Danubian Romania was a buffer zone during the third quarter of the nineteenth century. This was an inveterate situation. Muslim Turks of the Ottoman Empire (1300–1922) had taken advantage of the waning Byzantine Empire (325/330–1453) and had invaded the Balkan

Peninsula in the early fourteenth century, about the same time that Romanians formed their first independent principalities north of the Danube River in Wallachia (ca. 1310–ca. 1416) and Moldavia (1359–1456). Turkish victories in Southeastern Europe eventually engendered Turkish suzerainty over Wallachia around 1416 and Moldavia by 1456, a status that lasted until 1877. As a consequence, Romanian princes paid an annual tribute in coin and kind to Turkey in addition to assisting the Ottoman sultan's armies in wartime. Moreover, the Turks monopolized Romanian commerce until 1829: Romanians sold their livestock and crops solely to the Turks at fixed, marginal prices. But Moldavia and Wallachia were not fully integrated into Turkey as *paşalıks,* or provinces, nor was the *devşirme,* or boy-tax, levied on Romanians as it was on the Balkan Slavs. Further, Turks lacked the right to own property in the two principalities. Christian Romanians, in fact, enjoyed administrative autonomy, freedom of worship, and military protection owing to the shield they afforded against some of the Turks' enemies in Europe as well as to the Turks' reliance on Romanian money, millet, and meat.

The Ottoman Empire's westward thrust challenged Austria at the very moment that the Protestant Reformation disrupted the secular and spiritual repose of Europe. The Habsburg Empire (1452–1918) emerged as the champion of Catholic Christianity against Protestantism and Islam in the early modern era. The Austrian Habsburgs initially considered Orthodox Romanians to be potential allies; they thought that Catholic and Orthodox Christians, estranged since the great schism of 1054, might reconcile ecclesiastically and unite militarily to take up the Turks' gauntlet. Prospects for joint Christian efforts diminished, though, following the Turkish triumph at Mohács in 1526 and the Ottoman sultan's investment of Vienna in 1529. The Turkish conquest and control of Hungary (1541–1699) and Transylvania, indeed, effectively blocked cooperative essays by Austria and the Transylvanian Romanians. Ongoing divisions in the Islamic world, to be sure, turned the Sunni Turks' attention to the rising power of the Safavid dynasty (1501/2–1736) in Shia Persia, thereby benefiting the cause of European Christians. But while the first Turkish siege of Vienna in 1529 had spread Ottoman hegemony over much of Central Europe and assured Protestant success in Western Europe, the failure of the second assault in 1683 signaled the impending end of the Turkish threat and, concomitantly, the beginning of Austria's expansion in Eastern Europe. Austria acquired Hungary (1699–1918) with Transylvania by the Austro-Turkish Treaty of Karlowitz in 1699. Some Danubian Romanians worried henceforth about the prospect of being engulfed by Austria, being shackled by the Austrian administrative system—which was deemed to be far more pervasive than that of the Turks—or being drawn into the recently created Uniate Church (1698–1948) of some Transylvanian Romanians. The Austrian menace became tangible in the Turkish cession of Oltenia (1718–39), or western Wallachia, to Austria by the Treaty of Passarowitz (1718) and in the later Austrian occupation of Bukowina (Bucovina) (1775–1918) in northern Moldavia. Austria was, however, soon to return Oltenia to the Ottoman Empire, in accordance with the Treaty of Belgrade (1739), because of the ascending influence of Russia in Southeastern Europe plus the persisting vitality of the Turks. Instead of seeking to annex Moldavia and Wallachia, Austria next endeavored to employ the Danubian Romanians as a bulwark against Russia's aggrandizement in the Balkan Peninsula. Austria's policy in general, then, was to preserve the territorial integrity of the Ottoman Empire during the nineteenth century, particularly after the Austro-Hungarian Ausgleich of 1867 formed a dual monarchy in which Hungarian bureaucrats governed Transylvania (1867–1918). Danubian Romanian patriots therefore found little support for their state-building cause in the Habsburg Empire.

The Romanov rulers of Russia (1613–1917) recognized their need for ice-free ports on the Black Sea, owing to the inefficiency of exporting and importing goods through their often ice-bound windows on the Baltic and White seas. The drive to the south by Orthodox Christian Russians led inexorably to contact with Orthodox Romanians as well as to ten wars against the Turks between 1676 and 1878. Some Danubian Romanians, sensitive to their religious link with Russia, anticipated advantages to be won by aiding their northeastern neighbor. Thus, despite Turkish suzerainty over Moldavia and Wallachia, some Romanian princes endorsed Russian operations against the Ottoman Empire. But Romanian military cooperation with Russia's forces in the unsuccessful campaign against the Turks on the Prut River in 1711 had a disastrous sequel. To punish the Danubian Romanians, the Ottoman sultan replaced native princes with Greeks from the Phanar district in Constantinople (İstanbul). These so-called Phanariots in Moldavia (1711–1822) and Wallachia (1716–1822) obtained princely office by purchase and hence tried to reimburse themselves by exploiting the wealth of Romanian landlords and peasants. They were responsible, moreover, for the Hellenization of Romanian culture, a process that persisted down to the opening of the Greek War of Independence in 1821 and the restoring of indigenous Romanians to the princely Danubian thrones. Armies of the Russian Empire (1721–1918), for their part, continued to march against the Ottoman Empire. As a consequence of the Third Russo-Turkish War, concluded in 1774 at Küçük Kaynarca, the Turks agreed to the establishment of Russian consulates in Moldavia and Wallachia, with the consuls being granted the privilege of interceding at Constantinople on behalf of the Romanians. Russia and Moldavia became contiguous by a later Russo-Turkish pact signed at Iaşi in 1792. The next step was to annex Romanian territory in 1812, when the Russo-Turkish Treaty of Bucharest stipulated the alienation of Bessarabia, or eastern Moldavia, to Russia. Then came direct Russian intervention in Danubian Romanian internal affairs. By the Russo-Turkish Convention of Akkerman in 1826, Romanian assemblies in Moldavia and Wallachia were to elect their own princes, who were nevertheless subject to Russia's approval before being installed in office by the Turks. Russia enjoyed a protectorate (1829–56) over the Danubian principalities at the close of yet another Russo-Turkish war with a peace at Adrianople (Edirne). The Turkish monopoly of Romanian trade now collapsed, but Turkish suzerainty over Moldavia and Wallachia remained intact. And while Russian troops subsequently withdrew from the Danubian principalities in 1834, the Russian protectorate endured because accords in 1833 between Russia and Turkey at Hünkâr İskelesi and by Russia and Austria at Münchengrätz had temporarily guaranteed the status quo in Southeastern Europe.

Russia's presence in Southeastern Europe had both negative and positive effects on the Danubian Romanians. The loss of Bessarabia and the protracted lack of international commerce on the Danube until 1829 spelled, on the one hand, political instability and economic weakness in Moldavia and Wallachia. On the other hand, Russia's military administration of the principalities (1829–33) was enlightened: Russian officials supervised the drafting of the Organic Regulations, or constitutional charters, for Wallachia in 1831 and for Moldavia in 1832. These laws afforded the Romanian landholding and mercantile elites, which had begun to prosper from the amplification of trade after 1829, opportunities to gain practical experience in self-government and, concomitantly, to turn ambitious eyes toward the future. Patriotic aspirations were clearly manifest in the revolutionary declarations of 1848. The rebellions in Bucharest and Iaşi were, to be sure, suppressed by Russian and Turkish troops, who continued to occupy the principalities until 1851, when an autochthonous militia assumed the peacekeeping function. If sociopolitical and cultural attitudes may be objectively assessed, Orthodox Russians were nonetheless apparently somewhat more sympathetic to Orthodox Romanians than they were to the Catholic Poles, Lutheran Finns, or Monophysite Armenians, who likewise dwelled in the Russian Empire. But Russia's annexation of Orthodox Georgia in 1801 might well have served as a warning to the Danubian Romanians. The Romanians' already precarious geographical position seemed to become even more dangerous as some Russian Slavophils and Pan-Slavs contemplated Pan-Orthodox ideas. The importance of the Danubian Romanians in Russian calculations was again obvious when Russian soldiers invaded Moldavia and Wallachia in 1853, triggering the Crimean War.

The Crimean War (1853–56) enmeshed West European powers in the affairs of Southeastern Europe. Leaders of France, together with those of Great Britain and other Western states, made common cause in championing the Turks, opposing the Russians, and obliquely and quite incidentally assisting the Danubian Romanians. France's interests in Southeastern Europe stemmed primarily from political and indirectly from ideological roots. The Catholic French had crusaded for centuries against Islamic forces, yet the threat of Catholic Austrian preeminence in Western Europe during the sixteenth century dictated a reassessment of French policy, prompting France in 1535 to conclude a treaty with the Ottoman Empire. The Ottoman sultan therein awarded Frenchmen extraterritorial prerogatives and protection in Turkey in return for France's military measures against the mutual Habsburg foe. This covenant, among others, was the basis for the consular jurisdiction (1535–1923) enjoyed by some European powers, starting at various times in diverse portions of the Ottoman Empire.[2] Romanians would seek to abolish that authority by 1782, with the appointment of the first foreign consuls—initially by Russia and soon afterward by other powers—in the Danubian principalities down to, and even after, Romania's attaining independence.

Revolutionary concepts espoused in France circulated widely during the nineteenth century, and their role in stimulating the Danubian Romanians' national consciousness was indeed manifest in the revolts of 1821 and, especially, 1848. Romanians who studied in France after the 1848 insurrections, in particular, increasingly deemed their political bondage to the Turks and their Orthodox religious tie to the Russians to be irrelevant or contrary to their patriotic goals. They identified instead with the Latinity of French culture, which they recognized as being akin to their own, and endeavored to realize some of the romantic and radical notions they had encountered in Parisian salons. The French, for their part, hoped to enhance their country's international prestige by preserving the balance of power in Eastern Europe while encouraging nationalistic sentiments among Latin peoples, such as the Romanians, Italians, and inadvertently the Mexicans. France objected to Russia's protectorate over Danubian Romania and supported the unification of Moldavia and Wallachia. Its doing so convinced many Romanians that France was truly a reliable friend, ready to sponsor their quest for statehood.

For Great Britain, Moldavia and Wallachia had an economic and strategic importance. The British, along with the citizens of other European powers, enjoyed extraterritorial rights—that is, consular jurisdiction—in the Ottoman Empire; but the British as well as the French in early modern times were more deeply engaged in the Western Hemisphere than in Southeastern Europe and the Middle East. The loss of the thirteen American colonies by 1783, however, coupled with the extension of Britain's dominion in India, drew British attention to the Ottoman Empire. The Greek War of Independence (1821–29) elicited, to be sure, sympathy and succor from those Britons who admired the classical heritage of Hellas. Of more practical significance than romantic philhellenism was the wealth to be won via the trade route to India. The Suez Canal through the Turkish *hıdivlik,* or khediviate, of Egypt—which opened in 1869 owing to French initiatives—would become a vital link in Britain's passage to the East. Challenging Britain in the Middle East—in Persia, Afghanistan, and Turkey—was Russia. Russia's protectorate over Moldavia and Wallachia seemingly impeded Britain's grain traffic also, which had nonetheless begun to grow after 1829. In countering the Russians, the British defended the Turks, as was most notably apparent during the Crimean War. But Britain eschewed encouraging the Danubian Romanians' patriotic dreams. If Romanians and other peoples cohabiting the Ottoman Empire were sovereign, the privileged position of British merchants in the area would be sacrificed, the Suez Canal would be endangered, and Turkey itself might collapse, unlatching thereby the gate for Russia's expansion to the Bosporus and the Dardanelles. Hence British diplomats labored to preserve Turkey's territorial integrity.

Italy had much in common yet little to do with Danubian Romania in the modern era. Like the French, Italians shared membership with Romanians in the Latin family of nationalities, each speaking a Romance language. Many Romanians, who looked to Rome as the source of their own culture from the ancient Roman period (106–271) onward in Carpatho-Danubia, treasured their linguistic affinity and perceived consanguinity with the Italians. Religion and politics were, however, inhibiting factors. The Catholic traditions of the Italians, as those of the French, obviously differed from the Orthodox ones of the Danubian Romanians. Neither Italy nor Romania, moreover, had central governments before the mid-nineteenth century to coordinate contacts between the peoples of these two states-to-be. The necessary diplomatic conditions and administrative structure for Italian political and economic dealings with the Danubian Romanians eventually surfaced owing to Sardinia's military participation against Russia in the Crimean War and the ensuing foundation of a united Kingdom of Italy (1861–1946). Some Italian officials indeed supported Romanian aims, but most Italians kept so busy consolidating their own nation-state that they had scant time or energy for playing a major role in the Romanians' pursuit of sovereignty.

Prussia, among the various adversaries of Russia during the Crimean War, was practically indifferent to Southeastern Europe. Danubian Romania was nonetheless to evoke some strategic and economic concern among leaders of the Kingdom of Prussia (1701–1871) and later of the German Empire (1871–1918), especially after 1866. Hohenzollerns on the thrones in Berlin (1415/86–1918) and Bucharest (1866–1947), albeit representing different branches of the same house, confirmed to one and all that amicable relations existed between the two countries. Germany might find Romania useful in thwarting Berlin's potential or real rivals, Austria and Russia. The Hohenzollern dynastic connection would, in any case, embolden German financiers to put surplus capital in Romanian enterprises. Following its unification, Germany's diplomats endeavored to maintain the political equilibrium of Europe and protect German investments abroad. These policies, however, clashed with the Danubian Romanians' national goals.

The policy of self-interest determined the attitudes of the European powers toward Southeastern Europe and, in particular, toward Danubian Romania. Affecting the powers, too, were their involvements with one another. Russia, Austria, and Prussia cooperated in partitioning Poland, countering Napoleonic France, and opposing revolutionary movements. Still, they parted company over two major issues: Germany and the Eastern Question. The unification of Germany, for instance, triggered the Austro-Prussian War of 1866; moreover, Austria and Russia divided over the Turkish inheritance in Southeastern Europe. Of the Western powers, France and England competed for colonies throughout the world in modern times. In Europe itself, France was the focus of British animosity during the Napoleonic Wars, although France and Britain would subsequently join forces against Russia in the Crimean War. France had struggled with Habsburg Austria and Spain for the mastery of Western Europe in the sixteenth century, while in the nineteenth century France and Austria vied for influence in Central Europe, specifically in Italy and Germany after the Crimean War. Each European power, on the whole, sought to preserve the status quo in Southeastern Europe, save when a tangible advantage was to be readily won. The Romanians meanwhile watched patiently but anxiously for opportunities to achieve their national aims amid shifting international machinations and the ongoing decline of Turkey.

To be sure, Danubian Romanians enjoyed a privileged position under the suzerainty of the Ottoman sultan until the late 1870s, but they were dissatisfied with their dependent political station. Especially onerous was Phanariot Greek predominance in the secular and ecclesiastical affairs of Moldavia and Wallachia. Revolutionary waves occasionally rolled through Romanian lands, propelled in part by liberal and nationalistic ideas as well as by urgent needs. In 1821 Tudor Vladimirescu launched an uprising in Wallachia calling for a "representative assembly" to act on behalf of the people against the exploitative Phanariots and certain Romanian aristocrats.[3] Although the Turks suppressed this revolt, the Phanariots fell from office and were replaced by indigenous princes. Again in 1848, renewed seditious currents led Romanians to rebel; in Wallachia, for instance, they demanded "administrative and legislative independence" along with representative government and responsible ministers.[4] Russian and Turkish troops, as already noted, put down the insurgents in the Danubian principalities and restored the old order, including the Russian protectorate, by the Balta Limanı Convention of 1849. Some Romanian aspirations reached fruition, however, after the Crimean War by the Treaty of Paris (1856), which provided for a "national and independent administration" in the principalities.[5] This covenant also assured Danubian Romanians their freedom of lawmaking, worship, and commerce in addition to their right to a national army for maintaining public tranquillity and guarding the frontier. Further, the Paris accord exchanged the Russian protectorate for a collective guarantee by the European powers. This safeguard obviated the annexation of Moldavia and Wallachia by Austria or Russia, each of which had a sizable Romanian population by the 1860s—in Austrian Bukowina, Hungarian Transylvania and the Banat, and Russian Bessarabia. In the Moldavian and Wallachian divans ad hoc—or special assemblies—of 1857, Romanians insisted on forging an integrated and neutral Moldo-Wallachian principality under a foreign prince.[6] They gained their chief goal in the ensuing election by assemblies in both principalities during 1859 of a Romanian army officer from Moldavia, Prince Alexandru Ion Cuza (1859–66), together with the powers' recognition of that choice for Cuza's lifetime. The Danubian Romanians were thereby effectively united.[7] Some Danubian Romanians believed that only a foreign prince, one who would be unfettered by regional loyalties and jealousies, might successfully preserve the fragile Moldo-Wallachian union from being shattered on the reefs of political separatism and great-power rivalries. By

1866 they had one: Prince Carol of Hohenzollern-Sigmaringen (1866–1914). But they found themselves still confronted by the powers, who intervened repeatedly in Romanian domestic affairs so as to champion aliens' interests. An important consequence of such ongoing meddling was to raise still higher the level of Romanian national objectives. Danubian Romanians increasingly resented their dependence on the Ottoman Empire, which included the payment of annual tribute, adherence to the Turkish tariff, and consular jurisdiction. They endeavored to enlarge their prerogatives in Turkey by pursuing an independent foreign policy, such as concluding commercial conventions with Austria and Russia. At first Romanians asserted their neutrality in the Balkan Crisis of the mid-1870s. Yet when Russia prepared to fight Turkey, Romanian and Russian leaders negotiated military pacts that nullified neutrality. Danubian Romanians formally declared their independence during the next Russo-Turkish war and cooperated with Russian forces on the battlefield. The powers acknowledged the new situation after Turkey's defeat, thus ending their collective guarantee of Romania's autonomy and confirming the sovereignty of the Romanian state.

This tortuous road traversed by the Danubian Romanians toward independence in the late 1860s and 1870s is the focus then of our study. It is one that involves the aims and presumptions of Romanian patriots intertwined with the pretensions and conflicts of the great powers in Southeastern Europe.

Notes

1. For a discussion of this theme, see my "The Structure of Romanian Nationalism."

2. For more about consular jurisdiction, see Chapter Three below.

3. See Tudor Vladimirescu's proclamation of a revolution in Wallachia (23 January 1821), in *Documente privind istoria Romîniei: Răscoala din 1821*, 1:207–8.

4. See the relatively conservative program in Moldavia (Iaşi), 28 March/9 April 1848, and the more radical one in Wallachia (Islaz), 9/21 June 1848, in *Anul 1848 în principatele române: Acte şi documente*, 1:176–79, 490–501, and especially 495–96.

5. Article 23 of the Treaty of Paris, 30 March 1856, in *Recueil d'actes internationaux de l'Empire Ottoman*, 3:77.

6. Compare the almost identical programs of the divans in Moldavia, 7/19 October 1857, and Wallachia, 8/20 October 1857, in *Acte şi documente relative la istoria renascerei Romaniei*, vol. 6, pt. 1, 62–80; pt. 2, 28–30.

7. See the Paris conference protocols no. 21, 13 April 1859, and no. 22, 6 September 1859, in *Archives diplomatiques: Recueil de diplomatie et d'histoire*, vol. 6, pt. 2 (avril, mai, juin 1866), 162–64, 166–68.

Chapter Two

A FOREIGN PRINCE

Why a foreign prince? Did the choice of Carol from Hohenzollern-Sigmaringen to rule Danubian Romania violate the ideals of Romanian patriots? How could a foreigner be expected to attain Romanian national objectives?

Practical politics and historical precedents, even more than patriotic sentiments, prompted Danubian Romanians in selecting a prince. The *paşa* and later *hıdiv* of Egypt, the *knez* of Serbia, and *domns* of Moldavia and Wallachia were indigenous executives, yet each was a vassal of the Ottoman sultan. In Greece, conversely, West Europeans—first a Bavarian and subsequently Danes—held the scepter; and an independent Greece enjoyed the sympathy and support of Europe's great powers. Romanian patriots, for their part, believed that a foreign prince would amplify their voice in the European halls of puissance and would eventually steer them to freedom. They had experienced alien governors and found them wanting. The Greek Phanariots, who formerly controlled Moldavia and Wallachia for the Turks, had fostered Greek culture in the principalities, becoming thereby an anathema for many Romanians. Danubian Romanians therefore renounced another Greek and sought someone from a European dynasty. Such a person, they hoped, would impartially administer the land, standing apart from internal controversies and maintaining sociopolitical equilibrium. Already in the divans ad hoc of 1857, one statesman, Mihail Kogălniceanu in Moldavia, castigated the anarchy caused by the "rivalries and ambitions" of competing native candidates to the throne, while another, Ion C. Brătianu in Wallachia, anticipated that a foreign prince would somehow set his countrymen on the path to "progress and civilization."[1] Historical models might also be emulated. The Varangians had been called to Russia, the Angevins to Hungary and Poland, the Saxe-Coburg-Gothas to Belgium, and, of course, the Danes to Greece.

Delegates to the 1857 divans in the Danubian principalities had almost unanimously agreed that a foreign prince from one of the reigning European houses should preside over them; yet the powers collectively decided that only the sons of fathers born in Wallachia and Moldavia might ascend the thrones in Bucharest and Iaşi.[2] That is, a native leader was to be picked in each principality. The transition from two principalities to one was perhaps inevitable; and it certainly came quickly. Cuza's election in 1859 by assemblies in both principalities created in effect a new state: the United Principalities of Moldo-Wallachia (1859–66). The powers accepted it all by recognizing Cuza, but they denied his offspring the right to inherit the crown.[3]

Cuza reminded Europe immediately following the dual election that Danubian Romanians required a permanently unified regime and a foreign prince. He even promised to yield the helm as soon as the powers endorsed these "legitimate wishes" of the Romanian people.[4] As to his successor, Cuza seems to have favored Duke Nikolai of Leuchtenberg.[5] Nikolai's father, Maksimilian, had been a candidate to head an envisaged Danubian Romania in 1848; Nikolai's mother, Maria, was a sister of Emperor Alexander II of Russia (1855–81), and his paternal great grandmother, Josephine, had married Emperor Napoleon I of France (1799–1814/15).[6] The Leuchtenbergs' Russian and French familial ties, plus their Orthodox Christianity, made Nikolai an attractive choice for Orthodox Romanians, especially conservatives in Moldavia. Liberals in Wallachia, however, wanted a Latin prince from Western Europe and calculated that Duke Nikolai, who resided in St. Petersburg and served in Alexander II's army, would be motivated more by Russian than by Romanian interests. Some Romanians indeed feared that a Russian ruler in Danubian Romania would ultimately spell the annexation of their country by the Russian Empire. However, Romanians had little reason to worry inasmuch as the prospect of a Leuchtenberg on the Bucharest throne lacked encouragement from Alexander II, who remarked that no member of his family should become a vassal of the Ottoman sultan.[7]

Although Cuza initially appeared ready to step down, he would not willingly do so. He endeavored instead to reconstruct Romanian society. His reign witnessed wide-ranging reforms, such as the emancipation of the peasantry and the secularization of the so-called dedicated monasteries—which were under the ecclesiastical jurisdiction of the Holy Places and patriarchates in the Middle East since early modern times—along with major judicial, military, and educational improvements. These projects evoked opposition. Conservative landlords resisted socioeconomic changes that would benefit the peasants at the formers' expense; and urban liberals were deeply troubled by the absence of an effective, functioning constitutional government as well as by Danubian Romania's ongoing dependent political status. Diverse power-seeking individuals—including the liberals Brătianu and Constantin A. Rosetti, the moderate Ion Ghica, and the somewhat conservative Dimitrie Ghica—eventually formed, in 1863, a "monstrous" coalition to thwart Cuza's plans.[8] The idea of a foreign prince was also still in the air. Brătianu explained in the legislature that a Latin dynasty would ensure the existence of his country, continually threatened as it was by Austria, Russia, and Turkey.[9] This viewpoint, together with the coalition's obstructionist tactics, led Cuza to carry out a coup d'état in 1864 that enabled him, aided for a time by Kogălniceanu as prime minister, to promulgate his reforms.[10]

The autocratic methods, bureaucratic corruption, and financial mismanagement that accompanied Cuza's reforms encouraged the prince's opponents to act. Cuza himself lacked the requisite energy and perspicacity to reach his goals. The edict freeing serfs, for example, failed to redistribute the land equitably and was so vaguely worded as to bewilder both peasants and landlords. Cuza openly admitted his limitations; still, he attempted less to overcome them by practical policies and more to find solace in alcohol and in the arms of an attractive Moldavian widow, Maria Catargi Obrenović. His wife, Elena, née Rosetti, was barren, but Maria presented him with two sons, whom he adopted in 1865. On some Romanian palates, Cuza's amorous affair smacked of a scheme to establish a native dynasty with bastards as heirs to the crown.[11] Leaders of the "monstrous" coalition replied in June 1865 that "in case of a vacancy on the throne" they would strive to elect a "foreign prince from one of the ruling families in the West."[12] By the end of the year, Brătianu was in Paris trying in vain to obtain French support for the coalition's cause.[13] In Bucharest, the coalition—now involving also the conservatives Lascăr Catargiu and Petre P. Carp plus the liberal Dimitrie A. Sturdza—published the short-lived *Revista Dunării* (The Danubian Review), which called for a "full realization of the decisions of the *divans ad hoc*," meaning that a foreigner was to be head of state.[14] This propaganda affected army officers whose salaries had not recently been paid. Military conspirators—abetted by the palace guards—seized the initiative in the morning of 11/23 February 1866 by entering Cuza's bedroom and, while Maria concealed herself, forcing Cuza at gunpoint to abdicate.[15]

The same morning that Cuza abdicated, a regency was set up composed of Catargiu and two army officers along with a cabinet directed by Ion Ghica, with Dimitrie Ghica, Rosetti, and Sturdza among the ministers. Later that day, a joint session of deputies and senators chose a foreigner to guide the country, thereby propelling Romanian fortunes again into Europe's political corridors.[16]

The first question was: Who will lead us? Romanian legislators evidently wanted a foreigner. But they encountered opposition from the powers to such a choice as well as difficulty in selecting a suitable person who would accept subservience to the Ottoman sultan. Possible candidates included a Frenchman, a Russian, and a Belgian. One prospect, Prince Napoleon Joseph, was a first cousin of Emperor Napoleon III (1848/52–71) and second in line for the French imperial crown. Prince Napoleon had been mentioned for the Romanian throne after Cuza's double election in 1859, and was so again in 1864 and 1865.[17] Napoleon III eschewed, however, endorsing his cousin because the latter had publicly challenged the French emperor's pro-Austrian policy in mid-1865 by obliquely espousing the rights of submerged nationalities in Habsburg dominions while calling for an extension of liberty both at home and abroad.[18] Although Wallachian liberals would have been pleased with Prince Napoleon, they were unenthusiastic about the Russian, Nikolai of Leuchtenberg, who still enjoyed the support of Moldavian conservatives. The nomination and immediate approval of Count Philip of Flanders stemmed from sociopolitical exigencies in Bucharest, especially the need for dispatch to avoid disorder. Danubian Romanians were, moreover, undoubtedly impressed by the prestige of Philip's elder brother, King Leopold II of Belgium (1865–1909), and appreciated Philip's lack of ties to any Romanian faction. Many Romanians, in addition, admired Belgium's neutrality and constitutional framework, envisioning that their country might emulate Belgium's example.

The next question was: How do we win the powers and the suzerain Turks to our choice? Delegations seemed to be part of the answer. One delegation, headed by the first rector of Bucharest University, Gheorghe Costa-Foru, visited Constantinople to assure one and all of the new regime's peaceful intentions, promising that a foreign prince would not alter the "Romanians' secular sympathies for the Ottoman Empire." Another one, guided by a university law professor, Vasile Boerescu, traveled to Western Europe to receive Philip's reply and to convey the Romanians' wishes to the powers' representatives, who were meeting in Paris.[19]

Philip, however, quickly declined the Romanians' invitation.[20] He did so in order to avoid a Franco-Belgian rift. Inasmuch as Philip's mother, Louise of Orléans, was a daughter of the former French king Louis Philippe (1830–48), some considered Philip to be a pretender to the French throne, albeit a distant one, since by 1866 the long-dead Louis Philippe had four living sons and eight grandsons by direct male descent.[21] Might Danubian Romania become Philip's stepping-stone to France? Probably not. Of more immediate consequence for the Belgians was the fear that Napoleon III might try to expand France's Second Empire at Belgium's expense. Philip's refusal may have been expected by the Romanians. Earlier, in 1857 and again in 1865, Philip had been suggested as the chief executive of a united Danubian Romania.[22] From the prior reluctance of Belgian authorities to entertain such a prospect, we may assume that the Romanians fully anticipated Philip's negative response, which would avert compromising Belgium's neutrality. Romanians hoped nevertheless that by offering Philip their crown, the powers would recognize that none of them was inordinately influencing decisions at Bucharest and would therefore respect Romanian wishes regarding a prince.

Before a foreign prince could be selected, even before Cuza had abdicated, the powers toyed with projects to annex or partition Danubian Romania. These plans stemmed primarily from a need for equilibrium, to counter political instability due to the waning Turkish control of Southeastern Europe. Empress Catherine II of Russia (1762–96) and Emperor Joseph II of Austria (1765/80–90) had agreed in 1782 to divide Turkish holdings in Europe after a joint campaign against the Ottoman Empire. Austria was to get much of the northwest Balkan Peninsula along with western Wallachia, or Oltenia; a restored Byzantine Empire was to be headed by Catherine II's grandson, Konstantin; and the Danubian principalities—Moldavia and eastern Wallachia, or Muntenia—were to constitute an independent Dacian kingdom led by an Orthodox Christian.[23] Danubian Romania was again the object of a possible exchange in 1805 when the French foreign affairs minister, Charles-Maurice de Talleyrand-Périgord, in counseling Napoleon I about Franco-Austrian peace preliminaries, urged that Moldavia, Wallachia, and Dobrogea with the Danube Delta be conveyed to Austria as an indemnity for Austrian losses in Central Europe.[24] Nothing came of these probes because of the Turks' abiding military presence and the powers' own ongoing rivalries.

The powers contemplated anew territorial exchanges in the mid-nineteenth century. The Crimean War prompted proposals. While Russian troops occupied Moldavia and Wallachia in 1854, Napoleon III suggested to the Habsburg emperor, Francis Joseph (1848–1916), that Austria appropriate the Danubian principalities and renounce the troublesome Austrian holdings in Lombardy.[25] This blueprint encountered little enthusiasm in Vienna, yet the Romanian and Italian questions became intertwined in the powers' calculations. Napoleon III, for his part, persistently championed the cause of Italian patriots so as to demonstrate French leadership in European affairs. He apparently intimated to the Sardinian prime minister, Camillo di

Cavour, in Compiègne, toward the end of the Crimean campaign in December 1855, that the Danubian principalities be ceded to Austria, which had already militarily seized them; the childless Habsburg duke of Modena, Francis V (1846–60), was in turn to rule in the Danubian Romanian lands, and Francis Joseph was to deliver Lombardy to Sardinia.[26] Cavour amended Napoleon III's design, requesting that the independent duchies of Modena and Parma, rather than Austrian Lombardy, be assigned to Sardinia so as to avoid offending Austria, whereas Moldavia and Wallachia would be separately governed by Francis and the seven-year-old Bourbon duke of Parma, Robert (1854–60).[27] Napoleon III reverted to this matter at the ensuing Congress of Paris, which ended the Crimean War, proffering an idea, strongly endorsed by Cavour, that Francis go to the Danubian principalities; further, Robert and his mother, the Parma regent Luisa Maria, would transfer to Modena, and Parma would pass to Sardinia.[28] Austria's opposition to Sardinia's acquisition of Parma effectively thwarted this plan.[29] Such schemes were merely academic exercises preceding the decisive events in the unification of Italy. Napoleon III promised Austrian possessions in Italy, including Venetia, to Cavour in Plombières in 1858 as a reward for the anticipated armed Italian cooperation with France against Austria.[30] The Franco-Austrian war in the summer of 1859 did indeed bring Lombardy as well as Modena and Parma—but not Venetia—to Sardinia, and France received Savoy and Nice from Sardinia.

Venetia and Danubian Romania continued to be linked diplomatically. Abortive Franco-British-Italian talks during the Polish revolt and the Schleswig-Holstein crisis of 1863 included the offer of the Moldo-Wallachian principality to Austria in return for Austria's cession of Venetia to Italy.[31] Discussions revived in 1864, with a cash payment to Austria being proposed for Venetia. But the French foreign affairs minister, Édouard Drouyn de Lhuys, reckoned that plan would be repugnant to Austria; in any case, he preferred that Great Britain take the lead in posing an exchange of terrain, something the British were reluctant to do.[32] Napoleon III tentatively recommended again in 1865, despite his minister's hesitation, that Austrian dominions be extended to the mouth of the Danube River and that Venetia go to Italy. This initiative met with a solid rebuff from the Prussian foreign affairs minister, Otto von Bismarck, who indicated that Prussia's interest was more in maintaining cordial relations with Russia than in possibly affronting it by sponsoring territorial swaps involving Moldo-Wallachia.[33] Italian statesmen clearly understood that their French and British peers were loath to insist on a Romanian-Venetian trade so long as the success of that project appeared quite remote.[34]

Italian hopes still sprang eternal. Italy renewed efforts to switch territory on the eve of the palace revolution in Bucharest that swept Cuza from office, now adding Serbia and Bosnia to Moldo-Wallachia as Austria's compensation for Venetia.[35] Then, after Cuza's fall and before the Austro-Prussian War of 1866, Napoleon III espoused a scheme whereby Italy would receive Venetia; France, Genoa; Austria, Wallachia; Russia, Moldavia; and Prussia, Schleswig-Holstein.[36] We may only note here that Italy annexed Venetia, and Prussia annexed Schleswig-Holstein, following the Austro-Prussian War of 1866; Russia won southern Bessarabia after the Russo-Turkish War of 1877–78; and Austria-Hungary occupied Bosnia-Hercegovina in 1878 and formally incorporated it in 1908.

Austria and Russia strongly opposed territorial plundering prior to the Austro-Prussian War of 1866. Austria's foreign affairs minister, Alexander von Mensdorff-Pouilly, engrossed as he was in the contest with Prussia for Germany, repudiated trading Venetia for Moldo-Wallachia and furthermore thought the wresting of Turkish lands in Serbia, Bosnia, and Hercegovina to be a "most inopportune and inadmissible," premature reduction of the Ottoman Empire.[37] And Alexander II seems to have remarked that the apportioning of Danubian Romania by Russia and Austria was "inadmissible until the war."[38] He undoubtedly wanted to recover southern Bessarabia, which had been forfeited after the Crimean War, yet he was also committed to sustaining the status quo in Eastern Europe.[39] An Austrian victory over Prussia might endanger Russia's dominion over Poland; Russia would, moreover, profit little in seizing Moldavia if Austria procured Wallachia, thereby controlling the lower Danube and blocking Russia's overland route to the Bosporus and the Dardanelles. Russia's foreign affairs minister, Aleksandr M. Gorchakov, declared that neither the Romanians nor the Turks championed the Moldo-Wallachian principality, and contended that Cuza's deposition terminated the union of Danubian Romania. He, too, resisted a Venetia-Romania exchange and any extension of Austrian authority on the Danube.[40] Russia and Austria nonetheless tentatively considered cooperating diplomatically with one another in Moldo-Wallachia as well as in Schleswig-Holstein. What such collaboration would entail or accomplish in Southeastern Europe is unclear; southern Bessarabia and the clauses of the 1856 Treaty of Paris neutralizing the Black Sea may have been in Gorchakov's mind, but certainly not Austria's acquisition of Wallachia. Mensdorff-Pouilly, on his side, eventually rejected an Austro-Russian accord, fearing that it would engender the withdrawal of the anticipated British and French backing of Austria in the impending war with Prussia.[41]

The powers encountered insuperable obstacles in trying to resolve simultaneously the German, Italian, and Romanian questions in 1866. Hence, negotiations to partition Danubian Romania came to naught.

The future of Romania, along with the prospect of a foreign prince, was the focus of an ambassadorial conference of the powers that convened in Paris in March 1866. The product of the first session was a note that vaguely advised the provisional government in Bucharest to "maintain order" and to refrain from actions prejudicial to the conference's decisions.[42] Romanians did not participate in the meetings. Brătianu endeavored unsuccessfully to address the conference about Danubian Romania's longing for a ruler drawn from one of Europe's dynasties.[43] This wish, however, reached the delegates' ears via Drouyn de Lhuys. France had suggested the idea of a foreign prince at the 1858 Paris conference on Moldavia and Wallachia and raised this issue again in 1866.[44] Turkey, for its part, categorically rebuffed a foreign prince as abrogating the sultan's suzerainty.[45] Austria, Russia, and Britain likewise resisted the notion, foreseeing that any changes in Romania would imperil Europe's equilibrium. Austria had the most to lose in fostering the embryonic Romanian state, yet it was deeply engaged in the struggle with Prussia for Germany. Austria therefore abandoned its policy of preserving the territorial integrity of the Ottoman Empire as a hedge against Russian aspirations in Southeastern Europe; while sympathetic to a separate Moldavia, Austria was thus ready to accept a united Moldo-Wallachia in order to assure a working entente with France on the eve of the Austro-Prussian War. But Austria balked at a foreign prince, who might unduly enhance the international prestige of the Danubian Romanians and stir up Austria's own Romanian population.[46] Russia also objected to a foreign prince. It primarily wanted to overturn restrictions imposed by the 1856 Treaty of Paris and suspected Austria's aims in Southeastern Europe. Russia nevertheless deemed that a non-Romanian on the throne in Bucharest would spell Romania's independence and, in turn, signal the dismantling of the Ottoman Empire.[47] Britain rather ambiguously called for adherence to the 1858 convention, which had stipulated the parting of Moldavia and Wallachia at the end of Cuza's reign, and concurrently deferred an opinion about Danubian Romania's destiny.[48] Both Prussia and Italy had their own goals of national unification, which took precedence over other matters; so both powers evinced slight interest in Danubian Romania and were noncommittal about its affairs. Bismarck, for instance, welcomed the Paris conference as a diversion to veil Prussia's plan for regional aggrandizement in Central Europe, turning Austria's attention to the lower Danube River while continuing friendly relations with France and Russia.[49] Italy recognized that a foreign prince would provide a lasting regime, corresponding to the desires of the Romanian people; but Italy was more concerned about the possibility of gaining Venetia than about the status of Romania.[50] The divergent views of the European powers precluded an agreement as to what to do in Danubian Romania until May 1866; by that time, however, it was obvious that the powers had, collectively, little control over Romanian events.

Romanian patriots persistently demanded a foreign prince. As already noted, Brătianu was in Western Europe looking for one whom the powers would approve. Brătianu and the Romanian diplomatic agent in Paris, Ion Bălăceanu, probably failed to elicit serious applications from aspirants to Romania's crown owing to the principality's political and economic instability. Perhaps Prince Charles Anthony of Hohenzollern-Sigmaringen (1848–85) sponsored his second son, Carol, as he subsequently sought to place his eldest son, Leopold, on the Spanish throne. This is, at best, a remote possibility, for independent Spain was a far more attractive prize than dependent Danubian Romania. Brătianu was, for his part, optimistic in expecting strong support in France; he wrote to his wife: "once again I balance the destiny of Romania and . . . I alone defend the rights of the country. . . . The emperor [Napoleon III] is for us . . . all will be better than under the rule of Cuza."[51]

We still do not know who first proposed Carol.[52] Empress Eugénie of France said afterwards that Hortense Cornu, a confidante of Napoleon III's and a friend of Carol's, had been responsible.[53] Be that as it may, shortly after the ambassadorial conference opened in Paris, Brătianu presented a memorandum to France's ministry of foreign affairs that reaffirmed the need for a foreign prince, and asserted that Romanians "turned their hopes" to the "family of Prince Hohenzollern" as being indirectly akin to that of Napoleon III and because of the "impossibility" of finding anyone more closely related to France's emperor who might accept the Romanian offer.[54] A few days later, Drouyn de Lhuys asked Bălăceanu for Romania's candidate; the latter requested permission from the provisional government in Bucharest to name Carol, who was "very favorable in the eyes of Napoleon III."[55] At this juncture, the regency prorogued the senate and dissolved the chamber of deputies on account of the deputies' alleged plan to transform the chamber into a "national convention," whatever that might mean. Elections for the chamber were then held to replace Cuza's "muzhiks"—or ruffians— with merchants and landholders who would support a foreign prince from Western Europe and draft a new constitution.[56] Brătianu meanwhile met Charles Anthony in Düsseldorf to intimate that Napoleon III had given "favorable advice" about Carol's becoming prince of Romania.[57] Europe would readily recognize Carol, Brătianu explained, for the Hohenzollerns of Prussia were above suspicion, having no territorial ambitions on the lower Danube.[58] Carol was undoubtedly selected for his familial connections to the ruling houses of France and Prussia. But the overriding consideration was for speed; Romanian patriots lacked time to shop around for a candidate, fearing that any prolonged delay would result in the undoing of the uncertain Moldo-Wallachian union.

Would Carol take the Romanian crown? Would the powers allow him to do so? Brătianu promptly announced that Carol had unconditionally assented.[59] This claim was a sham. Moreover, Brătianu had not been candid in invoking France's blessing for Carol. France, to be sure, backed the Romanian call for a foreign prince in the conference of ambassadors; but Drouyn de Lhuys told Danubian Romanians that he favored a native prince, and Napoleon III characterized Carol's nomination as an escapade in which he himself played no part.[60] France presumably hedged in supporting Carol because of the state of flux in relations between the great powers—a result of coincident crises in Denmark, Italy, and Romania—and the attendant necessity to avoid isolation in case of war. In private, Cornu nonetheless urged Carol to exchange his "monotonous and little useful life" for a more "active role" as a "good and brave sovereign" of the Romanians. She shared the widely held belief that the princely power vacuum in Bucharest placed the Moldo-Wallachian union in jeopardy.[61] For Carol and his father, however, not France but the titular head of the house of Hohenzollern, King William I of Prussia (1861–88), should decide the matter. The first word from Berlin was ambivalent. William I was loath to have Prussia drawn into the Eastern Question, and hence he contended that no member of his family should become a vassal of the Ottoman sultan. He foresaw, moreover, the possible convergence of Austrian and Romanian interests against those of Prussia, yet would acquiesce in Carol's candidature if Russia and France consented.[62] This was a big order, for Russia had already opposed a foreign prince at the ambassadorial conference. William I's attitude reflected lessons from the campaigns of King Frederick II the Great (1740–86); on the eve of the Austro-Prussian War, William was unwilling to overextend Prussia's military strength by offending Russia or France.

Events in Romania outdistanced discussions by the ambassadors in Paris and within the Hohenzollern family. Without awaiting Carol's reply, the regency submitted his name to the public as "Prince of the Romanians."[63] The minister of interior, Dimitrie Ghica, who directed the plebiscite for Carol, enjoined prefects to "assure the happiness" of Romanians by a vote for union and a foreign prince.[64] Since the prefects conducted elections and controlled the militia, the outcome was predictable: Carol received 685,969 votes; 224 opposed him and 124,837 abstained; 167 of the negative ballots were cast in Iaşi, the capital of Moldavia.[65]

The results of the plebiscite gave merely an illusion of harmony. Opponents of a foreign prince and of the union of the principalities surfaced in Moldavia. The deposing of Cuza appeared to some in Moldavia to have been part of a conspiracy in Wallachia that fastened on political hegemony in Danubian Romania. Romanians in Moldavia resented the preeminence of Bucharest as the national capital, and the ensuing decline in importance and prestige of Iaşi. Danubian Romanians lacked a common educational background; sociopolitical notables in Moldavia had been primarily trained in Germany, while those in Wallachia studied in France. Potentially more significant was the orientation of Orthodox Romanian clerics in Moldavia toward Russia, and their apparent lack of confidence in a united Romanian state. Most momentous was the prospect of a Russian invasion to ensure the separation of the principalities; 60,000 Russian troops were reportedly on Moldavia's frontier, causing alarm throughout Danubian Romania.[66] Russia's delegate to the conference of ambassadors had, as already noted, resisted a foreign prince and reopened the question of union. So, too, did Russophil Romanians in Iaşi at the time of the plebiscite. A riot occurred after church services on Sunday, 3/15 April 1866, in protest against union and the "infidel" Carol the Catholic, led by a wealthy and ambitious magistrate, Neculai Rosetti-Roznovanu; a Russian subject, Constantin Moruzi; and the Orthodox metropolitan of Moldavia, Calinic Miclescu. Some of the slogans were "Down with Union," "Long Live Moldavia," and "Revolution: Fear Not, Hold on for a Few Hours, the Russians Are Coming to Help Us." Some Romanians later intimated that foreigners—Jews, Russian Old Believers (Lipoveni), Greeks, Poles, and Armenians—were involved in the tumult; they did so to convince the powers and to assure themselves that their cause was popular among fellow Romanians. Whatever the ethnic composition of the insurgents, the Romanian cavalry and infantry were to disperse an estimated five hundred persons who had broken the peace with their sticks and stones. The turbulence lasted three and a half hours; it left seventeen dead and about forty wounded, including the metropolitan, who was just scratched.[67]

Elsewhere, adversaries of Carol and union were less violent. In the Bucharest newspaper *Legalitatea,* Ion Heliade Rădulescu inveighed against a foreign prince as being a travesty of the nationality principle.[68] In Transylvania and the Banat, leaders of the Romanian National Party, such as Vincenţiu Babeş and Alexandru Mocsonyi, thought that Austria's annexation of Danubian Romania would be more desirable than a Moldo-Wallachian union under Carol.[69] By such an Austrian territorial expansion, according to Babeş and Mocsonyi, Romanians would gain a commanding numerical superiority over the Magyars and thereby might win considerable political and economic privileges. These Transylvanian Romanians envisioned a greater national union than already existed in Danubian Romania, yet one in which Danubian Romanians would probably have been far more subservient to the Habsburg emperor than they were to the Ottoman sultan.

The powers had earlier decreed in the 1858 Paris convention that solely electoral assemblies in the Danubian principalities might select new princes; hence the 1866 plebiscite was illegal. Furthermore, the ambassadors at Paris rejected the Romanians' call for a foreign prince, for only a native one would be acceptable to the powers.[70] This decision convinced William I of the impossibility of Carol's candidacy; he nevertheless equivocated by observing that Romanians clung firmly to their plebiscite, and so the matter was still open. Bismarck unofficially advised Carol: "You have been unanimously chosen by a whole nation to be prince; follow the call, go." Carol should eschew awaiting William I's blessing and instead request leave for a vacation abroad. He was to see Napoleon III to confirm France's support as well as to negotiate an understanding directly with Russia, Danubian Romania's chief "protector."[71] In concord with French diplomacy, Prussia publicly endorsed the stipulations of the ambassadorial conference to mollify Russia while encouraging Carol in private to ascend the Romanian throne, which would thereby divert Austria's military resources away from potential battlefields in Germany.

The regency and the chamber of deputies—now designated an electoral assembly—discerned that discord among the powers offered them an opportunity to act. The assembly reaffirmed on 1/13 May 1866 the union of "Romania: one and indivisible" under Prince Carol I. Some disagreed; the Bărnuţiu "school" of deputies from Moldavia opposed Carol. Simeon Bărnuţiu, a Transylvanian Romanian who had taught philosophy and law at Iaşi for almost a decade during and after the Crimean War, warned about the denationalizing effects of a foreign prince. Such a ruler would suspend the rights of Romanians, fill the bureaucratic ranks with foreign appointees, and give an alien orientation to public education; state income would be funneled into the pocketbooks of foreigners who would control Romanian trade and industry.[72] The outstanding spokesman of this "school" in the assembly, Nicolae Ionescu from Moldavia, suggested moreover that the naming of a foreign prince would anger Danubian Romania's neighbors and end the powers' collective guarantee of its existence. The only deputy from Wallachia to resist the Hohenzollern candidature was Heliade Rădulescu, who reminded his listeners about backslidings of foreign princes in earlier times as compared to the progress achieved by native leaders after 1821. But Heliade Rădulescu acknowledged his country's need for Carol in order to avert civil war. The deputies then voted overwhelmingly for union and Carol: 109 in favor, with 6 abstentions—all from Moldavia.[73] The assembly's resolution fulfilled provisions in the Paris convention of 1858 concerning union and a ruler in Danubian Romania, thereby clearing the way for the advent of the foreign prince.

Carol's ambitions overcame his ambivalence; he followed Bismarck's advice, accepted the Romanians' invitation, and went to Bucharest without William I's formal approval, without the powers' sanction, and without the backing of all segments of the Romanian populace. To get to his destination, Carol traveled incognito—under a pseudonym, with a Swiss passport, disguised with spectacles—by train and river steamer via the Habsburg Empire. It was a hazardous journey owing to Austro-Prussian rivalry over Germany plus the recent mobilization of Prussian troops. Carol abandoned his glasses upon reaching the Danubian port of Turnu-Severin. The short, slender, bearded, gray-eyed man of destiny, at age twenty-six, then rode with Brătianu through Wallachia, enjoying tumultuous welcomes in the larger villages and towns. En route, he wrote several letters: to William I resigning from the Prussian army, to Napoleon III and Alexander II seeking protection, and to Sultan Abdul Aziz (1861–76) requesting recognition.[74] Carol took office the same day he arrived in Bucharest. This Catholic prince heard a Te Deum sung by the Orthodox metropolitan of Ungro-Vlahia, Nifon; and in the presence of the assembly, he received his commission from the regency: "I swear to be faithful to the laws of the land, to preserve the religion of Romania as well as its territorial integrity, and to govern as a constitutional prince." In French, for of course he spoke no Romanian, he also indicated that he would be a "Citizen today, soldier tomorrow, if it is necessary,

I shall share with you good and bad fortune. . . . God alone knows what the future holds for our country."[75]

The first concerns of the prince and the government were to ensure the unity of the state, shore up its finances, adopt a constitution, and obtain the powers' approbation for the new situation in Danubian Romania. Carol immediately sought to mollify separatists in Moldavia by granting an amnesty to the Moldavian metropolitan in Iaşi, Calinic, and by establishing a coalition regime of liberals and conservatives from both Moldavia and Wallachia. He also sent diplomatic agents to St. Petersburg, Berlin, Vienna, and Constantinople to the end that the powers would acknowledge his title.[76]

Carol's arrival in Bucharest accentuated differences between the powers and rendered impossible any collective moves. Turkey strenuously protested the fait accompli and proposed direct military intervention to rectify the "abnormal and illegal" situation. Russia, while rejecting the entry of Turkish troops, recommended that an international commission be empowered to "annul the illegal acts" in Danubian Romania. Austria suggested further that if such a commission could not redress the matter, military force ought to be employed. France, Britain, Prussia, and Italy, on the contrary, repudiated armed meddling. Drouyn de Lhuys, for example, warned about the inevitable bloodshed that an occupation of Danubian Romania would entail; hence he argued that Carol be allowed to govern.[77]

The powers' postures had dramatically changed since the Crimean War, when the Western powers cooperated in preserving the integrity of the Ottoman Empire. Britain was more avid in 1866 about suffrage reform at home and in keeping an entente with France than in the future of Turkey. Italy still longed to obtain Venetia, in concord with Prussia and an understanding with France; loath to offend either power, Italy was sympathetic to the Hohenzollern candidate. For France, the presence of a foreign prince in Bucharest spelled the maintenance of the Moldo-Wallachian union and thereby of a roadblock on Russian and Austrian paths of expansion in the Balkan Peninsula. Austria was, of course, deeply involved in a struggle with Prussia for mastery of Germany as well as in a contest with Hungarians for political control within the Habsburg Empire, and so had little energy left for dealing with Danubian Romania. Austria nonetheless opposed a Hohenzollern in Bucharest as being a potential military threat to the Habsburg Empire and a challenge to Austrian political predominance in Southeastern Europe. For Prussia, friendship with Russia was more important on the eve of war with Austria than a foreign prince in Romania. Bismarck informed Gorchakov that Carol had acted on his own personal "risk and responsibility," and not on that of the Prussian government. Bismarck indicated that Russia should decide whether Carol was to stay in Bucharest.[78] Even so, Danubian Romania might assist Prussia against Austria. If Hungarians attacked Germans in Austria, then Romanians would join the fray.[79] This possibility was stillborn owing to the speed with which Prussia defeated Austria and to the lack of compensation available for the Romanians. Bismarck was unable to offer the Romanian-inhabited regions of Bessarabia, Transylvania, Bukowina, or the Banat. Russia would resist the creation of a large Romanian state under Carol's direction and would certainly refuse to cede northern Bessarabia to Romania. Nor was Prussia ready to antagonize the Hungarians in the Habsburg Empire, whose support would be more valuable than that of the more distant and less concerned Danubian Romanians. The possibility still remained that Prussia would become the advocate for an independent Romania if Bucharest's aid was helpful in winning the war. What was to be accomplished a decade later in Romania's alliance with Russia against Turkey might have been achieved in league with Prussia against Austria. Russia, in turn, sought a quid pro quo on the Romanian question; in exchange for a foreign prince, restrictions on Russia's naval activity in the Black Sea were to be rescinded.[80] But once Carol was ensconced in Bucharest, Russia heeded the Catholic Polish refugees in Danubian Romania and Romania's dedicated monasteries more than Carol. Many Poles had sought asylum abroad following the failure of the Polish rebellion of 1863, and Russia feared the consequences of a Polish conspiracy developing on its frontier. This presentiment proved to be a fantasy, as most Polish exiles found life in Catholic France more compatible religiously and culturally than in Orthodox Romania. Further, the dedicated monasteries embraced much wealth, having Greek monks who siphoned off monastic revenues to the Holy Places and patriarchates. Romania's secularization of these monasteries in 1863 meant that their property passed to the state. Russia, in its traditional role as champion of Orthodox Christianity in the Ottoman Empire, objected. Monastic estates, Russia demanded, were to be returned, or a large indemnity was to be paid. Danubian Romania nevertheless kept these monastic lands without recompense, despite Russia's efforts and the Romanians' willingness to compromise regarding financial claims.[81]

More dangerous than the attitudes of the other powers were those of the Ottoman Empire; a Turkish invasion of Danubian Romania would compel Carol to abdicate. Turkey's foreign affairs minister, Ali Mehmed Paşa, disregarded the plebiscite in favor of Carol and bid the provisional government in Bucharest to select an indigenous prince for a five-year term.[82] Moreover, the Turks concentrated troops at Shumen and at the fortresses of Ruse and Tulcea south of the Danube River in April and May 1866.[83] One estimate had 5,000–7,000 Turkish soldiers at Silistra and 10,000–15,000 at Ruse preparing for operations north of the Danube.[84] A Romanian district prefect reported that 65,000 Turks, led by Osman Nuri Paşa, were set to cross the Danube at three points: Giurgiu, Calafat, and Galaţi.[85] The Turkish grand vezir, Fuad Paşa, thought the Romanians were about to strike the Ottoman Empire; in addition, Ali Paşa wanted to overrun Danubian Romania because of its "flagrant violation" of treaties.[86] Turkey's council of ministers then ordered its army to traverse the Danube, advance to Bucharest, and, presumably, expel the foreign prince.[87] No offensive was launched, for all that, due to inadequate Turkish military preparations and to Turkey's status in European politics: the Ottoman Empire existed in large measure on the sufferance of the other powers, and so it abjured interceding in Danubian Romania without their approval.

The Turkish military machinations nonetheless triggered a vigorous response. Romania's prime minister, Ion Ghica, declared: "If the Turks cross the Danube, we shall resist."[88] The Romanian army mobilized, and the deputies voted a war budget. Forty thousand men and one hundred cannon in one cavalry and three infantry brigades deployed on the Argeş River with advance posts at Giurgiu and Olteniţa on the Danube.[89] Serbian military aid was requested. Dumitru Brătianu, Ion's elder brother, went to Belgrade (Beograd) seeking bullets and powder. Serbia's ruler, Prince Michael Obrenović (1860–68), then empowered Filip Hristić to promise supplies and, according to Carol, to declare that all Orthodox Christians of the Ottoman Empire placed their hopes in Carol's guidance.[90] Yet Romania's ability to withstand a Turkish incursion was slight. Morale was low among the officers, and discipline lax among the troops. Officers were somewhat unreliable, for many were upset by the dismissal or resignation of some Cuza loyalists.[91] Soldiers lacked enthusiasm for combat. One frontier battalion, composed principally of peasants, refused to be mustered. And 80 peasants deserted from a battalion of 350 at Giurgiu in May 1866, for they had insufficient food, shelter, and pay; moreover, they were heavily taxed.[92] Nor, as already noted, were the Turks braced for hostilities; the Romanian prefect in Giurgiu was even able to purchase ammunition from the Turks across the Danube in Ruse.[93] The significance of Romania's tough response to the Turkish challenge lay less in whether it was realistic and more in the success it had in solidifying public opinion for union and the foreign prince. Indeed, the specter of separatism, though still lingering, no longer haunted Romanian patriots after this crisis.

Threats and counterthreats of war between Danubian Romania and the Ottoman Empire evaporated when Ion Ghica, who had once served the sultan as *bey* (governor) of Samos, and Ali Paşa began to negotiate. The Turks rescinded orders to attack, and Romanian troops withdrew from forward positions.[94] Both sides backed away from hostilities for which neither was prepared and for which neither was supported by any of the powers. At the outset of deliberations, Ali Paşa enumerated conditions for the sultan's recognition of Carol. Several of them infringed on Romania's autonomy: namely, a Romanian fortification of the Prut River in wartime, a Turkish occupation of Ismail in southern Bessarabia and Calafat in Wallachia, and an interdiction on Hungarian refugees returning to Transylvania.[95] These terms indicated the defensive posture of Turkish policy and again identified the Russian menace to Southeastern Europe. Ali Paşa also called on Carol to swear loyalty to the sultan and to acknowledge that the "United Principalities of Wallachia and Moldavia" were an "integral part" of the Ottoman Empire; Carol was to respect the sultan's "suzerainty" and "never interfere with the bonds of vassalage" joining Danubian Romania to the empire. Ghica, in his turn, proposed the substitution of "Romania" for "United Principalities" and suggested that the phrase "secular bonds" replace "bonds of vassalage." Ali Paşa required Carol to go to Constantinople for investiture as an elective, nonhereditary prince. Ghica argued that Carol should meet the sultan only after being accredited as Romania's ruler with the prerogative of direct male inheritance to the throne. Ghica and Ali Paşa concurred on the indisputable need for Danubian Romania's "prosperity" and its "rights," yet they had conflicting views about collaboration between vassal and suzerain. Ali Paşa insisted that Romania cooperate fully in defending Turkish "rights and general interests"; Ghica consented merely to take measures in common with the Ottoman Empire in order to repel "all foreign aggression." Ghica nonetheless accepted the applicability in Romania of Turkish international treaties so long as their provisions heeded domestic privileges. But he resolutely opposed Turkish demands that Romania pledge to forswear conspiring against Turkey, that Romanian diplomatic agents be restricted to nonpolitical functions of a "purely local nature," that the Turks have a representative residing in Romania to supervise Ottoman commercial affairs, and that the dedicated monasteries be further discussed. Other areas of disagreement involved the internal administration of Danubian Romania, the size of its army, the emission of money, and the conferment of decorations. Romanians and Turks agreed that the tribute be increased in proportion to the "actual resources" of the country, and that it be fixed by a separate convention.[96] These were the major points of friction and accord. At stake was less a break with the past than the prestige of both parties.

Turkish-Romanian negotiations were tortuous and time-consuming. Carol meanwhile journeyed in Moldavia and brought about a rapprochement with separatists in Iaşi.[97] Carol's chief problems—separatism, financial chaos, and recognition—also concerned his primary booster, Napoleon III, who pledged monetary aid to Danubian Romania if Carol promptly obtained the sultan's approval.[98] Carol finally went to Constantinople after corresponding with the new grand vezir, Mehmed Rüştü Paşa. The latter endorsed Carol as the hereditary prince of Romania in exchange for Carol's approbation of the "secular bonds" of Ottoman "suzerainty" over the "United Principalities"—an "integral part" of the empire—and for his promise that Turkish subjects in Romania would enjoy "security and protection."[99] The moment had come for investiture.

Carol's sojourn in Constantinople was highly ceremonial, resembling Cuza's visits in 1860 and 1864 as well as earlier ones by the *voievods* (princes) of Moldavia and Wallachia.[100] Carol traveled by train to Giurgiu on the Danube and to Varna on the Black Sea coast, accompanied by a representative entourage of Romanian statesmen. At Varna, he sailed to the Palace of the Sweet Water on the Anatolian side of the Sea of Marmara. Carol met the ecumenical patriarch, Sōphronios III (1863–66), donated alms to the poor, and called on diplomats. He traded assurances of friendship with Ali Paşa, and together they smoked from long pipes and drank much coffee. Ali Paşa continued to employ the expression "Moldo-Wallachians," while Carol said "Romanians." In his first meeting with Sultan Abdul Aziz, Carol rejected an assigned chair, shook hands with him, and sat beside him on the imperial sofa. The sultan handed Carol a *ferman*, or edict of investiture, which was then passed unopened to Gheorghe Ştirbei, Romania's minister of foreign affairs. The second and last audience with Abdul Aziz involved the awarding of presents and decorations. In all, Carol received five Arabian stallions, a bejeweled saber from Damascus, and the Order of Osman. His reception was magnificent, but it differed from the ones accorded to Cuza mainly in Carol's delegating to his private secretary, Émile Picot, the distribution of *bahşiş*, or gifts.[101]

Carol's *ferman* revealed how little and how much Romanian diplomacy had achieved. The hereditary prince of the United Principalities of

Moldavia and Wallachia was to "respect constantly" the sultan's rights of suzerainty over Danubian Romania—an "integral part" of the Ottoman Empire—and to maintain the "secular bonds" that linked them together. Additional signs of dependence included stipulations that the maximum size of the army be 30,000 men; Romanian money was to bear an Ottoman insignia; the principality was not to bestow military decorations; Romania was not to be a haven for conspirators; and the tribute was to be augmented. Treaties between the Ottoman Empire and other powers were binding in Danubian Romania, except when their provisions contravened international acts concerning the principality. The *ferman* expressly prohibited Romania from concluding pacts with foreign powers yet allowed nonpolitical arrangements with Russia and Austria that might serve local interests.[102]

Ştirbei worked out final details of the Romanian-Turkish settlement following Carol's departure from Constantinople. He succeeded in gaining authorization for his country to issue a medal, to mint gold and silver money—but carrying an imperial insignia—and to appoint a Romanian commercial agent in Varna.[103] More important was the tribute. Danubian Romania had paid the sultan in coin and in kind from the time of the Turkish conquest in the fifteenth century. Agreements between Turkey and Russia had regulated tribute at the end of the eighteenth century. Such was also the situation after the Crimean War, when the amount was 1.5 million piastres from Moldavia and 2.5 million from Wallachia.[104] Carol conceded that the tribute should be increased, but he likewise reckoned that any increase needed the Romanian legislature's approval.[105] It was to be remitted each April to the Zarifi bank in Constantinople.[106] Carol was, however, to send no more and no less than had Cuza. Nor was the tribute reported in the budget. Turkey refrained from pressing this matter, being apparently convinced of its bargaining weakness; Romania, on its side, behaved as if what was not urgently claimed did not, or would not, pose a problem. The tribute was hardly exorbitant, being equal to what Danubian Romania spent each year for managing prisons or for operating rural schools; the 4 million piastres amounted to 5 percent of the state's expenditures. In contrast, Serbia owed 2.3 million piastres in annual tribute, or 8 percent of its distributions; and Egypt, 75 million piastres, or 13 percent of its total outlay in 1869.[107] Though only a nominal burden, the tribute still symbolized Danubian Romania's vassalage.

After the investiture in Constantinople, the powers recognized Carol, the first foreigner in a dynasty that lasted until 1947.[108] The powers had done next to nothing to prevent a foreign prince in Danubian Romania; they had been too involved in other quarrels, especially in questions attending the

Austro-Prussian War, to prevent or overturn Romania's decisions. Austria's defeat at Königgrätz emasculated its foreign policy; its primary concern was then to reorganize itself internally. Russia required Prussia's support in eventually abrogating clauses in the 1856 Treaty of Paris that neutralized the Black Sea, and therefore cultivated Prussia's favor. Prussia's reemergence as a potent military force ensured Russia's and Austria's acceptance of Romania's Hohenzollern. The foreign prince signified stability to some European financiers and statesmen. The Ottoman sultan's conferral of a *ferman* on Carol and the powers' approbation of this act led West European bankers to invest in Romania.[109] Romania's economic dependence on foreign countries would, as we shall see, gradually replace political dependence on the Ottoman Empire.

One of the patriots' goals—the foreign prince—had been achieved. The aspirations of many Danubian Romanians would, however, await fulfillment until complete independence was won.

Notes

1. Procès-verbal no. 7 of the divan in Moldavia, 7/19 October 1857, and no. 6 of the one in Wallachia, 9/21 October 1857, in *Acte şi documente relative la istoria renascerei Romaniei*, vol. 6, pt. 1, 66; pt. 2, 33.

2. Procès-verbal no. 7 of the divan in Moldavia, 7/19 October 1857, and no. 5 of the one in Wallachia, 8/20 October 1857, in *Acte şi documente relative la istoria renascerei Romaniei*, vol. 6, pt. 1, 68, 79; pt. 2, 28, 30; article 13 of the Paris convention, 19 August 1858, in *Recueil d'actes internationaux de l'Empire Ottoman*, 3:112.

3. Paris conference protocol nos. 21 and 22, 13 April and 6 September 1859, in *Archives diplomatiques*, vol. 6, pt. 2 (avril, mai, juin 1866), 162, 166–67.

4. Note from Cuza, 25 January/6 February 1859, to the powers that signed the Treaty of Paris, 30 March 1856, in *Acte şi documente relative la istoria renascerei Romaniei*, 8:639–40.

5. Henri Tillos (Bucharest) to Édouard Drouyn de Lhuys (Paris), 20 October 1865, no. 40, in Archives du Ministère des Affaires Étrangères, Correspondance Politique—Turquie: Consulat Bucarest, vol. 26 (hereinafter cited AMAE[F], CP); Tillos to Drouyn de Lhuys, 9 January 1866, no. 3, in ibid., vol. 27; Karl von Eder (Bucharest) to Alexander von Mensdorff-Pouilly (Vienna), 10 April 1866, no. 51, in Paul Henry, *L'abdication du prince Cuza et l'avènement de la dynastie de Hohenzollern au trône de Roumanie: Documents diplomatiques*, 296; see Brătianu's speech in the assembly (Bucharest), 11/23 February 1863, in *Din scrierile şi cuvîntările lui Ion C. Brătianu*, vol. 1, pt. 1, 302–3.

6. Henri de Ségur (Bucharest) to Jules Bastide (Paris), 5/17 November 1848, in *Anul 1848 în principatele române*, 5:375–76.

7. Aleksandr M. Gorchakov to Nikolai P. Ignat'ev (Constantinople), 10/22 October 1865, in Gerhard Hilke, "Russlands Haltung zur rumänischen Frage," 204.

8. Constantin C. Giurescu, *Viaţa şi opera lui Cuza Vodă*, 159–71; Apostol Stan, *Grupări şi curente politice în România între unire şi independenţă (1859–1877)*, 158–68.

9. Brătianu's speech in the assembly, 11/23 February 1863, in *Din scrierile şi cuvîntările lui Ion C. Brătianu*, vol. 1, pt. 1, 297, 310.

10. Dan Berindei, *Epoca unirii*, 106–15; Gerald J. Bobango, *The Emergence of the Romanian National State*, 159–69.

11. Alexandru D. Xenopol, *Domnia lui Cuza-Vodă*, 2:30–31; Slobodan Jovanović, *Vlada Milana Obrenovića*, 1:156–57. Maria's first son, Prince Milan (1854–1901), from her marriage to a landholder in Wallachia, Miloš Obrenović (1829–60), would later rule Serbia (1868–89). Cuza adopted his first son, Alexandru, on 11/23 May 1865 and his second son, Dumitru, on 5/17 November 1865.

12. *Domnia regelui Carol I: Fapte-cuvântări-documente*, 1:xix.

13. Brătianu (Paris) to Pia (wife) (Florica), 9/21 January 1866, in *Din corespondenţa familiei Ion C. Brătianu*, 1:67.

14. *Revista Dunării* appeared in Bucharest from 19/31 December 1865 to 1/13 January 1866; see *Publicaţiunile periodice româneşti: Ziare, gazete, reviste*, 1:569.

15. Giurescu, *Viaţa şi opera lui Cuza Vodă*, 374–76; Thad W. Riker, *The Making of Roumania: A Study of an International Problem, 1856–1866*, 491–92.

16. *Monitorul: Jurnal oficial al României*, 15/27 February 1866. Other members of the regency were General Nicolae Golescu and Colonel Nicolae Haralambie; Tillos to Drouyn de Lhuys, 23 February 1866, telegram no. 3421, in AMAE(F), CP—Turquie: Consulat Bucarest, vol. 27. See a legislative decision, 11/23 February 1866, in *Archives diplomatiques*, vol. 6, pt. 2 (1866), 284–85.

17. Ludwika Sniadecka (Kaba Taş/Constantinople) to Jan L. Gradowicz (Bucharest), 11/23 February 1859, in *Documente privind unirea principatelor*, vol. 3: *Corespondenţa politică (1855–1859)*, 523, 525; Tillos to Drouyn de Lhuys, 16 August 1865, no. 30, in AMAE(F), CP—Turquie: Consulat Bucarest, vol. 26.

18. *Discours prononcé par Son Altesse Impériale le Prince Napoléon le 15 mai 1865 pour l'inauguration du monument élevé dans la ville d'Ajaccio à Napoléon Ier et à ses frères*, 9, 16–23, 29–32. For a conversation at the Tuileries Palace, 19 June 1865, see *Napoléon III et le Prince Napoléon: Correspondance inédite*, 373–82. The rift between the emperor and the prince lasted from May 1865 to June 1866.

19. Procès-verbal by the Romanian delegation from the legislature, 24 February/8 March 1866, in *Charles Ier, Roi de Roumanie: Chronique, actes, documents*, 1:9–11.

20. Charles Rogier (Brussels) to Jacques Poumay (Bucharest), 14/26 February 1866, in *Charles Ier, Roi de Roumanie*, 1:3. Philip married Carol's younger sister, Maria, in 1867; owing to the death of King Leopold II's only son, Leopold (1859–69), Philip's son, Albert, would eventually rule Belgium (1909–34).

21. *Almanach de Gotha: Annuaire diplomatique et statistique, 1867*, 19–23.

22. See letters from Austria's envoy in Belgium, Vrintz (Brussels) to Karl F. von Buol-Schauenstein (Vienna), 2 April, 7 May, 5 and 8 June 1857, in Henry, *L'abdication du prince Cuza*, 181–84. See the Romanians' appeal to the Paris conference, 30 March 1866, in *Din scrierile şi cuvîntările lui Ion C. Brătianu*, vol. 1, pt. 1, 407; for Brătianu's speech (Bucharest), 3/15 February 1869, see *Ion C. Brătianu:*

Acte şi cuvântări, vol. 1, pt. 2, 101; Gheorghe Platon, "Le diplomate belge Édouard Blondeel van Cuelebroeck dans les Principautés roumaines (1856–1857)," 43, 51–52, 58–65.

23. Empress Catherine II (Tsarskoe Tselo) to Emperor Joseph II, 10/21 September 1782, and Joseph (Vienna) to Catherine, 13 November 1782, in *Joseph II und Katharina von Russland: Ihr Briefwechsel,* 153–56, 172–73.

24. Talleyrand (Strasbourg) to Emperor Napoleon I, 17 October 1805, in *Lettres inédites de Talleyrand à Napoléon, 1800–1809,* 162–64, 168, 171–72.

25. See notes on a conversation with Napoleon III, March 1854, and with Francis Joseph I, 1 June 1854, in Ernst II von Sachsen-Coburg-Gotha, *Aus meinem Leben und aus meiner Zeit,* 2:139, 174, 186.

26. Cavour (Paris) to Massimo d'Azeglio, 8 December 1855, in *Lettere edite ed inedite di Camillo Cavour,* 2:158.

27. Cavour (Torino) to Salvatore di Villamarina (Paris), 29 December 1855, in *Tutti gli scritti di Camillo Cavour,* vol. 4 (1850–61), 1872–73.

28. Cavour (Paris) to Emanuele d'Azeglio (London), 26 February 1856, in *La politique du comte Camillo di Cavour de 1852 à 1861: Lettres inédites avec notes,* 103; see Cavour's notes (February 1856), in *Tutti gli scritti di Camillo Cavour,* 4:1881–82, 1883–84.

29. Cavour (Paris) to Michelangelo Castelli (Torino), April 1856, in *Lettere edite ed inedite di Camillo Cavour,* 2:227.

30. See point no. 7 of the Pact of Plombières-les-Bains, 21 July 1858, in *Tutti gli scritti di Camillo Cavour,* 4:1979.

31. John W. Bush, *Venetia Redeemed: Franco-Italian Relations, 1864–1866,* 10–11.

32. Temple Viscount Palmerston to John Russell, 7 January 1864, in *The Later Correspondence of Lord John Russell, 1840–1878,* 2: 288; Costantino Nigra (Paris) to Alfonso di La Marmora, 26 November 1864, in Alfonso La Marmora, *Un po' più di luce sugli eventi politici e militari dell' anno 1866,* 39; Drouyn de Lhuys's circular (Compiègne), 29 November 1864, in Ministère des Affaires Étrangères, *Les origines diplomatiques de la guerre de 1870–1871: Recueil de documents,* 5:105–6.

33. Bismarck (Biarritz) to King William I, 11 October 1865, in *Bismarck: Die gesammelten Werke—Politische Schriften,* 5:310.

34. Nigra to La Marmora, 19 January 1866, in Eugenio Passamonti, "Constantino Nigra ed Alfonso Lamarmora dal 1862–1866," 441–42.

35. Robert von der Goltz (Paris) to Bismarck, 16 February 1866, reporting a conversation with the Italian envoy, Nigra, in *Die auswärtige Politik Preußens, 1858–1871: Diplomatische Aktenstücke,* 6:587; cf. Nigra to La Marmora, 1 March 1866, relating an interview with Napoleon III, omitting Bosnia and Serbia but suggesting that Austria take Moldo-Wallachia, and Turkey receive financial compensation, in Passamonti, "Constantino Nigra ed Alfonso Lamarmora dal 1862–1866," 447–49.

36. See the report of Helmuth von Moltke (chief of the Prussian general staff) concerning a Prussian crown council meeting, 28 February 1866, referring to information from Goltz, the Prussian envoy in Paris, in *Die auswärtige Politik Preußens,* 6:618.

37. Mensdorff-Pouilly to Richard von Metternich-Winneburg (Paris), 16 March 1866, in Hermann Oncken, *Die Rheinpolitik Kaiser Napoleons III von 1863 bis 1870 und der Ursprung des Krieges von 1870/71,* 1:110–11.

38. Heinrich von Redern (St. Petersburg) to Bismarck, 10 March 1866, in *Die auswärtige Politik Preußens,* 6:649; Charles-Angél de Talleyrand-Périgord (St. Petersburg) to Drouyn de Lhuys, 14 March 1866, in Henry, *L'abdication du prince Cuza,* 242.

39. Cf. Werner E. Mosse, *The Rise and Fall of the Crimean System, 1855–71: The Story of a Peace Settlement,* 133–35.

40. Gorchakov to Andrei Budberg (Paris), 23 February/7 March 1866, in *Archives diplomatiques,* vol. 8, pt. 1 (1868), 271–73; Redern to Bismarck, 25 February and 15 March 1866, in *Die auswärtige Politik Preußens,* 6:605, 674; Talleyrand-Périgord to Drouyn de Lhuys, 21 March 1866, in *Les origines diplomatiques de la guerre de 1870–1871,* 8:51; Evgenii E. Chertan, "Velikie derzhavy i gosudarstvennyi perevorot 1866 g. v Rumynii," 26.

41. Werner E. Mosse, *The European Powers and the German Question 1848–71, with special reference to England and Russia,* 225–26.

42. Paris conference protocol no. 1, 10 March 1866, in *Archives diplomatiques,* vol. 7, pt. 2 (avril, mai, juin 1867), 614.

43. [Brătianu], *Appel des Roumains à la Conférence.*

44. Paris conference protocol no. 4, 22 May 1858, in *Archives diplomatiques,* vol. 6, pt. 2 (1866), 114–15; protocol no. 2, 19 March 1866, in ibid., vol. 7, pt. 2 (1867), 615–16, 618–20.

45. Lionel de Moustier (Constantinople) to Drouyn de Lhuys, 28 February and 11 April 1866, in *Archives diplomatiques,* vol. 7, pt. 1 (janvier, février, mars 1867), 240, 249; Moustier to Drouyn de Lhuys, 8 March 1866, in Henry, *L'abdication du prince Cuza,* 227.

46. Mensdorff-Pouilly to Metternich-Winneburg, 1, 22, and 26 March 1866, in Henry, *L'abdication du prince Cuza,* 204, 258, 263–64.

47. Gorchakov to Ignat'ev, 14/26 February 1866, in Hilke, "Russlands Haltung zur rumänischen Frage," 205–6; Gorchakov to Filipp I. Brunnov (London), 22 February/6 March 1866, and Gorchakov to Budberg, 23 February/7 March 1866, in *Archives diplomatiques,* vol. 8, pt. 1 (1868), 274–75, 273; Paris conference protocol no. 2, 19 March 1866, in ibid., vol. 7, pt. 2 (1867), 616; Redern to Bismarck, 15 March 1866, in *Die auswärtige Politik Preußens,* 6:674.

48. Henri de La Tour d'Auvergne (London) to Drouyn de Lhuys, 22 March 1866, in Henry, *L'abdication du prince Cuza,* 258.

49. Bismarck to Goltz, 14 March 1866, in *Bismarck: Die gesammelten Werke,* 5:403–5; Bismarck to Goltz, 23 March 1866, in *Die auswärtige Politik Preußens,* 6:723–24.

50. Paris conference protocol no. 2, 19 March 1866, in *Archives diplomatiques,* vol. 7, pt. 2 (1867), 619–20; cf. Nigra to La Marmora, 17 March 1866, in Passamonti, "Constantino Nigra ed Alfonso Lamarmora dal 1862–1866," 452–53.

51. Brătianu (Paris) to Pia Brătianu, 14/26 February 1866, in *Din corespondenţa familiei Ion C. Brătianu,* 1:73.

52. Petre P. Panaitescu, "Urcarea în scaun a principelui Carol de Hohenzollern," 256.

53. Marcel Emerit, *Madame Cornu et Napoléon III,* 66, 68; Cornu was born Hortense Lacroix, the daughter of a chambermaid of Napoleon III's mother, Hortense de Beauharnais; Émile Ollivier, *L'empire libéral: Études, récits, souvenirs,* 8:71–72.

54. Brătianu's memorandum (Paris), 12 March 1866, in AMAE(F), Mémoires et documents—Roumanie, 1862–1869, vol. 18.

55. Bălăceanu's telegram of 14/26 March 1866, in *Charles Ier, Roi de Roumanie,* 1:46.

56. *Monitorul: Jurnal oficial al României,* 19/31 March 1866; Gheorghe Georgescu-Buzău, "Instaurarea şi organizarea regimului burghezo-moşieresc (1866)," 525–26. Deputies, but not senators, were to be elected.

57. See Carol's notes for March 1866, in *Aus dem Leben König Karls von Rumänien: Aufzeichnungen eines Augenzeugen,* 1:3–4; Emerit, *Madame Cornu et Napoléon III,* 8, 63–64, and n.2.

58. Prince Charles Anthony to William I, 4 April 1866, in *Aus dem Leben König Karls von Rumänien,* 1:5–6.

59. Brătianu's telegram (Berlin), 20 March/1 April 1866, in *Charles Ier, Roi de Roumanie,* 1:64.

60. Boerescu and Ludovic Steege (Paris) to Ion Ghica (Bucharest), 18 April 1866, in Arhivele Statului, Arhiva Istorică Centrală, Casa Regală, dosar no. 18/1866 (hereinafter cited AIC, CR); Drouyn de Lhuys to Adolphe d'Avril (Bucharest), 13 April 1866, no. 9, in AMAE(F), CP—Turquie: Consulat Bucarest, vol. 27; Drouyn de Lhuys to Avril, 11 May 1866, no. 12, and Drouyn de Lhuys to Ion Ghica, 18 May 1866, in ibid., vol. 28; Drouyn de Lhuys's circular, 18 April 1866, in *Archives diplomatiques,* vol. 7, pt.1 (1867), 250–52.

61. Cornu (Versailles) to Bălăceanu (Paris), 2 April 1866, in Fond Ion Bălăceanu, no. 29320, Biblioteca Academiei Române, Secţia de corespondenţă (hereinafter cited BAR, SC); Cornu to Carol, 4/16 April 1866, in *Charles Ier, Roi de Roumanie,* 1:110–11; Paris conference protocol no. 6, 24 April 1866, in *Archives diplomatiques,* vol. 7, pt. 2 (1867), 647–55.

62. William I's undated draft of a repy to Charles Anthony, in *Bismarck: Die gesammelten Werke,* 5:447; William I to Charles Anthony, 14 April 1866, in *Aus dem Leben König Karls von Rumänien,* 1:11–14.

63. Journal of the council of ministers, 30 March/11 April 1866, in *Monitorul: Jurnal oficial al României,* 2/14 April 1866.

64. Dimitrie Ghica (Bucharest) to Matei Sturdza (Roman), 7 April and 13 April 1866, in Fond Dimitrie A. Sturdza, XX/161, 162, BAR, SC.

65. George Lecca (prefect of Bacău) to the prefect of Roman (Matei Sturdza), 17 April 1866, in Fond Dimitrie A. Sturdza, XXVII/70, BAR, SC; Ion Ghica to Drouyn de Lhuys, 16/28 April 1866, in AMAE(F), CP—Turquie: Consulat Bucarest, vol. 27; Ferdinand Haas (Iaşi) to Mensdorff-Pouilly, 30 April 1866, no. 29, copy in Arhiva Consul Austriaci, IX, Biblioteca Academiei Române (hereinafter cited BAR, ACA); cf. *Monitorul: Jurnal oficial al României,* 12/24 1866. Cuza's coup d'état in 1864 was submitted to a plebiscite and approved by a vote of 682,621 to 1,307 with 70,220 abstentions; see Grigore Chiriţă, "România în 1866: Coordinate ale politicii interne şi internaţionale," 2206.

66. Haas to Mensdorff-Pouilly, 16 March 1866, no. 13, in BAR, ACA, XIX; Ion Ghica to Bălăceanu, 16 April 1866, in AMAE(F), CP—Turquie: Consulat Bucarest, vol. 27.

67. For accounts of the riot and conflicting casualty reports, see the initial issue of *Vocea nationala,* 5 April 1866; reports by Ştefan Golescu, 3/15 and 4/16 April 1866, in *Romanulu,* 4–5/16–17 April 1866; Haas to Mensdorff-Pouilly, 17 April 1866, no. 25, in BAR, ACA, XIX; see reports by Austrian and French representatives, 17 April 1866, in Henry, *L'abdication du prince Cuza,* 311–17; Golescu (Iaşi) to Dimitrie Ghica, 28 March/9 April and 2/14 April 1866, in *Din vremea renaşterii naţionale a Ţării Româneşti: Boierii Goleşti,* 4:407–8; Barbara Jelavich, "Russia and Moldavian Separatism: The Demonstration of April, 1866," 82–86.

68. Nicolae Iorga, *Istoria Românilor,* 10:24; Gheorghe Cristea, "Manifestări antidinastice în perioada venirii lui Carol I în România (aprilie-mai 1866)," 1090.

69. Avril to Drouyn de Lhuys, 8 September 1866, in Henry, *L'abdication du prince Cuza,* 450.

70. See article 12 of the Paris convention, 19 August 1858, in *Recueil d'actes internationaux de l'Empire Ottoman,* 3:112; Vasile Boeresu, Ludovic Steege, and Scarlat Fălcoianu, "Mémoire presénté à la Conférence de Paris par les délégués des Principautés Unies Roumaines, 15 April 1866," in Arhiva Dimitrie A. Sturdza, II/471–84, Biblioteca Academiei Române, Secţia manuscriselor (hereinafter cited BAR, SM); Paris conference protocol no. 7, 2 May 1866, in *Archives diplomatiques,* vol. 7, pt. 2 (1867), 657.

71. Carol's conversation with Bismarck, 19 April 1866, in *Aus dem Leben König Karls von Rumänien,* 1:17; Bălăceanu to Ion Ghica, 27 April 1866, in Arhiva Dimitrie A. Sturdza, II/158, BAR, SM; John Green (Bucharest) to George Villiers, Earl of Clarendon (London), 5 July 1866, no. 110, in Public Record Office, Foreign Office, 78/1920 (hereinafter cited PRO, FO).

72. See a review of Simeon Bărnuţiu, *Dreptulu publicu alu Romanilor* (Iaşi: Tribunei Romane, 1867), in *Titu Maiorescu: Critice,* 2:166–68, 190–92.

73. *Monitorul: Jurnal oficial al României,* 5/17 May and 7/19 May 1866; cf. Dimitrie Ghica's circular to prefects, 13 May 1866, in Fond Dimitrie A. Sturdza, XX/169, BAR, SC; "Autoritatea faptului îndeplinit executat în 1866 de cei îndreptăţiţi," 961–62, 977–81.

74. Carol's passport bearing the name Karl Hettingen, dated 15 May 1866, in Arhiva Palatului, XXVII/113, Biblioteca Academiei Române (hereinafter cited BAR, AP); Carol's letters to William I, 12 May 1866, as well as to Napoleon III, Alexander II, and Abdul Aziz, 13 May 1866, in *Aus dem Leben König Karls von Rumänien,* 1:31–32, 33–49.

75. See Carol's notes, 10/22 May 1866, in *Aus dem Leben König Karls von Rumänien,* 1:52–53.

76. Boerescu and Costa-Foru went to St. Petersburg and Berlin, Dimitrie Ghica to Vienna and Berlin, Ion Ghica to Constantinople, and Dumitru Brătianu to Paris; Dumitru Brătianu (Paris) to Carol, 30 August 1866, in *Din arhiva lui Dumitru Brătianu: Acte şi scrisori din perioada 1840–1870,* 2:259–60; Nicolae Corivan, *Relaţiile diplomatice ale României de la 1859 la 1877,* 204.

77. Paris conference protocols no. 9, 25 May 1866, and no. 10, 4 June 1866, in *Archives diplomatiques,* vol. 7, pt. 2 (1867), 665–69, 669–73.

78. Bismarck to Redern, 30 May 1866, in *Bismarck: Die gesammelten Werke,* 5:517–18.

79. Bismarck encouraged Hungarian émigrés, including István Türr, to attack Austria, possibly in league with Italy as well as with Romania and Serbia, in order to gain an independent Transylvania under the crown of Hungary; see a copy of Bismarck's letter to Türr in Bălăceanu to Carol, n.d., Fond Ion Bălăceanu, no. 28507, BAR, SC; Bismarck to Goltz, 14 June 1866, in *Bismarck: Die gesammelten Werke,* 5:549; cf. Bismarck to Saint Pierre (Bucharest), 5 July 1866, in ibid., 6:37.

80. Chester W. Clark, "Prince Gorchakov and the Black Sea Question, 1866: A Russian Bomb That Did Not Explode," 52.

81. For the monasteries, see Mircea Păcurariu, *Istoria bisericii ortodoxe române,* 1:551–52, 595–603; 2:216–28, 560–72, 641–51; 3:116–20, 369–73; see also Chapter Eight below.

82. Report by Alexandru Golescu, (Constantinople), 22 April/4 May 1866, in Constantin N. Velichi, "Relaţiile romîno-turce în perioada februarie-iulie 1866," 848; cf. Paris conference protocol no. 8, 17 May 1866, in *Archives diplomatiques,* vol 7, pt. 2 (1867), 661.

83. E. Joy Morris (Constantinople) to William H. Seward (Washington), 11 April and 17 May 1866, in 39th Congress, 2nd Session, House of Representatives, Executive Documents, 1866–1867, 240, 441–42 (hereinafter cited 39th Cong.).

84. Ion Ghica (Bucharest) to Bălăceanu (Paris), n.d. (end of April or beginning of May), in Fond Ion Bălăceanu, no. 29465, BAR, SC; Haralambie (Giurgiu) to Dimitrie Creţulescu (Olteniţa), 28 May/9 June 1866, in Velichi, "Relaţiile romîno-turce în perioada februarie-iulie 1866," 850.

85. Cf. Morris to Seward, 17 May 1866, in 39th Cong., 441–42.

86. Vasile Mihordea, *Răscoala grănicerilor de la 1866,* 13n. 8, 16; Ali Paşa (Constantinople) to Savfet Paşa (Paris), 24 May 1866, in Henry, *L'abdication du prince Cuza,* 391.

87. Morris to Seward, 22 May 1866, in 39th Cong., 244.

88. Ion Ghica (Bucharest) to Bălăceanu (Paris), 19 May 1866, in Fond Ion Bălăceanu, no. 29470, BAR, SC.

89. Riker, *The Making of Roumania,* 552–54; Petru Mavrogheni (Bucharest) to Bălăceanu (Paris), 5/17 June 1866, in Mihordea, *Răscoala grănicerilor de la 1866,* 17, 247–48.

90. See Carol's notes, 25 May/6 June, 17/29 June, and 9/21 July 1866, in *Aus dem Leben König Karls von Rumänien,* 1:67, 75, 89–90; cf. Slobodan Jovanović, *Druga vlada Miloša i Mihaila (1858–1868),* 210; Grgur Jakšić and Vojislav J. Vučković, *Spoljna politika Srbije za vlade kneza Mihaila: Prvi balkanski savez,* 236–37, 269; see also Carol to Michael Obrenović (Belgrade), 15/27 May and 13 August 1866, and Michael to Carol, 14/26 June, 5/17 July, and 13 August 1866, in AIC, CR, dosar 83/1866.

91. Riker, *The Making of Roumania,* 497n. 2; Carol's speech to army officers, 24 May/5 June 1866, in *Aus dem Leben König Karls von Rumänien,* 1:65–66; Savel Manu (Bucharest) to Ministerul de Interne, 16/28 February 1866, in Mihordea, *Răscoala grănicerilor de la 1866,* 120–21.

92. Report from the Vlaşca district prefect, 6/18 May 1866, and Mavrogheni's circular, 26 May/7 June 1866, in Mihordea, *Răscoala grănicerilor de la 1866*, 124, 208–9.

93. Carol's notes, 14/26 June 1866, in *Aus dem Leben König Karls von Rumänien*, 1:74.

94. Morris to Seward, 25 May 1866, in 39th Cong., 244.

95. Diplomatic pressure from France and Great Britain on the Ottoman Empire reportedly kept Turkish troops out of Romania; Anton von Prokesch-Osten (Constantinople) to Mensdorff-Pouilly, 2 June 1866, in BAR, ACA, XX; Dimitrie Sturdza to Bălăceanu, 9 July 1866, in Henry, *L'abdication du prince Cuza*, 435–36.

96. Ion Ghica (Constantinople) to Bălăceanu, 12 July 1866, in Fond Ion Bălăceanu, no. 29473, BAR, SC; see the Romanian and Turkish projects in Carol's notes, 5/17 July 1866, in *Aus dem Leben König Karls von Rumänien*, 1:85–89n. 1; Ghica's report, 21 June/3 July 1866, and Moustier to Drouyn de Lhuys, 11 July 1866, in Henry, *L'abdication du prince Cuza*, 430–32, 437–38.

97. Carol's journey lasted seventeen days, 9/21 August–26 August/7 September 1866; see *Charles Ier, Roi de Roumanie*, 1:313–18; *Aus dem Leben König Karls von Rumänien*, 1:101–18.

98. Bălăceanu (Paris) to Carol, n.d., in Fond Ion Bălăceanu, no. 28495, BAR, SC; Drouyn de Lhuys to Avril, 4 August 1866, no. 18, AMAE(F), CP—Turquie: Consulat Bucarest, vol. 28. See Carol's notes for 16/28 July, 22 August/3 September, and 29 August/10 September 1866, and his letter to Napoleon III, 5/17 August 1866, in *Aus dem Leben König Karls von Rumänien*, 1:92, 99, 115, 120; a Romanian translation of Napoleon III's letter to Carol, 22 August/3 September 1866, in *Domnia regelui Carol I*, 1:335.

99. Carol to Napoleon III, 9 October 1866, and Moustier (Paris) to Avril, 5 and 12 October 1866, in AMAE(F), CP—Turquie: Consulat Bucarest, vol. 29; French diplomatic letters from Constantinople and Bucharest to Paris, 26 September to 12 October 1866, in Henry, *L'abdication du prince Cuza*, 452–55; Mehmed Rüştü Paşa (Constantinople) to Carol, 18 October 1866, and Carol (Cotroceni) to Mehmed Rüştü Paşa, 19 October 1866, in *Aus dem Leben König Karls von Rumänien*, 1:132–35.

100. Giurescu, *Viaţa şi opera lui Cuza Vodă*, 102–3, 259–62; for ceremonials in visits by *voievods* from Moldavia and Wallachia to Constantinople during the eighteenth century, see Hagop Dj. Siruni, *Domnii Români la Poarta Otomană*, 9–10, 49–51n. 44, 51–52n. 46, 80–81n. 143.

101. This trip lasted twelve days, 9/21 October–21 October/2 November 1866; *Aus dem Leben König Karls von Rumänien*, 1:137–51; Picot (Bucharest) to Cornu, 2/14 November 1866, in "Correspondance d'un secrétaire princier en Roumanie: Émile Picot," 108. Picot (1844–1918) was appointed Carol's secretary owing to the influence of Cornu and Napoleon III. Approximately 240,000 francs were expended for *bahşiş*.

102. See Carol's *ferman*, 23 October 1866, in *Recueil d'actes internationaux de l'Empire Ottoman*, 3:257–59.

103. Mehmed Rüştü Paşa (Constantinople) to Carol, 16 December 1866, in Colecţia Kogălniceanu, XLIX/10, Biblioteca Naţională a României, Secţia manuscriselor (hereinafter cited BNR, SM).

104. See the *hatt-ı hümayuns,* or imperial decrees, of 1776, in *Documente privind istoria Romîniei: Colecţia Eudoxiu de Hurmuzaki,* Serie nouă, *Rapoarte consulare ruse (1770–1796),* 1:116–18, 120–22; *Regulamentul Organik,* 23, article 65; *Reglementul Organik a Prinţipatului Moldovei,* 15–16, article 74; see also article 8 of the Paris convention of 1858, in *Recueil d'actes internationaux de l'Empire Ottoman,* 3:111.

105. Carol to Mehmed Rüştü Paşa, 19 October 1866, in *Aus dem Leben König Karls von Rumänien,* 1:134–35.

106. Report by Richard von Pfuel (Bucharest), 4 January 1876, no. 3, in Hauptarchiv des Auswärtigen Amtes (Prussia), Politischer Schriftwechsel: Türkei, 24, vol. 52 (hereinafter cited HAA, PS). The bank of Hagop Zarifi became Turkey's chief creditor.

107. *Almanach de Gotha, 1871,* 765, 772, 778, 782–83.

108. Ignat'ev to Ali Paşa, 28 November/10 December 1866, and identic notes to Ali Paşa from the diplomatic representatives of France, Austria, Britain, Italy, and Prussia, 29 January 1867, in Foreign Office, *British and Foreign State Papers, 1866–1867,* 57:603–4.

109. Bălăceanu negotiated a loan on 12/24 October 1866 from a banking syndicate headed by the house of Oppenheim by which Romania received 18.5 million francs, to be repaid by 1889 at a highly unfavorable annual interest rate of 13 percent. Romania guaranteed this loan by a mortgage on state lands; Green to Edward H. Stanley (London), 8 December 1866, no. 155, in PRO, FO, 78/1922; see Carol's notes, 23 October/4 November–29 October/10 November 1866, in *Aus dem Leben König Karls von Rumänien,* 1:152–54.

Chapter Three

FOREIGNERS AND
THE JEWISH QUESTION

Romania had a foreign prince by 1866, but its patriots wanted more—much more. Carol's arrival marked the beginning of a new era, one aspect of which was a problem with resident foreigners. Vassalage to the Ottoman Empire had become troublesome for Danubian Romanians, despite the mild nature of Turkish suzerainty and the benefits of protection by the great powers of Europe. Autonomy in conducting Romania's internal affairs appeared to be challenged by special privileges enjoyed by foreigners dwelling in the country. Romania attempted to deal with those persons via its own laws and customs, without outside intervention or control, as a way of shucking the ties of Turkish bondage.

An obvious sign of Danubian Romania's dependent status was consular jurisdiction, which was based on *ahdname,* or capitulations awarded by the Ottoman sultans. The Danubian principalities received them in the early modern epoch: Wallachia in 1402 and 1467/68, Moldavia in 1512.[1] They guaranteed the principalities' autonomy and released citizens from paying the *haraç,* or tax, customarily remitted by the *reaya,* or non-Muslim subjects, of Turkey. The Danubian princes, in return, annually sent tribute to Constantinople and cooperated militarily with the sultan in time of need. The powers recognized these capitulations in the 1858 Convention of Paris after the Crimean War.[2] They themselves obtained such charters for prerogatives yet without obligations. The first ones that contained such provisions went to France in 1535 and England in 1675, followed by commercial accords between the Ottoman Empire and Austria in 1718, Prussia in 1761, Russia in 1783, and Sardinia in 1823.[3] The powers had thereby the right to establish consuls in the Ottoman Empire; citizens of the powers might, moreover, trade freely in Turkey, be spared the *haraç,* and have consular jurisdiction. This authority meant that civil and criminal affairs involving the powers' citizens were to be handled by their respective officials in accordance with the laws of their own land and without Turkish interference. Romanians, for their part, objected, for this safeguard violated the principalities' rights of domestic autonomy that had been assured by their capitulations.

The early Ottoman capitulations and later commercial compacts were at first of little importance in Moldavia and Wallachia owing to the powers' inconsequential trade with the principalities and the attendant absence of envoys residing there. Consuls began to appear in Danubian Romania, however, after the Russo-Turkish war that ended in 1774. The first one in Bucharest was from Russia by 1782, and later others from Austria in 1783, Prussia in 1785, France in 1798, Great Britain in 1802, and Sardinia in 1838.[4] The principalities' law codes had indicated that foreigners were to be treated equally with Romanians, without reference to consuls; but after another Russo-Turkish war concluded in 1829, Romanian regulations acknowledged that the powers indeed shielded various foreigners.[5] Consular jurisdiction became more obnoxious for Romanians as trade between Danubian Romania and the powers eventually increased. Consuls encouraged their own compatriots' business in the principalities and sold patents of citizenship that exempted purchasers from Romanian taxes, laws, and military service. Some Jewish, Armenian, and Greek merchants—and even some of their Romanian counterparts—were under foreign aegis. Romanian patriots now faced significant questions. How might Romanian national ideals be achieved as long as aliens enjoyed advantages that Romanians did not? How might Romanian commerce and industry develop effectively if foreigners had a substantial competitive edge? The answers seemed to lie in ridding Danubian Romania of consular jurisdiction.

Romanians considered several ways to terminate this regime. They might ignore it altogether, as they did with codes stipulating that Romanian laws applied to foreigners; yet the powers opposed this course. They might publicly denounce it, a tack that would have been highly presumptuous given Danubian Romania's weak political-military standing. Or they might sign bilateral consular conventions with each power. By such pacts, Romanians anticipated that the privileges they had once received from the Ottoman Empire would be confirmed and foreign jurisdiction thus quashed. But why should the powers negotiate this matter with Danubian Romania? By and large, the powers had no incentive to abandon their prerogatives. Only Austria-Hungary and Russia had an interest in accommodating Bucharest, because they might need the Romanians. That is, Danubian Romania might become an ally in case of a crisis in Southeastern Europe. Austria-Hungary and Russia viewed Romania as a pivotal area that contained a dynamic elite whose energies might be harnessed so as to promote the powers' individual designs.

The Habsburg Empire was the first power to deal with Danubian Romania on consular jurisdiction. Ştirbei, Romania's minister of foreign affairs, proposed in 1867 that relations between the two countries be regularized by agreements regarding consuls, commerce, railroad junctions, the extradition of criminals, and the establishment of a Romanian diplomatic agency in Vienna. Austria-Hungary's minister of foreign affairs, Friedrich F. von Beust, conceded that these were important issues that needed to be resolved.[6] Dumitru Brătianu, a former Romanian minister of public works, went to Vienna to discuss this matter. He contended that the Habsburg Empire, along with the other powers, should unilaterally renounce its jurisdiction in Romania, after which consular conventions could be negotiated. Beust was reluctant to forsake privileges in Romania. Still, he would explore this topic so long as Habsburg-Ottoman treaties were not thereby violated. The founder of the Alliance Israélite Universelle, Adolphe Crémieux, advised Beust that Romania's Jews would be ill served if consular jurisdiction stopped.[7] Beust concurred, calculating that Austro-Hungarian nationals might be treated inequitably if the Habsburg Empire dropped or circumscribed its extraterritorial rights.[8] He informed Romania that the powers reckoned further debate on this subject was "inopportune."[9] Again in 1870, Alexandru G. Golescu, who had become Romania's minister of foreign affairs, instructed his representative in Vienna, Ludovic Steege, to seek a halt to consular jurisdiction.[10] Beust was, however, merely willing to confer about some lesser judicial and administrative concerns.[11] Not until 1887 did the two sides exchange notes by which Austria-Hungary withdrew its protection over non-Habsburg citizens in Romania.

Although the many Jews under Austria-Hungary's wing in Romania posed an obstacle to resolving the consular jurisdiction problem between Vienna and Bucharest, the same circumstance was inconsequential in deliberations between St. Petersburg and Bucharest. Jews in Russia suffered various disadvantages, and some wished to move elsewhere, including to Romania. Russia, for its part, was disposed to forgo its extraterritorial prerogatives in Romania owing to its dearth of commercial interest there and its apathy about safeguarding Jews. Early in 1868, a former minister of justice, Ion C. Cantacuzino, visited St. Petersburg to put forth the notion that consular jurisdiction led to disputes between foreign consuls and Romanian courts because the latter disregarded it. Gorchakov, Russia's minister of foreign affairs, indicated a readiness to renounce Russian claims in Romania and to adjust the position of Russian citizens there.[12] Romania's cabinet of ministers entrusted Steege to consult the Russian consul general in Bucharest, Genrikh G. Offenberg, about a Russo-Romanian consular convention that would contribute significantly to the "complete reentry" of Romania into its ancient "rights and privileges."[13] St. Petersburg enjoined Offenberg to acknowledge the authority of Romanian courts over Russian subjects and to end the practice of granting or selling patents of protection to non-Russians. Offenberg formulated a compact that, by the way, admitted in the preamble a new title for the ruler at Bucharest: Prince of Romania, instead of Prince of the United Principalities of Moldavia and Wallachia. Romanian statesmen objected to some aspects of Offenberg's scheme, especially measures allowing Russians to enter Romanian chambers of commerce and to deliberate economic questions in villages.[14] Steege and Offenberg then jointly prepared another draft that envisioned the cessation of Russian consular jurisdiction in Romania. This meant that Romanian judges would handle—according to Romanian laws—Russians accused of crimes and misdemeanors; Romanian tribunals would decide whether a Russian who had already received a Russian permit to emigrate might become a Romanian citizen; and Romanian obligations, save for the poll tax and military service, were to apply to Russians just as to Romanians. The projected Russo-Romanian convention elicited so much opposition from the Ottoman Empire and other powers,[15] however, that Gorchakov modified his stance. No longer would Russia contemplate equality and reciprocity for Romania, but it did yield its extraterritorial perquisites—its control over landed property and fiscal immunities for Russians.[16] Steege journeyed to St. Petersburg, where he and Offenberg initialed an agreement that was subsequently signed in Bucharest in November 1869.[17] Romania's legislature refused, nevertheless, to confirm this covenant. One of its reasons was a fear that pursuing an independent foreign policy would undermine support from the other powers. Russia accepted one postponement in ratification yet rejected a further Romanian effort to delay.[18] The two parties eventually exchanged notes in 1871 that limited Russia's consular jurisdiction, approving some articles in the pact but essentially continuing the protection of Russians in Romania.[19] The recognition of Romania's independence in 1880 would effectively snuff out such consular authority.

Foreigners would attract the attention of Romanian legislators at the outset of Carol's reign. The electoral assembly of deputies, which had hailed Carol's arrival, transformed itself into a constituent assembly to formulate a charter for the state, one modeled on that of Belgium. Debates on the constitution revealed Romanian attitudes toward foreigners, especially toward Jews.

The provisional government, led by Ion Ghica, offered a constitutional project to the chamber even before Carol arrived in Bucharest in 1866. A committee of deputies subsequently modified it.[20] The committee's reporter, Aristid Pascal, a civil law professor at Bucharest University, commented on the relationship between religion and naturalization. He observed that Jews from backward, uncivilized lands were inundating Romania, forming an "illiterate population, totally lacking in the culture of the age." Jews should nevertheless, he advocated, gain civil and political rights, without endangering the nation's development, being gradually emancipated by legislative action corresponding to their "moral amelioration" through obligatory schooling. To deny Jews the privilege of becoming Romanian citizens would injure Romanian interests, for Romania needed more people and more foreign capital. When aliens owned property in Romanian towns, those towns prospered, enlarged, and grew more beautiful. Pascal concluded that if the first generation of foreigners had not completely assimilated, the next one would certainly be fully Romanian in "heart, spirit, and language just as were the descendants of Traian's colonists" in ancient Dacia.[21]

Should non-Christians be naturalized? A deputy from Moldavia, Alexandru Sihleanu, said no. He argued that the constitutional program, which provided freedom of faith, would usher in a "most dreadful fear" that spread throughout the land. When faced with danger, he continued, we yell "kikes" in one voice, for we see ourselves menaced by an "incurable illness." For the government, Ion Brătianu, as minister of finance, responded by deploring the intrigues and passions engendered by the Jewish issue. He promised not to give the country to the Jews nor to award them anything that would imperil Romania's well-being. Hence he withdrew from the plan a stipulation on Jewish enfranchisement.[22] Brătianu's declaration failed, however, to calm tempers in Bucharest, where an anti-Jewish mob ravaged a recently built synagogue. Carol donated monies from his private purse to help reconstruct it. Romania's Jews, those who were subjects of the great powers, wanted more. They appealed to the powers, telling about the threat to their persons and properties and requesting a collective note be addressed to the Romanian regime to the effect that preventive measures should be taken against further attacks.[23]

Next on the assembly's agenda was a discussion of immigration. Some deputies warned against Romania's being colonized by a "foreign race." Ion

Brătianu agreed. He referred to a speech he had delivered in 1861 in which he rebuffed foreigners because he thought Romanian serfs ought to have the land they tilled before letting aliens purchase it. The deputies then adopted a nonimmigration clause.[24]

The assembly subsequently returned to the question of naturalization with a government proposal that only Christian foreigners might become Romanian citizens. Pascal reminded his colleagues that the 1864 civil code allowed non-Christian aliens to acquire citizenship after a ten-year wait. Other views prevailed. Ion D. Strat, a professor of political economy at Bucharest University, recommended that Jews be denied political rights until they were more civilized; thenceforward, they might be enfranchised individually but not en masse. A surveyor in Wallachia, C. Pană Buescu, remarked that Jews in Bucharest felt for the first time the fury of the Romanian populace, all owing to an article in the projected constitution. He admitted that Jews ought to enjoy privileges in accord with modern principles of toleration, yet Romania was still too weak to emancipate them. An eminent politician from Moldavia, Manolache Costache Epureanu, reckoned that Romania might be so overwhelmed by Jews that Romanians themselves would be transformed into "helots" in their own country. Romanians should refrain, he contended, from attacking Jews, because doing so would undermine Romania's prosperity: if Romania expelled its Jews, it would lose Jewish capital. Romania had too few native merchants; and those who were businessmen, once they became wealthy, wished to abandon their calling in favor of an aristocratic life-style. No one hating Romanians should, to be sure, live in the state; what Romanians needed was to "Romanize" its Jews. Ion Brătianu responded that Jews were a "social plague"; Jews were more boorish than Romanians, with solely the Gypsies being worse. When Romanians are threatened, he continued, they turn not "intolerant, but cautious." He agreed with Epureanu that affluent Jews ought not to be banished; rather, "proletarian" Jews, who brought no money with them and produced none in Romania, should go. He had already withdrawn a proviso for freeing the Jews and would next endeavor to stop the influx of all indigents—including Jews—so as to keep Romania from developing into a colony of "sluggards."[25]

An even tougher stance was taken by some deputies, primarily from Moldavia, who insisted that Jews be barred from entering Romania without prior approval via a special statute. Ionescu, who was a history professor at Iaşi University, maintained that Romania should not be Jewish booty. Furthermore, indigenous Jews should, forbear assimilating with Jewish vagabonds from Austrian Galicia and Russia. This suggestion foundered. In another article of the constitutional blueprint, foreigners were to have the same privileges as Romanians, except for political perquisites. Strat, Buescu, and Ionescu sought to amend this so that non-Christian aliens would be excluded from acquiring property in rural areas. This scheme failed, as did one curbing real-estate ownership in general for naturalized foreigners. The article was, however, modified to provide legal protection to aliens and their assets.[26] The assembly unanimously adopted the constitution at the close of its deliberations, which had amply illustrated deep-seated feelings stemming from long experience.[27]

Romania's Jews had different origins. The expulsion of Jews from major states in Western Europe during early modern times meant that some Sephardic Jews moved from Spain to the Ottoman Empire and reached Wallachia; some Ashkenazic Jews subsequently left German-speaking lands, Galicia, and Russia for Moldavia. Sephardic Jews spoke Ladino, which evolved from Spanish, and were more readily absorbed into Romanian society than Ashkenazic Jews, who spoke Yiddish, which was based on German. Sephardic and Ashkenazic Jews lacked a mutual culture and a common past. They would nonetheless cooperate in protesting anti-Jewish acts. The Jewish question became acute in Moldavia, where ever larger numbers of Jews arrived. Many Ashkenazic Jews in Russia sought refuge in Moldavia when confronted by compulsory military service for twenty-five-year terms according to a decree issued by Emperor Nicholas I (1825–55) in 1827. In Danubian Romania by the 1830s, foreigners accounted for more than 2 percent of the population, yet in Moldavia 3 percent were Jews. By the first census in 1859/60, Jews in Moldavia had increased to a remarkable 8.53 percent, while throughout the Danubian principalities they constituted 3.03 percent of the inhabitants. The second census, that in 1899, had the Jews at 4.48 percent of the total.[28]

The Jews' enterprise was more challenging to Romanians than their numbers. Thrifty Jewish entrepreneurs earned distrust as well as profit from Danubian Romanian aristocrats and peasants. In Moldavia, Jews were bankers—moneylenders and moneychangers—innkeepers, lessees of taverns in villages, shopkeepers in towns: grocers, rug merchants, peddlers, besides being artisans—tailors, turners, glass makers, and carpet makers. Romanians reckoned Jewish moneylenders in particular to be dangerous to the social order owing to their pervasive influence on impoverished farmers and perennially indebted landed proprietors. *Boiers,* or aristocrats, regarded commerce and industry to be beneath their dignity, thereby leaving the door open for their Jewish creditors to seize control of an important segment of the economy. An additional problem was the Jewish way of life in Moldavia. The Jews' exclusive family circles and non-Romanian customs clearly identified them as outsiders. Romanians considered them to be aliens, and some were indeed foreign subjects protected by one or another of the great powers. Romanian leaders strove to guard national interests; and thus they sought to divert public attention away from failures in domestic and foreign affairs, and toward humiliating Jews as scapegoats. Fear and pride, including a belief in the superiority of Romanians over Jews, were governing factors in the anti-Jewish equation.

Some Romanians' views of foreigners is evident in their spiritual art, in which Jews, Muslim Turks and Tatars, Monophysite Christian Armenians, and Roman Catholics were depicted on a lower level than Orthodox Christians. Frescoes of the Last Judgment on the exterior walls of the Moldavian monasteries of Humor (1535), Voroneţ (1547), and Suceviţa (1596) showed contemporary Jews along with other non-Orthodox peoples in limbo—between Heaven and Hell—awaiting damnation.[29] Moldavian frescoes conveyed attitudes about ethnic and religious outsiders more effectively than sixteenth-century artistic pieces by Orthodox South Slavs, Greeks, Russians, or Roman Catholic Italians.

Laws regarding foreigners were even more revealing and certainly more pervasive than works of art. Byzantine jurisprudence formed the basis of Romanian regulations. In the seventeenth century, aliens in the Danubian principalities paid no imposts and had no obligation to serve the state. Enactments in Moldavia and Wallachia during that era—inspired by the Byzantine compendium, *Hexabiblios* (1345), by Kōnstantin Armenopoulos —nonetheless forbade non-Christians from testifying in court and from marrying Christians.[30] These measures were undoubtedly as much anti-Muslim as anti-Jewish, yet they were springboards for subsequent anti-Jewish laws. By the first half of the eighteenth century, Jews had a higher tax rate than Romanians, could not build synagogues of stone, and might make a living only as merchants and innkeepers.[31] At the end of that century, Jews in Moldavia could not lease estates, inns, and taverns, nor reside in villages. In Wallachia at the same time, aliens were unable to purchase farms, vineyards, houses, mills, and shops.[32] The major codes of the early nineteenth century, by Prince Scarlat Callimachi (1812–19) in Moldavia and Prince Ioan Caragea (1812–18) in Wallachia—both predicated on the ninth-century Byzantine *Basilika*—renewed a ban on non-Christians wedding Christians; also, Jews in Moldavia might buy property in towns, but not in villages.[33] The Organic Regulations in each principality incorporated and amplified these provisions. Jews henceforth might operate butcher shops and distilleries in Moldavia yet could still not let land and were subject to a special tax. Jewish children might attend Romanian schools if they dressed in the style of their Romanian contemporaries. Jews who lacked visible means of support or a useful trade were to be expelled as vagabonds. In both principalities, only Christians had the possibility of becoming citizens.[34] Enforcement of such limits, especially those concerning derelicts, curbed Jewish immigration. Still, many Jews in Moldavia circumvented these restrictions by taking Romanian names, bribing bureaucrats, or moving to Wallachia—despite a prohibition against this—where anti-Jewish edicts were less onerous.[35]

Fresh winds blew in 1848. Revolutionaries in Wallachia proclaimed the "emancipation of Jews and political rights for all fellow countrymen of a different faith"; and in Moldavia, Kogălniceanu advocated a "gradual emancipation" of the Jews.[36] Neither course prevailed, for the Romanian rebellions collapsed. Following the union of Moldavia and Wallachia, Cuza issued several assizes in 1864 that are nominally still in force. Articles in them resemble those in the Organic Regulations. The civil code—modeled on that of France (1804) and earlier Romanian prescripts—opened citizenship only to Christian aliens; and the penal code—fashioned on a French ordinance (1810) and Romanian rules—stipulated the banishment of foreign vagrants. Cuza's communal law excluded Jews, except under particular circumstances, such as military service or education, from enjoying privileges in villages until they adopted "Romanian sentiments and customs." Romanians, but not Jews, participated in the newly formed chambers of commerce, thus bypassing the most significant traders in Danubian Romania.[37] This, then, is the legal backdrop to the debates that shaped the Romanian constitution of 1866.

Danubian Romanians faced a financial crisis in the mid-1860s, for the country was heavily in arrears. As a result, taxes were raised, as was the price of salt—which was a government monopoly—and the army was reduced in size at a moment when many Romanians feared an invasion by the Ottoman Empire, Austria, or Russia for having contravened the wishes of the powers in choosing a foreign prince.[38] Ion Brătianu proposed a monetary remedy: bills guaranteed by some state domains would be emitted. These notes were to circulate, as Russian and Austrian notes occasionally did in Danubian Romania earlier in the century. The assembly, however, rejected Brătianu's suggestion.[39] The deputies reckoned that such money would signify bankruptcy; not until the war of 1877 would Romanians employ paper currency. Had Brătianu's initiative been accepted in 1866, Romanian indebtedness to

Jewish moneylenders might not have been as pivotal a consideration as it was in deliberations about the constitution. Jews from abroad—from the Alliance Israélite Universelle—offered aid at this juncture. The Alliance had been established in Paris in 1860 with the goal of the "emancipation and spiritual progress of Jews everywhere." Local committees of the Alliance formed in large Romanian towns; in 1864 a committee in Iaşi aimed at persuading Romanians to grant civil prerogatives to Jews.[40] Crémieux, the president of the Alliance, visited Bucharest and spoke eloquently to nearly fifty deputies about the absurdity of religious intolerance. He also concluded with Brătianu an agreement whereby Jewish financiers in France would supply Romania with funds to cover the annual tribute and other expenses in return for a relatively moderate rate of interest and a clause in the constitution admitting Jews to citizenship.[41] As we have seen, this bore no fruit. Romania endorsed no pro-Jewish article in its charter and received no loan on favorable terms from bankers in France.

Anti-Jewish incidents in Danubian Romania during the early years of Carol's reign along with diplomatic intervention by the powers on behalf of the Jews helped more to sharpen Romanians' awareness of their political need to end consular jurisdiction and to win national independence than to evoke a humanitarian concern for the Jews.

Romania's policy about its Jews corresponded to the country's constitution and laws. But were anti-Jewish provisions in those documents the result of internal conditions, or were they a patriotic reaction to outside interference in Romania's domestic affairs? Both components were unquestionably involved. Conservative and liberal leaders pursued anti-Jewish programs, yet not always for the same reasons or with equal vigor. Conservatives in Moldavia, on the one hand, opposed enfranchising the Jews for fear of forfeiting their own estates to their Jewish creditors. Conservatives, however, stood relatively aloof from anti-Jewish demonstrations and persecution. So long as Jews lacked land in the countryside, large landholders tolerated them and even depended on Jewish moneylenders for cash to purchase foreign manufactured goods. Liberals, on the other hand, generally possessed comparatively little agricultural land and had less to lose from freeing the Jews. Liberals, who resided mainly in towns, nonetheless exploited the distrust and apprehension that Romanian townspeople and peasants had for the Jews in order to build a popular base for political authority. Hence some liberals, such as Ion Brătianu, were more aggressively anti-Jewish than some conservatives, such as Catargiu. Jews—both those protected by the powers and indigenous ones—for their part confronted

Romania's regard for economic independence and ethnic exclusiveness on one side and reckoned on the powers' solicitude for their welfare on the other.

Romania's Jews faced restrictive enactments, as already noted, but little harassment until they sought civil rights in 1866. The Romanian government henceforth used the Jew as a scapegoat in a quest for national homogeneity and safety. Ion Brătianu, now as minister of interior, urged district prefects in 1867 to implement decrees about vagabonds. Romania should be rid of "helpless and filthy Jews" who were unable to find jobs; a person without work was an itinerant, and was to be expelled.[42] After visiting a Jewish hospital in Iaşi that wanted adequate space, beds, cleanliness, and ventilation, Brătianu also suggested that "security and hygienic" measures be taken against Jewish humanitarian foundations. His directive on primary instruction was even more telling: "All children . . . [will] be compelled to attend public schools where the Romanian language . . . [is] taught." The police were to enforce this stipulation; failure to carry it out was a "crime against posterity" and against "Romanism."[43] Although the Romanian educational system was quite limited, and an overwhelming majority of Romanians were illiterate, Brătianu attempted to ensure national unity via the classroom.

The immediate result of Ion Brătianu's orders on vagrants was the arrest of about ninety Jews in Iaşi; thirty-seven of them were banished.[44] Two of the latter drowned upon being cast overboard from a Turkish vessel at Galaţi. This incident aroused European opinion against Romania, but not against the Ottoman Empire, and evoked diplomatic intervention on behalf of the Jews. Crémieux characterized the killings as "a scandal of religious persecution."[45] Napoleon III thought that Carol had personally authorized steps "contrary to humanity and to civilization."[46] The power's representatives, who were accredited to the European Danube Commission in Galaţi, sent a collective note of protest to the local district prefect.[47] Ştefan Golescu, Romania's minister of foreign affairs, reminded the powers that Turks had been responsible. The Turkish governor of the Danubian *vilâyet,* or province, Midhat Paşa, proposed that a mixed delegation investigate the deaths. Romania, however, rejected Midhat's recommendation.[48] Self-conscious Romanian statesmen, who were sensitive about previous censure by the powers and were still in a position of evident weakness, withheld pressing charges against the suzerain Ottoman Empire.

Not every Romanian rallied to support the government. Sturdza, who was a liberal landowner from Moldavia, condemned Ion Brătianu's policy as demagoguery, one that "sacrificed the interests" of the country. Sturdza described Brătianu as being hypocritical, immoral, and traitorous; his political program evinced "patriotic gloom."[49] Brătianu, in turn, wrote to his wife that his problems stemmed from an "intrigue of the *boiers*," who hoped to "deceive Europe in our affairs."[50] The vivid language invoked against Brătianu and the latter's stance may be attributed to long-standing differences among Romanian politicians. Diplomatic action at Galați nonetheless ended the deportation of Jews as vagabonds. A British philanthropist, Moses Montefiore, visited Bucharest in the summer of 1867 and found no evidence of religious oppression.[51] Events in Galați, nevertheless, brought about the replacement of the cabinet headed by Constantin A. Krețulescu for one conducted by Ștefan Golescu. Brătianu remained as minister of interior, and so this change was one more in name than in fact.

Difficulties for the Jews intensified in 1868. In Călărași in Wallachia, a child of a nurse in a Jewish household died. A mob deemed the Jewish family to be at fault and so sacked the local synagogue. In Bîrlad in Moldavia, the suspicion that a monk had been poisoned by a Jew prompted the beating of Jews and the pillaging of their synagogue. These disturbances evoked remonstrations from Jews in Britain and elsewhere, but no diplomatic protests, mainly because Ștefan Golescu promised to indemnify the wronged.[52]

More serious was the discussion of anti-Jewish legislation in Bucharest. Thirty-one deputies from Moldavia—the "free and independent fraction," as they called themselves—designated as a vagabond every Jew who resided permanently in a rural commune or was in an urban one without the authorization of the communal council. These deputies proposed that Jews were to be forbidden to own both urban and rural land; nor were they to lease property, taverns, mills, distilleries, bridges, vineyards, pasturages, stables, grazing fields for sheep, or inns on major roads; nor were they to engage in any state or communal business; nor were they to sell food or drink to Christians.[53] What these deputies envisioned was a law so restrictive that Jews would be forced to emigrate. Crémieux and others attacked this motion, as did representatives of the powers, and the chamber ultimately repudiated it.[54] Still and all, this project reflected the attitudes of many Romanians. Ion Brătianu insisted on a provision about itinerants in the rural law of 1868. Carp rejoined that Romania should leave its Jews in peace, in accord with the Calimach Code of Moldavia, rather than treat them illegally. Prefects nevertheless received orders to stop Jews—whom Brătianu believed could never be "Romanized"—from trading in the countryside, letting real estate, and establishing taverns and inns in rural communes.[55] Liquor licenses of Jews in Bacău in Moldavia were also revoked, and about five hundred Jews were thus left without visible means of subsistence. The national guard consequently deported some of them—twenty-five of whom were Austro-Hungarian subjects—as vagrants.[56] The Israelite Union in Iaşi rejected a governmental whitewash of this incident and requested aid from abroad.[57]

The powers would respond to the Jews' plea. The Alliance Israélite Universelle solicited the assistance of individual statesmen and served as a press agent in publicizing the plight of Romania's Jews. Foreign consuls in Iaşi, Galaţi, and Bucharest reported extensively to their respective governments about the maltreatment of Jews. What was the position of the powers? Just recently, if at all, had the powers themselves ameliorated the political status of their own Jews. In Russia a large number of Jews lived in colonies in the southwestern part of the country and were exposed to Russification. Hence Russia rarely censured Romania's anti-Jewish doings. Jews in Prussia tardily gained full citizenship in 1869. Bismarck nonetheless decried Bucharest's proposed anti-Jewish legislation.[58] Romania's Jews won sympathetic attention especially in Western Europe owing to liberal traditions there. Jews had been emancipated in France by 1791, in Sardinia by 1850, and in Britain by 1858. Napoleon III objected to Romania's persecution of its Jews and thought that Ion Brătianu was personally responsible. If Brătianu were no longer in the cabinet, the abuse would end.[59] Britain's minister of foreign affairs, Edward Henry Stanley, urged that Romania fulfill stipulations in the 1856 Treaty of Paris to the effect that each class be dealt with equally without regard to race or creed. He considered Romania to be inconsistent in complaining about the "oppression of Christians by Mussulmans of Turkey" while undertaking a "still greater degree of oppression against the Jewish inhabitants of their soil."[60] Italy was more interested in cultivating Romania's friendship than in the Jewish question, but as a former ally of France and Britain in the Crimean War and unwilling to pursue a separate foreign policy in Danubian Romania, it joined in the protests. Jews in the Habsburg Empire were relatively numerous and influential, but they had only become citizens in 1867. Austria-Hungary adhered to the Western powers' criticism of Romania more because it required a rapprochement with France in case of war with Prussia than for humanitarian reasons. Beust strongly condemned the Bacău outrage, demanding that the guilty be punished and the victims indemnified.[61] The first fruit of this international concern was a protocol signed by the consuls in Iaşi denouncing the Bacău disorder.[62]

Ion Brătianu was now apparently convinced that the powers meant business about the Jews, for he resolved to "repress with energy any deed having the character of persecution"; yet he also refused to "permit any interference in the administration of public order." Ştefan Golescu informed the powers that Romania would indeed solve its Jewish problem but would do so without damaging its national interests.[63] Foreign pressure kept mounting with the result that Nicolae Golescu replaced his elder brother, Ştefan, as prime minister; Brătianu, who, according to Carol, was "one of the most capable Romanian statesmen," still remained minister of interior. This cabinet change again signified little, and so the French, British, and Austrian consuls in Bucharest presented a collective note of protest about the Bacău matter to the Romanian government. Brătianu replied that injured Jews would receive restitution: "any losses suffered by them through the acts of the authorities will be made good."[64] This moderate reaction may be explained by Romania's need for extrinsic financial support: Jewish bankers abroad might withhold credit, and this prospect gave Brătianu pause about Romania's Jews. Brătianu's promise did not, however, prevent the ravaging of the synagogue in Galaţi by a mob motivated by the erroneous belief that Christian blood was being used in Jewish religious services. Thirty-eight Jews were wounded, thirty of whom were subjects of the Habsburg Empire.[65] Romania eventually paid an indemnity of one thousand ducats to Austria-Hungary's consul for damages to its subjects.[66] The pattern was then clear. Jews shielded by foreign consuls were also protected by Romania; indigenous Jews were not.

Ion Brătianu had company in advocating an anti-Jewish policy. His views coincided with those of many of his Romanian political contemporaries and with those of the prince. Although Carol discreetly refrained from proclaiming openly his opinion about Jews, his defense of Brătianu and the continuation of Brătianu's course following the latter's fall from the cabinet in late 1868 attests that Carol himself was anti-Jewish, or that many Romanians supported Brătianu's steps, or both. Probably both. Recurrent queries by the powers regarding Romania's Jews brought about yet another cabinet shift at the end of 1868. Dimitrie Ghica, who stood somewhere between the liberals and the conservatives, became prime minister. Brătianu was finally out of office; still, Kogălniceanu, his successor as interior minister, followed Brătianu's program.

Kogălniceanu managed domestic affairs according to the needs, passions, and prejudices—as he saw them—of Danubian Romanians. To do so, he decided to expel Jewish tax collectors and tavern keepers from rural districts on Saint George's Day, 23 April, when contracts were usually renewed.

Kogălniceanu argued that Romania's Jews were a "foreign nationality" by their origin, language, customs, and sentiment. The "spirit of modern civilization" gave Jews the right to build synagogues, publish religious books, and be teachers, doctors, pharmacists, lithographers, officials, and soldiers, as well as to be mechanics, artisans, and distillers in villages. Romania protected its Jews' life and property while ensuring their freedom of religion, free public education, and liberty of thought, assembly, and press. But Jews might not run taverns or serve as tax collectors.[67] In the chamber of deputies, Kogălniceanu pointed out that Jews constituted an economic problem, not an ecclesiastical one, and that "we seek to defend our nationality and all our interests against every peril."[68] The prime minister and prince concurred. Dimitrie Ghica explained that Jewish tavern keepers compromised the "security" of the country; Carol remarked that rural taverns contributed to peasant alcoholism. Boerescu, the minister of justice, contended moreover that canceling the contracts of Jewish tax gatherers and tavern keepers signified no "abuse of power."[69] Kogălniceanu next proposed that vagabonds—that is, Jewish itinerants—be resettled in southern Bessarabia, on the Danube Delta, and on the Black Sea coast.[70] This project came to naught owing to the potential cost entailed therein. Then Kogălniceanu, who was deeply worried about anti-Jewish opinion in the Moldavian countryside, closed the frontiers to poor Jews from Russian Podolia and Austrian Galicia, and enforced the 1868 rural police code that provided for the banishment from agrarian communes of vagrants without work or money.[71] In all of this, Kogălniceanu believed he was fulfilling the will of the Romanian populace; and he deprecated attendant remonstrances by the powers as "mere words" to satisfy influential Jews in foreign capitals.[72] Most Romanian statesmen recognized that restrictions on Jews stemmed from patriotism. Jews functioned as a safety valve to relieve social tension and were thus a useful part of society. Had the Jews been absent, another scapegoat would have been found—perhaps one of the cohabiting Balkan peoples.

Action by the powers followed a now familiar scenario of protests, threats, collective notes, and, in the final analysis, a failure to cooperate that spelled support for Jewish subjects of the individual powers but neglect of Romania's indigenous Jews.

Further anti-Jewish disturbances erupted in the early 1870s. Romanians in Tecuci in Moldavia, accompanied by some foreign railway workers, attacked local Jews in 1870. A court in Galaţi, however, acquitted those accused of the disorder. The government lamely regretted this judgment yet balked at authorizing a retrial.[73] Carp, the current minister of foreign affairs, sought nonetheless to grant privileges to Jews residing in rural communes and to remove restrictions on Jewish immigration.[74] The latter promise remained a paper concession because Romania was unable to stop the illegal influx. Although Bismarck refused to pressure Romania into changing its laws and policy regarding Jews, Prussia joined in a note signed by each of the powers calling upon Romania to maintain tranquillity for its aliens.[75]

In southern Bessarabia—in Ismail, Cahul, and Vîlcov—anti-Jewish riots burst forth in 1872, and some Jews fled into the Ottoman Empire looking for a better life. The powers, except Russia, protested this outrage.[76] Germany's agenda in Romania remained primarily economic and only secondarily humanitarian; but Bismarck, influenced by Jewish financiers in Berlin, adhered to the identic note presented in Bucharest.[77] Carol and Costa-Foru, the minister of foreign affairs, promised that the perpetrators would be punished. The Buzău tribunal ruled nevertheless in favor of the Christian troublemakers and against the Jewish victims. Bismarck remarked that this was a "sad symptom" that demonstrated the "impossibility of an impartial administering of justice in Romanian courts." The Buzău decision also prompted a fresh protest by the powers, save Russia.[78] Gorchakov was consistent. He opposed all proposals affording political rights to Romania's Jews. He argued that Jews in Eastern Europe differed somehow from those in Western Europe and were unready for citizenship.[79] Persistent diplomatic clamor ultimately led Carol, nonetheless, to pardon some Jews convicted in Buzău for having provoked trouble.[80] Costa-Foru visited Constantinople to assure the Ottoman Empire of Romania's "calm and prosperity."[81] Such pledges notwithstanding, in 1873 the Romanian legislature renewed the prohibition on Jews' managing village taverns and precluded them from selling tobacco. On the one hand, Gerson von Bleichröder, Bismarck's banker, who was himself a Jew, worried that such measures would dispossess fifteen thousand families.[82] On the other hand, Gorchakov contended that Romania's Jewish question was an internal matter that should be left to Romania to resolve.[83] Bismarck recognized the failure of earlier remonstrances and reckoned that intervention would be detrimental to the interests of Romania's Jews.[84] A causal relationship did indeed exist between anti-Jewish acts, foreign meddling, heightened patriotic feeling, and additional turmoil.

Foreign concern for Romania's Jews waned owing to the powers' ongoing inability to cooperate effectively in Romania and because the Balkan Crisis of the mid-1870s commanded Europe's attention. Jews in Danubian Romania reemerged as an important issue at the Congress of Berlin following the Russo-Romanian-Turkish war of 1877–78. The powers then granted, as we shall see, Romania's independence on condition that its Jews be treated equally with other Romanians.

Notes

1. For the *hatt-ı hümayuns,* or imperial decrees, to the *voievods,* or princes, of Wallachia in 1402 and 1467/68, see Dionysios Phōteinos, *Historia tēs palai Dakias, ta nyn Transilvanias, Vlachias kai Moldauias,* 3:369–72; for the *hatt-ı şerif,* or imperial edict, to Moldavia in 1512, see Nicolae Costin, "Tractaturile prin cari s'aŭ închinatŭ ţéra, de către Bogdanŭ Vv. Domnŭ alŭ Moldaviĕ, împĕrăţindŭ Sultan Baiazet II," 451–52; for the capitulation of 1529 for Moldavia, see *Archives diplomatiques,* vol. 6, pt. 2 (avril, mai, juin 1866), 296–97.

2. See article 2 of the Paris convention of 19 August 1858, in *Recueil d'actes internationaux de l'Empire Ottoman,* 3:110.

3. See the capitulations for France in 1535, 1569, 1604, 1673, and 1674 as well as one for England in 1675, in *Recueil d'actes internationaux de l'Empire Ottoman,* 1:84–87, 91–92, 97, 101, 141–42, 280 ff., and 149. For commercial treaties with Austria in 1718, Prussia in 1761, Russia in 1783, and Sardinia in 1823, see ibid., 1:222–24, 317–18, 359–72, and 2:100–101.

4. *Reprezentanţele diplomatice ale României, 1859–1917,* 1:187, 156, 285, 102, 306, 236.

5. *Codul Calimach,* p. 66, para. 6, and p. 80, para. 45 of this Moldavian code, promulgated in 1817; *Regulamentul Organik,* p. 160, art. 239; *Reglementul Organik a Prinţipatului Moldovei,* p. 192, art. 297; *Codice Civile,* p. 5, art. 11; *Codicele penale şi de procedura criminala,* p. 4, art. 5 of the 1864 penal code; see *Desbaterile Adunărei Constituante din anul 1866 asupra Constituţiunei şi legei electorale din România,* p. 292 for art. 11 of the 1866 constitution.

6. George B. Ştirbei (Vienna) to Beust, 12 March 1867, and Beust to Ştirbei, 17 March 1867, in Haus- Hof- und Staatsarchiv (Austria), Politisches Archiv—XXXVIII, Konsulate: Bukarest, Varia (hereinafter cited HHS, PA).

7. Crémieux (Paris) to Beust, 4 February 1868, in HHS, PA—XXXVIII, Konsulate: Bukarest, Karton 178.

8. Beust to Eder (Bucharest), 14 March 1868, in HHS, PA—XXXVIII, Konsulate: Bukarest, Karton 179.

9. Beust to Eder, 5 November 1868, in HHS, PA—XXXVIII, Konsulate: Bukarest, Karton 179.

10. Vasile Netea, "Viena," *Reprezentanţele diplomatice ale României,* 1:168.

11. Beust to Nikolaus Zulauf von Pottenburg (Bucharest), 14 November 1870, in HHS, PA—XXXVIII, Konsulate: Bukarest, Karton 188.

12. Cantacuzino (St. Petersburg) to Carol, 24 February/8 March 1868, in AIC, CR, dosar 40 (1868); Gorchakov (St. Petersburg) to Ştefan Golescu (Bucharest), 5 March 1868, in Arhiva Ministerului Afacerilor Externe (Romania), Fond Convenţii, vol. 108, fol. 28 (hereinafter cited AMAE[R], FC).

13. Offenberg (Bucharest) to Ştefan Golescu, 17 March 1868, and journal of the council of ministers, 3 April 1868, no. 1, in AMAE(R), FC, vol. 108, fols. 1, 5.

14. Evgenii E. Chertan, "Iz istorii zakliucheniia russko-rumynskoi konsul'skoi konventsii 1869 g.," 46–47; Dimitrie Ghica (Bucharest) to Offenberg, 18 July 1869, no. 5307, in AMAE(R), FC, vol. 108, fols. 88–89.

15. See, for example, France's attitude in Strat (Vienna) to Dimitrie Ghica, 23 June 1869, in Fond Ion C. Brătianu, L/1/14, BNR, SM; Beust to Rudolf von Filek (Bucharest), 1 August 1869, in HHS, PA—XXXVIII, Konsulate: Bukarest, Karton 184.

16. Chertan, "Iz istorii zakliucheniia russko-rumynskoi konsul'skoi konventsii 1869 g.," 49–50.

17. Dimitrie Ghica to Steege, 8 April 1869, no. 2496, in AMAE(R), FC, vol. 108, fol. 81; Ghica to Offenberg, 19 April 1869, no. 6182, in ibid., vol. 108, fol. 91; instructions to Steege, 18 September 1869, telegram no. 8645, in ibid., vol. 108, fol. 93. The convention was initialed in St. Petersburg on 14/26 June 1869 and signed in Bucharest on 29 November/11 December 1869; ibid., vol. 108, fols. 109–10, 121ff. See the convention itself in ibid., vol. 108, fols. 324–32.

18. Carp (Bucharest) to Offenberg, 2/14 June 1870, no. 3764, in AMAE(R), FC, vol. 108, fol. 291; Offenberg to Carp, 2 July 1870, no. 33, in ibid., vol. 108, fol. 292; protocol of 26 July/7 August 1870 signed by Carp and Offenberg, in ibid., vol. 108, fol. 333; Offenberg to Nicolae Calimaki-Catargi, 6 March 1871, in ibid., vol. 108, fol. 295.

19. Project of a protocol approved by the Romanian cabiniet of ministers, 20 May 1871, in AMAE(R), FC, vol. 108, fol. 321; Offenberg to Boerescu (Bucharest), 30 June 1871, no. 36, in Fond Alexandru Saint-Georges, CXXVI/3, BNR, SM; Vladislav Ia. Grosul and Evgenii E. Chertan, *Rossiia i formirovanie rumynskogo nezavisimogo gosudarstva*, 172; Barbara Jelavich, *Russia and the Formation of the Romanian National State, 1821–1878*, 195.

20. For the project of 1 May 1866, and the committee's modifications, see *Desbaterile Adunării Constituante din anul 1866 asupra Constituțiunei*, 1–12, 34–46.

21. Session of 16/28 June 1866, in *Monitorul: Jurnal oficial al României*, 17/29 June 1866.

22. Session of 18/30 June 1866, in *Monitorul: Jurnal oficial al României*, 19 June/1 July 1866. Sihleanu used a pejorative term, "jidani," for Jews.

23. Carol allegedly spent 6,000 ducats for the restoration of the synagogue; see his notes, 18/30 June–20 June/2 July 1866, in *Aus dem Leben König Karls von Rumänien*, 1:76–78. But Picot, his secretary, noted that only 2,000 ducats were expended for this purpose; see Picot (Bucharest) to Alexandru Golescu (Constantinople), 27 December 1866/8 January 1867, in Fond Ion C. Brătianu, L1/3/2, BNR, SM; Avril (Bucharest) to Drouyn de Lhuys (Paris), 1 July 1866, no. 37, in AMAE(F), CP—Turquie: Consulat Bucarest, vol. 28. For a petition by Jews (Bucharest) to the powers, 19 June/1 July 1866, see Carol Iancu, *Les Juifs en Roumanie, 1866–1919: De l'exclusion à l'émancipation*, 283.

24. Session of 20 June/2 July 1866, in *Monitorul: Jurnal oficial al României*, 21 June/3 July 1866 and 22 June/4 July 1866; cf. Brătianu's speech in the legislative assembly, 10/22 January 1861, in *Din scrierile și cuvîntarile lui Ion C. Brătianu, 1821–1891*, vol. 1, pt. 1 (1848–68), 244–50.

Ionitorul: Jurnal oficial al României,
ice Civile, pp. 5–6, art. 16.
Ionitorul: Jurnal oficial al României,

ind 12 abstained from voting; see ses-
Jurnal oficial al României, 5/17 July
ution on 30 June/12 July 1866; see
July 1866. For the constitution, see
866 asupra Constituțiuñei, 290–308.
arles J. Bois-le-Comte, 11 and 14 May
or, vol. 17: *Corespondență diplomatică*
35–37, 359–60; *Analele statistice alle*
h de Gotha, 1871, 772; *Almanach de*
European Russia (including Poland)
3.23%, in Germany 1.30%, in Turkey
n 0.14%, and in Italy 0.11%.
)1, 370, 387; Ion Solcanu, "Realizări
recognize the Roman Catholic doc-

sile Lupu, issued in 1646, see *Carte*
!, para. 30, and p. 146, chap. 42, para.
iarab, see *Îndreptarea Legii, 1652,* p.
!, para. 7.

ui et hodierni status Moldaviæ, 296,

Prince Grigore A. Ghica of Moldavia
n Brezoianu, *Vechile institutiuni alle*

. . . . , . . . , . . . , . . . p. 508, paras. 1430, 1431; *Legiuirea*
Caragea, p. 75, chap. 16, para. 2. The latter code was promulgated in 1818.

34. *Reglementul Organik a Prințipatului Moldovei,* p. 199, art. 318, p. 27, art.
94, pp. 146–47, annex P, arts. 50–54, and p. 245, annex X, arts. 1, 4; *Regulamentul
Organik,* p. 160, art. 231, and pp. 196–97, art. 379.

35. *Codul Calimach,* 891, circular of 1843; Dimitrie Alexandresco, *Droit ancien
et moderne de la Roumanie,* 20; Verax [Radu D. Rosetti], *La Roumanie et les Juifs,*
77–91.

36. For point 21 of the Wallachian declaration in Izlaz, 9/21 June 1848, see
Anul 1848 în principatele române, 1:496; for point 27 in Kogălniceanu's brochure
"Dorințele Partidei Naționale în Moldova," which appeared in August 1848, see
ibid., 4:102.

37. *Codice Civile,* p. 5, art. 9; *Codicele penale și procedura criminala,* p. 52,
art. 220; *Reformele Romanilor,* p. 175, art. 26 of the communal law of 1864 and p.
686, art. 7 of the chambers of commerce law of 1864.

38. Ion Ghica to Alexandru Golescu (Bucharest) (1866), in Fond Mihail
Kogălniceanu, LXXXV/14, BNR, SC; Carol to Charles Anthony, 16/28 July 1866,
in *Aus dem Leben König Karls von Rumänien,* 1:93–94, 69n. 1.

39. Costin C. Kirițescu, *Sistemul bănesc al leului și precursorii lui*, 1:217–18. Brătianu offered his proposal to the chamber on 29 May/10 June 1866. Foreign paper tender had been used during the Russian occupation (1828–34) and the Austrian occupation (1854–57). For the currency law of 22 April/4 May 1867, see Kirițescu, 1:165–67 n.

40. *Statutele Uniunei Israelite din Jassi.*

41. Avril (Bucharest) to Drouyn de Lhuys (Paris), 16 June 1866, no. 31, and 29 June 1866, no. 34, in AMAE(F), CP—Turquie: Consulat Bucarest, vol. 28. Isidore Loeb, *La situation des israélites en Turquie, en Serbie et en Roumanie*, 147–57; Solomon Posener, *Adolphe Crémieux (1796–1880)*, vol. 2 (1840–80), 150. According to Carol, the loan was to be for 25,000,000 francs; see his notes, 2/14 June 1866, in *Aus dem Leben König Karls von Rumänien*, 1:70–71.

42. Brătianu's circular to Moldavian prefects, n.d., in *British and Foreign State Papers, 1867–1868*, 58:887; Carol dates this circular 2/14 April 1867 in *Aus dem Leben König Karls von Rumänien*, 1:188–89; Alexander B. Saint Clair (Iași) to Green (Bucharest), 21 May 1867, in *British and Foreign State Papers, 1867–1868*, 58:885.

43. Brătianu to the Iași mayor, 12/24 May 1867, in *British and Foreign State Papers, 1867–1868*, 58:887–88.

44. According to one allegation, in Czernowitz (Cernăuți), the provincial capital of Bukowina, three hundred families were buried owing to the persecution; Chajim Goldner to the Reverend Dr. Nathan M. Adler (London), May 1867, in HAA, PS: Türkei, 24, vol. 35.

45. See a report from the Romanian prefect of Covurluiu district (Galați), 2/14 July 1867, in Foreign Office, *Further Correspondence respecting the Persecution of the Jews in Moldavia*, 3:4; Crémieux and Narcisse Leven (Paris) to Bismarck, 1 June 1867, in HAA, PS: Türkei, 24, vol. 35.

46. Napoleon III to Carol, received 14/26 May 1867, in *Aus dem Leben König Karls von Rumänien*, 1:201.

47. Note dated 3/15 July 1867, in *British and Foreign State Papers, 1867–1868*, 58:904.

48. Midhat Paşa to Golescu, 18/30 July 1867, Golescu to Midhat Paşa, 28 July/9 August 1867, and Henry P. T. Barron (Constantinople) to Stanley, 10 September 1867, in *British and Foreign State Papers, 1871–1872*, 62:713–17.

49. See letters by Sturdza to Ion Ghica, 13 May (Nagyenyed/Aiud), 15 June (Eisenach), 16 November (Paris), and 23 December 1867 (Paris), in Fond Ion Ghica, XIV, 321, 322, 328, and 328 [*sic*], BAR, SC.

50. Brătianu (Paris) to Pia Brătianu, 25 September/7 October 1867, in *Din corespondența familiei Ion C. Brătianu*, 1:88.

51. See notes by Montefiore, 18 July and 18/30 August 1867, in Foreign Office, *Correspondence respecting the Condition and Treatment of the Jews in Servia and Roumania, 1867–76*, 31–32, 60; see Carol's notes, 13/25 August 1867, in *Aus dem Leben König Karls von Rumänien*, 1:218–19; Iancu, *Les Juifs en Roumanie*, 83–84.

52. Green to Stanley, 3, 10, and 16 January and 4 February 1868, Stanley to Green and Augustus Loftus (Berlin), 31 January 1868, and Loftus to Stanley, 15 February 1868, in *British and Foreign State Papers, 1871–1872*, 62:719–24.

53. See the deputies' project (1868) in *British and Foreign State Papers, 1871–1872*, 62:724–25.

54. Robert von der Goltz (Paris) to Bismarck, and Albert von Bernsdorff (London) to Bismarck, 27 March 1868, in HAA, PS: Türkei, 24, vol. 35.

55. See Carp's speech in the chamber, 26 April/8 May 1868, in Petre P. Carp, *Discursuri, 1866–1888*, 1:5, 13, 18; for Brătianu's speech in the chamber, 30 April/12 May 1868, see *Din scrierile şi cuvîntarile lui Ion C. Brătianu*, vol. 1, pt. 1, 454, 456.

56. Saint Clair (Iaşi) to Green, 18 April 1868, and Green to Stanley, 28 April 1868, in *Correspondence respecting the Condition and Treatment of the Jews in Servia and Roumania, 1867–76*, 110–11. See Carol's notes, 3/15 April 1868, in *Aus dem Leben König Karls von Rumänien*, 1:262.

57. See the protest by Jews in Iaşi to Gerson Bleichröder in Berlin, Montefiore and Francis Goldsmid in London, and Abraham Oppenheim in Cologne, 6 April 1868; Jonas Byk and Jacques Kaufman (Iaşi) to Bleichröder, 10 April 1868, in HAA, PS: Türkei, 24, vol. 37; Byk to Crémieux, 14 April 1868, in *Correspondence respecting the Condition and Treatment of the Jews in Servia and Roumania, 1867–76*, 104–5.

58. Bismarck to Heinrich von Keyserling-Rautenburg, 31 March and 7 April 1868, in *Die auswärtige Politik Preußens*, 9:821, 835.

59. Charles Anthony to Carol, 5/17 April 1868, in *Aus dem Leben König Karls von Rumänien*, 1:263.

60. Stanley to Green, 24 April 1868, in *British and Foreign State Papers, 1871–1872*, 62:727–29. Stanley referred to article 46 of the 1858 convention.

61. Beust to Eder, 6 and 12 April 1868, 21 May 1868, in HHS, PA—XXXVIII, Konsulate: Bukarest, Karton 179; Beust to Rudolf von Apponyi (London), 21 April 1868, in *Correspondence respecting the Condition and Treatment of the Jews in Servia and Roumania, 1867–76*, 106.

62. Protocol of 15 April 1868, in *British and Foreign State Papers, 1871–1872*, 62:729. Italy was not represented, but the Greek consul adhered to the note.

63. Brătianu to Golescu, 16 April 1868, in *British and Foreign State Papers, 1871–1872*, 62:737–38. See Golescu's note to the consuls in Bucharest, 17/29 April 1868, in *Aus dem Leben König Karls von Rumänien*, 1:276–77.

64. Carol to Prince Frederick William of Prussia, 18/30 June 1868, in *Aus dem Leben König Karls von Rumänien*, 1:277–78; protocol of 10 June 1868, Green to Stanley, 12 June 1868, and Brătianu to Eder, 25 June/7 July 1868, in *British and Foreign State Papers, 1871–1872*, 62:743–46.

65. G. B. Ward (Galaţi) to Green, 9 October 1868, Green to Stanley, 10 October 1868, Alfred G. Bonar (Vienna) to Stanley, 20 October 1868, and Green to Stanley, 26 October 1868, in *British and Foreign State Papers, 1871–1872*, 62:747–50; Beust to Eder, 9 October 1868, in HHS, PA—XXXVIII, Konsulate: Bukarest, Karton 179.

66. Keyserling to the Auswärtiges Amt (Berlin), 13 April 1869, in HAA, PS: Türkei, 24, vol. 40.

67. Kogălniceanu to Dimitrie Ghica, n.d., and Kogălniceanu's circulars, 15/27 January, 7 April, and 4/16 September 1869, in *British and Foreign State Papers, 1871–1872*, 62:759–68, 752–53, 771–74, 783.

68. See Kogălniceanu's speech in the chamber, 22 May/3 June 1869, in Mihail Kogălniceanu, *Opere*, vol. 4: *Oratorie II, 1864–1878*, pt. 2 (1868–70), 226–27.

69. Ghica to Green, 21 June/3 July 1869, Green to Clarendon (London), 17 July 1869, Boerescu's circular to Moldavian prefects, 25 June/7 July 1869, and Clarendon to Green, 13 October 1869, in *British and Foreign State Papers, 1871–1872*, 62:757–58, 775–78, 783–84.

70. Kogălniceanu to the Bolgrad prefect, 16 August 1869, in *Correspondence respecting the Condition and Treatment of the Jews in Servia and Roumania, 1867–76*, 179–80.

71. Kogălniceanu (Iaşi) to Dimitrie Ghica, n.d., in Fond Ion C. Brătianu, L/8/16, BNR, SM; Kogălniceanu's circular, 3/15 January 1870, in *British and Foreign State Papers, 1871–1872*, 62:797–98.

72. Green to Clarendon, 1 October 1869, in *British and Foreign State Papers, 1871–1872*, 62:784–85.

73. Joseph M. von Radowitz (Bucharest) to Bismarck, 2 May 1870, no. 28, in HAA, PS: Türkei, 24, vol. 42; Arthur C. Green (Bucharest) to Granville George, Earl Granville (London), 7 July 1870, in *British and Foreign State Papers, 1871–1872*, 62:806.

74. Carp to Steege, 29 April/11 May 1870, in Fond Ion C. Brătianu, LVI/D4, BNR, SM.

75. Loftus to Clarendon, 5 March 1870, in *British and Foreign State Papers, 1871–1872*, 62:799–800; note dated 31 May 1870, in HAA, PS: Türkei, 24, vol. 43; cf. John Green to Clarendon, 7 June 1870, no. 77, in PRO, FO, 195/966.

76. John Green to Granville, 29 January and 8 February 1872, and Ward to Green, 30 January 1872, in *Correspondence respecting the Condition and Treatment of the Jews in Servia and Roumania, 1867–76*, 224–27; Benjamin F. Peixotto (Bucharest) to William Hunter (Washington, D.C.), 9 February 1872, and an identic note to the Romanian government, 9 February 1872, in 42nd Congress, 3rd session, *Papers relating to the Foreign Relations of the United States, 2 December 1872*, 682–83, 685 (hereinafter cited 42nd Cong.).

77. Bismarck to Heinrich VII von Reuss (St. Petersburg), 11 February 1872, no. 9, and 14 February 1872, in HAA, PS: Türkei, 24, vol. 47.

78. Bleichröder to Bismarck, 30 March 1872, Bismarck to Bleichröder, 2 April 1872, Bismarck to Wilhelm Otto von Theilau (Bucharest), 2 April 1872, no. 5, and Bismarck to William I, 19 April 1872, in HAA, PS: Türkei, 24, vol. 47. The United States and Greece joined the protest, 18 April 1872; see 42nd Cong., 690.

79. Loftus to Granville, 22 May 1872, in *Correspondence respecting the Condition and Treatment of the Jews in Servia and Roumania*, 246, 249; *The Diplomatic Reminiscences of Lord Augustus Loftus, 1862–1879*, 2:19–23. See Carol's notes, 18/30 May 1872, in *Aus dem Leben König Karls von Rumänien*, 2:266.

80. Costa-Foru's circular, 27 April/9 May 1872, in 42nd Cong., 693–96.

81. See Carol's notes, 27 May/8 June 1872, in *Aus dem Leben König Karls von Rumänien*, 2:267.

82. Carol to Charles Anthony, 16/28 February 1873, in *Aus dem Leben König Karls von Rumänien*, 2:304–5; Bleichröder to Bismarck, 1 March 1873, in HAA, PS: Türkei, 24, vol. 47.

83. See Russian memorandum of 17 March 1873, in *Correspondence respecting the Conditions and Treatment of Jews in Servia and Roumania, 1867–76*, 293–94.

84. Bismarck to Bleichröder, 6 March 1873, in HAA, PS: Türkei, 24, vol. 47.

Carol (1839–1914)

Ion C. Brătianu (1821–91)

Mihail Kogălniceanu (1817–91)

Constantin A. Rosetti (1816–85)

Ion Ghica (1817–97)

Dimitrie Ghica (1816–97)

Lascăr Catargiu (1823–99)

Petre P. Carp (1837–1918)

Dimitrie A. Sturdza (1833–1914)

Vasile Boerescu (1830–83)

Nicolae Ionescu (1820–1905)

Manolache Costache Epureanu (1824–80)

Chapter Four

FOREIGN CONSTRUCTION

The modernization of Europe's economy in the nineteenth century depended in large part on rapid communication and transportation. Railroads provided the means for the relatively inexpensive and speedy movement of goods and persons the year round. Railways offered the prospect of ending food shortages caused by regional droughts and crop failures, although peasants used them, primarily during summer months, to send agricultural products to major markets. Rail construction was, however, costly and complicated. Romania lacked the requisite capital and skills and so looked to foreign contractors and technicians to do the job. Alien investors were, in the main, responsible for Romania's lines, which turned into arteries for the foreign commercial penetration of the country. Modernization, for many Romanians, became synonymous with outside interests, and so it aroused patriotic, anti-alien sentiments.

The great powers had somewhat different views as to the purposes of railroads in Southeastern Europe, but their primary considerations were economic and strategic. The British had originally developed locomotives and railways to exploit coal resources in England. Economic designs were also preeminent in creating lines in territories of the British Empire—Canada, India, Australia, and South Africa—as well as in the Ottoman Empire. British initiative was responsible for the first Turkish railroad, running in Egypt from Alexandria to Cairo by 1852 and on to Suez by 1861, linking thereby the Mediterranean and Red seas before the Suez Canal was ready for vessels in 1869. The British identified the lower Danubian area as an agricultural supply base and consequently built the initial line there from the Danube to the Black Sea. John Trevor Barkley, a British entrepreneur, constructed one railway from Cernavodă on the Danube River in Dobrogea to Constanța on the seashore, which opened in 1860, plus another from Ruse on the Danube to Varna on the coast by 1866. In 1865 he began forty-three miles of track from Bucharest to Giurgiu on the Danube opposite Ruse—inaugurated in 1869—that tied the Romanian capital to the Black Sea.[1] No Romanian rail bridge crossed the Danube, however, until the erection of the span at Cernavodă in 1895. These early lines nonetheless gave British merchants in the 1860s and 1870s access to the farm products of the Danube Valley. In addition, Great Britain was potentially able, with its ships and trains, to bring troops to the Danube at two separate points and so to challenge a possible Russian march on Constantinople.

Russian railroads emerged slowly at the outset; but following the Crimean War and the introduction of Henry Bessemer's open-hearth method of making inexpensive steel, railways spread rapidly in western Russia. In 1842 Nicholas I ordered a Moscow-St. Petersburg line, which was ready in 1851. This railroad had no major military purpose, although it united Russia's two largest towns. No longer was Sweden the principal enemy. More important were Russia's western and southern frontiers: to the west, Russian Poland, wedged between the two Germanys of Prussia and Austria; to the south, the Ottoman Empire, which might again be the source, if not the site, of a future war. Hence the military and economic goals were clear in Alexander II's edict of 1857: to fashion a rail network extending west from St. Petersburg to Warsaw and the Prussian border, west from central Russia to the Baltic Sea, and south from Moscow via the lower Dnieper River to the Crimea.[2]

A Russian railroad linked Moscow to Kiev by 1871, and then to Odessa on the Black Sea coast; in addition, a line joined Odessa to Kishinev (Chişinău), the capital of Russia's northern Bessarabia. This railway pushed westward during the early 1870s to Ungeny (Ungeni) on the Prut River frontier with Romania.[3] The gauge of the Russian track was 5 feet, wider than the 4.71 feet customarily used elsewhere in Europe, including Romania. Gauge was an issue in building the only Romanian-planned and financed railroad during the 1860s and 1870s, from Iaşi in Moldavia to the Russian border. Grigore Eliad, a Romanian engineer, supervised the construction of the Iaşi-Ungeny line from 1873 to 1874, and a rail bridge across the Prut at Ungeny built by April 1877 was the work of both Romanians and Russians. The thirteen miles of this line had the same width as Russian railroads, and so Russia had easier access to Romania than vice versa.[4] Another Russian railway was built during the Russo-Romanian-Turkish war in 1877, coupling the Kishinev-Odessa course at Bendery (Bender) on the Dnestr (Dniester) River to Reni in Romania's southern Bessarabia, opposite Galaţi at the confluence of the Prut and Danube rivers. This line, hastily set up by the Russian engineer Samuil S. Poliakov, facilitated the movement of Russian troops and supplies to Balkan battlefields.[5] The Bendery-Reni railroad fell into disuse after the war.

Some Romanians opposed a direct rail tie to Russia. Dimitrie Ghica, the minister of public works, remarked in 1869 that although rail passage between the two countries might facilitate the export of Romanian salt to Russian markets, Russia had a high tariff on salt. He warned moreover that rail contact from southern Bessarabia to Odessa would imperil the prosperity of Romania's Danubian ports of Galați and Brăila.[6] Romania persevered after the 1877 war in striving to protect its economy. Thus traffic from Galați to Reni was by water until Romania annexed northern Bessarabia after World War I—when a rail span crossed the Prut to Reni. Romania also weighed political and strategic factors. If Russia gained a preponderant position in Romania through railroads, perhaps the other powers would withdraw their collective guarantee of Romania's autonomy. Russia certainly desired a rail route to the Balkan Peninsula for its army in case of war with the Ottoman Empire. Romanians, for their part, fully perceived Russia's military and economic interests, which potentially threatened their land.

Many Romanians saw greater economic, political, and military challenges from the Habsburg Empire than from Russia, especially after the latter's defeat in the Crimean War. Railroads in Austria developed according to a patent issued by Emperor Ferdinand (1835–48) in 1841. Thereby, Austria's railways were to run north from Vienna to Prague and Saxony, west to Bavaria, and south to Trieste on the Adriatic Sea; lines in Hungary pointed from Budapest to Vienna, via Zagreb to Fiume on the Adriatic, to Galicia, to Transylvania, and to the Banat of Temesvár. Austria's first track led to Krakau, eventually extending to Warsaw as well as through Galicia to Bukowina. By the 1870s, Austria-Hungary's lines reached Romania's borders.[7] Some Danubian Romanians fretted that the Habsburg Empire sought to enlarge itself at their expense. Would Austria-Hungary, after being denied supremacy in Germany, turn southward and try to annex Romania? The empire's later military occupation of Bosnia and Hercegovina in 1878 indicated that Vienna did indeed envision territorial aggrandizement in Southeastern Europe. After the Ausgleich of 1867 and the political emergence of the Magyars, however, a debate ensued about the ethnic mix in the Dual Monarchy. How might the Germans in Austria and the Magyars in Hungary effectively handle their respective domains if more non-Germans and non-Magyars came into the Habsburg realm? Germans and Magyars would themselves become minorities by taking in many Slavs and Romanians. On the one hand, Austria-Hungary had less to fear because of geographical and historical divisions among the Slavs: the Catholic West Slavs of Bohemia and Galicia were cut off by the Magyars from the Catholic South Slavs of

Slovenia and Croatia, so the addition of Orthodox Slavic Serbs of Bosnia and Hercegovina to Austria might not upset German hegemony. On the other hand, Hungary had to cope with a large Romanian population in Transylvania and the Banat. The inclusion of almost five million more, contiguous Romanians from Moldavia and Wallachia into Hungary would overwhelm the narrow numerical superiority then enjoyed by the Magyars. Hence Magyars resisted the acquisition of more Romanians. The regime in Vienna was cordial toward the one in Bucharest and wanted rail connections between the two countries. Beust, Austria-Hungary's minister of foreign affairs, commented that he was indifferent as to who built Romania's railroads, yet he hoped for a solid rail link from Brassó (Braşov) in Transylvania to the Danubian port of Galaţi.[8]

What was Romania's interest in railroads? Would railways benefit the powers more than Romania itself? Or was the threat from abroad more illusory than genuine? Prince Carol thought that only a line from Bucharest to Iaşi would "really cement Moldavia and wither every separatist tendency."[9] Boerescu later recalled that the "union was in danger" in 1868 and thus concluded that railroads were an "urgent necessity."[10] Railways in Moldavia and Wallachia might, to be sure, facilitate an alien military invasion in case of a Russo-Turkish war or one between the Habsburg and Romanov empires. Romania might become a battlefield, with trains transporting troops and munitions. Far more important still were Romania's needs in the 1860s and 1870s to firmly unify itself, to assure its political viability, and to end the prospect of famine. Railroads were essential for such purposes as well to tie Romania's commerce to foreign markets and to provide an efficient means for its affluent individuals to visit cultural centers at Paris, Vienna, and Berlin.

Before railroads, communications were slow and cumbersome. The principal routes were rivers, along which were roads. The Danube, Prut, Siret, and Olt rivers had been the ways of trade and travel from earliest times. Moldavia and Wallachia each had two main avenues. In Moldavia one course led southward down the Siret River valley from Bukowina to the Danube at Galaţi; the other one went from northern Moldavia through Iaşi, parallel to the Prut River, to Galaţi. In Wallachia roads bisected the land. An east-west artery ran from the mouth of the Ialomiţa River south of Brăila on the Danube to Bucharest, Craiova, and Vîrciorova near the Banat; the major north-south way was in the Prahova Valley from Predeal, near Transylvania, to Ploieşti, and then to Bucharest and Giurgiu on the Danube.[11] These roads would, in essence, become the paths of the railroads. The first Moldavian rail project in 1842 envisioned a line from Bukowina down the Siret to Galaţi;

the first Wallachian proposal in 1855 foresaw passage from east to west and from north to south following the roads. In 1861 and 1862, Danubian Romania authorized a rail network in Moldavia and Wallachia, with branch lines to the Tîrgu Ocna salt mines, to Iaşi, to Giurgiu and Galaţi on the Danube, and to Transylvania—north of Craiova in the Jiu River valley.[12] Romanians were unable to realize these plans by themselves owing to their inadequate financial resources and expertise.

Railway contracts were consequently offered by the Romanian legislature to foreign entrepreneurs for constructing a rail grid uniting the country and tying Romania's lines to those in the Habsburg Empire. Two groups received the chief contracts. Austrian and British financiers, headed by Victor von Ofenheim of Vienna, formed one syndicate; Bethel H. Strousberg organized Prussian investors into a second company. Ion Brătianu later reckoned that Vienna was less interested than Berlin in building Romania's railroads—especially in Wallachia—for a direct line from Paris to Constantinople via Serbia or Bosnia and Hercegovina would bypass Romania. On the one hand, Danubian Romanians needed a track from Bucharest to the Banat so as to allow a rapid mobilization of troops in Oltenia, or western Wallachia, and thereby to contest an Austro-Hungarian attack.[13] On the other hand, some Romanians in the Banat wanted rail contact with Romania in order to facilitate the transit of the Habsburg army in case of war with Russia.[14] Austro-Hungarian forces might, to be sure, reach Russia more rapidly by way of Galicia or Bukowina than through Romania. Still, the prospect of conflict between Russia and Austria-Hungary in Southeastern Europe would persist until the collapse of both empires in World War I.

The Austro-Hungarian syndicate was responsible for Romania's railroad in northern Moldavia from Suczawa (Suceava) in Bukowina to Iaşi, Roman, and Botoşani. Its 138 miles opened on schedule in 1871.[15] Yet Romania denied this firm's proposal to push the line southward to Bucharest and Galaţi, awarding instead a concession for the rest of the rail network to Strousberg's Prussian company. One reason for this decision may have been fear of Habsburg leverage. Prince Charles Anthony had reportedly invested in Austria-Hungary's state railway company—which built many railways in the Habsburg Empire and had actually forged the line in Moldavia—a rumor seemingly substantiated by Carol's preference for the Viennese consortium's offer.[16]

The next questions were economic and diplomatic. Where should rail junctions be established between Austria-Hungary and Romania? In negotiations about couplings, patriotic feelings percolated in Romanians. One link already existed between Bukowina and Moldavia. Beust called for another that would open Transylvanian trade from Kolozsvár (Cluj) and Brassó to Galaţi and to the Black Sea—something that Romania did not initially favor. The Habsburg Empire eschewed, however, pressing for a tie between the Banat and Romania's rails in Oltenia; in any case, Austria had yet to complete its Banat railroad owing to the difficulties and expenses of constructing in mountainous terrain.[17] Romania wanted a link with the Banat in part because the Prussian contract entailed a line westward to the Banat, but not northward to Transylvania. This disagreement irked many Romanians in Austria-Hungary and in Romania who sought to be almost everywhere bound by rail as they were bound in spirit. Formalities also played a role. In insisting on a special convention to identify and regulate the junctions, Romanian minister of foreign affairs Costa-Foru demanded in addition that "Romania" ("Roumanie") be used in the text instead of "Moldo-Wallachia" ("Moldo-Valachie") or "United Principalities" ("Principautés-Unies"). Beust had stipulated "United Principalities" in the Habsburg Empire's postal accord of 1868 with Romania. Russia was the first power to employ the name "Romania" in 1869 but was the only one to do so until Austria-Hungary yielded to Romanian national pride in a telegraph agreement in 1871 and a rail connection compact in 1872.[18]

Romania's covenant with Austria-Hungary prescribed five rail junctions: the one already in place between Bukowina and northern Moldavia, plus others between the Banat and Oltenia, between Oltenia and Transylvania, between Transylvania and Muntenia, and between Transylvania and western Moldavia.[19] The Habsburg Empire's railroads would thereby join those in all portions of Romania. In the chamber of deputies, Boerescu maintained that such links would help in developing barren sectors and would enhance the prosperity of currently productive regions in his country.[20] Kogălniceanu opposed this treaty. He had once warned that Romania's railways might ease Russia's capture of Iaşi and facilitate the entry of Turkey's troops; now he suggested that Austria-Hungary might seize Bucharest from Brassó. Romanians needed no further connections, he contended, for they could journey to Western Europe by water up the Danube in summer and by rail through northern Moldavia in winter.[21] He ignored a potential Habsburg invasion of Moldavia. The upshot of the chamber's debates was to approve the existing tie between Bukowina and Moldavia but to reject the others. The convention itself failed.

Negotiations for rail junctions began anew in the mid-1870s. Adolf von Hansemann, a German banker who would finance a Romanian railway, saw the "immense advantages" and "grand interest" in such links, a subject that "deeply preoccupies the court at Berlin."[22] An agreement was ultimately adopted in 1874 for connections in Muntenia and Oltenia.[23] A railroad extended westward in Oltenia to the Austro-Hungarian border by 1875, but not northward in Muntenia; therefore Romania needed a line going north to Transylvania. A concession for track from Ploieşti to Predeal was first offered to Ernest Gouin, an engineer with Prussia's state railway company; but political machinations in Bucharest, which may have included bribery, led to a deal with the British contractor George B. Crawley.[24] Its 53 miles was an expensive deal. The cost was about twice that paid per mile for the Austrian and Prussian undertakings because of rough terrain and a steep route, rising from an altitude of 499 feet to 3,468 feet.[25] Dissatisfaction with this engagement was, in part, the reason for the resignation of some deputies in 1875 and the fall of Catargiu's ministry in 1876.[26] The Russo-Romanian hostilities with Turkey interrupted Crawley's work. Romanian legislators then sought to cancel his project and to have Romanian engineers finish the job. The British diplomatic agent at Bucharest, Charles E. Mansfield, hinted that the powers might withhold recognizing Romania's independence, which the legislature proclaimed in 1877, if Crawley were denied "justice."[27] Crawley eventually lost his concession yet received compensation in state bonds guaranteed by the liquor tax.[28] Léon Guilloux, who directed the Prussian-built lines for several years, completed the Ploieşti-Predeal railway.[29] The Hungarian prime minister, Kálmán Tisza, then successfully persuaded Romania to couple its trade to that of Hungary in return for Austria-Hungary's aid at the Congress of Berlin.[30] The Transylvania-Muntenia tie opened in 1879. The Banat track met the Romanian frontier at Orsova (Orşova) in 1878, and the link with Oltenia was in service by 1880. Later, in 1899, Hungarian and Romanian railroads sped traffic from Moldavian salt deposits; the planned rail passage from Oltenia to the coal mines of Petrozsény (Petroşani) in Transylvania would nevertheless wait until 1948—well after another line in 1901 stretched northward up the Olt River valley to Nagyszeben (Sibiu) in Transylvania.

Romania's most significant railway joined northern Moldavia to the Danube and then passed through Wallachia to the Austro-Hungarian border. It followed, in general, early trade routes ranging southward along the Siret River to its confluence with the Danube between the ports of Galaţi and Brăila, and from Brăila westward to Bucharest, Ploieşti, Craiova, and Vîrciorova—north of Serbia and east of the Banat. This railroad's 568 miles connected Romania's major towns and was to facilitate its produce in reaching West European markets.

Strousberg—popularly known as the Railway King—was to build this railroad. His attention to Romania's railroad was, however, less than Danubian Romanians expected, for he was already immersed in rail construction in Prussian Poland, Silesia, and Hanover. Strousberg promised to raise capital abroad for the Romanian project, something Ofenheim had refused to do.[31] The Strousberg concession hence appeared to be financially advantageous for the Romanians. Strousberg was to issue shares for the lines he had begun work on but had not yet finished. A rail commissioner in Berlin representing the Romanian government was to vend the stock corresponding to certificates of completion from the principal engineer.[32] Strousberg was to pay dividends on the shares until the lines were ready for operation; Romania would thereafter be responsible for remuneration. A shareholders' association was formed in Berlin to manage the company for ninety years, after which the lines would go to Romania. Romania, in essence, lacked control over the quality and length of the railways and over the sale of rail securities. This situation was nevertheless devoid of substantial controversy until Strousberg later declared bankruptcy, and rumors surfaced about collusion between the Berlin commissioner and the chief engineer.

Beforehand, however, Romanian legislators had been reluctant to award Strousberg a contract without a full discussion of its provisions. Deputies coveted a measure of authority over the company. Carp proposed tight governmental supervision yet lacked adequate support for this recommendation, since his colleagues thought it would have made the concession "more tangled" than necessary.[33] Ion Brătianu, who was then minister of finance, described the Strousberg enterprise as an "association composed of persons who by their social status, by their material position, [and] by their important standing would inspire confidence in Europe's capitalists, who would aid in constructing the railroad."[34] Brătianu also praised German technical skill, concluding that the next generations "will laugh much about our theories today and will thank us that we gave them railroads."[35] Some legislators were less enthusiastic and called for more time to consider the pact. Carol intervened at this juncture, offering the senate's two vice presidents the opportunity to organize a new cabinet if they could gain a speedy approval of the Strousberg transaction. The senate still balked, and so Carol, who was adamant, brought about its dissolution.[36] The deputies eventually yielded to Carol's ongoing pressure and authorized the cabinet to arrange with Strousberg to start construction.[37] The chamber of deputies was then dissolved as well. This procedure was high-handed and quite illegal, but the constitutional mode sat lightly on Romanian shoulders; even two years after adopting their charter, few Romanians understood either its letter or its spirit. Building got underway in the summer of 1868. Carol again exerted his influence during and after the elections in the fall of 1868 so as to win the senate's endorsement of the rail bargain.[38]

Many were the difficulties that Strousberg encountered in Romania, and many were the doubts among Romanians about his railroad. Some Romanians suspected complicity between Strousberg, the chief engineer, and Romania's commissioner in Berlin in reaping unearned profits from unbuilt lines. The commissioner, Otto V. Ambronn, who was said to be an "honorable and eminent" man—albeit neither a Romanian citizen nor Romania's salaried official—was a Prussian privy councilor for high finance employed by the house of Hohenzollern, with orders from Carol to cooperate closely with Strousberg.[39] Kogălniceanu remarked that Ambronn had been selected because Romania required German capital; Ambronn was the sine qua non for vending rail securities in Prussia inasmuch as earlier Romanian loans prohibited Danubian Romania from making new ones at that time.[40] Ambronn invested funds from the marketing of rail shares in companies owned by Strousberg; but according to rumor, he unloaded more stock than justified by certificates of completion emitted by the chief engineer.[41] Romania then set up a technical committee to verify the engineer's reports.[42] All of this was crucial for the Romanians. Strousberg had, after all, obtained his concession mainly owing to his promise to build at his own expense; Romania was only to pay dividends on the rail warrants after the lines opened. If more shares had been issued than the cost of the railroad in place, Romania would be remitting for nonexistent lines. Hence Bucharest insisted that the chief engineer's accounts be accurate and that the amount of stock sold abroad correctly represent the completed construction.[43] The chamber approved a resolution asking the Romanian diplomatic agent in Berlin to ascertain the number of outstanding shares. Sturdza, a former minister of public works, then went to Berlin to take control over the emission of rail securities. After studying the matter in the Prussian capital, however, Sturdza expressed his trust in Ambronn and his feeling that the latter's ouster would shake public confidence in the shares, thus lessening their value.[44] One of Carol's confidants, Teodor Văcărescu, investigated the rail firm anew in Berlin during the Franco-Prussian War of 1870–71. He discovered a difference of 7.4 million francs between the worth of the stocks and that of the rail work. Strousberg had apparently gotten the extra money directly from Ambronn. The eventual result of Văcărescu's revelation was Ambronn's being replaced as commissioner by Steege, Romania's envoy in Berlin.[45]

The evident lack of progress in building the railroad and the attendant hostility toward Strousberg had political reverberations that led to changes in Romania's cabinet of ministers.[46] Strousberg responded bitterly to allegations leveled against him. Had he received more cash than he deserved? Had he evaded the rail plan agreed to by the Romanian government?[47] Strousberg cataloged his troubles: Romania had no railroad to bring supplies to his construction sites and no trained technicians; many rivers needed bridging, and quicksand posed a problem. He encountered snags also in obtaining rights of way and found himself hindered by local administrators and courts. Most important, an anti-German attitude surfaced in Romania during the Franco-Prussian War.[48] The unsettling effects of those hostilities on Strousberg's financial situation provoked him to declare bankruptcy. He suggested that Romania defray dividends on the rail warrants for incomplete lines. When Bucharest rejected this proposal, he stopped work on the railroad, which—by the end of December 1870—merely reached eastward from Bucharest to Galaţi in Wallachia and thence northward to Roman in Moldavia. He next announced his inability to pay the rail shares' dividend that was due on 1 January 1871.[49]

Strousberg's insolvency was a blow for Carol as well as for Romania. Many Romanians were strongly pro-French and anti-Prussian during the Franco-Prussian War, and Carol had been accused of secretly aiding Germans in that conflict. Carol admitted he had adversaries and remarked that four hundred of five thousand voters in Ploieşti were rebels with the backing of a foreign power—presumably France—but without secure roots in the populace at large. The prince's opponents viewed the railroad as a means for Carol to consolidate his authority, and so they confronted the rail company with numerous difficulties in the hope that Strousberg would shut down.[50] Anti-Carol agitators unexpectedly proclaimed a republic in Ploieşti on 8/20 August 1870, solemnly deposed the prince, and set up a new regime. The government quickly suppressed this revolt and incarcerated the insurgents, who were headed by Alexandru Candiano-Popescu and Eugeniu Carada.[51] Were Romanians, in general, loyal to Carol? Was he able to direct the fortunes of the state in a crisis? Carol pondered these questions. He contemplated abdicating and informed the powers guaranteeing Romania's autonomy about his intentions; later, he conveyed his ideas also to the suzerain Ottoman Empire and to an influential German newspaper in Bavaria.[52] The powers, who were primarily occupied with the Franco-Prussian War, offered sympathy but no support. Ali Paşa, Turkey's minister of foreign affairs, promised nonetheless to help in fighting "anarchical tendencies," something Romanians were loath to accept from the sultan.[53] Some Romanians saw in Carol's demission threat an "act of high treason."[54] Others, chastened by the abortive uprising, expressed in the chamber their "devotion to the throne and to the dynasty"; the senate adopted a motion endorsing Carol.[55] These were faithful words and, in light of the Ploieşti insurrection, were in keeping with propriety. Would this attitude extend to protecting the prince against renewed seditious outbursts? Fortunately for Carol and for Romania's internal order, Strousberg's bankruptcy became more of a political football than a rallying cry for revolution.

Following the Ploieşti revolt, a Romanian engineer, Panait Donici, investigated the railroads. Donici reported faulty and inadequate construction. The lines had too few stations, warehouses, optical signals, and sentry boxes; locomotives were too light and too weak, carriages and watchhouses were inferior, and earthworks needed reshaping.[56] Donici left no doubt that Strousberg had duped the Romanians. Diplomatic quarrels compounded national chagrin. The German consul in Bucharest and his Austro-Hungarian colleague adopted the stand of the foreign shareholders and demanded that Romania pay dividends on Strousberg's obligations.[57] The chamber of deputies responded by annulling the rail concession, sequestering the lines, and turning to a court of arbitration to resolve differences between Strousberg and the state.[58] The deputies failed to provide financial compensation, and so the investors rejected Romania's actions.

Romanian antagonism toward Germans continued to grow after the foundation of the German Empire in 1871. The German company had, after all, yet to finish Romania's railroad, and the German government had intervened in a Romanian domestic matter. Some frustrated Romanian patriots decided to unveil their anti-German animosity. A demonstration erupted at a banquet in Bucharest's Slătineanu Hall, where local German residents had gathered to celebrate the birthday of the German emperor, William I. Although the capital's prefect had assured the Germans a peaceable setting, a group of students assaulted the hall with stones while police stood passively by. Church bells tolled, and cries reverberated far and wide: "Long live the republic," "Free the country from foreigners," and "To the palace."[59] Troops brought to the scene forbore suppressing the riot owing to a reluctance to see bloodshed. The German consul, Joseph M. von Radowitz, and about one hundred guests received no protection in making their way homeward. Radowitz and Ion Ghica, the prime minister, then went to the palace, where Ghica conceded: "This is a great misfortune." Carol agreed, and Ghica resigned.[60]

Once again Carol considered abdicating. He called the available members of the regency of 1866—Catargiu and Nicolae Golescu—to hear his intentions. He would remain in Romania only if peace was restored and a budget adopted incorporating expenditures necessary for paying dividends on the rail investments. Catargiu and Golescu opposed Carol's demission as heralding anarchy; a new ministry, led by Catargiu, was then formed that would last until 1876.[61] Bismarck, now German chancellor, appreciated the cabinet change but indicated that he would seek help from the Ottoman Empire if Romania denied adequate compensation to victims of the riot.[62] Bucharest awarded sixteen thousand francs to the Germans in Bucharest, and that satisfied Bismarck.[63] Bismarck nonetheless encouraged Ali Paşa to write Carol about the lack of harmony and tranquillity that compromised Romania's "peace and public security."[64] Carol replied to Ali that his chief concern was to assure a "solid and durable" basis for order in the country.[65] The Ottoman Empire still exercised some indirect influence in Romania's internal affairs, and this troubled Carol. To William I, he complained: "the future lies impenetrably dark before me."[66] If Carol had shown sympathy for the Germans during the Franco-Prussian War, was the time now ripe for him to fully embrace the Romanians' national cause? Since arriving in Bucharest, Carol had merged his own destiny with that of Romania; and the events of 1871 served to strengthen his resolve, despite some lingering doubts and hesitation, to be rid of Turkish suzerainty.

Strousberg's rail shares continued to be a critical issue. Strousberg and the German government insisted that Romania pay the dividends. Romania refused. Ion Brătianu would later admit that he had put "too much faith in the honor and honesty of some, and in the intelligence, patriotism, character, ability, and prudence of others" in this matter; he had, moreover, failed to foresee the German victory over France and the resulting shift in the locus of European power.[67] Germany and Romania were not, of course, contiguous, and so Romania anticipated no military attack by Germany. Bismarck's primary policy henceforth was to maintain the political status quo in Europe. Germany would nevertheless exert leverage in Romania via diplomatic channels.

Romanian legislators discussed several proposals about the railroads. According to one proposal, the discredited Strousberg was to continue building his line from Piteşti to Turnu-Severin in eastern Oltenia; the rail shares were, in addition, to be converted from Strousberg's obligations, which yielded 7.5-percent dividends, to state bonds bearing 5-percent interest.[68] Romania's finance minister, Petru Mavrogheni, at first sponsored this plan but soon reversed himself, asking: "who will guarantee to us that Strousberg will keep this engagement?"[69] Deputies talked so much about this question, suggesting and dismissing so many programs, that Ion Brătianu character-ized them as being "stuck in the mud" of this "scandalous" affair.[70] The cham-ber eventually adopted a blueprint elaborated by Constantin Boerescu and his elder brother, Vasile, among others, as being "most practicable" and "most just." It would annul the Strousberg concession and offer the shareholders an opportunity to create their own society, having the rights and duties of the original association. If they declined to do so, the state would expropri-ate the railway and reimburse them with a sum equivalent to the nominal value of the line. Strousberg's 7.5-percent shares were to be converted into state debentures returning 4 percent.[71] Carol, facing again the prospect of abdication or accommodation, chose the latter course and approved the Boerescu project.[72] This measure signified a decrease in the stock's worth yet also formally recognized Romania's responsibility for the dividends.

Danubian Romanians thought the Boerescu project would be approved in Berlin, but they were to be sorely disappointed. Bismarck actively cru-saded for the shareholders. He requested and won Turkish support in pro-tecting German investors.[73] Ottoman suzerainty was quite flimsy in Romania, but the Turks still welcomed the chance to demonstrate anew their political influence. Ali Paşa wrote to Carol about the importance of the rail stock and called for a "definite arrangement" to "safeguard the interests" of the own-ers.[74] Carol acquiesced to such entreaties by withdrawing his endorsement of the Boerescu plan and by declaring rather vaguely that he was working for a "satisfactory" solution.[75] However, Bismarck was unable to gain the assistance of other powers in exerting pressure on Romania to render divi-dends on the securities; even the Ottoman Empire backed away from this issue.[76] Costa-Foru argued with some justification that Bismarck had again intervened in Danubian Romania's internal affairs in contravention of the 1856 Treaty of Paris and convention of 1858.[77] Sturdza mistakenly imag-ined that Bismarck covertly sought to transfer southern Bessarabia to Rus-sia and to change the Romanian constitution in favor of foreigners—that is, the Jews.[78] Foreign diplomatic machinations certainly heightened Romanians' fears about their destiny, which in turn stimulated their patriotic spirits. Sturdza's foreboding appeared unrealistic in 1871, yet it could only be consid-ered visionary by the end of the decade, when Romania lost southern

Bessarabia and was pressured to amend its constitution to benefit the Jews. Some Danubian Romanians viewed both experiences as national calamities.

Romania's legislators attempted once more to settle the railway question. Some proposed to rescind Strousberg's concession and require shareholders to form societies in Berlin, Breslau, and Vienna that would take over Strousberg's equity.[79] A syndicate of stockholders, led by Hansemann of the Disconto Gesellschaft and Bleichröder, was to control, complete, and run the railroad.[80] Strousberg's 7.5-percent shares were to be converted into 5-percent ones guaranteed by the Romanian state. Romania would be responsible for dividends due on the lines opened by Strousberg, namely, Bucharest-Galaţi-Roman.[81] A majority of the deputies nevertheless demurred, for this plan was more favorable for the German investors than the Boerescu project. Ion Ghica denounced this scheme as being less advantageous to Romania than the original Strousberg contract. The deputies then resolved that the shareholders should simply assume Strousberg's perquisites and responsibilities in return for a cash remittance of 72 million francs.[82] This award was about half what the Berlin bankers wanted, and so they rejected it.

Bismarck intervened again, this time having the German emperor court the Ottoman sultan into safeguarding German investments in Romania.[83] The new grand vezir, Mahmud Paşa, let Carol know that Turkey still supported the shareholders, and called for a "prompt and definitive solution" to the rail problem.[84] Bismarck also informed Austria-Hungary, Russia, and Britain that Carol's tenure in Romania depended on an outcome in the railway issue that was satisfactory to Germany.[85] Bismarck reckoned that Carol's allegiance to the house of Hohenzollern was stronger than his loyalty to Romania. He may have been correct. Bismarck explained that, in any case, he wished only to shield German investors, and by doing so he "protected" Carol.[86] Carol condemned, on the one hand, Bismarck's petition to the Ottoman Empire; but he appealed, on the other, to Germany for aid "to transplant German culture to the East."[87] Some Romanians suspected Carol of being financially involved in the railroad. Carol derided this idea as being "too absurd and ridiculous," for he held merely one railway share.[88]

Romania's pride eventually gave way in the face of pressure from Germany as well as promptings from Austria-Hungary, Turkey, Britain, and Russia. The chamber adopted yet another project, which would soon be accepted by the bankers in Berlin. The shareholders were thereby to receive the rights and tasks of the Strousberg concession. Strousberg was responsible for dividends due in 1871; thereafter, the Romanian government was to pay them.[89] Strousberg ceded his prerogative of directing the railroad to a syndicate in Berlin and rendered to it 22.5 million francs.[90] The syndicate, in turn, subcontracted the building and managing of the lines to Austria-Hungary's state railway company.[91] To assuage Romanian ill will about this transaction, the consortium appointed a supervisory commission consisting of prominent Romanian statesmen, such as Vasile Boerescu, Epureanu, and Dimitrie Ghica.[92] This plan, according to the German consul in Bucharest, was the most that could be obtained without the "use of extensive political measures" and an antidynastic revolution.[93] Bismarck advised the shareholders to endorse Romania's proposal, and they did so.[94] The immediate result was an increase in the value of the rail stock despite the nonpayment of the 1871 dividend.

Germany's diplomatic and economic victory in Romania followed its major military and political triumph in France. But the railway question was still open. So long as the railroad was in large part owned by foreign investors, it posed a problem for Romania. Danubian Romanians might vilify the alien entrepreneur and financier who grew fat at Romania's expense, but the railroad was unprofitable. A loan in 1872 for 78 million francs—based on the railroad's worth—was insufficient to enable the Berlin syndicate to finish construction. Moreover, a European economic crisis beginning in 1873 forced Bleichröder and Hansemann to announce in 1874 and 1875 that their firm needed more money. They called for an additional advance of 75 million francs that would be guaranteed by a mortgage on the railway.[95] This demand clearly contravened a provision in the convention between the syndicate and the Romanian government. Bucharest at first refused, yet negotiations for a loan continued. Hansemann hinted broadly that if Romania rejected the proposed encumbrance, Germany would again intervene in the name of "justice." [96]

Romania's reaction to Germany's claim was mixed. Few Romanian statesmen wished to discuss the matter, being reluctant to get embroiled in an issue that had brought down the previous ministry. Catargiu preferred to resign his premiership than be responsible for another railway deal. Vasile Boerescu, who was now the minister for foreign affairs, thought the government should ask the chamber's approval before acting on the propounded loan and mortgage.[97] In 1874 and 1875, however, Romania was seeking to conclude commercial treaties with the powers in order to demonstrate its economic independence. Boerescu and Carol feared that the powers would spurn such important transactions so long as Germany was dissatisfied about the railroad. Hence Romania offered a counterproposal that seemingly met the Berlin syndicate's requirements. One third of the annual dividends, or six million francs, was for interest on a new loan, which in turn was to be deducted from the original cost of the railroad.[98] Romania would thereby become a coproprietor of the line.

Romania's minister of public works, Teodor Rosetti, went to Berlin to confer on the railway affair. He encountered a complicated situation. Bismarck continued to support the syndicate, explaining that "hardly any other foreign undertaking has involved such a large amount of German capital" and advising that the railroad would be decisive in developing Romania's resources.[99] The Berlin consortium suggested to Rosetti that Romania raise a loan of 75 million francs to cover the firm's liabilities in exchange for one third of the initial shares. Romania would then, indeed, own one third of the railroad.[100] If Romania had genuinely desired to acquire the line at this juncture, it might have done so and saved funds by buying rail warrants on the open market, because their price had sunk to 35 percent of the par value.[101] The chamber adopted in 1875 Rosetti's recommendation, by which Romania would receive 137 miles of track—including the stretch in Wallachia, from Bucharest to Vîrciorova on the Austro-Hungarian frontier, which had been operational by the outset of 1875—in return for 7-percent state bonds.[102] The syndicate refused, however, to relinquish the railroad for debentures that might rapidly depreciate in worth and so vetoed Rosetti's plan. Vasile Boerescu subsequently visited Berlin to negotiate for the complete purchase of the lines but had little success.[103] The corporation undoubtedly wanted more than Romania was willing or able to pay. Nonetheless, after consulting Germany's minister of foreign affairs, Bernhard Ernst von Bülow, Titu Maiorescu, Romania's minister of religion and education, considered the sale of the railroad to be a political necessity rather than a commercial question.[104]

The railway matter was essentially shelved during the Balkan Crisis of 1875–78;[105] still, it reemerged after the Congress of Berlin. One condition for the powers' recognition of Romania's independence would be its purchase of the lines. Foreign diplomatic pressure undoubtedly secured advantages for foreign investors. The protracted deliberations about rail stock were mainly due to Romania's hostility toward alien contractors and shareholders as well as toward the foreign government that sponsored them. Moreover, Danubian Romanians were apparently too poor to afford the railroad yet too proud to admit their poverty.

The railroads had a profound effect on the course of Romanian history. Militarily, they would convey a Russian army south of the Danube River to fight the Turks in the 1877–78 war. Economically, they conquered time and space by facilitating the rapid transport of perishable fruits and dairy products to markets that might not otherwise have been easily reached. Socially, foreign tourists and merchants would pass from the English Channel to the Black Sea—in part on Romania's railroads—via the Orient Express beginning in 1883. Despite a direct rail connection through Serbia and Bulgaria to Constantinople that opened later in 1883, many travelers preferred the fascinating journey through Romania, and the Orient Express continued to traverse the country once a week. For Romanians, however, only wealthy aristocrats had the means for trips to the West. The railways nonetheless helped to forge a united, national society in place of the self-contained regional milieus of northern and southern Moldavia on the one hand and Wallachia's Muntenia and Oltenia on the other, assisting thereby to create a heightened sense of national identity. Moreover, resentment against foreign intervention on behalf of foreign rail investors furthered an ever rising spirit of Romanian patriotism.

Notes

1. The cost of construction for the line to Giurgiu was 196,500 francs per kilometer for 69.821 kilometers, or 43.36 miles, with a total cost of 13,755,000 francs, and 7-percent rail stock was issued with an annual dividend of 1,650,000 francs; Brezoianu, *Vechile institutiuni alle Romaniei,* 200–201; cf. Constantin Botez, "Concesiunile de construcții feroviare și implicațiile lor," 68–72.

2. Aleksandr I. Chuprov and Boris F. Brandt, "Zheleznye dorogy"; *Khrestomatiia po istorii SSSR,* vol. 3 (1857–94), 185–86. Russia was also to have a line eastward to Nizhnii Novgorod.

3. Sergei Iu. Vitte, *Vospominaniia,* vol. 1 (1849–94), 85–86, 91, 94–95; *Istoriia Moldavskoi SSR,* 1:492.

4. The construction cost was 176,022 lei per kilometer for 21.419 kilometers, or 13.30 miles—that is, 3,770,215 lei; Russia's gauge was 1.524 meters, Romania's 1.435 meters; Dumitru P. Ionescu, "Construirea liniei ferate Iași-Ungheni." On 6/18 May 1872, a Russian diplomatic agent, Ivan A. Zinov'ev, and Costa-Foru signed a rail junction convention, which was ratified on 9/21 January 1873; *Tractate, conventiuni și invoiri internationale ale Romaniei actualmente in vigóre,* 33–43.

5. Friedrich Johann von Alvensleben (Bucharest) to Bernhard Ernst von Bülow (Berlin), 11 July 1877, no. 202, in HAA, PS: Türkei, 24, vol. 61; Alvensleben to Bülow, 11 September 1877, no. 273, and 28 November 1877, no. 377, in ibid., Türkei, 24, vol. 62.

6. Ghica (Bucharest) to Kogălniceanu, 12/24 April 1869, in Fond Mihail Kogălniceanu, XVIII, no. 2, BAR, SC.

7. *Brockhaus' Konversations-Lexikon,* 12:708–12; *Eisenbahn-Jahrbuch der österreichisch-ungarischen Monarchie,* 4:48–49.

8. Beust (Vienna) to Eder (Bucharest), 2 October 1868, no. 410, in HHS, HA—Konsulate: Bukarest, Fach 34, Karton 69.

9. Prince Carol to Prince Charles Anthony, 13/25 January 1868, in *Aus dem Leben König Karls von Rumänien,* 1:241.

10. See Boerescu's speech in the chamber of deputies, 28 February/12 March 1871, in Vasile Boerescu, *Discursuri politice, 1859–1883,* vol. 1 (1859–73), 330.

11. Dan Berindei and Valerian Popovici, "Dezvoltarea economică şi socială a Principatelor în anii 1848–1864," 198; Aurel Maier, "Drumurile şi transportul rutier," 429; Leonid Boicu, "Transporturile în Moldova între 1848 şi 1864," 430–31.

12. For the Galaţi-Bukowina rail concession of 1862, see *Reformele Romanilor,* 216–31.

13. Brătianu to Catargiu, 3/15 May and 10/22 May 1873, in *Ion C. Brătianu: Acte şi cuvântări,* vol. 1, pt. 2, 385–86, 389–92.

14. George Klapka (Temesvár/Timişoara) to Alexandru Golescu (Bucharest), 8 March 1870, in Arhiva Mihail Kogălniceanu, LXI/4, BNR, SM.

15. The cost of construction was 270,000 francs per kilometer for 222.411 kilometers, or 138.12 miles—that is, 60,050,970 francs—and 7.5-percent rail shares were issued to 51,520,000 francs, with an annual dividend of 3,857,025 francs; see Carol's notes, 4/16 October 1867, in *Aus dem Leben König Karls von Rumänien,* 1:226–27.

16. See Ofenheim's proposal of 12/24 September 1867, in AIC, CR, dosar 13/1867; Eder to Beust, 10 March, no. 23, and 10 June 1868, no. 70, in HHS, HA—Konsulate: Bukarest, Fach 34, Karton 69.

17. Gyula Andrássy (Budapest) to Beust, 14 January 1869, Zulauf (Bucharest) to Beust, 17 March 1870, no. 17, and Andrássy to Beust, 24 March 1870, no. 510, in HHS, HA—Konsulate: Bukarest, Fach 34, Karton 69.

18. Beust to Andrássy, 7 January 1870, Zulauf to Beust, 12 February 1870, no. 17, and Beust to Zulauf, 6 March 1870, in HHS, HA—Konsulate: Bukarest, Fach 34, Karton 69. For Romania's postal convention with Austria-Hungary (Vienna), 24 July 1868, see *Tractate, conventiuni şi invoiri internationale ale Romaniei,* 1; for Romania's telegraph convention with Austria-Hungary, 8 August 1871, and their unratified rail junction convention (Bucharest), 27 October/8 November 1872, see *Collectiune de tratatele si conventiunile Romaniei cu puterile straine de la annulŭ 1368 pânĕ în zilele nóstre,* 254, 330.

19. See Romania's convention with Austria-Hungary, 27 October/8 November 1872, for rail junctions—Moldavia (Burdujeni)-Bukowina (Itzkany/Iţcani), Oltenia (Vîrciorova)-Banat (Orsova/Orşova), Oltenia (Filiaşi)-Transylvania (Petrozséni/Petroşani), Muntenia (Predeal)-Transylvania (Brassó), Moldavia (Adjud)-Transylvania (Gyimes/Ghimeş or Oituz)—in *Collectiune de tratatele si conventiunile Romaniei,* 330–37.

20. Boerescu's speeches in the chamber, 27 October/8 November 1872 and 20 February/4 March 1873, in Vasile Boerescu, *Discursuri politice, 1859–1883* 1:549–50, 567.

21. See Kogălniceanu's speech in the chamber, 25 May/6 June 1868, in Kogălniceanu, *Opere,* vol. 4: *Oratorie II, 1864–1878,* pt. 1 (1864–68), 587–88; see also his chamber speeches of 16/28 March 1872 and 19 February/3 March 1873, in ibid., pt. 3 (1870–74), 167–68, 252.

22. Nicolae Kreţulescu (Berlin) to Boercscu (Bucharest), 9/21 April 1874, in Arhiva Vasile Boerescu, CXXVII/3, no. 284, BNR, SM.

23. Kreţulescu to Boerescu, 11/23 April 1874, in Arhiva Vasile Boerescu, CXXVII/3, no. 285, BNR, SM. See *Tractate, conventiuni şi invoiri internationale ale Romaniei,* 90–107, for Romania's rail convention with Austria-Hungary, 19/31 May 1874. Ratifications were exchanged on 5/17 August 1874, but the convention was not in operation until 14 April 1879 owing to delays in building to Predeal.

24. Pfuel (Bucharest) to Max von Philipsborn (Berlin), 6 July 1875, in HAA, PS: Türkei, 24, vol. 51.

25. See a proposal by the minister of public works, Teodor Rosetti, 6 June 1875, in Arhiva Mihail Kogălniceanu, XIX, no. 1112, BAR, SC. For a report by Strat, the minister of finance, 31 January 1876, about Crawley's rail concession and the law of 22 July/3 August 1875, see *Documente privind istoria Romîniei: Războiul pentru independenţă,* vol. 1, pt. 1, 302–3. The cost of construction was 500,000 francs per kilometer for 84.654 kilometers, or 52.57 miles, with a capital of 42,500,000 francs and 7-percent rail shares.

26. For a joint letter of resignation signed by Ion Brătianu, Kogălniceanu, Epureanu, Alexandru Golescu, and six other deputies, 30 June and 1 July 1875, see *Ion C. Brătianu: Acte şi cuvântări,* vol. 1, pt. 2, 492.

27. Mansfield (Bucharest) to Ion Brătianu, 9 June 1877, in Fond Mihail Kogălniceanu, XXVII, no. 54, BAR, SC; Alvensleben to Bülow, 29 June 1877, no. 184, in HAA, PS: Türkei, 104, vol. 3.

28. Crawley received 13,810,000 francs. For the law on the Ploieşti-Predeal concession, 2/14 July 1877, see *Ion C. Brătianu: Acte şi cuvântări,* 3:338–44.

29. Alvensleben to Bülow, 2 August 1878, no. 130, in HAA, PS: Türkei, 24, vol. 65; Dumitru P. Ionescu, "Construirea liniei ferate Ploieşti-Predeal."

30. Bălăceanu (Vienna) to Dimitrie Sturdza (Bucharest), 23 June 1878 and 15 January 1879, in Fond Dimitrie A. Sturdza, II, nos. 245, 250, BAR, SC; Bălăceanu to Ion Brătianu, 6 February 1879, in Fond Ion C. Brătianu, LVIII/2/1, BNR, SC; Alvensleben to Bülow, 7 May 1878, no. 94, in HAA, PS: Türkei, 24, vol. 65. For additional arrangements on Romania's rail convention with Austria-Hungary of 31 May 1874, signed in Vienna, 24 March 1879, see *Tractate, conventiuni şi invoiri internationale ale Romaniei,* 103–7. This route opened on 1 December 1879.

31. See the concession agreed to by Dimitrie Ghica and the company's representative, Conrad Busse, 21 November/3 December 1868, in AMAE(R), FC, 9:5–14; *Dr. Strousberg und sein Wirken von ihm selbst geschildert,* 338–39. See Ion Brătianu's chamber speech, 4/16 March 1871, in *Ion C. Brătianu: Acte şi cuvântări,* vol. 1, pt. 2, 290, 293. The cost of construction was 270,000 francs per kilometer for 914.8 kilometers, or 568.09 miles—that is, 248,130,000 francs—and 7.5-percent rail shares had an annual dividend of 18,609,750 francs.

32. See Boerescu's speech in the chamber, 28 February/12 March 1871, in Vasile Boerescu, *Discursuri politice,* 1:333, 340–41, 367, 388–89; *Dr. Strousberg und sein Wirken,* 344–45; Ion Brătianu to Catargiu, 10 May 1873, in *Ion C. Brătianu: Acte şi cuvântări,* vol. 1, pt. 2, 391.

33. See Boerescu's speech in the chamber, 28 February/12 March 1871, in Vasile Boerescu, *Discursuri politice,* 1:386–87.

34. See Brătianu's speech in the chamber, 4/16 March 1871, in *Ion C. Brătianu: Acte şi cuvântări,* vol. 1, pt. 2, 290.

35. See Boerescu's speech in the chamber, 28 February/12 March 1871, in Vasile Boerescu, *Discursuri politice,* 1:343.

36. John Green (Bucharest) to Stanley (London), 14 June 1868, no. 74, in PRO, FO, 78/2031.

37. G. G. A. Anneke (Bucharest) to Bismarck (Berlin), 28 July 1868, no. 74, in HAA, PS: Türkei, 24, vol. 38. See Carol's speech in the chamber, 10/22 June 1868, in *Charles Ier, Roi de Roumanie,* 1:434.

38. Charles Vogel (Cotroceni) to Ion Brătianu, 5/17 September 1868, in Fond Ion C. Brătianu, VI/3, BNR, SM.

39. Ion Brătianu to Alexandru Golescu, 1 April 1870, in *Ion C. Brătianu: Acte şi cuvântări,* vol. 1, pt. 2, 192–93. See Vasile Boerescu's speech in the chamber, 28 February/12 March 1871, in Vasile Boerescu, *Discursuri politice,* 1:367–71. Both Ambronn and the chief engineer, Brand, were Germans; see Carol to Charles Anthony, 7/19 June 1871, in *Aus dem Leben König Karls von Rumänien,* 2:200–201.

40. See Kogălniceanu's speech in the chamber, 5/17 March 1871, in Kogălniceanu, *Opere,* vol. 4: *Oratorie II, 1864–1878,* pt. 3, 97–102.

41. *Dr. Strousberg und sein Wirken,* 358–59.

42. C. Bellioc (Bucharest) to Dimitrie Sturdza (Constantinople), 20 March/1 April 1870, in Dosar Dimitrie A. Sturdza, 7:331–32, BAR, SM.

43. See Carol's notes, 16/28 January 1870, in *Aus dem Leben König Karls von Rumänien,* 2:56.

44. Zulauf to Beust, 29 March 1870, no. 30, in HHS, HA—Konsulate: Bukarest, Fach 34, Karton 69.

45. Journal of the council of ministers, 11 May 1870, in AMAE(R), FC, 9:36; Dimitrie Sturdza's notice (Berlin), 2/14 June 1870, in Dosar Dimitrie A. Sturdza, 7:414–17, BAR, SM. See Carol's notes, 17/29 July 1870, in *Aus dem Leben König Karls von Rumänien,* 2:109–10.

46. Bellioc to Dimitrie Sturdza, 20 March/1 April 1870, in Dosar Dimitrie A. Sturdza, 7:331–32, BAR, SM; Ambronn to Carol, 5 October and 22 October 1870, in AIC, CR. See Carol's notes, 22 July/3 August and 5/17 September 1870, in *Aus dem Leben König Karls von Rumänien,* 2:110–11, 122; *Dr. Strousberg und sein Wirken,* 359, 367–68. During the Franco-Prussian War, Strousberg's rail shares declined from 80 percent to less than 20 percent of their nominal value.

47. For earlier cases of seemingly superfluous kilometers of track near the village of Ghergani and between Brăila and Galaţi, see Ion Ghica (Ghergani) to Alexandru Golescu, 12 May 1869, in Fond Mihail Kogălniceanu, LXXXV/14, no. 17, BNR, SM; Keyserling (Constantinople) to Bismarck, 15 June 1869, no. 66, in HAA, PS: Türkei, 24, vol. 41.

48. *Dr. Strousberg und sein Wirken,* 341, 346–47, 355.

49. *Dr. Strousberg und sein Wirken,* 359–67.

50. Carol to Felix Bamberg (Messina), 16/28 April 1870, in Fond Dimitrie A. Sturdza, XII, no. 11, BAR, SC.

51. Ion Ghica to Dimitrie Sturdza, 12/24 August, 19/31 August, and 6/18 September 1870, in Fond Dimitrie A. Sturdza, XX, nos. 320–22, BAR, SC; *Monitorul officiale: România,* 9/21 August and 11/23 August 1870; *Romanulu,* 9/22 August–22 August/3 September 1870.

52. See Carol's notes, 27 November/7 December 1870 and 28 December 1870/
9 January 1871, in *Aus dem Leben König Karls von Rumänien*, 2:134–35, 146–47.
Carol's open letter (Bucharest) to a "friend," 10/22 December.1870, was published
in the *Augsburger Allgemeine Zeitung*, 15/27 January 1871; see ibid., 2:138–40.

53. Ali Paşa to Carol, 8/20 January 1871, in *Aus dem Leben König Karls von
Rumänien*, 2:149; letters to Carol from William I (Versailles), 13 January, from
Emperor Francis Joseph (Budapest), 29 January, as well as from King Victor
Emmanuel II and from Alexander II, which Carol received respectively on 12/24
February and 16/28 February 1871, in ibid., 2:152–53, 157–58, 161–62, 163–64.

54. For Nicolae Blaremberg's interpellation in the chamber, 30 January/11 February 1871, see Gheorghe Cristea, "La guerre Franco-Allemande et le mouvement
républicain de mars 1871 à Bucarest," 281.

55. See Carol's notes, 30 January/11 February, as well as 3/15 and 5/17 February 1871, in *Aus dem Leben König Karls von Rumänien*, 2:158–59, 160.

56. *Romanulu*, 12/24 January 1871.

57. See the protocol of 24 February 1871, in AMAE(R), FC, vol. 9; John Green
to Granville (London), 15 March 1871, no. 16, in PRO, FO, 195/977; Beust to Zulauf,
17 March 1871, in HHS, HA—Konsulate: Bukarest, Fach 34, Karton 69. See Carol's
notes, 1/13 March 1871, in *Aus dem Leben König Karls von Rumänien*, 2:173.

58. Nicolae Calimaki-Catargi (Bucharest) to Bălăceanu (Constantinople), 15
March 1871, in Fond Ion Bălăceanu, no. 29232, BAR, SC. For a commission report
about malfeasance in the railway question, see Cristea, "Le guerre Franco-Allemande," 281.

59. Radowitz (Bucharest) to Bismarck, 23 March 1871, no. 18, in HAA, PS:
Türkei, 24, vol. 45; Radowitz to Bismarck, 15 July 1871, no. 45, in ibid., vol. 46.

60. See Carol's notes, 10/22 March 1871, in *Aus dem Leben König Karls von
Rumänien*, 2:174–76; John Green to Granville, 23 March 1871, in PRO, FO, 78/
2183.

61. See Carol's notes, 11/23 March 1871, in *Aus dem Leben König Karls von
Rumänien*, 2:176–79.

62. Bismarck to Radowitz, 26 March 1871, no. 5, and 28 March 1871, no. 6, in
HAA, PS: Türkei, 24, vol. 45.

63. Radowitz to Bismarck, 29 March 1871 and 1 April 1871, in HAA, PS: Türkei,
24, vol. 45.

64. Ali Paşa to Carol, 21 March/2 April 1871, in *Correspondance diplomatique
roumaine sous le roi Charles Ier (1866–1880)*, 75–76.

65. Carol to Ali Paşa, 1/13 April 1871, in *Aus dem Leben König Karls von
Rumänien*, 2:186–87.

66. Carol to William I, 6 April 1871, in HAA, PS: Türkei, 24, vol. 45.

67. Brătianu to Catargiu, 10 May 1873, in *Ion C. Brătianu: Acte şi cuvântări*,
vol. 1, pt. 2, 393.

68. Ladislaus von Hengelmüller (Bucharest) to Beust, 30 June 1871, no. 67, in
HHS, HA—Konsulate: Bukarest, Fach 34, Karton 69.

69. Ion Ghica to Dimitrie Sturdza, 24 June/5 July 1871, in Fond Dimitrie A.
Sturdza, XX, no. 324, BAR, SC; Mavrogheni (Bucharest) to Teodor Rosetti (Berlin), 7/19 June 1871, in AMAE(R), FC, 9:260.

70. Brătianu to Pia Brătianu (Florica), 16/28 June 1871, in *Din corespondenţa familiei Ion C. Brătianu,* 1:150.

71. For the Chamber committee report of 4/16, 5/17, and 6/18 July 1871; see Constantin Boerescu, *Discursuri politice, 1866–1891,* 236–54; Costa-Foru to Strat (Constantinople) and Carp (Vienna), 6/18 July 1871, in AMAE(R), FC, 9:307–8; Radowitz to Bismarck, 20 July 1871, no. 51, in HAA, PS: Türkei, 24, vol. 46; John Green to Granville, 18 July 1871, no. 62, in PRO, FO, 78/2183.

72. Radowitz to Bismarck, 26 July 1871, no. 55, in HAA, PS: Türkei, 24, vol. 46; John Green to Granville, 30 July 1871, in PRO, FO, 78/2183; see Vasile Boerescu's speech in the chamber, 4/16 December 1872, in Vasile Boerescu, *Discursuri politice,* 1:485–86.

73. Bismarck to Friedrich zu Limburg-Stirum (Constantinople), 18 July 1871, no. 12, in HAA, PS: Türkei, 24, vol. 46; cf. Lothar Maier, "Die innen- und aussen-politischen Auseinandersetzungen um die Gründung der 'Rumänischen Eisenbahn-gesellschaft' 1871–1872," 494.

74. Ali Paşa to Carol, 2 August 1871, no. 30663, in AMAE(R), FC, 9:390.

75. Carol to Ali Paşa, 8/20 July 1871, in HAA, PS: Türkei, 24, vol. 46.

76. Bismarck's circular, 28 July 1871, in HAA, PS: Türkei, 24, vol. 46; Ottokar von Schlechta-Wssehrd (Bucharest) to Beust, 6 August 1871, no. 41, in HHS, HA—Konsulate: Bukarest, Fach 34, Karton 69; Carp to Costa-Foru, 2 August 1871, in AMAE(R), FC, 9:360–61; Costa-Foru to Strat, 23 July/4 August 1871, in ibid., 374–75; Strat to Costa-Foru, 10/22 August 1871, in ibid., 429–31.

77. Costa-Foru to Strat, 3/15 August 1871, in AMAE(R), FC, 9:422–25.

78. Dimitrie Sturdza (Miclăuşeni) to Ion Ghica, 7 August 1871 and 2 September 1871, in Fond Ion Ghica, XIX, nos. 312, 313, BAR, SC.

79. Hengelmüller to Beust, 20 October 1871, no. 66, in HHS, HA—Konsulate: Bukarest, Fach 34, Karton 69; Green to Granville, 17 October 1871, no. 90, in PRO, FO, 195/977. A court of arbitration annulled Strousberg's concession on 3/15 October 1871.

80. Ion Ghica to Dimitrie Sturdza, 21 October/3 November 1871 and 14/26 January 1872, in Fond Dimitrie A. Sturdza, XX, nos. 328, 330, BAR, SC; *Dr. Strousberg und sein Wirken,* 375–76; Fritz Stern, *Gold and Iron: Bismarck, Bleich-röder, and the Building of the German Empire,* 365–66.

81. This maneuver would have exchanged 7.5-percent shares at 245,160,000 francs for 5-percent stock at 367,740,000 francs; cf. *Aufzeichnungen und Erin-nerungen aus dem Leben des Botschafters Joseph Maria von Radowitz,* vol. 1 (1839–77), 227.

82. Ghica (Ghergany) to Dimitrie Sturdza, 12/24 November 1871, in Fond Dimitrie A. Sturdza, XX, no. 329, BAR, SC; William Otto von Theilau (Bucharest) to Bismarck, 26 December 1871, no. 24, in HAA, PS: Türkei, 104, vol. 1.

83. Bismarck to Radowitz (Constantinople), 24 November 1871, no. 24, in HAA, PS: Türkei, 24, vol. 46.

84. Mahmud Paşa to Carol, 20 November/2 December and 22 December 1871, in AMAE(R), FC, 10:77, 111.

85. Bismarck's circular to Vienna, St. Petersburg, and London, 22 December 1871, in HAA, PS: Türkei, 104, vol. 1. Bismarck promptly responded to Bleichröder's

appeal by sending a circular message about the railroad to Constantinople, St. Petersburg, and Vienna, 19 December 1871; see Lothar Maier, *Rumänien auf dem Weg zur Unabhängigkeitserklärung, 1866–1877: Schein und Wirklichkeit liberaler Verfassung und staatlicher Souveränität*, 202.

86. Bismarck to Carol, 12 April 1872, in HAA, PS: Türkei, 24, vol. 47.

87. Carol to Bismarck, 26 February/9 March 1872, in *Aus dem Leben König Karls von Rumänien*, 2:248–50.

88. Carol to Charles Anthony, 16/28 January 1872, in *Aus dem Leben König Karls von Rumänien*, 2:238.

89. Beust (Gastein) to Schlechta, 2 August 1871, Karl von Franckenstein (St. Petersburg) to Beust, 11/23 August 1871, Beust to Hengelmüller, 4 October 1871, no. 581, Andrássy to Schlechta, 24 November, 21 December, no. 719, and 27 December 1871, no. 724, and Schlechta to Andrássy, 5 January 1872, in HHS, HA—Konsulate: Bukarest, Fach 34, Karton 69; John Green to Henry Elliot (Constantinople), 30 December 1871, in PRO, FO, 195/977; Evgenii E. Chertan, *Velikie derzhavy i formirovanie rumynskogo nezavisimogo gosudarstva*, 180–81. See articles 5 and 7, in *Statutes: Articles of Association of the Roumanian Railways' Share Company*. Par value of the stock was 196,276,875 francs, but it could be increased to a maximum of 247,500,000 francs. The chamber vote, 21 December 1871/2 January 1872, was 75 to 48; the senate ballot, 24 December 1871/5 January 1872, was 31 to 6.

90. *Dr. Stousberg und sein Wirken*, 377–78, 431. Strousberg sold some of his property to the Disconto-Gesellschaft to help raise the sum of six million thalers, or 22.5 million francs.

91. Ion Ghica to Dimitrie Sturdza, 14/26 January 1872, in Fond Dimitrie A. Sturdza, XX, no. 330, BAR, SC; Andrássy to Gustav Kálnoky (Berlin), 21 January 1872, and Hans von Schweinitz (Vienna) to Bismarck, 26 January 1872, no. 21, in HAA, PS: Türkei, 104, vol. 1; Moritz von Wodianer (Vienna) of the Österreichisch-Ungarische Staatseisenbahngesellschaft to Andrássy, 20 January 1872, in HHS, HA—Konsulate: Bukarest, Fach 34, Karton 69.

92. A railway protocol was signed in Berlin on 1 February 1872; Arhiva Vasile Boerescu, CXXVII/3, no.12, BNR, SM; Ion Ghica to Sturdza, 2/14 February 1872, in Fond Dimitrie A. Sturdza, XX, no. 331, BAR, SC. Donici was also on the commission.

93. Theilau to Bismarck, 9 January 1872, no. 3, in HAA, PS: Türkei, 104, vol. 1; Schlechta to Andrássy, 8 January 1872, no. 30, in HHS, HA—Konsulate: Bukarest, Fach 34, Karton 69.

94. Alajos Károlyi von Nagy-Károly (Berlin) to Andrássy, 27 January 1872, no. 6a–b, in HHS, HA—Konsulate: Bukarest, Fach 34, Karton 69; Bismarck to Schweinitz and Heinrich VII von Reuss (St. Petersburg), 30 January 1872, in HAA, PS: Türkei, 104, vol. 1.

95. See Carol's notes, 3/15 and 6/18 July 1872, and Carol to Charles Anthony, 14/26 January 1875, in *Aus dem Leben König Karls von Rumänien*, 2:275–76, 290, 412.

96. Krețulescu (Berlin) to Vasile Boerescu (Bucharest), 30 September/12 October 1874, in Arhiva Vasile Boerescu, CXXVII/3, no. 368, BNR, SM. See article 7, in *Statutes: Articles of Association of the Roumanian Railways' Share Company*.

97. Boerescu to Krețulescu, 14/26 October 1874, in Arhiva Vasile Boerescu, CXXVII/3, no. 374, BNR, SM.

98. Carol to Charles Anthony, 14/26 January 1875, and Carol's notes, 15/27 January 1875, in *Aus dem Leben König Karls von Rumänien,* 2:412–14, 417.

99. Bismarck to Carol, [March 1875], in *Aus dem Leben König Karls von Rumänien,* 2:427.

100. Hussey C. Vivian (Bucharest) to Stanley, 19 April 1875, no. 29, in PRO, FO, 78/2398.

101. Vivian to Stanley, 16 May 1875, no. 37, in PRO, FO, 78/2398.

102. See Carol's notes, 1/13 July 1875, in *Aus dem Leben König Karls von Rumänien,* 2:452. The 7-percent state bonds were to be issued at 91 percent of par, with a nominal value of 63.5 million francs; the amount due annually was to be reduced from 18 to 14 million francs. By September 1872, the railroad reached westward from Bucharest to Pitești, and by January 1875 from Pitești to Vîrciorova, for a total of 220 kilometers.

103. Vivian to Stanley, 30 September 1875, no. 55, in PRO, FO, 78/2398; Carol's notes, 2/14 September and 26 October/7 November 1875, in *Aus dem Leben König Karls von Rumänien,* 2:459, 474.

104. Titu Maiorescu, *Istoria contimporană a României (1866–1900),* 79. He refers to his report to Catargiu of 5 August 1875.

105. Cf. muted, abortive rail negotiations in 1876 and 1877, discussed in Maier, *Rumänien auf dem Weg zur Unabhängigkeitserklärung,* 237–52.

Chapter Five

FOREIGN TRADE

After the Crimean War, Danubian Romanians utilized all available means to assert their country's autonomy. One way of doing so was to invoke their old treaties with the Ottoman Empire along with recent international agreements. They had, as we have seen, been unable to rid themselves of consular jurisdiction; yet they hoped that their railroads and the attendant augmented trade would somehow aid in achieving their national goals. If they concluded commercial conventions with the great powers, they would assure their right to self-government and thus shed the remnants of Turkish suzerainty. The sultan's overlordship would fall into desuetude as Romania successfully pursued its own foreign policy. Mercantile pacts would therefore be steps on the path leading inexorably to Romania's independence.[1]

The origin of Romania's commercial accords may be found in the political and economic needs of Romania and the powers. Danubian Romania's exports and imports especially affected its neighbors. Its most significant trading neighbor was Austria-Hungary. The Habsburg Empire's exports to Southeastern Europe rose in value and volume during the nineteenth century; Romania in particular became an extraordinarily important marketplace for Austro-Hungarian goods. The Dual Monarchy had an obvious interest in facilitating the access of its products to locales where substantial earnings could be won. The existence of a railway network linking it to many regions of Romania by the 1870s decreased the risk and cost of transport and increased profits. Hence when Romania launched a protectionist program of encumbering foreign imports, Vienna responded by treating diplomatically with Bucharest about mercantile matters.

Danubian Romania's commercial position improved during the course of the nineteenth century. The Turkish monopoly, by which the Ottoman Empire enjoyed preferential treatment in purchasing Moldavian goods in Galați, had depressed the native economy for three centuries.[2] In the 1830s, this regime terminated with the establishment of a Russian protectorate and the concomitant promulgation of the Organic Regulations, which guaranteed the Danubian Romanians' liberty of commerce.[3] A 3-percent Turkish tariff on exports and imports was valid in Moldavia and Wallachia from 1718 to 1838; this impost fell on merchandise directly entering the principalities notwithstanding duties already defrayed on the same items when they had previously entered another portion of the Ottoman Empire. Austria's products, for example, paid 3 percent ad valorum in Wallachia, while articles passing through the Ottoman Empire from abroad had a double charge: 3 percent in Turkey and 3 percent in Wallachia. Austria's favorable mercantile situation in the principalities would nonetheless erode in the latter half of the nineteenth century owing to the extension of British shipping into the Black Sea and the international supervision of the lower Danube River. The abolition of internal economic barriers would stimulate the growth of Romanian trade. A customs frontier between Moldavia and Wallachia had impeded the easy exchange of products: Wallachian goods going to Moldavia faced the 3-percent Wallachian export toll in addition to the Moldavian 3-percent import fee. This system ended in 1847 with a Moldo-Wallachian agreement that stipulated the economic unification of the two principalities. The Ottoman Empire, for its part, raised its import tariff from 3 percent to 5 percent in 1838, and to 8 percent in 1861; its export tariff was, however, reduced to 1 percent. These changes essentially applied as well to Danubian Romania; in 1866 the Romanian tariff was 7.5 percent ad valorum on imports plus 0.50 percent on merchandise coming via Danubian ports.[4] This still relatively low tariff, along with enhanced roads, expanded Danubian dock facilities, and in particular Romania's railroads, resulted in a market bonanza for Romanian grain. Danubian Romania exchanged its agricultural commodities for foreign currency, which was in turn used to buy foreign wares. This intercourse nevertheless inhibited the simultaneous development of Romanian industries.

Patriotic Romanian statesmen sought in various ways to assert their country's autonomy. One method was to rock the economic equilibrium, thereby alarming trading circles in Austria-Hungary. Romania's 1871 excise duties and its 1874 tariff compelled the Habsburg Empire to reassess its relations with Romania. By the Law of the Maximum of 1871, Romania's rural communes could tax foreign goods entering villages. This measure was to raise funds for local purposes, but it also protected indigenous products from foreign competition. The excise levies devolved chiefly on alcoholic beverages—of keen interest to peasants, who distilled, imbibed, and sold them—as well as on candles, sugar, coffee, and oil. The burden on some foreign imports thereupon rose roughly 10 percent above the level set in the Turkish tariff. Moreover, Romania's legislature adopted in 1874 and revised in 1875 a protective tariff with tolls ranging as high as 20 percent.[5] Danubian Romanians probably wished, nonetheless, to retain the principle of free trade, which had been inaugurated in 1860 by the Cobden-Chevallier Treaty between Great Britain and France; Romania lacked, after all, an important industry to safeguard and had perforce to import manufactured articles. They hoped rather to engage the powers in commercial conventions so as to provide further evidence of their independent posture in international affairs. Romania actually suspended its tariff until an accord with Austria-Hungary was in place and then abrogated the tariff altogether.

The Habsburg Empire launched its first, if unsuccessful, probes at regulating mercantile relations with Danubian Romania in 1848 and 1856. Later, Ştirbei propounded in 1867 a commercial understanding, an idea that Beust endorsed.[6] The two sides would, however, discount a formal covenant until their economic ties became markedly strained. Following the application of the Law of the Maximum, Costa-Foru, a later minister for foreign affairs, put forth in 1872 the notion that a bilateral trade agreement be negotiated without reference to existing treaties between the Ottoman Empire and the other powers.[7] Gyula Andrássy, Austria-Hungary's new foreign affairs minister, "provisionally" approved this proposal; the Hungarian minister responsible for commercial affairs, József Szlávy, likewise supported an accord with Romania. Szlávy's main concern was to remove Romania's protective excise tolls, which adversely affected the sale of Hungarian goods. In return, he suggested that Romanian goods be given most-favored-nation treatment in the Habsburg Empire; import duties on Romanian grain were to be canceled as well; and Austria-Hungary's consular jurisdiction was to end.[8] These were indeed major concessions. Costa-Foru's successor as Romania's minister of foreign affairs, Vasile Boerescu, eventually sent a draft convention to Vienna in 1874.[9] The projected pact depended, of course, on the interests of both parties and on the positions of the powers.

This embryonic understanding, as well as Romania's new tariff and excise duties, challenged the status quo. Despite the freedom of its trade as guaranteed by the 1856 Treaty of Paris, the 1858 Convention of Paris barred Danubian Romania from contravening pacts made by the suzerain Ottoman Empire, and so Bucharest was supposed to hold its tariff at or below that established by Turkey and the powers. Besides, Romania lacked the right to conclude international concords.[10] The powers protested Romania's tariff and excise tolls, but to no avail. The same would be the case with the commercial covenant. The powers, which had worked in concert after the Crimean War, disengaged by the 1870s, as was clearly evident in the Balkan Crisis.

Andrássy nonetheless sought the support of the other powers for an Austro-Hungarian economic agreement with Romania so as to preserve a semblance of conformity to international law. He contended that the Austro-Turkish trade compact of 1862 was inapplicable to Romania because the latter was fully independent in the administration of its domestic affairs. Andrássy suggested that since Egypt, also a vassal of the Ottoman sultan, had received a Turkish *ferman* in 1873 to sign commercial accords, this privilege should be extended as well to Romania.[11]

The Ottoman Empire protested vigorously against Romania's "inadmissible" pretensions to sign conventions. Turkey noted the irrelevance of the Egyptian example. Turkish laws applied to Egypt, while international treaties regulated Romania; Egypt was a province, Romania a principality; the Turkish tariff operated in Egypt, but not in Romania. Egypt also had a resident Turkish commissioner, which Romania did not. Moreover, financial chaos in Egypt rendered its *ferman* meaningless, as Britain and France would manage Egypt's finances by 1876, and the British occupied it in 1882. The Turks reckoned in 1874 that Danubian Romanians would disregard a *ferman* allowing Bucharest to conclude covenants. To avoid being insulted, the Ottoman Empire refused Austria-Hungary's suggestion.[12] Vasile Boerescu indeed rejected a Turkish *ferman,* for the sultan had no prerogative to control Romania. He would instead treat directly with the other powers, but not the Ottoman Empire, in adjusting Romania's tariff according to the Turks' interests.[13] Turkey got only modest backing from Britain, France, and Italy in its protests against Romania's making mercantile accords. Stanley, now Earl of Derby, expressed the attitude of the Western powers when he characterized the proposed concord as being prompted more "by political than commercial considerations." He declined, however, to actively oppose an agreement so long as the Ottoman Empire suffered no "substantial injury."[14]

Austria-Hungary found solid encouragement for its position from its colleagues in the League of Three Emperors. Russia and Germany declared their willingness to forge separate commercial compacts with Romania after the anticipated Austro-Hungarian convention with the principality.[15] Bülow applauded Andrássy's initiative and denied Berlin's having infringed Turkey's sovereignty.[16] Gorchakov, the Russian chancellor, fruitlessly suggested that the Ottoman Empire append an additional article to its commercial accords with the powers to the effect that Romania would have the privilege of treating with them on questions relating to its commercial and industrial concerns.[17] The Ottoman Empire balked, the Western powers were neutral, and the League of Three Emperors supported Austria-Hungary.

Andrássy then dealt solely with Russia and Germany with the result that the *dragomen,* or interpreters—not the ambassadors—of these powers presented an identic note to the Turkish government. This missive told of the powers' "right to conclude direct and special arrangements of customs, tariff, and commerce with the vassal principalities of Turkey." These empires would not "weaken or strengthen the ties that unite the vassal principalities with the suzerain court," yet they also disavowed that their "positive interests be endangered on account of questions of mere form."[18] The Ottoman foreign affairs minister, Arifi Paşa, condemned this note: "We hold more than ever to the belief that this pretension, which is as presumptuous in form as it is untenable in reality, is the exact negation of [our] rights." He indicated nonetheless the value Turkey placed on the powers' advice and would "meet their wishes so far as that is possible." To solve the impasse, Arifi Paşa recommended that Romania ask Turkey for permission to contract covenants.[19] The Romanians refused, however, to go to Canossa. Turkey next suggested a European ambassadorial conference to settle the issue. The Three Emperors' League categorically rebuffed this scheme because it had already stated its opinion.[20] And so matters stood. The upshot of the collective demarche in Constantinople was to set the stage for the negotiation of Austria-Hungary's commercial convention with Romania.

Deliberations between Romania and the Habsburg Empire began even before Vienna gained the backing of St. Petersburg and Berlin. Romania first proposed a 9-percent conventional tariff on Austro-Hungarian imports. The Dual Monarchy rejected this rate as being prohibitively high. Representatives of the joint Austro-Hungarian ministries of foreign affairs and finance, along with the Austrian and Hungarian ministries of commerce, then drafted a counterproject, which was subsequently discussed with Costa-Foru in Vienna.[21] This plan—based on the principle of most-favored-nation treatment—became, in essence, the final accord.

Negotiations in Vienna included topics relating to reciprocity and rates, Danubian navigation, and the rights of foreigners. Costa-Foru insisted on mutuality: if Romania's tariff on Austria-Hungary's fabricated goods were to be low, the Habsburg Empire's tariff on the principality's agricultural produce also had to be low. The key issue here was the grain trade. Andrássy favored the duty-free import of Romania's cereals, but the Austrian and Hungarian ministers of commerce, Jan Chlumecký and György Bartal, respectively, opposed the unrestricted entry of Romania's grain into the Habsburg Empire. Bartal contended that such a concession, which had been envisioned by Szlávy in 1872, would weaken Austria-Hungary's economic position.[22] Hungarian landlords in particular feared the competition of inexpensive Romanian cereals and so viewed tariff reciprocity as being more advantageous to Austrian manufacturers than to themselves.[23] In order to assuage Hungarian misgivings for the moment, Andrássy suggested that this aspect of the projected pact be kept confidential until after the Hungarian elections of July 1875.[24] This ruse appeared necessary, as the new Hungarian minister of commerce, Lajos Simonyi, insisted that an increased number of Hungarian products were to enter the principality duty-free in return for unrestrained cereal trade. When this demand was not met, Simonyi recommended that the stipulation regarding grain be deleted.[25] Vasile Boerescu refused to consider Simonyi's agenda. He realized that Hungary's grain was of higher quality and so was more valuable than Romania's; Hungarians would therefore benefit from the convention by exporting their cereals to the West for a substantial profit while importing relatively cheap Romanian grain for domestic consumption.[26] Andrássy sought Emperor Francis Joseph's aid in convincing Hungarians to yield in this matter and warned that Austria-Hungary's bargaining position vis-à-vis Romania was weakening inasmuch as the Ottoman Empire contemplated raising its tariff to 20 percent.[27] The outcome of dealings with Romania and consultations within the Habsburg Empire was the acceptance of the free trade of grain to and from the principality.

Less important than tariff reciprocity in the deliberations were questions about the prerogatives of foreigners—especially Jews—in Romania, Danubian navigation, and specific tariff duties. At this point, Romanians did not distinguish between Jews born in Romania and those who had immigrated there. According to the draft accord, citizens in one country were to enjoy equal civil rights with citizens in the other. Costa-Foru thought this provision corresponded to Romania's customary and statutory regulations.[28] Yet Boerescu fully recognized the political implications of this topic and worried that Jewish Austro-Hungarian subjects would be able to obtain real estate in Romania. He maintained that they could merely own urban, not rural, land.[29] Vienna eventually concurred. The convention therefore indicated that the principality's laws were to be observed; only indigenous Romanians, not aliens, might "acquire and possess" immovable property in the countryside, and municipal councils continued to determine the eligibility of foreigners to reside in rural communes.[30]

The Danube River also figured in the convention. After the Crimean War, Turkey and the powers had established the European Danube Commission to clear silt from the waterway's mouths—from Isaccea to the Black Sea—so as to facilitate navigation. The powers later extended the commission's jurisdiction upstream to Galați in 1878 and Brăila in 1883. Austria-Hungary's economy benefited remarkably from this commission's work. Austria's Danube Steamship Company, which had been founded in Vienna in 1830, served Orsova on the Wallachian frontier by 1834, Galați by 1835, and Constantinople by 1836. No effective international arrangement existed, however, for the stretch from Orsova to Isaccea, along which Austria-Hungary wanted depots at Romania's ports. Romania did not seriously vie with the Habsburg Empire for transport and trade on the river, and so statesmen at Bucharest reluctantly accepted a proposal from Vienna that the steamship companies be granted the privilege of procuring land for wharves, offices, shops, and warehouses on Romania's Danubian bank.[31]

The 1875 convention specified tariff rates, which would be in effect during the agreement's ten-year term. Bucharest allowed the free import of the Habsburg Empire's machinery, iron, art objects, and books—along with cereal, flour, petroleum, wood, tallow, coal, and hides, which contested for markets with Romania's products. Austria-Hungary, in turn, permitted duty-free import of Romanian salt, tobacco, flour, spiritous beverages, petroleum, and minerals. Austro-Hungarian wine was taxed 5.5 percent ad valorum in Romania—down from 17.5 percent—whereas the principality's wine in the Habsburg Empire was subject to the latter's most-favored-nation terms, in this case 13.5 percent. The cattle trade between the two sides was also based on most-favored-nation treatment. Romania imposed various tolls, ranging from 7.5 percent to 15 percent, on the Dual Monarchy's sugar, alcoholic beverages (except wine), soap, paper, candles, wax, and leather—some of which competed with local output. A 7-percent levy applied to Austro-Hungarian merchandise not mentioned in the accord.[32] This duty, plus the protection of the nonexistent Romanian sugar and paper industries, was a quid pro quo for Bucharest's concession regarding the duty-free import of Habsburg cereals. Goods in transit to a third country bore no charges. Romania's income from customs duties almost doubled after the convention's implementation.[33]

The relatively low conventional tariff, together with Romania's expanding rail network and increased agrarian productivity, resulted in a remarkable growth of Romania's exports and imports. The worth of Romania's total exports in 1883 more than quadrupled that of 1874, and imports trebled; the same pattern held for Romania's trade with Austria-Hungary. In the early 1880s, about 95 percent of the principality's exports to the Habsburg Empire were raw materials, such as crops, wool, and animals, whereas 84 percent of Romania's imports from Austria-Hungary were manufactured goods, such as clothes, iron, woolens, and leather articles. About 8 percent of the

Dual Monarchy's aggregate exports in 1874 and 1881—and 13 percent of its fabricated wares in 1881—went to Romania.[34] Trade statistics are notoriously unreliable in this period, mingling commodities destined for one country with those in transit to a third. The following chart nonetheless gives the approximate value in percentages of Romania's commerce with the powers and shows the predominant role of Austria-Hungary therein:[35]

Exports to:	1874	1883
Austria-Hungary	41.16	38.83
Ottoman Empire	29.55	3.82
Great Britain	9.71	28.83
France	7.44	9.57
Italy	3.04	0.90
Russia	1.47	3.00
Germany	0.17	8.34
Total	92.54	93.29

Imports from:	1874	1883
Austria-Hungary	39.34	42.78
Great Britain	26.75	21.88
France	12.77	10.14
Ottoman Empire	10.16	3.79
Germany	5.03	12.19
Russia	2.42	2.56
Italy	0.60	0.84
Total	97.07	94.18

The commercial covenant served to encourage Romania's agricultural production, to inhibit its industrial development, and to assure the ongoing colonial nature of its economy. In Vienna Costa-Foru proudly declared the convention to be "good" and "very acceptable";[36] yet some of his contemporaries in Bucharest disagreed. Members of the legislative opposition saw Romania's interests threatened by clauses dealing with foreigners and free trade. In the chamber of deputies, Epureanu expressed his fear that Austro-Hungarian subjects—that is, Jews, despite being elided from the accord—would be able to conduct business in Romania while being exempt from military service and from the garrisoning of troops; as a consequence, the

principality would be occupied by privileged aristocratic Jews. The poet
Vasile Alecsandri argued that the powers might absorb Jews, but small countries were unable to do so. Romania was faced by "an invasion organized by
a powerful freemasonry": a torrent of fanatics was forming a gigantic ghetto
in the heart of Romanian society. Kogălniceanu and Ion Brătianu also em-
phasized the pact's negative aspects. Kogălniceanu depreciated the advantages of free trade. Only during droughts did Romania export much grain to
the Habsburg Empire; when crops were abundant, Hungary alone produced
enough cereals to feed all Europe. Free trade benefited mighty states that
imported raw materials and needed foreign outlets for their industrial merchandise. Romania had, of course, an agrarian economy, and so free trade
would stifle the further emergence of its incipient industry. Kogălniceanu
also thought that Romania would lose the Ottoman Empire as an excellent
customer and would, in effect, complete an exchange of the former Russian
political protectorate for Austro-Hungarian economic hegemony. As to the
rights of aliens, he considered that the understanding virtually denied mutuality; 100,000 Jews in Moldavia would gain special prerogatives, whereas
only three Romanian merchants were in Brassó in Transylvania and two in
Czernowitz (Cernăuţi) in Bukowina. He also spoke categorically against
the incursion of vagabonds, a term denoting Jewish immigrants. Notwithstanding a stipulation in Romania's constitution prohibiting aliens from settling, the compact—under the banner of free trade—would open the door to
a colonization of Romania by Jews from Galicia, who had already "dena-
tionalized" Bukowina. Brătianu enlarged on Kogălniceanu's comments. He
noted that the three or four "ignorant" peasants in each of the rural councils,
which were responsible for deciding who might dwell in the countryside,
were incompetent to shield Romania from the Jews. He regretted that a foreign steamship company might set up stations on Romanian soil, and he
deplored an article allowing people living along the border between Austria-Hungary and Romania to trade freely. These provisions, for Brătianu,
would lead to an Austro-Hungarian occupation of Romania's frontiers, ports,
and markets. He also asserted that tariff reciprocity on cattle came too late;
foreign investors, borrowing at 3–5-percent interest rates—compared to the
15–30-percent available to Romanians—had earlier purchased most of
Romania's livestock. For Brătianu, "national salvation" lay in ending the export
of the country's wealth.[37] This contention was highly unrealistic. The Romanian economy had changed during the nineteenth century; the raising of
cattle, sheep, and other animals for export had declined with the intensifica-
tion of agriculture. Romania had transformed from a pastoral to an agrarian

community.[38] Had the export of grain been stopped, as Brătianu proposed, the flow of foreign capital into the country would have ceased, and Romania's economy would thereby have become isolated from international commerce.

Representatives of the government and their backers, as was expected, sought to refute or minimize their opponents' objections. Carp rejected Epureanu's allegation about the Jews. He suggested furthermore that Danubian Romanians should be more concerned with supporting their country's agricultural commodities and less with its "nonexistent" local industry. For Carp, the signing of a major convention with a great power signified "our economic independence." George G. Cantacuzino, Romania's minister of finance, enumerated benefits accruing to the principality from the deal: duty-free entry in Austria-Hungary of Romania's grain—without the former 10-percent import tax—reduced fees on livestock, protection of some Romanian goods, and most-favored-nation treatment. He calculated that had the convention been in effect in 1873, state revenues would have increased by 3.5 million lei. More persuasive were Vasile Boerescu's remarks. Romania's Jews constituted a "very delicate" social question that Romania would eventually resolve in harmony with "modern ideas" and "our social interests." The treaty had ignored this issue; hence, prior restrictions on foreigners remained in force. Boerescu deemed the accord to be "so favorable to us as rarely is to be seen in Europe," for it ensured a safe and important market for Romanian cereals in Hungary. The pact was a "consecration of the country's autonomy and assures the future exercise of that autonomy."[39]

The opposition wanted more time to scrutinize the convention, but the governmental majority cut off discussion. The deputies thereupon adopted, without amendments, the covenant by a vote of 68 to 22; two days later—on 1/13 July 1875—the senators, without much ado, concurred by 25 to 5; the next day, the legislature closed. Prominent opponents then renounced their legislative seats owing to bitter disagreements about the compact and about the adoption of a rail concession from Ploieşti to Predeal that would tie Romania's commerce directly to Transylvania. Those who resigned would form the core of a new cabinet headed by Ion Brătianu and Kogălniceanu following elections in 1876.[40]

Controversy over the convention persisted after the legislature's prorogation. Constantin Rosetti's newspaper, *Romanulu,* launched a vitriolic attack against the agreement. The first page of the issue announcing the pact's approval was edged in black. The lead article declared: "Yesterday . . . a knife was stuck up to the hilt in the belly of Romania, whose body, still palpitating, was pushed to the feet of Count Andrássy. . . . All Romanians, Christians and even native Jews if they consider themselves to be Romanians, must don mourning clothes and sigh, for Count Andrássy is the ruler, the absolute sovereign of Romanian slaves." *Romanulu* contended that the "midnight" cabinet headed by Catargiu had rushed the accord through the legislature and thereby opened the door to a conflict between Romanians and Jews. It observed moreover that an international contract between parties of unequal strength signified not autonomy—as Vasile Boerescu had claimed—but a loss of stature by the weaker party. Boerescu's organ, *Pressa,* responded to *Romanulu's* funereal edition by disparaging these complaints, which only discredited the demagogic opposition; arguments against the covenant were indeed merely the lamentations of whining "nihilists." *Pressa* pointed out that Romanian statesmen had investigated the country's mercantile interests for two years and relied on two years of negotiations in Vienna by the "intelligent and patriotic" Costa-Foru before deciding to treat seriously with Austria-Hungary. The understanding was, *Pressa* maintained, designed to protect Romania's national autonomy against pretensions by the Ottoman Empire, to shield its fledgling industry, to encourage the export of cereals and other products, and to prevent the immigration of Jews into Moldavia.[41] The Romanian government was, however, extraordinarily sensitive to its opponents' criticisms. Catargiu, in his capacity as minister of interior, informed district prefects that the convention had avoided the Jewish question, and so restrictions on foreigners were still in force. Boerescu, for his part, was less firmly convinced about the pact's advantages for Romania than he had indicated in the chamber. He proposed to Vienna that Austria-Hungary's privilege of establishing warehouses on the Danube River bank be interpreted as a "nominal" or "fictitious" right, since aliens in rural communes wanted comparable prerogatives. Costa-Foru replied that it was too late to change the deal.[42] And it was.

The convention received perfunctory treatment in the Hungarian National Assembly and the Austrian Imperial Council. The Hungarian assembly, after a brief debate in which the accord's adversaries suggested it would tie the government's hands in concluding future treaties, voted 216 to 41 in favor of the agreement on 18 December 1875. Opposition in the Austrian council ranged from outrage at dealing diplomatically with a vassal principality and concern for the integrity of the Ottoman Empire to fear of Romanian agricultural competition. Some councilors regretted that Austria-Hungary's Jews would still lack the same rights as Christians in Romania. Others doubted that by recognizing Romania's claim to pursue an independent foreign policy, the Habsburg Empire would thereby gain an ally in case of an emergency. The pact's proponents pointed out that Romania had already raised its tolls without regard to the suzerain Ottoman Empire; Austria-Hungary therefore needed to acquire, via a covenant, benefits for its trade—especially for its textiles—with Romania. The failure of the compact to protect all Austro-Hungarian subjects in Romania was dismissed as a price that had to be paid for important commercial advantages. On 28 February 1876, the Austrian council approved the concord by a vote of 145 to 33.[43]

Chlumecký had endeavored to mollify the convention's adversaries in the Habsburg Empire by noting that the privileges of Austro-Hungarian merchants would be safeguarded by provisions in understandings with Turkey and with third states, in line with most-favored-nation treatment. Kogălniceanu, the new Romanian minister of foreign affairs, denounced this idea as a "curious pretension" to be disregarded. At the same time, he indicated he would be "loyal and sincere" in executing the covenant because of its endorsement by the legislatures in Vienna, Budapest, and Bucharest.[44] Kogălniceanu and Ion Brătianu had won control of the government partly because of their protests against the agreement, but once in power they followed—with Carol's support—the same path as had their predecessors. Austria-Hungary and Romania exchanged ratifications of the accord on 1 June 1876, and it was implemented one month later.

Economic ties with Russia were far less significant for Romania than links with Austria-Hungary, as can be seen in the chart above. Romania's trade played a similarly minor role in Russia's commerce. Before a Russo-Romanian commercial accord was in place, Romania's imports from Russia constituted only 0.42 percent of Russia's total exports, whereas Romania's exports were 0.57 percent of Russia's imports in 1874. With a convention, Romania received more of Russia's exports (1.61 percent) yet had less of Russia's imports (0.18 percent in 1881). The chief commodity that Russia sent to Romania before and after their compact was grain; Russia's main imports from Romania were wool and paper goods in 1874, and forest products together with cereals in 1881.[45] The agrarian nature of society in both countries dictated that about two thirds of Russia's trade to Romania were in transit elsewhere.[46]

Russia had proposed in the early 1860s that Romania share in regulating the transit trade on the Prut River. Russia thereupon concluded a convention with Austria and Romania in 1866 respecting the Prut, which strengthened economic relations between Russia and Romania. This pact was, notwithstanding, blocked owing to objections of some Romanians, such as Kogălniceanu, who contended that Austria should withdraw from the agreement, since it was not a riparian state for the navigable portion of the river. However, he later recognized, as minister of interior, that Romania's interest in the concord was four times that of the Habsburg Empire and twice that of Russia; he was then successful in winning his countrymen to support the deal.[47] Henceforward, until the opening of the Iaşi-Odessa railroad in 1874, about one fourth of Russia's agricultural merchandise in Romania moved via the Prut; this river was, besides, an avenue for Russia's imports of manufactured articles and raw materials from Western Europe.[48]

Negotiations for a Russo-Romanian commercial convention began in earnest in 1875. Russia desired to protect its transit trade in Romania, calling for six months for Russian goods to traverse Romania and for most-favored-nation treatment. Romania in turn wished to facilitate the transport of its farm commodities on the Iaşi-Odessa railway. Vasile Boerescu noted that a trade pact with Russia would scarcely benefit Romania economically, yet he viewed such a covenant as further evidence of Romania's prerogative to deal internationally without regard to the suzerain Ottoman Empire.[49] George Cantacuzino and the Russian consul in Bucharest, Ivan A. Zinov'ev, drafted an accord by the end of 1875; Romania's diplomatic agent in Russia, Gheorghe C. Filipescu, then went to St. Petersburg to endorse this document with Russian chancellor Gorchakov.[50] Some Russians thought, however, that it ought to be confirmed instead by Russia's minister of finance, Mikhail Kh. Reitern, an idea Carol rejected.[51] Bălăceanu, who was minister of foreign affairs in the new cabinet, was also annoyed at Russia's reluctance to grant formal approval and so asked Austria-Hungary to intervene on Romania's behalf, which Andrássy was loath to do.[52] Russia eventually acceded to Romania's request about the sanctioning of the agreement[53] because of disturbances in the Balkan Peninsula that required Russia to have a friend on the Danube. Russia got what it wanted: most-favored-nation perquisites, no customs duties on Russian merchandise traveling through Romania, and the right of Russian raw materials to remain in Romanian warehouses for six months without fees. Overlooked was the passage of Romania's products along the Iaşi-Odessa railway. Russia's subjects, like Austria-Hungary's, were barred from holding or owning rural estates in the principality. Russians in Romania and Romanians in Russia were nevertheless exempt from paying more taxes than those levied on citizens in the host country and were free from military service except during a war.[54]

Legislators in Bucharest heatedly discussed the Russo-Romanian convention. Some landowners feared the potential competition of Russian grain and so opposed the entry or even the transit of Russian wheat. One deputy, Nicolae Fleva, remarked that the accord could hardly affect the Habsburg Empire's corner on Romania's imports because Russia's industry was much inferior to Austria-Hungary's. Another deputy, Vasile Maniu, contended that the pact would create a bridge between Slavs in Russia and those in the Balkan Peninsula. Ion Brătianu rejoined for the government: "We will not be Russia's tool in the East." Kogălniceanu said the most-favored-nation clause would win respect from other powers. Romania's transit trade in Galaţi and Brăila was more important than that by rail from Iaşi to Odessa; but on that rail-road, Kogălniceanu noted, Romania's wood and skins actually had free passage. Furthermore, this covenant was a political act, ending Austria-Hungary's commercial monopoly in Romania. Kogălniceanu also assured that Russia's Jews would have no more privileges than Austria-Hungary's; that is, they would still be unable to purchase land or houses in rural communes. At the close of debates, the legislators adopted the agreement without amendments.[55]

Romania also concluded commercial conventions with Britain, Italy, and Germany as well as with Greece, Holland, Belgium, and Switzerland from 1878 to 1882. Negotiations with Germany began in 1875, yet ratification of a covenant would be stalled until 1881. Germany insisted first upon the sale of the German-owned railroad in Romania to the Bucharest government.[56] In 1876 France, Italy, and Britain exchanged diplomatic notes with Romania providing for most-favored-nation access for a short term.[57] The Western powers wanted Romania first to grant political equality to all of its subjects without religious distinctions. Italy's foreign affairs minister, Luigi Amedeo Melegari, worried about the negative reaction of the Jewish-controlled press in his country if Italian citizens were denied the right to obtain rural property in Romania. Kogălniceanu refused, however, to consider the Jewish question as part of a trade agreement.[58] Concords with Italy and Britain would await the revision of the Romanian constitution in favor of the Jews in 1879 and the subsequent recognition of Romania's independence by the powers.[59] France was satisfied with the most-favored-nation privileges that it enjoyed, a concession Romania offered to every state indicating a willingness to make a commercial pact with it. Not until Romania's conventional tariff had expired in 1886 did a Franco-Romanian mercantile deal come to pass in 1893.[60] The Ottoman Empire also struck a commercial accord with Romania in 1887.[61] By that time, however, the direction of Romania's trade was no longer toward Turkish markets.

Romania's commercial convention with the Habsburg Empire was the key. This covenant surfaced when the powers were reconsidering the efficacy of free trade after the financial crisis of 1873 and were beginning to adopt protective measures against foreign imports. The cost of manufactured wares declined in the 1870s, output increased, and the demand for industrial machines and equipment sagged. Moreover, a rapid and inexpensive means of transport and the growth of agricultural production flooded Europe with relatively cheap goods. Competition in cereals tended to depress the price of that commodity. Thus, on the one hand, the value of Romania's exports to Austria-Hungary did not rise as much as did the value of its imports from the Habsburg Empire, despite the free trade in grain. The Dual Monarchy's fabricated articles, on the other hand, found a secure and profitable outlet in Romania. This accord confirmed the principality's colonial posture. Romania's raw materials supplied Austria-Hungary's industries, and the latter's surplus products went to Romanian markets; the conventional tariff encouraged Habsburg exports and inhibited Romanian industrial development. Economic dependence led, in part, to political dependence; Romania's secret treaty with Austria-Hungary in 1883, which was in force until World War I, was mute evidence of this situation.

Danubian Romanians trembled at seeing their country become a satellite of any power. Hence a patriotic spirit, which had been a factor in making commercial conventions with Austria-Hungary and Russia in the first place, found expression in the legislative debates about these compacts. Romanian statesmen—both government spokespersons and those in opposition—nevertheless recognized that these accords marked the beginning of a new era in their country's international affairs. No other vassal of the Ottoman Empire had heretofore signed a trade agreement with a great power. Turkish suzerainty perforce still existed under the powers' supervision; the annual tribute and consular jurisdiction continued to remind Romanians of their bondage. But the commercial pacts appeared to buttress Romania's quest to manage its own autarchic foreign relations. In this sense, the covenants with Austria-Hungary and Russia were moves toward Romania's political independence.

Notes

1. Frederick Kellogg, "Convenţia comercială din 1875: Un pas către independenţă?"

2. See article 8 of the Moldavian-Turkish treaty of 1634, in *Acte şi documente relative la istoria renascerei Romaniei,* 1:6.

3. According to the treaty and separate act signed by Russia and Turkey in Adrianople, 2/14 September 1829, the Danubian Romanians were to enjoy "full lib-

erty of commerce" and were no longer bound to supply Turkish consumers in Constantinople or in the Danubian fortresses; *Archives diplomatiques,* vol. 6, pt. 2 (avril, mai, juin 1866), 311–15. See articles 154 and 156 of *Regulamentul Organik,* 101–2; and articles 148, 150, and 155 of *Reglementul Organik a Prinţipatului Moldovei,* 161–62.

4. For the Moldo-Wallachian customs union of 1847, see *Relaţiile internaţionale ale României în documente (1368–1900),* 309–25. For the rise in Turkish customs duties, see treaties with Great Britain in 1838 and 1861 in *Recueil d'actes internationaux de l'Empire Ottoman,* vol. 2 (1789–1856), 252, and vol. 3 (1856–78), 138; Constantin I. Băicoianu, *Geschichte der rumänischen Zollpolitik seit dem 14. Jahrhundert bis 1874,* 21–131.

5. Vasile Boerescu's circular, 21 June 1874, no. 225, in Arhiva Vasile Boerescu, CXXVII/3, BNR, SM; Constantin I. Băicoianu, *Istoria politicei nóstre vamale şi comerciale de la Regulamentul Organic până în present,* vol. 1, pt. 1, 52–54, 95–116; Corneliu Antonescu, *Die rumänische Handelspolitik von 1875–1910,* 39–42.

6. Adolf Beer, *Die österreichische Handelspolitik im neunzehnten Jahrhundert,* 418–19; Ştirbei (Vienna) to Beust (Vienna), 2 March 1867, and Beust to Ştirbei, 17 March 1867, in *Collectiune de tratatele si conventiunile Romaniei,* 129–32; see Carol's notes, 5/17 March 1867, in *Aus dem Leben König Karls von Rumänien,* 1:184.

7. Schlechta (Bucharest) to Andrássy (Vienna), 25 January 1872, no. 9C, in HHS, HA—Konsulate: Bukarest, Fach 34, Karton 118.

8. Andrássy to Adolf von Auersperg (Vienna) and Melchior Lónyay (Budapest), 9 March 1872, and Szlávy to Anton Banhans, 16 August 1872, no. 8223, in HHS, HA—Konsulate: Bukarest, Fach 34, Karton 118.

9. Uta Bindreiter, *Die diplomatischen und wirtschaftlichen Beziehungen zwischen Österreich-Ungarn und Rumänien 1875–1888,* 55.

10. See article 23 of the 1856 Treaty of Paris and article 8 of the 1858 Convention of Paris, in *Archives diplomatiques,* vol. 6, pt. 2 (1866), 30, 104.

11. Andrássy to Ferenc Zichy (Constantinople), 14 June 1874, in HHS, PA—XII, Türkei, Varia I, Karton 107; Andrássy to Beust, 11 June 1874 (abstract), in Foreign Office, *Correspondence respecting the Question of the Negotiation of Commercial Conventions by the Principalities,* 1–3.

12. Zichy to Andrássy, 23 June 1874, no. 47, and Andrássy (Budapest) to Zichy, 25 December 1874, in HHS, PA—XII, Türkei, Varia I, Karton 107; Arifi Paşa (Constantinople) to Musurus Paşa (London), 19 August 1874, and Edward Henry Stanley, Earl of Derby (London) to Elliot (Constantinople), 31 October 1874 and 5 December 1874, in *Correspondence respecting the Question of the Negotiation of Commercial Conventions by the Principalities,* 4, 11–12, 24–25. For the *ferman* of 8 June 1873, see *Recueil d'actes internationaux de l'Empire Ottoman,* 3:349.

13. Boerescu's circular, 12/24 July 1874, in AIC, CR, dosar no. 11/1874.

14. Derby to Elliot, 20 November 1874, in HAA, PS: Türkei, 111, vol. 3; Vasile Boerescu to Constantin Esarcu (Rome), 22 April and 30 October 1874, and Esarcu to Boerescu, 13 November 1874, in Raoul V. Bossy, *Politica externă a României între anii 1873–1880, privită dela agenţia diplomatică din Roma,* 103, 106–9, 112.

15. Louis Decazes, duc de Glücksberg (Paris) to Louis-Emmanuel d'Harcourt (Vienna), 9 April 1874, in HHS, PA—XII, Türkei, Varia I, Karton 107; Reuss (St.

Petersburg) to Bismarck (Berlin), 11 April 1875, and Bülow (Berlin) to Rudolf von Delbrück (Berlin), 13 June 1875, in HAA, PS: Türkei, 111, vol. 4.

16. Bülow's memo, 8 June 1874, and Auswärtiges Amt to Pfuel (Bucharest), 13 June 1874, no. 3, in HAA, PS: Türkei, 111, vol. 1; Károlyi (Berlin) to Andrássy, 27 June 1874, no. 37B, in HHS, PA—XII, Türkei, Varia I, Karton 107.

17. Adolphe Le Flô (St. Petersburg) to Jacques, duc de Broglie (Paris), 21 March 1874, in HHS, PA—XII, Türkei, Varia I, Karton 107.

18. Auswärtiges Amt (Berlin) to Vienna, 7 July 1874, no. 353, in HAA, PS: Türkei, 111, vol. 1; Bülow to Pfuel, 10 July 1874, no. 104, Bülow to William I, 31 July 1874, Karl von Werther (Bujukdere) to Auswärtiges Amt, 22 October 1874, no. 78, in ibid., vol. 2; note to William I, 16 November 1874, in ibid., vol. 3; identic note of 20 October 1874, in HHS, PA—XII, Türkei, Varia I, Karton 107.

19. Arifi Paşa to Musurus Paşa, 10/22 October 1874, in *Correspondence respecting the Question of the Negotiation of Commercial Conventions by the Principalities,* 14–15; Arifi Paşa to Aristarki Bey (Berlin), 11/23 October 1874, in HAA, PS: Türkei, 111, vol. 2.

20. Zichy to Andrássy, 25 November 1874, no. 84, and Andrássy's note, 26 November 1874, in HHS, PA—XII, Türkei, Varia I, Karton 107.

21. Băicoianu, *Istoria politicei nóstre vamale şi comerciale,* vol. 1, pt. 1, 119–20; Bindreiter, *Die diplomatischen und wirtschaftlichen Beziehungen zwischen Österreich-Ungarn und Rumänien,* 59–60, 66–72.

22. Bartal (Budapest) to Andrássy, 16 August 1874, and Heinrich von Calice (Bucharest) to Andrássy, 23 November 1874, no. 75, in HHS, HA—Konsulate: Bukarest, Fach 34, Karton 118; L. von Waecker-Gotter (Budapest) to Bismarck, 13 November 1874, in HAA, PS: Türkei, 111, vol. 3; Bindreiter, *Die diplomatischen und wirtschaftlichen Beziehungen zwischen Österreich-Ungarn und Rumänien,* 74–76.

23. Lajos Simonyi to Andrássy, 30 May 1875, in HHS, HA—Konsulate: Bukarest, Fach 34, Karton 166.

24. Andrássy to Calice, 3 and 15 June 1875, in HHS, HA—Konsulate: Bukarest, Fach 34, Karton 166; Pfuel to Bismarck, 7 April 1875, no. 30, Schweinitz (Vienna) to Philipsborn (Berlin), 17 June 1875, no. 54, and Andrássy to Bismarck, 24 June 1875, in HAA, PS: Türkei, 111, vol. 4.

25. Simonyi to Andrássy, 10 and 30 May 1875, in HHS, HA—Konsulate: Bukarest, Fach 34, Karton 166.

26. Calice to Andrássy, 18 February 1875, no. 8, and 7 June 1875, in HHS, HA—Konsulate: Bukarest, Fach 34, Karton 166.

27. Andrássy to Tisza, 31 May 1875, in HHS, HA—Konsulate: Bukarest, Fach 34, Karton 166.

28. Costa-Foru (Vienna) to Vasile Boerescu (Bucharest), 12/24 January 1875, nos. 18–20, in Arhiva Vasile Boerescu, IV, dosar 423, BNR, SM.

29. Calice to Andrássy, 18 February 1875, no. 8, in HHS, HA—Konsulate: Bukarest, Fach 34, Karton 166.

30. See articles 1 and 4 of the convention, and article 1 of the final protocol, each signed (Vienna) on 22 June 1875 and ratified (Bucharest) on 1 June 1876, in *Nouveau recueil général de traités et autres actes relatifs aux rapports de droit international,* vol. 2, pt. 1, 372, 374, 389–90.

31. See article 29 of the 1875 convention, in *Nouveau recueil général de traités,* vol. 2, pt. 1, 379–80; see also articles 16 and 18 of the 1856 Treaty of Paris for dispositions establishing the European Danube Commission, originally for a two-year term, in *Archives diplomatiques,* vol. 13, pt. 3 (juillet, août, septembre 1873), 88–89.

32. See tariffs A, B, and C of the convention, in *Nouveau recueil général de traités,* vol. 2, pt. 1, 381–87; Calice to Andrássy, 16 April 1875, in HHS, HA—Konsulate: Bukarest, Fach 34, Karton 166; Băicoianu, *Istoria politicei nóstre vamale şi comerciale,* vol. 1, pt. 1, 121–40.

33. Theodor C. Aslan, *Finanţele României dela Regulamentul Organic până astăzi, 1831–1905,* 173.

34. *Österreichische Statistik,* vol. 4, pt. 1: *Die Statistik des auswärtigen Handels der österreichisch-ungarischen Monarchie im Jahre 1882,* 102–3; Josef Pizzala, "Die österreichisch-ungarische Handelsbilanz für das Jahr 1877"; Pizzala, "Der Export Österreich-Ungarns nach Rumänien."

35. Ministeriu de Interne, Oficiu Central de Statistică, *Statistica din Romania—Comerciul exterior: Import şi export pe anu 1874,* 4–5, 15–19; Ministerul Financelor, Direcţiunea Vămilor, Timbrului şi Inregistrărei, Biuroul statisticei comerciului exterior, *Tablou general indicând comerciul României cu Terile straine in anul 1883,* 8–9, 40, 58.

36. Costa-Foru to Vasile Boerescu, 12/24 January 1875, no. 18-20, in Arhiva Vasile Boerescu, IV, dosar 423, BNR, SM.

37. For debates in the chamber of deputies on 27/9 July–29 June/11 July 1875, see *Monitorul oficial al României,* 12/24 July, 3414–17, 13/25 July, 3443–44, 15/27 July, 3465–68, 3470–76, 16/28 July, 3492, 17/29 July, 3506–8, and 24 July/5 August 1875, 3633–34; see also Brătianu's speeches in the chamber, 28–29 June/10–11 July 1875, in *Ion C. Brătianu: Acte şi cuvântări,* vol. 1, pt. 2, 437–39, 450, 453–54, 456, 468.

38. Gheorghe Zane, "Die österreichischen und die deutschen Wirtschaftsbeziehungen zu den rumänischen Fürstentümern, 1774–1874," 275–76.

39. For debates in the chamber on 27 June/9 July and 29 June/11 July 1875, see *Monitorul officiale al României,* 12/24 July, 3417–20, 22 July/3 August, 3590–94, and 24 July/5 August 1875, 3635–41; see also Carp's speech in the chamber, 29 June/11 July 1875, in Carp, *Discursuri,* 1:84–92.

40. For debates in the chamber on 30 June/12 July 1875, see *Monitorul officiale al României,* 27 July/8 August 1875, 3736. Ion Brătianu, Kogălniceanu, Epureanu, Alexandru Golescu, and Alexandru Candiano-Popescu were among those who resigned.

41. *Romanulu,* 27, 28, 30 June–1 July, 11, 13, 17, 21–22, 25, 27 July, 1, 7–8, 11–12, 14, 15 August 1875; *Pressa,* 28 June, 1, 2, 3, 4, 23 July, 26 July–7 August 1875.

42. Catargiu to prefects, 10/22 July 1875, in *Monitorul officiale al României,* 11/23 July 1875, 3889–91; Boerescu to Costa-Foru, 30 August 1875, and Costa-Foru to Boerescu, 18/30 October 1875, in Arhiva Vasile Boerescu, IV, dosar 423, BNR, SM.

43. *Neue Freie Presse,* 20 December 1875; Cauldonoff (Vienna) to Bülow, 12, 20, 29 February 1876, in HAA, PS: Türkei, 111, vol. 5. See an unsigned report from

Chapter Five

Budapest, [December 1875], in Alliance Israélite Universelle, *Bulletin* (2e semestre 1875), 9; Bindreiter, *Die diplomatischen und wirtschaftlichen Beziehungen zwischen Österreich-Ungarn und Rumänien,* 94–95, 166–69; Antonescu, *Die rumänische Handelspolitik,* 51–54; Băicoianu, *Istoria politicei nóstre vamale şi comerciale,* vol. 1, pt. 1, 150–52.

44. Bindreiter, *Die diplomatischen und wirtschaftlichen Beziehungen zwischen Österreich-Ungarn und Rumänien,* 170; Kogălniceanu's petition to the council of ministers, 20 May/1 June 1876, in *Charles Ier, Roi de Roumanie,* 2:50–53; see Carol's notes, 15/27 May and 20 May/1 June 1876, in *Aus dem Leben König Karls von Rumänien,* 3:32–33.

45. Ministerstvo finansov, *Obzor vneshnei torgovli Rossii po evropeiskoi i aziatskoi granitsam za 1874 god,* 117–41, 493–549; Ministerstvo finansov, *Obzor vneshnei torgovli Rossii po evropeiskoi i aziatskoi granitsam za 1881 god,* passim.

46. Evgenii E. Chertan, "Iz istorii russko-rumynskikh torgovykh vzaimootnoshenii v 1860–1875 godakh," 28.

47. See Kogălniceanu's speeches in the chamber, 29 May/10 June 1869, and in the senate, 6/18 June 1869, in Kogălniceanu, *Opere,* vol. 4: *Oratorie II, 1864–1878,* pt. 2, 250, 254, 269–70. See the Russo-Romanian convention regarding navigation on the Prut River (Bucharest), 3/15 December 1866, in *Tractate, conventiuni şi invoiri internationale ale Romaniei,* lviii–lxviii. Romania's chamber approved this, on 29 May, as did the senate, on 6 June 1869; it was ratified on 13 June 1869.

48. Evgenii E. Chertan, "Konventsiia o sudokhodstve po reke Prut 1866 goda."

49. Evgenii E. Chertan, "Russko-rumynskaia torgovaia konventsiia 1876 goda," 451, 453–54.

50. Pfuel to Bülow, 28 December 1875, no. 87, in HAA, PS: Türkei, 111, vol. 5.

51. Bülow to Delbrück (Berlin), 6 Dec. 1875, in HAA, PS: Türkei, 111, vol. 5.

52. Calice to Auswärtiges Amt (Vienna), 22 February, no. 32, and 29 February 1876, no. 35, and Auswärtiges Amt to Calice, 2 March 1876, in HHS, PA—XXXVIII, Konsulate: Bukarest, Karton 211.

53. Calice to Andrássy, 18 March 1876, no. 43, in HHS, PA—XXXVIII, Konsulate: Bukarest, Karton 211; Dr. Reitz (Bucharest) to Bülow, 31 March 1876, no. 29, in HAA, PS: Türkei, 111, vol. 5.

54. See especially articles 1, 3, and 16 of the Russo-Romanian commercial convention (Bucharest), 15/27 March 1876, in *Nouveau recueil général de traités,* vol. 2, pt. 1, 571–72, 574–75. This pact was ratified on 21 October/2 November 1876.

55. Alvensleben (Bucharest) to Bülow, 28 July 1876, no. 98, in HAA, PS: Türkei, 111, vol 5. See Kogălniceanu's speech in the chamber, 13/25 and 14/26 July 1876, in Kogălniceanu, *Opere,* vol. 4: *Oratorie II, 1864–1878,* pt. 4 (1874–78), 212–22; Victor Jinga, *Principii şi orientări ale comerţului exterior al României (1859–1916),* 170; Chertan, "Russko-rumynskaia torgovaia konventsiia 1876 goda," 457. The chamber of deputies adopted the convention by a vote of 78 to 18 with 10 abstentions on 15/27 July 1876, followed by the senate by 25 to 2 on 20 July/1 August 1876; ratifications were exchanged in Bucharest on 21 October/2 November 1876.

56. Auswärtiges Amt to Pfuel, 14 July 1875, no. 11, in HAA, PS: Türkei, 111, vol. 4; Bülow to Pfuel, 16 November 1875, no. 99, Bülow to Delbrück, 6 December 1875, note by Nicolae Kreţulescu (Berlin) to Auswärtiges Amt, 14/26 April 1876, in

HAA, PS: Türkei, 111, vol. 5; Alexandru Degré (Berlin) to Kogălniceanu, 29 September 1877, in Fond Mihail Kogălniceanu, XVI, no. 40, BAR, SC. For the convention of 14 November 1877, which was ratified on 10 July 1881, see *Tractate, conventiuni şi invoiri internationale ale Romaniei,* 149–66.

57. See the accords with France, Italy, and Britain of 5 November, 16 November, 30 November 1876, respectively, in *British and Foreign State Papers, 1875–1876,* 67:50–51, 601–2, and 68:665–66. These agreements expired 12 May 1877.

58. Esarcu to Bălăceanu, 4 April 1876, and George Cantacuzino (Rome) to Ionescu (Bucharest), 26 August 1876, in Bossy, *Politica externă a României,* 135–36, 139–40.

59. For the convention with Italy, 23 March 1878, which was ratified on 1/13 March 1881, and the one with Britain, 24 March/5 April 1880, which was ratified on 30 June/12 July 1880, see *Tractate, conventiuni şi invoiri internationale ale Romaniei,* 185–98, 214–28.

60. For ongoing negotiations with France, see Ministère des Affaires Étrangères, *Documents diplomatiques: Negociation commerciale avec Roumanie, 1876–1885,* 3–14 and passim. For the convention of 16/28 February 1893, which was ratified on 22 March/3 April 1893, see *Conventions de la Roumanie avec les états étrangères concernant le commerce et les marques de fabrique,* 96–97.

61. Constantin I. Băicoianu, *Relaţiunile noastre comerciale cu Turcia de la 1860 până în present,* 7–70. For the convention of 10/22 November 1887, which was ratified on 31 December 1887, see *Recueil d'actes internationaux de l'Empire Ottoman,* 4:443–45.

Chapter Six

FOREIGN ENTANGLEMENTS

Intervention by the great powers to protect foreign commercial interests, railroad investors, and Jews certainly nurtured aspirations among Danubian Romanians for independence. Also of importance in this mosaic were Bulgarian revolutionaries domiciled in Romania and projects for alliances aimed against the Turks. The powers strongly disapproved of any disruption of the status quo in Southeastern Europe and so opposed any Bulgarian political agitation that might lead to the formation of a Bulgarian state; and they contested the prospect of an entente by Christian Romania, Greece, and Serbia against the Muslim Ottoman Empire, which might spell the end of the Turkish presence in Europe.

Was a coalition of national entities in Southeastern Europe possible? Some thought so. Yet negotiations for one foundered on the lack of direct, mutual concerns.

The Greek government aimed at expanding its lands into Greek-speaking but Turkish-controlled Epirus, Thessaly, and Crete following the winning of Greece's independence in 1821. The outbreak of a revolt in Crete during 1866 triggered an immediate response in Athens. The Greek minister in Paris, Gregorios Ypsilantis, visited Bucharest to solicit aid against the Turks. Carol declined. Carol, who had just been confirmed in office by the Ottoman sultan, recognized the weakness of his army and was more heedful of consolidating his position in Bucharest than of pursuing an aggressive foreign policy. He nonetheless donated money for Cretan refugees and supported Ypsilantis in raising funds in Romania for the Greek cause.[1]

Discussions focusing on a Greco-Romanian entente still continued. Mihaēl Antonopoulos, a Greek diplomat, was in Bucharest early in 1867 with instructions to "tighten the bonds of friendship that unite Greece and Romania."[2] At the same time, Bălăceanu, the Romanian diplomatic agent in Paris, went to Athens to confer about the future of Orthodox Christian peoples of Southeastern Europe. He conveyed Carol's fear that common action against the Ottoman Empire at that juncture would be dangerous and would provoke the "armed intervention of the great powers." Greece's minister of foreign affairs, Kharilaos Trikoupis, understood this stand and remarked that Greece itself was exhausted from championing the rebellion in Crete and was apprehensive about further nationalistic agitation in Epirus and Thessaly. Bălăceanu told King George I (1863–1913) that Greece, Serbia, and Romania should come together in a "confederation of the East"—without the participation of the powers—directed at solving the Eastern Question by a unified governmental engagement. George declared: "The Prince of Romania has in me a sincere and true ally." [3] George and Carol, of course, shared a conservative, paternalistic ideology. Greece and Romania were, however, far too weak, despite the intentions of their leaders, to defeat the Ottoman Empire without the assistance of one of the powers. No alliance flowed from this exchange of felicities.

Greco-Romanian relations remained cordial. Greece once more sought Romania's aid after a resolution by the powers at the outset of 1869 to restore Turkish control over Crete. Ypsilantis was again in Bucharest in the spring of 1869 with a letter from George to Carol telling of the need for "Christian nationalities of the East" to forcibly assert their rights and thereby to escape the Turkish yoke. Carol replied evasively by simply acknowledging the mutual political, religious, and commercial interests that linked the two countries.[4] Ypsilantis prepared a draft accord for joint military operations by Greece and Romania to win the independence of Romania and the incorporation of Turkey's Greek provinces into the Greek kingdom.[5] Romania responded with a project stipulating, on the one hand, the avoidance of untimely, isolated acts that would endanger the peace and impede the realization of patriotic goals; yet it anticipated, on the other hand, a joint Greco-Romanian campaign against the Ottoman Empire if the two allies were provoked by Turkey. This plan also envisioned Serbia's cooperation in a tripartite league against Turkey.[6] Ypsilantis observed that the aims of Greece and Romania would abort without the backing of the powers, especially that of Russia—which was known to be sympathetic to fellow Orthodox Christians.[7] Ypsilantis returned to Bucharest at the end of 1869 to put the final touches on the blueprint. By this time, Greece clearly wanted Romania to sponsor Bulgarian bands north of the Danube that would raid south.[8] Carol delegated the matter to his minister of finance, Alexandru Golescu, noting that as a constitutional ruler his ministers had to participate in state decisions. No treaty ensued, since Ypsilantis had only been empowered to deal directly with Carol.[9] The prince undoubtedly recognized that Romania was ill prepared for war and lacked the powers' support for achieving its national aspirations.

Although Greco-Romanian negotiations failed, Serbia and Romania reached an agreement. Serbia's Prince Michael hoped to rid his country of Turkish troops and to rule an independent state. To do so, he concluded treaties with Montenegro, Greece, and Romania. Serbia and Montenegro secretly allied in 1866 for a joint effort to gain freedom and unify into a greater Serbia, which would be led by Michael.[10] Serbia backed away, however, from a proposal by the Bulgarian conspiratorial Virtuous Company in Bucharest for a "Yugoslav Empire."[11] Serbia's reluctance was no doubt due to the nonexistence of a Bulgarian state; also, the Virtuous Company represented merely a few Bulgarian émigrés. Turkish garrisons quit Serbia in the spring of 1867, owing in part to the Ottoman Empire's troubles in Crete and its desire to discourage revolutionary activities in Southeastern Europe. But Serbia wanted more and thus treated with Greece for a covenant that would involve hostilities against the Ottoman Empire. By this compact, after a victorious war Serbia was to get Bosnia and Hercegovina, while Greece was to have Thessaly and Epirus.[12]

Almost immediately after Carol ascended the throne, he wrote to Michael about the necessity for cordial relations between the two neighbors.[13] Dumitru Brătianu, who delivered Carol's letter, also—so it seems—requested, to no avail, Serbia's military support in case of a Turkish occupation of Romania or a Russo-Turkish war.[14] Brătianu later learned from Serbia's diplomatic agent in Constantinople, Jovan Ristić, that Belgrade would not be "responsible for agitation that might arise" in Serbia if Turkey invaded Romania.[15] Michael visited Bucharest in the spring of 1867, at which time Carol declared that their two countries shared "bonds of friendship" and an identical interest in being rid of Turkish vassalage.[16] Soon thereafter, Ştefan Golescu, Romania's minister of foreign affairs, suggested a concord among the Christian population of the Ottoman Empire and assured Serbia that Romania did not seek to create a "Kingdom of Romania-Bulgaria."[17] Romania's agent in Belgrade, Radu Ionescu, then proposed a "close alliance" and "intimate union" of the two states that would last "forever" in "all circumstances." This project was to favor the "prosperity and progress" of both parties as well as to regulate and encourage commercial ties. A provision for "aid and assistance" was nevertheless dropped from the final treaty.[18] France's consul in Belgrade, Édouard Engelhardt, indicated that this pact possibly included additional desiderata. Further aims were to end consular jurisdiction and to cooperate militarily in liberating Turkey's Christian peoples. If the battles were successful, Romania would receive the Danube Delta with Dobrogea north of a line from Ruse on the Danube to Varna on the Black

Sea, while Serbia would acquire Bosnia, Hercegovina, Old Serbia (western Macedonia), and what was left of Bulgaria.[19] The assassination of Michael did not shake Serbo-Romanian amity. Ristić, who acted as Serbia's regent, affirmed that his government "would not hesitate to take part in a war into which Romania was drawn."[20]

A more ambitious scheme was for a Serbian-Greek-Montenegrin-Romanian compact. The Greco-Serbian agreement of 1867 had called for Serbia to work with Montenegro and for both Greece and Serbia to deal with Romania. One of the probably apocryphal clauses of the Serbo-Romanian covenant also stipulated negotiations between Serbia and Montenegro on the one hand and between Greece and Romania on the other to expand an understanding among the states of Southeastern Europe.[21] Rumors in Constantinople about the existence of such a four-sided agreement caused the Turks to mobilize 120,000 troops on the Danube.[22] The intentions of the principals may be gleaned from a missive in which the Montenegrin prince, Nicholas (1860–1918), told Carol that their comity was "the best guarantee for gaining the object that God has assigned us."[23] That object was undoubtedly independence. The project of the alliance is practically identical in phraseology to the Serbo-Romanian treaty of 1868 regarding common interests and the encouragement of commercial relations. The draft, preserved in Romania's archives, omits the phrase "aid and possible assistance" but adds the term "autonomy."[24] Autonomy was inapplicable to the independent Greek kingdom. Hence we may assume that the four-country plan preceded and then served as a model for the Serbo-Romanian accord. Although this plan remained a dream for Christians in Southeastern Europe, it prompted nightmares for the Muslim Turks. An effective league in this area against the Ottoman Empire was nevertheless highly improbable without the powers' support, and the powers applied diplomatic pressure to restrain the Romanians, Serbs, and Greeks. The formers' influence plus the latters' national jealousies precluded regional unity.

Romania's relations with Bulgarians differed markedly from those with Serbia and Greece. Serbia and Romania were, after all, autonomous principalities, and Greece was an independent kingdom, whereas the Bulgarians had no recognized political station either within or outside the Ottoman Empire. Bulgarians, Serbians, and Romanians nonetheless shared common aims: to overthrow Turkish tutelage and to establish their own independent states. Bulgarian revolutionaries would therefore find in Romania and Serbia relatively safe havens and launching pads for their nationalistic undertakings.[25]

Bulgarian émigrés in Romania (in Brăila and Bucharest) and in Serbia (in Belgrade) as well as in Russia (in Odessa) organized themselves to achieve statehood. Bulgarians were especially active in Romania. They discovered inspiration in the words and deeds of Georgi S. Rakovski, who had fought the Turks in the name of all Bulgarians and for his own profit. He founded in Bucharest a short-lived newspaper, *Bŭdushtnost* (The Future) (1864), and by 1867 set up there a command post for *khaiduk,* or brigand, endeavors. Some idealistic and impatient Bulgarian adventurers in Romania then formed military units, crossed the Danube River, and attacked the Turks in Bulgaria. In the spring of 1867, Panait Khitov was in Tutrakan and Filip Totiu in Svishtov. The following year, Khadzhi Dimitŭr and Stefan Karadzha conducted a band into Bulgaria, only to meet defeat in the Letnitsa Forest.[26] These campaigns failed to rouse Bulgarians in Bulgaria to assert their national claims. The agitators themselves lacked unity, and Turkish troops in Bulgaria inhibited a Bulgarian patriotic revolt.

The ineffectiveness of the raids to provoke a general rising led some Bulgarians abroad to reconsider their immediate aims and methods. Already in 1866, Ivan Kasabov had organized some émigrés into the Bulgarian Central Secret Committee, which had its headquarters in Bucharest and branches in several communities on the left bank of the Danube.[27] Secrecy was required in order to allay Romanian fears that Bulgarian revolutionary activity might—as it indeed did—stir the powers, including the Ottoman Empire, to intervene. Counting on Romanian aid, Kasabov called for an insurrection against the Turks. A "sacred coalition," directed by Kasabov and embracing prominent Romanians—such as Eugeniu Carada, the editor of Bucharest's premier newspaper, *Romanulu;* and Constantin Ciocîrlan, the Bucharest police prefect—pressed Bulgarians, Romanians, and Serbs to create their own "autonomous and independent states," all "united in a confederation."[28] Also important was the Virtuous Company inaugurated at Bucharest by a few Bulgarians, Romanians, and Serbs—guided by the merchant Khristo Georgiev—which promoted Bulgarian-Serbian cooperation in building a South Slavic empire.[29] This company materially supported the Khitov and Totiu raids. In a similar vein, Liuben Karavelov advocated a Christian Balkan federation in his Bucharest newspaper, *Svoboda* (Freedom) (1869–72).[30] Another expatriate, Pandeli Kisimov, in his Bucharest journal, *Otechestvo* (Fatherland) (1869–71), suggested a Bulgarian-Turkish state under the sultan's sovereignty similar to the Dual Monarchy created by the Austro-Hungarian Ausgleich of 1867.[31] Furthermore, by 1869 the Bookman's Association of Brăila, which would be the springboard for the future Bulgarian Academy of Sciences, was non-militant.[32] The moral backing of foreign radicals such as Mikhail Bakunin and Giuseppe Mazzini for Young Bulgaria, which was briefly espoused by Kasabov and his colleagues in 1869, was for naught. And Vasil Levski had meager success at first in fashioning insurrectionary committees inside Bulgaria. Many Bulgarian émigrés seemed to prefer the conservative Bulgarian Society, which was also initiated by Kasabov in 1868. Although society members abetted the Dimitŭr-Karadzha expedition in 1868, they were thereafter primarily interested in simply preaching the cause of a free Bulgaria via Kasabov's Bucharest newspaper, *Narodnost* (Nationality) (1867–69), and the *Dunavska Zora* (Danubian Dawn) (1867–70), edited by Dobri P. Voinikov in Brăila.[33] From this sketch, it should be evident that Bulgarian rebels in exile differed markedly about their objectives and tactics.

The powers intervened diplomatically with the Turks and Romanians to protect their own individual interests, and this had the eventual effect of quelling Bulgarian insurrectionary agitation in Danubian Romania. Turkish officials feared contemporary nationalistic movements throughout the Ottoman Empire: among the Greeks (especially in Crete), Kurds, and Armenians, as well as the Romanians and Bulgarians. After Khitov's raid of 1867, Turkey's grand vezir, Ali Paşa, protested to Carol that Bulgarian revolutionary committees in the Danubian ports of Galaţi, Brăila, and Giurgiu financed incursions by teams of outlaws into Bulgaria.[34] Romania then assured the powers that "everything possible [was being done] . . . to annul completely propagandistic tendencies by these clandestine [Bulgarian] committees."[35] Such pledges failed, notwithstanding, to forestall Totiu's foray in May 1867. In 1868 Offenberg, Russia's consul in Bucharest, warned Ion Brătianu that almost one hundred dangerous men had assembled on the Danube between Giurgiu and Zimnicea, and he advised Romanians to take "rapid and energetic" measures to prevent "reprehensible and inconsiderate" deeds.[36] After the Crimean War, Russian diplomats, despite Russia's traditional role in embracing Slavic, Orthodox Christian causes, usually resisted Pan-Slavic ideas and instead generally sought to maintain the status quo in Southeastern Europe. On the one hand, Russian statesmen evinced more concern for the Catholic Polish rebels of 1863 and for Prussia's military machinations than for the Orthodox Christian Balkan peoples. Their desire, on the other hand, to overturn provisions in the Treaty of Paris that neutralized the Black Sea, and their concomitant need for the assistance of the other powers to do so, dictated a passive Russian policy in Romania and Bulgaria.

As had the Russians, so also the Turks objected to bandits in Romania who disrupted the "tranquillity of Bulgaria." Romanian officials asserted the impossibility of stopping individuals from wandering across the Danube into the Ottoman Empire; some of these vagabonds, moreover, carried alien passports, and so foreign consuls, not Romanian bureaucrats, bore responsibility for them.[37] Ali Paşa contended that Bulgarian revolutionary committees still enjoyed "full liberty of action"; he signaled therefore the "urgent necessity" for an "immediate remedy" via a European commission to investigate the situation.[38] Such a body was stillborn, however, owing to the difficulty some of the powers had themselves in controlling their own frontiers. Prussia, for example, was unable to keep armed Poles from crossing its border into Russia. Neither Prussia nor Russia supported Turkey's proposal.[39] French leaders, for their part, worried about Prussia's territorial designs and suspected the Romanians of covertly sponsoring Bulgarian rebels. The French minister for foreign affairs, Lionel de Moustier, imaginatively tied Romania's encouragement of the Bulgarians to its aspirations in Transylvania.[40] In 1868 France pursued an alliance with Austria to offset a Russo-Prussian accord about Poland. If Paris could convince Vienna that Danubian Romania, with the tacit approval of Berlin and St. Petersburg, wanted to attack the Habsburg Empire, France would find an Austro-Hungarian ally in case of a Franco-Prussian war. Habsburg statesmen in fact closely watched events in Romania.[41] They anxiously contemplated the prospect of a greater Dacia—including Romania, Transylvania, Bukowina, and the Banat—but they were far more concerned about diplomatic and military matters in neighboring German, Italian, and Russian lands than about relatively remote Bulgaria. Hence Austria-Hungary's diplomats did not support Turkey's project.[42] Nor did Great Britain, which thought more about the status of Romanian Jews than about any Romanian-Bulgarian threat to the Ottoman Empire.[43]

How did Romania respond to the powers' protests? Carol believed his ministers had no complicity in the Bulgarian raids and, by August 1868, declared that Bulgarian detachments were no longer in Romania. He opposed the suggestion of some powers to dismiss Ion Brătianu for having countenanced disturbances.[44] Brătianu was one of the most persuasive orators of his era and would perhaps have been more troublesome for Carol as an opposition deputy at this juncture than as a government official. Possibly prompted by Carol, Brătianu took repressive steps against the Bulgarian community in Brăila and revoked Totiu's privilege of residing in Zimnicea on the Danube, while allowing him to stay in the countryside.[45] Brătianu seems as well to have cautioned Kasabov to conduct his seditious agitation secretly so as not to imperil Romania's international position.[46] A spirited debate ensued in the Romanian legislature. Carp accused Brătianu of "high treason" and warned about Bulgarian independence being purchased at the price of Russian supremacy in the Balkans.[47] Brătianu then argued that Romanians lacked the powers' "liberty and intelligence" and so were incompetent to "hang and butcher men"; Romanians were "unable to betray Bulgarians in Romania," and if "we should send them to the gallows . . . God would damn us and Romania would indeed perish."[48] Yet without the backing of any great power, Brătianu had to acquiesce to Turkey's demands. Kasabov was informally incarcerated for two months; in addition, a half dozen of Dimitŭr's accomplices—together with a Romanian baker, Teodor Mărgineanu—stood trial in Giurgiu and were sentenced to terms from two to six months in prison. Furthermore, Nicolae Golescu, Romania's prime minister, visited Constantinople with a pledge to preserve quiesence.[49] This was not enough. Unremitting foreign diplomatic pressure in connection with the Romanian-Bulgarian imbroglio, the Transylvanian Romanian issue, and the Romanian Jewish problem contributed to the fall of the Golescu-Brătianu ministry and to the formation of one headed by Dimitrie Ghica.[50] Kogălniceanu, the new interior minister, directed Danubian prefects to maintain strict surveillance of the frontier. This measure, plus assurances of pacific intentions to the powers and the suzerain Ottoman Empire, apparently placated one and all.[51] Order had, for the moment, been restored in Southeastern Europe.

The outbreak of the Balkan Crisis of 1875, commencing with a revolt in Hercegovina, presented Danubian Romanians with several options. They might join Balkan Christians to expel the Turks from Europe, unite with the suzerain Ottoman Empire to suppress the rebels, ally with Austria-Hungary or Russia to intervene militarily to restore peace, or avoid any involvement in the crisis. Vienna would probably counteract St. Petersburg in pacifying the Balkan Peninsula owing to their long-standing animosity. Both powers were still recovering from military defeats and both pursued cautious foreign policies, neither side then wishing to upset the uneasy balance of power in Europe. Romanian patriots, for their part, were unwilling to assist the Turks against the Slavs. Therefore Romanians seriously contemplated only two possibilities at first: they might fight the Ottoman Empire or remain aloof. Neutrality jarred the rising spirit of Romanian patriotism, but Romanian statesmen nonetheless sought to contain popular sentiment in favor of the Orthodox Christian insurgents. Frequent violations of neutrality would create a climate of distrust at home and abroad, and liberal and conservative leaders thus espoused an uncommitted stance as a means of survival. The Romanian army was too weak, the neighboring powers too strong, and the course of events too uncertain for Romania to adopt another posture.

Vasile Boerescu, minister of foreign affairs at this juncture, explained Romania's neutrality in August 1875. The tumult in Hercegovina would find no echo in Romania; although Bucharest had "sympathy" for the South Slavs, its national agenda dictated a hands-off program—"separate and independent of our neighbors." Boerescu endorsed the adage that "the East begins on the right bank of the Danube, the West begins on the left"; thus Romania's attitude must be differentiated from that of Serbia or Montenegro. His position toward the Ottoman Empire was "completely peaceful and friendly"; Romania's aspirations might be realized nonviolently in "perfect understanding" with Turkey, whose concerns on the Danube were identical with Romania's. Hence Danubian Romanians would employ the "strictest vigilance," in Boerescu's words, so as not to "compromise in any way our neutrality." The Hercegovina insurrection would receive neither "aid nor encouragement"; that is, neither military enlistments nor contributions for the rebels would be tolerated on Romanian soil. Despite this statement, Boerescu admitted that Romania should not "close all the doors," for "we must profit by events."[52] In Romania's chamber of deputies, Boerescu later declared that "in this knotty epoch in which we live, we need not only much patriotism but also much cold blood—much prudence and abnegation."[53] He evidently scoffed at invoking the alliances that had been proposed with Greece and concluded with Serbia in the late 1860s. The portal nevertheless remained open, in case the powers interceded, to cancel tribute to the Ottoman Empire, whereby Romania would become the "Belgium of the East," with international treaties protecting it.[54] Bălăceanu, Boerescu's successor as minister of foreign affairs, reaffirmed Romania's passive role. Romania's middle road was, he said, due to Danubian Romanians' disjunction from Balkan Slavs by blood, language, family, and spirit.[55] He saw no community of interest, notwithstanding the common bond of Orthodox Christianity, between South Slavs and Romanians. Romanians viewed themselves as culturally superior to the Balkan Slavs and hesitated to be inextricably tied to the mutual cause of independence from the Muslim Turks.

Romania had to strengthen itself militarily so as to preserve its neutrality. How else might the government control the activities of Slavs on Romanian soil? Carol attended carefully to the army; he reorganized it and increased its size. The permanent standing army, together with the territorial army and urban militia, which had the task of maintaining order in villages and towns, had in all about 150,000 men. The regular forces with reserves had between 15,000 and 35,000 and were armed with German needle guns and advised by Prussian officers.[56] The minister of war, Ioan E. Florescu, called for extra appropriations to purchase "munitions, equipment, ambulances, and other necessities of the army." He stressed the "innocent" aim of conducting topographical and statistical studies that were not an "act of military aggression."[57] Ion Brătianu, now an opposition leader, rejected an increase in the budget for the troops and deplored that millions had been used for "vanities [and] fortifications" to fashion an "army of parade, of show only."[58] Catargiu, the prime minister, hinted that if the legislature withheld the requested funds, the annual tribute to the Ottoman Empire could not be paid when due. And if monies destined for the tribute went instead to the troops, would Turkey construe this as meaning that Romania had declared its independence? Catargiu described this impost as a "personal" engagement with the sultan that might easily be broken, and thereby Romania would indeed become a state similar in status to Belgium.[59] Neither the Romanian legislature nor the army, however, was ready for such a step. Nor did the powers encourage a unilateral proclamation by Romania, for in 1876 they had nothing to gain by its independence.

Catargiu's cabinet, which had held office for five years, then collapsed. The opposition party's strength crested in 1876 owing to controversy over the commercial accord with Austria-Hungary, negotiations for buying the railroad, and neutrality. Some generals formed a short-lived ministry. The tribute no longer commanded attention, and Romania's foreign policy remained set. The new minister of foreign affairs, Dimitrie Cornea, repeated earlier promises to conserve the "strictest neutrality and respect for treaties."[60] Florescu, now the prime minister, instructed prefects of Danubian districts to prevent armed Bulgarians from crossing the river and thus compromising Romania's neutrality.[61]

Another coalition government eventually emerged, directed by Epureanu, in which the liberals constituted a majority. The liberals retained the same foreign course as their predecessors, despite having opposed the conservatives' agenda for almost half a decade in salons, chamber, and senate. Even before the insurrection in Hercegovina, the liberals issued a program that called for a "Romanian policy, a policy of peace" in accord with existing covenants.[62] Kogălniceanu, the new minister of foreign affairs, was quite circumspect in ordering Danubian port captains to supervise carefully the movement of aliens and munitions so as to preserve neutrality.[63] Epureanu explained that "our foreign policy will be peaceful . . . with full respect for international treaties establishing the political conditions of Romania, [treaties] which assure its independence, which assure its neutrality." [64] By "independence" Epureanu undoubtedly meant autonomy in Romania's internal matters. The Treaty of Paris and the 1858 convention had, moreover, omitted any reference to Romania's "neutrality"; that is, Turkey's suzerainty and the powers' protection or guarantee had not specifically neutralized Romania. Epureanu's declaration provoked little response abroad, for the powers interpreted it as signifying no change in Romania's stance.

Bulgarian radicals on the left bank of the Danube posed the chief threat to Romania's neutrality. In the early 1870s, Karavelov, who had served about half a decade as chairman of the Bulgarian Philanthropic Society of Bucharest and edited the newspapers *Svoboda* and *Znanie* (Knowledge) (1875–76), inspired Bulgarian nationalists. Yet Turkish protests against his propaganda prompted the Catargiu ministry to deport him, despite the favor and encouragement he had met in Bucharest. [65] Leadership then passed to a fresh generation of activists, headed by Khristo Botev. Botev's primary focus was on Bulgaria. He and his associates in local committees in Brăila, Ploieşti, Galaţi, and Craiova proclaimed a Bulgarian rebellion in August 1875. [66] This move evoked few reverberations across the Danube; still, Botev, who now ran the Bulgarian Central Revolutionary Committee, continued to sow the seeds for conflict in his countrymen.

The eruption of insurgency in Bulgaria itself again incited the Bulgarian émigrés to overt measures. Botev led several hundred Bulgarians across the Danube on an Austro-Hungarian steamship, the *Radetzky*. The ship's captain, with a gun pointed at his head, had no choice but to comply with the Bulgarians' demands. Botev's band landed at a deserted spot between Lom and Rakhovo, unfurled a flag, sounded a trumpet, and yelled "Long live Bulgaria." [67] The revolt was, however, unsuccessful; Turkish *başıbozuks,* or irregular troops, suppressed the rebels in a bloodbath.

The *Radetzky* business had certainly violated Romania's neutrality. The minister of the interior, George Vernescu, therefore ordered prefects of police to accord only travelers with valid passports the right of traversing the Danube. Furthermore, baggage on trains was to be thoroughly searched; port captains were to be replaced if similar incidents occurred. [68] Kogălniceanu was nonetheless well disposed to the two thousand Bulgarians living in Romania. He found it difficult to "bear the cry of indignation and protest" against the Bulgarian "horrors." Romania appeared to be giving tacit support to "hideous crimes" through the silence imposed by neutrality. The time for passivity had, he thought, ended, for even the "army is rustling under the yoke of discipline, desiring to take part in the fight." [69] This was hardly a neutral attitude, and Kogălniceanu's colleagues would later repudiate him for it.

The Balkan Crisis became more complex with the outbreak of the Serbo-Turkish War in June 1876. The Serbs had, of course, a direct interest—ethnic, economic, and political—in the insurgents in neighboring Hercegovina and Bosnia. Serbs hoped not only for independence but for the creation of a large Serbian state. To achieve their goals, they needed weapons. Prince Milan (1868–89) purchased guns and swords in Germany and obtained transport for them by way of Russia.[70] Austria-Hungary's neutrality in the imbroglio barred the guns from going directly to Serbia. Would Romania assent to the passage of these weapons? Kogălniceanu sympathized with the Serbs yet reminded them that part of the Moldavian railroad was in the hands of an Austro-Hungarian company. The shipment of the arms would be manifest, and knowledge of that act would compromise Romania's own neutrality. Hence he refused. Still, as we have noted, Kogălniceanu had begun to change his view of neutrality and had allowed the recruitment of troops and the collection of money and goods that were destined for Serbia.[71]

Kogălniceanu nonetheless retained the pretense of neutrality in discussions about the Danube River. Romanians considered the Danube to be a possible avenue for Turkish operations against Serbia. Kogălniceanu accordingly petitioned the powers to recognize the neutrality of the Serbo-Romanian frontier, that is, the Danube between Negotin and Vîrciorova.[72] Ristić, Serbia's minister of foreign affairs, likewise favored neutralization but desired a channel for the import of guns.[73] While Romania had indeed prohibited the transport of weapons to Serbia over Romanian territory, Ristić still optimistically anticipated Romanian military cooperation against the Ottoman Empire. Although neutralization of the Danubian boundary would impede the movement of Russians and others who wished to join the Serbian cause, it would also legally shield Serbia from attacks by Turkish gunboats. A Romanian observation corps established camp at Gruia, opposite Negotin, to assure neutrality. Turkey's minister of foreign affairs, Savfet Paşa, agreed to keep warships away from this area so long as neutrality reigned. Neutrality meant that "no arms, munitions, objects of war, volunteers, [or] cattle" were to reach Serbia via the Romanian-Serbian border. Romania engaged, moreover, to protect and supply the Turkish garrison on the Danubian island of Ada Kale.[74]

To preserve Romania's neutrality, Vernescu next ordered his prefects to prevent the entry or exit of all travelers—with or without valid passports.[75]

He apparently concurred with Ion Brătianu, who feared that either the Russians or the Turks would invade Romania and that the country was in a "most difficult, most uncertain and . . . most dangerous position." [76] Notwithstanding Vernescu's instructions, Russian volunteers arrived in Serbia. Serbia also received—through Romania—supplies, doctors, and funds from Russia.[77] Kogălniceanu explained that neutrality obliged Romania to ban merely the transit of groups, not individuals.[78] Russian volunteers therefore reached Serbia via the neutralized Danubian frontier and fought with the Serbs in an unsuccessful campaign on the Timok River. Turkish enemies even used the Romanian Red Cross. Romania offered ambulances to both Serbs and Turks, yet only the Serbs accepted. The Ottoman Empire punctiliously regarded the Serbs as rebels and not belligerents. Turkey had balked at subscribing to the Geneva Convention of 1864 regarding ambulances; still, it tolerated Romania's ambulances. Savfet Paşa nevertheless later accused Romania of employing the Red Cross as a front for sending men and munitions to Serbia.[79]

Kogălniceanu's policy of neutrality was, as already mentioned, more on paper than in practice. He saw the Serbo-Turkish War as an opportunity to wrest major concessions from the Ottoman Empire, and so he formulated seven demands that reflected the ambitions of many Danubian Romanians. First, the Ottoman Empire was henceforth to convert the country's name from "United Principalities of Moldavia and Wallachia" to "Romania." Second, Romanian representatives were to be sanctioned as diplomats, not agents. Third, Romanians were to enjoy their own consular jurisdiction in Turkey. Fourth, Romanian territory was to be inviolable, and the Danubian islands were to be delimited. Fifth, covenants relating to commerce, extradition, post, and telegraph were to be concluded between Romania and Turkey. Sixth, Romanian passports were to be recognized, and Turkish officials were to eschew meddling in the affairs of Romanians abroad. Seventh, part of the Danube Delta was to be ceded to Romania, and the border on the southern, Sf. Gheorghe, branch was to be delimited.[80] Savfet Paşa rejected all of these calls.[81] Kogălniceanu omitted the word "independence," but Turkey's assent to his wants would have been tantamount to it. Vassal states lacked consular jurisdiction. The cession of land, however, had some precedents; Egypt and Serbia had both enlarged their dominions at Turkish expense during the nineteenth century. Kogălniceanu's desiderata would possibly have simply served as topics for negotiation had they not been published in Paris. He thought, though, that this "indiscretion" would give Europeans an opportunity to appreciate the "legitimacy and moderation" of Romania's claims.

Given the insurrection in the Ottoman Empire, substantial changes were imperative; if Romania's needs were ignored, it might abandon its neutrality.[82]

The powers reacted negatively to the "indiscretion," and Kogălniceanu's ministerial colleagues demurred at an agenda that endangered the country's neutrality. Consequently, Nicolae Ionescu replaced Kogălniceanu as minister of foreign affairs. Kogălniceanu would return to office, but only after Russia had promised military aid and Romanian statesmen had become convinced of the necessity to participate actively in the Balkan Crisis. A crown council reevaluated Romania's program. Epureanu declared that Kogălniceanu's statement had indeed violated Romania's neutrality; Ionescu reckoned that Kogălniceanu had behaved as a private individual, misrepresenting the cabinet's opinion. Kogălniceanu had undoubtedly obtained Carol's approval, for the prince recommended a posture of "benevolent neutrality." This benevolence implied a flexible attitude. The council agreed that the best path for the government to follow was that of continued neutrality.[83] Ionescu pledged that he would "religiously respect . . . absolute neutrality" and would persist in supervising the border.[84] Nonetheless, from 31 July to 11 September 1876, according to one Romanian estimate, 1,194 persons crossed the Danube into Serbia at Turnu Severin; of these, 1,130 held valid passports—mainly Russian ones—44 were with the Red Cross, and 20 were vagabonds deported from Danubian Romania.[85] Ionescu moreover reiterated several of Kogălniceanu's demands. He called for the demarcation of the Danubian boundary and for the signing of conventions of commerce, extradition, post, and telegraph with the Ottoman Empire; yet he disregarded consular jurisdiction. Still, the Romanian agent in Constantinople contemplated that the only allowance Turkey might make was to employ the appellation "Romania."[86]

Assurances of neutrality notwithstanding, Romania persevered in girding itself for war. The legislature allocated an extraordinary credit of 500,000 lei, from which 200,000 was designated for the training and maneuvers of permanent and territorial troops.[87] Nicolae Ionescu considered "we must be ready for any eventuality"; still, he also insisted that "our desire for peace is sincere," for Romania shunned any secret plan to invade Bulgaria.[88] Even after Serbia encountered defeat at Aleksinac and hostilities had ceased, Romania kept its military reserves under arms.[89] The legislature appropriated an additional four million lei to buy guns and munitions.[90] The same day that the chamber approved the military monies, the senate's president, Calinic, or Calinic Miclescu—the metropolitan-primate of Wallachia—observed that "neutrality is in the traditions of this land."[91] A few days later, the legislature allotted 961,000 lei to pay servicemen until the end of the year.[92] Would

Romania's military preparedness ensure the powers' respect of Romania's neutrality? Although Ionescu wanted an international guarantee of Romania's neutrality, the powers received this plea with deaf ears.[93]

During the Balkan Crisis, the powers worried that the collapse of the Ottoman Empire might spell far-ranging, dangerous complications involving the nationalities of Southeastern Europe and directly affecting the powers themselves. They at first adhered to a note of 30 December 1875 by Andrássy requesting Turkish reforms in Hercegovina and Bosnia. The insurgents wanted more; some were for union with Serbia, while others sought a collective warranty for their political security from the powers. As the crisis continued, the League of Three Emperors signed a memorandum in Berlin on 13 May 1876 calling for an armistice of two months, the resettlement of the rebels, and the concentration of Turkish forces in areas supervised by the powers. France agreed to the memo, but Great Britain now pursued a separate policy of supporting the Ottoman Empire. As the crisis turned into a Serbo-Turkish war, Russia and Austria-Hungary concurred in Reichstadt on 8 July 1876 that should Serbia and Montenegro be defeated, peace would be restored on the basis of the status quo ante bellum. If the Ottoman Empire fell, most of Bosnia and Hercegovina was to go to the Habsburg Empire, Bulgaria and Rumelia were to be autonomous or independent principalities, and Russia was to regain southern Bessarabia. Gorchakov thus renounced the idea of a large South Slavic state yet required the retrocession of Romania's portion of Bessarabia.

After the Serbo-Turkish War, the powers eventually convened a conference of ambassadors in Constantinople—which met from 11 December 1876 to 20 January 1877—to discuss reforms in the Ottoman Empire and the destiny of the defeated Serbs and Bulgarians. In preliminary talks before the sessions opened, the powers recognized that the time was unripe to divide Turkey. The immediate quest was to make peace and to institute improvements in Turkey's European regions. Danubian Romania's statesmen saw the conference as a vehicle for redefining their country's international position, and with that in mind, Dumitru Brătianu went to Constantinople to argue the Romanian case. Brătianu was to call for the "consecration of the political status of Romania by a special guarantee for its perpetual neutrality." In the event of war between Turkey and one of the powers, Romania would receive instructions from the other powers as to its "line of conduct" and an affirmation of its "rights, neutrality, and territorial integrity."[94] The powers, however, ignored Romania's demands and disregarded the Romanian question in Constantinople.

Andrássy supported Romania's policy of arming for defense even against the unlikely prospect of a Turkish attack. He suggested that if Russia invaded, Romania should declare that it yielded to a superior force; Romania's army ought to move away from advancing Russian troops, thereby preserving neutrality. If Romania remained neutral, Andrássy promised—despite the Reichstadt agreement, which foresaw southern Bessarabia going to Russia—to endeavor to maintain indivisibly Romania's territory.[95] Savfet Paşa also favored Romania's neutrality. The Turks viewed their vassal as a defensive buffer against Russia. Savfet was willing to deal on some Romanian claims, but not at the ambassadorial conference.[96]

Failure to win a hearing at the conference in Constantinople, plus Savfet Paşa's apparent willingness to discuss neutrality and some of Romania's requests, prompted Dumitru Brătianu to ask for new instructions.[97] Nicolae Ionescu empowered Brătianu to negotiate on the basis of Kogălniceanu's seven demands. Ionescu had earlier disavowed Kogălniceanu's points about consular jurisdiction and the possession of the Danube Delta. Now, however, Ionescu—while still disregarding consular jurisdiction—called for the cession of the delta to Romania. He insisted, moreover, that Romania's neutrality be guaranteed by a treaty.[98] Romanians had previously assumed that their neutrality came from the powers; now they wanted a special covenant confirming this situation. Brătianu was nevertheless loath to conclude a commercial convention with the Ottoman Empire. Romania's exporters and consumers had shelter from the relatively high Turkish tariff so long as Romania was part of Turkey. Romania's trade to the Ottoman Empire was about four times what Turkish trade was to Romania, and so a commercial accord might encumber Romanian trade.[99] One area of concord was that of neutrality. Savfet Paşa declared that the Turks would forbear crossing the Danube River in case of war.[100] Romania's neutrality would hence be safeguarded; and, more important for the Turks, a protective shield would be raised against a Russian offensive in Southeastern Europe. As to the Danube Delta, Brătianu gained the support of neither Savfet nor the representatives of the other powers. The latter were more concerned with other subjects. The British representative, Robert Arthur Cecil, Marquess of Salisbury, explained to Brătianu that the conference aimed at keeping the peace, not at debating Romania's needs.[101]

Full political independence appeared to be a long way off for Romania in 1876 and early 1877. The new Ottoman sultan, Abdul Hamid II (1876–1909), promulgated a constitution at the outset of the ambassadorial conference that enumerated his prerogatives. He invested the "chiefs of the privileged provinces, according to forms determined by the privileges granted them." Savfet Paşa remarked that this passage referred to the United Principalities of Moldavia and Wallachia, Serbia, and Egypt.[102] Romania strongly protested against this wording, and Prime Minister Ion Brătianu considered "null and void" any stipulation that listed Romania as one of the "provinces and possessions" of the Ottoman Empire.[103] Legislators in Bucharest asked the Turks to recognize Romania's ancient rights, which had been sanctioned by the 1858 Paris convention.[104] Supported by Britain, however, Savfet replied that the Turkish charter was not an "international act" and that Moldo-Wallachia remained an "integral part" of Turkey.[105] Andrássy backed Romania's objections, yet he thought that Savfet's rationale closed the incident.[106] Romania was obviously still within the Ottoman Empire, but the Turkish constitution had put the matter rather baldly by ignoring Romania's protection by the powers.

An assembly of Turkish notables in Constantinople on 18 January 1877 rejected the reforms prescribed by the powers. Soon thereafter the ambassadorial conference halted its work. The Turks had been emboldened by British advice and aid and therefore spurned the other powers' demands. Britain was certainly less concerned with the Balkan peoples than it was with preserving the Ottoman Empire as a buffer against Russian expansion. Russia, for its part, recognized a duty to the Orthodox Christian Slavs of Southeastern Europe; if the Ottoman Empire would not institute reforms, then Russia must intervene to secure the requisite changes. Russians also recalled their humiliation in the Crimean War, a memory that might be erased by a successful campaign against the Turks, but only if they could dodge the diplomatic isolation they had experienced in 1854–56. Russia required Austria-Hungary's cooperation or at least neutrality. On 15 January 1877, Russia and Austria concurred at Budapest to follow, in general, the terms of the Reichstadt agreement: in case of war, the Habsburg Empire would stay neutral, and no large state would be created in Turkish lands in Europe. An additional convention in Budapest on 18 March 1877 repeated these provisions. The failure of the ambassadorial conference in Constantinople and the making of Habsburg-Romanov covenants in Budapest brought Eastern Europe close to armed conflict.

Danubian Romanians worried also about the South Slavs. As we noted, Romania aided Bulgarians living in the country in the late 1860s and supported the Serbs during the Serbo-Turkish War. Romania eluded, however, overt hostilities. The accord with Serbia in 1868 remained a pious dream. In the mid-1870s, the Balkan Crisis appeared to offer Romania a chance to break its political bonds with the Ottoman Empire; yet by seizing this opportunity, the Romanian countryside might become a battlefield. Danubian Romania's military weakness dictated a posture of neutrality, especially since the powers resisted Romanian aspirations.

Notes

1. See Carol's notes, 14/26 November and 19/31 December 1866, in *Aus dem Leben König Karls von Rumänien*, 1:161, 168.

2. Leften S. Stavrianos, "Balkan Federation: A History of the Movement toward Balkan Unity in Modern Times," 95.

3. Bălăceanu (Athens) to Carol, 9 February 1867, no. 2, in AIC, CR, dosar 41/1866.

4. George to Carol, [May 1869], and Carol's reply, 3/15 June 1869, in *Charles Ier, Roi de Roumanie*, 1:511–12.

5. Ypsilantis (Bucharest) to Carol, 10/22 May 1869, in AIC, CR, dosar 25/1867.

6. See the draft in pencil by Carol(?), 6/18 June 1869, in AIC, CR, dosar 57/1869.

7. Ypsilantis's comments, no date, in AIC, CR, dosar 57/1869.

8. Notes by Dimitrie Sturdza and Alexandru Golescu, 19 November/1 December 1869, on Ypsilantis's project, in Fond Ion C. Brătianu, XXIII/2 (1869), BNR, SM.

9. Ypsilantis (Bucharest) to Carol, 26 November/6 December, Carol to Ypsilantis, 27 November/7 December, and Ypsilantis to Carol, 29 November/11 December 1869, in AIC, CR, dosar 25/1867.

10. See the Treaty of Cetinje, 23 September/5 October 1866, in Jakšić and Vučković, *Spoljna politika Srbije*, 486–89.

11. See the project of 5/17 April 1867, in Jakšić and Vučković, *Spoljna politika Srbije*, 505–6.

12. See the Treaty of Voeslau, 14/26 August 1867, in Jakšić and Vučković, *Spoljna politika Srbije*, 510–14.

13. Carol to Michael, 15/27 May 1866, in AIC, CR, dosar 33/1866.

14. Jakšić and Vučković, *Spoljna politika Srbije*, 236, 237, 239; see also Michael to Carol, 14/26 June 1866, in AIC, CR, dosar 33/1866.

15. Report by Ion A. Cantacuzino (Constantinople), 17 February 1867, in *Correspondance diplomatique roumaine sous le roi Charles Ier*, 15.

16. See Carol's toast at a dinner for Michael, 1/13 April 1867, in *Charles Ier, Roi de Roumanie*, 1:371; see also Carol's notes, 1/13 April 1867, in *Aus dem Leben König Karls von Rumänien*, 1:188.

17. Golescu to Ilija Garašanin, 24 June 1867, in Jakšić and Vučković, *Spoljna politika Srbije*, 408–9.

18. See the Treaty of Bucharest signed by Ionescu and Kosta Magazinović, 20 January 1868, in AIC, CR, dosar 33/1866.

19. Engelhardt (Belgrade) to Moustier (Paris), 1 March 1868, in Jakšić and Vučković, *Spoljna politika Srbije*, 410–11; see also articles 3, 6, 7, and 8 of an "apoc-

ryphal" Serbo-Romanian arrangement (Bucharest) [January 1868] that reached Constantinople (March 1868), in Édouard Engelhardt, "La confédération balcanique," 36–38.

20. Ionescu (Belgrade) to Nicolae Golescu, 17 September 1868, in AIC, CR, dosar 57/1868.

21. See article 11 of the Greco-Serbian Treaty of Voeslau, 14/26 August 1867, in Jakšić and Vučković, *Spoljna politika Srbije,* 512; see also article 9 of the Serbo-Romanian pact [January 1868], in Engelhardt, "La confédération balcanique," 38.

22. Report by Alexandru Golescu (Constantinople) to Bucharest, 24 January/4 February 1867, no. 1, in BAR, AP, LVII, Varia I.

23. Nicholas to Carol, 2/14 June 1867, in *Aus dem Leben König Karls von Rumänien,* 1:205.

24. See an undated project for a Montenegrin-Romanian pact, in AIC, CR, dosar 64/1867.

25. See Frederick Kellogg, "The Bulgarian Revolutionary Movement in Romania, 1867–1868."

26. Constantin N. Velichi, *La Roumanie et la mouvement révolutionnaire bulgare de libération nationale (1850–1878),* 39–54, 61, 71–73, 95–99; see also Zakhari Stoianov, *Chetite v Bŭlgariia na Filip Totia, Khadzhi Dimitra, i Stefan Karadzhata (1867–1868),* passim; Kukuri S. Liluashvili, *Natsional'no-osvoboditel'naia bor'ba bolgarskogo naroda protiv fanariotskogo iga i Rossiia,* 145–46. The Khitov raid was in April 1867, Totiu in May 1867, Dimitŭr and Karadzha in July 1868.

27. Stepan I. Sidel'nikov, *Bolgarskii revoliutsionnyi tsentral'nyi komitet (1868–1872 gg.),* 23–24; Aleksandŭr Burmov, *Bŭlgarski revoliutsionen tsentralen komitet (1868–1876),* 18.

28. See the Bulgarian-Romanian act (Bucharest), [May] 1867, in Bŭlgarska Akademiia na Naukite, *Dokumenti za bŭlgarskata istoriia,* 1:438–39; cf. Velichi, "Relaţiile romîno-turce în perioada februarie-iulie 1866," 851–58, 862–65. Also to be independent were Montenegro, Hercegovina, Epirus, and Albania. Velichi concludes that the disputed date of this undated pact was sometime in the second half of May 1866.

29. See the protocol of a Serbo-Bulgarian agreement (Bucharest), 5/17 April 1867, in Jakšić and Vučković, *Spoljna politika Srbije,* 505–6. One member of the Virtuous Company was a Romanian, Dimitrie Ghiculescu, of Bucharest.

30. See *Svoboda,* 1 June 1870; Liuben Karavelov, *Sŭbrani sŭchineniia,* 7:176–77; cf. Krumka Sharova, *Liuben Karavelov i bŭlgarskoto osvoboditelno dvizhenie, 1860–1867,* 334.

31. Dimitŭr Kosev, *Kŭm istoriiata na revoliutsionnoto dvizhenie v Bŭlgariia prez 1867–1871,* 13–14.

32. See the daily reports of the Bookman's Association (Brăila), 21, 26–30 September/3, 8–12 October 1869, in *Dokumenti za istoriiata na bŭlgarskoto knizhovno druzhestvo v Braila, 1868–1876,* 25–26, 31–37; Nikolai Zhechev, *Braila i bŭlgarskoto kulturno-natsionalno vŭzrazhdane,* 116–20; Mikhail Arnaudov, *Bŭlgarskoto knizhovno druzhestvo v Braila, 1869–1876,* 116–22.

33. Velichi, *La Roumanie et la mouvement révolutionnaire bulgare,* 92–94, 120–25; Kosev, *Kŭm istoriiata na revoliutsionnoto dvizhenie v Bŭlgariia,* 17–21.

34. Ali Paşa (Constantinople) to Carol (Bucharest), 18/30 April 1867, in Fond Dimitrie A. Sturdza, VII, no. 40, BAR, SM.

35. Constantin N. Velichi, "C. A. Rosetti şi 'Comunitatea Bulgară,'" 530; Traian Ionesku Nishkov, "Za otnoshenieto na rumŭnskata obshtestvenost kŭm bŭlgarskoto natsionalnoosvoboditelno dvizhenie prez 70-te godini na XIX v.," 1:384.

36. Offenberg to Brătianu, 5/17 July 1868, in *Charles Ier, Roi de Roumanie,* 1:438; Filip Stoianov-Simidov, *Prochutiia Filip Totiu Voivoda,* 2:501–2.

37. Ali Paşa to Carol, 9/21 July 1868, in *Charles Ier, Roi de Roumanie,* 1:438–39; Velichi, *La Roumanie et la mouvement révolutionnaire bulgare,* 88–91, 101–3.

38. Ali Paşa to Carol, 5/17 September 1868, in *Charles Ier, Roi de Roumanie,* 1:452–54; cf. Vladimir Diculescu, "Rumänien und die Frage der bulgarischen Freischaren (1866–1868)," 480.

39. Hermann von Thile [Berlin] to Uebel [Constantinople], 17 August 1868, memo by Heinrich Abeken (Berlin), 27 August 1868, and Abeken's dispatch to Bucharest, 1 September 1868, in *Die auswärtige Politik Preußens,* 9:146–47, 154–55.

40. Eberhard zu Solms-Sonnenwalde (Paris) to Bismarck (Berlin), 7 July 1868, in *Die auswärtige Politik Preußens,* 9:678–79; Solms to Bismarck, 31 July 1868, in ibid., 10:133–34.

41. Nishkov, "Za otnoshenieto na rumŭnskata obshtestvenost," 388–89.

42. Auswärtiges Amt (Vienna) to Eder (Bucharest), 7 August 1868, in HHS, PA—XXXVIII, Konsulate: Bukarest 1868, Karton 179.

43. John Green (Bucharest) to Stanley (Constantinople), 10 February 1868, no. 16, in PRO, FO, 78/2030.

44. Carol to Charles Anthony, 1/13 August 1868, in *Aus dem Leben König Karls von Rumänien,* 1:283–84.

45. Angelaki Savich, *Insurgenţii bulgari della 1868 sub commanda lui Hagi Dumitru şi Stefan Caradge,* 178–88; Stoianov, *Chetite v Bŭlgariia,* 2:486–87; Nishkov, "Za otnoshenieto na rumŭnskata obshtestvenost," 392–97; Albin de Vetsera (Constantinople) to Beust (Vienna), 5 July 1867, in *Dokumenti za bŭlgarskata istoriia,* 5:74.

46. Mikhail Arnaudov, *Liuben Karavelov: Zhivot, delo, epokha, 1834–1879,* 294.

47. Constantin Gane, *P. P. Carp şi locul său în istoria politică a ţării,* 1:119–20.

48. See Brătianu's speech in the chamber, 29 November/10 December 1868, in *Din scrierile şi cuvîntările lui Ion C. Brătianu,* vol. 1, pt. 1, 517.

49. Kosev, *Kŭm istoriiata na revoliutsionnoto dvizhenie v Bŭlgariia,* 32; Velichi, *La Roumanie et la mouvement révolutionnaire bulgare,* 111–13, 116–17. Dr. Ghiculescu was the defense attorney at the trial.

50. Werther (Vienna) to Thile (Berlin), 11 November 1868, no. 393, and Bismarck (Varzin) to Keyserling (Bucharest), 22 November 1868, in HAA, PS: Türkei, 24, vol. 38; Keyserling to Bismarck, 4 December 1868, no. 108, in ibid., vol. 39; cf. Bismarck via Thile/Robert von Keudell (Berlin) to Keyserling, 14 November 1868, and Bismarck (Varzin) to Keyserling, 22 November 1868, in *Bismarck: Die gesammelten Werke,* 6a:431, 445; see Carol's notes, 5/17 November and 16/28 November 1868, in *Aus dem Leben König Karls von Rumänien,* 1:303–4, 310.

51. See letters from Abdul Aziz and Ali Paşa to Carol that Carol received on 27 November/9 December 1868, in *Charles Ier, Roi de Roumanie,* 1:479.

52. Boerescu to Ion G. Ghica (Constantinople), 9/21 August 1875, in *Independenţa României: Documente,* 4:47–49. The Russophil diplomat Ion G. Ghica is not to be confused with the Turcophil statesman Ion Ghica.

53. See Boerescu's speech in the chamber of deputies, 25 November/7 December 1875, in *Documente privind istoria Romîniei: Războiul pentru independenţă,* vol. 1, pt. 2, 50.

54. Boerescu's circular, 4/16 February 1876, in *Correspondance diplomatique roumaine sous le roi Charles Ier,* 104–6.

55. Bălăceanu's circular, 23 March/4 April 1876, in *Charles Ier, Roi de Roumanie,* 2:14–16.

56. Some Romanian politicians resented the presence of Prussian officers in Romania's army; see Ion Popescu (Bucharest) to Babeş (Kolozsvár/Cluj), 18/30 January 1869, in Arhiva Vincenţiu Babeş, Institutul de Istorie—Cluj-Napoca; Vivian (Bucharest) to Derby (London), 17 February 1875, in PRO, FO, 78/2398; *La guerre d'Orient (1877–1878): Revue d'opérations militaires,* sections 22–25.

57. Florescu spoke in the chamber, 26 January/7 February 1876; the vote by the chamber was 58 to 16, 26 January/7 February, and the senate approval was 37 to 3, 31 January/12 February 1876; see *Documente privind istoria Romîniei: Războiul pentru independenţă,* vol. 1, pt. 2, 93, 114.

58. Speeches in the chamber by [George Brătianu and] Catargiu, 26 January/7 February 1876, in *Documente privind istoria Romîniei: Războiul pentru independenţă,* vol. 1, pt. 2, 87–88, 96; Pfuel (Bucharest) to Auswärtiges Amtes (Berlin), 4 January 1876, no. 3, in HAA, PS: Türkei, 24, vol. 24.

59. Catargiu's circular, 4/16 January 1876, in *Independenţa României,* 4:56.

60. Cornea's circular, 9/21 April 1876, in *Correspondance diplomatique roumaine sous le roi Charles Ier,* 115.

61. Florescu's order, 10/22 April 1876, in *Documente privind istoria Romîniei: Războiul pentru independenţă,* vol. 1, pt. 2, 141.

62. For the liberal's program, 2–4 June 1875, see *Ion C. Brătianu: Acte şi cuvîntări,* vol. 1, pt. 2, 488.

63. Kogălniceanu's circular, 29 April/11 May 1876, in *Mihail Kogălniceanu: Documente diplomatice,* 94.

64. The government's program, 28 April/10 May 1876, in *Independenţa României,* 1:1.

65. Stoian Zaimov, *Minaloto: Ocherki i spomeni,* 3:2–29.

66. Protocol of the Bulgarian Central Revolutionary Committee (Bucharest), 12/24 August 1875, in *Osvobozhdenie Bolgarii ot turetskogo iga: Dokumenty,* 1:70–71.

67. See Romanian documents of 18/30 May 1876 about the Bulgarian raid, in *Documente privind istoria Romîniei: Războiul pentru independenţă,* vol. 1, pt. 2, 158–61; Zinov'ev (Bucharest) to Nikolai K. Girs (St. Petersburg), 22 May/3 June 1876, in *Osvobozhdenie Bolgarii ot turetskogo iga,* 1:229–30. Botev had 400 napoleons, or 5000 Romanian lei, to support this expedition.

68. Kogălniceanu (Bucharest) to Vernescu (Bucharest), 22 May/3 June 1876, Vernescu to the prefect of Vlaşca, 20 May/1 June 1876, and Kogălniceanu to port captains, 22 May/3 June 1876, in *Documente privind istoria Romîniei: Războiul pentru independenţă*, vol. 1, pt. 2, 164, 166. See a letter from the Austro-Hungarian Danube Steamship Company to Kogălniceanu, 24 May/5 June 1876, in *Charles Ier, Roi de Roumanie*, 2:61–62; the company agreed to cooperate in restoring order by excluding Bulgarians, together with their arms and munitions, from its ships.

69. Kogălniceanu's circular, 20 July/1 August 1876, in *Documente privind istoria Romîniei: Războiul pentru independenţă*, vol. 1, pt. 2, 293–94.

70. Alexandru Sturdza (Belgrade) to Ministerul Afacerilor Străine (Ministry of Foreign Affairs) (Bucharest), 12/24 June 1876, in *Charles Ier, Roi de Roumanie*, 2:76–77. Serbia bought 120,000 rifles, 12 field guns, and 5,000 swords.

71. Kogălniceanu to Alexandru Sturdza, 14/26 June 1876, in *Documente privind istoria Romîniei: Războiul pentru independenţă*, vol. 1, pt. 2, 183–84; Kogălniceanu to Sturdza, 16/28 June 1876, in *Charles Ier, Roi de Roumanie*, 2:81.

72. Kogălniceanu to Ion G. Ghica (Constantinople), and Kogălniceanu's circular, 16/28 June 1876, in *Charles Ier, Roi de Roumanie*, 2:85–88. See also Radowitz's report of his discussion with Titu-Liviu Maiorescu (Berlin), 3 July 1876, in HAA, PS: Türkei, 24.

73. Milan A. Petronijević (Bucharest) to Kogălniceanu, 24 June/6 July 1876, in *Documente privind istoria Romîniei: Războiul pentru independenţă*, vol. 1, pt. 2, 238.

74. Savfet Paşa (Constantinople) to Ion G. Ghica, 26 June/8 July 1876, and Ghica to Savfet Paşa, 2/14 July 1876, in *Charles Ier, Roi de Roumanie*, 2:125–26; Ghica to Kogălniceanu, 3/15 July 1876, in *Documente privind istoria Romîniei: Războiul pentru independenţă*, vol. 1, pt. 2, 265–66; Kogălniceanu to the prefect of Turnu-Severin, 2/14 July 1876, in *Mihail Kogălniceanu: Documente diplomatice*, 126–27.

75. Vernescu's circular, 21 June/3 July 1876, in *Documente privind istoria Romîniei: Războiul pentru independenţă*, vol. 1, pt. 2, 217–18.

76. Brătianu to Pia Brătianu, 28 June/10 July 1876, in *Din corespondenţa familiei Ion C. Brătianu*, 1:160.

77. Dmitrii F. Stuart (Bucharest) to Gorchakov (St. Petersburg), 27 July/8 August 1876, and Stuart to Gorchakov, 29 July/10 August 1876, in *Rossiia i natsional'noosvoboditel'naia bor'ba na Balkanakh, 1875–1878*, 138–39; Stuart to Aleksandr I. Vasil'chikov (St. Petersburg), 10/22 September 1876, in *Osvobozhdenie Bolgarii ot turetskogo iga*, 1:389. Stuart received 3,000 rubles, or 9,690 francs, from the St. Petersburg Slavonic Benevolent Society.

78. Kogălniceanu's circular, 15/27 July 1876, in *Charles Ier, Roi de Roumanie*, 2:143.

79. Ion G. Ghica (Pera) to Ministerul Afacerilor Străine, 17/29 July 1876, in *Correspondance diplomatique roumaine sous le roi Charles Ier*, 156–57; Alexandru Sturdza (Semlin) to Ministerul Afacerilor Străine, 18/30 July 1876, in *Documente privind istoria Romîniei: Războiul pentru independenţă*, vol. 1, pt. 2, 288; Savfet Paşa to Cabuli Paşa (St. Petersburg), 17/29 August 1876, in *Charles Ier, Roi de Roumanie*, 2:156–57.

80. Kogălniceanu's circular, 16/28 June 1876, and Kogălniceanu to Savfet Paşa, 25 June/7 July 1876, no. 6555, in Dosar relativ la misiuni diplomatice: Causele isbucnirei resbelului româno-turc, AMAE(R), 88–91.

81. Ion G. Ghica to Kogălniceanu, 14/24 July 1876, in AMAE(R), 154–55; Ghica to Ministerul Afacerilor Străine, 17/29 July 1876, in *Documente privind istoria Romîniei: Războiul pentru independenţă,* vol. 1, pt. 2, 286.

82. Kogălniceanu's circular, 24 July/5 August 1876, in AMAE(R), 168.

83. Ionescu's circular, 26 July/7 August 1876, in AMAE(R), 208; Epureanu's declaration, 29 July/10 August 1876, in AMAE(R), 214; Alexandru D. Xenopol, *Resboaele d'intre Ruşi şi Turci şi inriurirea lor asupra ţerilor române,* 2:327–29.

84. Ministerul Afacerilor Străine to Ion G. Ghica, 4/16 August 1876, in *Correspondance diplomatique roumaine sous le roi Charles Ier,* 159.

85. Nicolae D. Popescu (chief archivist) to Ministerul Afacerilor Străine, 4/16 September 1876, in *Documente privind istoria Romîniei: Războiul pentru independenţă,* vol. 1, pt. 2, 343; Emil I. Ghica (St. Petersburg) to Ministerul Afacerilor Străine, September 1876, in *Correspondance diplomatique roumaine sous le roi Charles Ier,* 169. These figures included, by the end of September, approximately 225 Russian soldiers, of whom 45 were officers.

86. Ionescu to Ion G. Ghica, 3/15 September 1876, no. 9342, in AMAE(R), 172–77; Ghica to Ionescu, 13/25 September 1876, no. 196, in AMAE(R), 184–86.

87. See Carol's decree (Bucharest), 20 September/2 October 1876, and the council of ministers' authorization, 24 September/6 October 1876, in *Documente privind istoria Romîniei: Războiul pentru independenţă,* vol. 1, pt. 2, 362, 365. The 200,000 lei were divided as follows: regular infantry, 93,000; regular cavalry, 6,200; artillery, 12,400; engineers, 6,200; territorial infantry, 55,800; territorial cavalry, 26,400. An additional 20,000 lei went for arms and munitions.

88. Ionescu's circular, 25 September/7 October 1876, and Ionescu to Bălăceanu (Vienna), 28 September/10 October 1876, in *Documente privind istoria Romîniei: Războiul pentru independenţă,* vol. 1, pt. 2, 365, 366.

89. The chamber approved this measure for military preparations by a vote of 74 to 7 on 29 October/10 November 1876, while the senate favored it by 45 to 1 on 6/18 November 1876; see *Documente privind istoria Romîniei: Războiul pentru independenţă,* vol. 1, pt. 2, 426–36.

90. The chamber approved this step to purchase military supplies by 67 to 4 on 9/21 November 1876, and the senate concurred by 50 to 4 on 19 November/1 December 1876; see *Documente privind istoria Romîniei: Războiul pentru independenţă,* vol. 1, pt. 2, 444–45, 461–62.

91. Calinic's speech in the senate, 9/21 November 1876, in *Documente privind istoria Romîniei: Războiul pentru independenţă,* vol. 1, pt. 2, 446.

92. The chamber approved this expenditure by a vote of 61 to 3 on 25 November/7 December 1876; the law was then promulgated on 29 November/11 December 1876; see *Documente privind istoria Romîniei: Războiul pentru independenţă,* vol. 1, pt. 2, 468–70, 490–92.

93. Ionescu's speech in the chamber, 25 November/7 December 1876, in *Documente privind istoria Romîniei: Războiul pentru independenţă,* vol. 1, pt. 2, 471–76.

94. Brătianu's instructions, 26 November/8 December 1876, and his memo to the ambassadorial conference (Constantinople), 13/25 December 1876, in *Charles Ier, Roi de Roumanie*, 2:275–76, 398–99.

95. Andrássy (Vienna) to Carl Bosizio von Thurnberg (Bucharest), 5/17 December 1876, in HHS, PA—XXXVIII, Konsulate: Bukarest, Karton 211.

96. Ion G. Ghica (Constantinople) to Radu Ionescu (Bucharest), 13/25 December 1876, in *Independența României*, 4:170–72; cf. İbrahim Halil Sedes, *1875–1878 Osmanlı ordusu savaşları: 1877–1878 Osmanlı-Rus ve Roman savaşı*, 1:38.

97. Brătianu (Pera) to Nicolae Ionescu, 9/21 December 1876, in *Documente privind istoria Romîniei: Războiul pentru independență*, vol. 1, pt. 2, 513.

98. Ionescu to Brătianu (Constantinople), 10/22 December 1876, in *Independența României*, 4:168–70.

99. Brătianu (Constantinople) to Ionescu, 17/29 December 1876, in *Documente privind istoria Romîniei: Războiul pentru independență*, vol. 1, pt. 2, 529.

100. Brătianu (Constantinople) to Ionescu, 3/15 December 1876, in *Documente privind istoria Romîniei: Războiul pentru independență*, vol. 1, pt. 2, 500.

101. Salisbury (Pera) to Brătianu, 4/16 January 1877, in *Charles Ier, Roi de Roumanie*, 2:458.

102. See article 7 of the Turkish constitution, 11/23 December 1876, in *The Map of Europe by Treaty*, 4:2533; Ion G. Ghica (Pera) to Ministerul Afacerilor Străine, 20 December 1876/1 January 1877, in *Independența României*, 4:181.

103. Brătianu to Ion G. Ghica, 22 December 1876/3 January 1877, in *Independența României*, 1:20–21.

104. See the debates in the chamber, 22 December 1876/3 January 1877, and in the senate, 23 December 1876/4 January 1877, in *Charles Ier, Roi de Roumanie*, 2:424–27, 428–41. The chamber approved Romania's request by a vote of 79 to 0 with 9 abstentions, while the senate did so by 27 to 12.

105. Savfet Paşa to Ion G. Ghica, 27 December 1876/7 January 1877, in *Independența României*, 4:192.

106. Andrássy to Bosizio, 5/17 January 1877, in *Charles Ier, Roi de Roumanie*, 2:459–60.

Chapter Seven

A FOREIGN ALLIANCE

Romanian statesmen frequently sought the advice of the great powers during the Balkan Crisis. That counsel and Romania's military weakness dictated Bucharest's policy of neutrality. Many Danubian Romanians believed indeed that their goal of independence could be won solely with the powers' aid in a victorious war against the Turks.

The powers, however, no longer cooperated as they had immediately after the Crimean War. The alliance among Great Britain, France, and Italy had ceased to exist. France was shattered by its war with Germany, after which the French thought more about Alsace and Lorraine than about Southeastern Europe. The first business in France was to rebuild the country, and so French officials eschewed intervening actively in the Balkan Crisis. Following the unification in 1870, Italy's leaders concentrated on making their state viable and lasting. Italian irredentism might arouse Italians in Austria-Hungary's Trentino and Trieste and would indeed become a powerful force, but not in the 1870s, when bureaucrats in the Italian heartland were finishing the work of political consolidation. Thus Italy also shunned interceding directly in the Balkan Crisis. Only Britain, then, supported the Ottoman Empire. The British had an immediate interest in maintaining the status quo in Turkey, especially after their purchase of the Suez Canal shares in 1875. If Egypt were to declare its sovereignty and confiscate the canal, the Suez route to India plus Britain's heavy investment in the canal might be lost in Turkey's subsequent collapse. Another threat to India came from Russia's advance into Central Asia. The nominal British protectorate over Afghanistan dissolved because the Afghan emir, Shir Ali (1863–79), favored Russia. Hence Britain was pro-Turkish and anti-Russian during the 1870s.

Austria-Hungary, Russia, and, to a much lesser degree, Germany, were deeply concerned about the Balkan Crisis. As in Italy, so too in Germany the focus was on national consolidation. Germany needed peace to successfully complete its task of political unification. One consequence of that requisite was the formation of the Three Emperors' League in 1873. This was, to be sure, merely an informal dynastic association of Hohenzollerns, Habsburgs, and Romanovs; yet it was also a vehicle for consultation and cooperation.

Austria-Hungary also required peace. Conditions in the Habsburg Empire in the 1870s had changed dramatically from what they had been before 1866. After being defeated by Prussia at Königgrätz in 1866, the newly constituted Austria-Hungary, as per the Ausgleich of 1867, was occupied with the rise of Czech national sentiment; and Hungary became absorbed in the Magyarization of its minorities. The delicate balance between Hungary's nationalities would have been disrupted by a Habsburg annexation of Danubian Romania. Moreover, Hungary had no stake in encouraging Romanians in Transylvania and the Banat of Temesvár to look across the border for guidance from what could become an independent Romania. Austria-Hungary consequently advocated that Romania be neutral during the Balkan Crisis.[1] The Habsburg Empire would expand territorially in Bosnia and Hercegovina after an anti-Turkish revolt, but it lacked a militant foreign policy and was ill prepared for war. Austria-Hungary therefore remained neutral throughout the crisis.

Nor was Russia ready for war in 1875 and 1876. Russia's interest in the Balkan Peninsula was partly emotional. Many Russians identified with their fellow Orthodox Christians, the South Slavs. Russia's repression of the Slavic Poles in the nineteenth century may be explained by Polish revolutionary movements and by a basic distrust that Orthodox Russians had for Catholic Poles. But humanitarianism had become a potent force in the nineteenth century. It led to the abolition of slavery in the United States of America and of serfdom in Russia and to the assumption of Britain's "White Man's Burden" in India. Some Russians were eager to fulfill the humanitarian objective of breaking Turkey's grip on the South Slavs. Others went further, hoping to erect a new South Slavic state dependent on Russia. Russia also wanted to rectify its boundaries. From 1812 to 1856, Russia had held all of Bessarabia. One humiliating result of its debacle in the Crimean War was losing the southern portion of Bessarabia to Moldavia. Furthermore, some Russians dreamed of extending their empire's borders even farther —to the Bosporus and the Dardanelles—something opposed by Britain and Austria-Hungary. A Russian attack in the Balkans had to have Austria-Hungary's approval or at least forbearance so that Russia's western flank would not be threatened by a hostile army. The British had, as already noted, endeavored to protect the Ottoman Empire in case of a Russo-Turkish war; still, the absence of a strong ally primed for joint military action caused British statesmen to balk at joining Turkey, despite their desire to block Russia's advance in Southeastern Europe.

Danubian Romanians had several alternatives to a pact with Russia. They could remain aloof and rely on Austria-Hungary to protect them. But according to the 1877 Budapest conventions, the Habsburg Empire was to be noninvolved in case of a Russo-Turkish war. Vienna was unwilling to employ its resources in defending Romania's neutrality, notwithstanding its need for an autonomous or sovereign state on the lower Danube River that might prevent Russia's hegemony in the Balkans. Romanians also had the option of staying in the Ottoman Empire. Some Romanians indeed wished to retain their country's autonomy, for Russians were deemed to be a greater menace than Turks. Under Turkish suzerainty, Romania had its own constitution, conducted its own foreign policy, and raised its own army and taxes. Tribute to the Ottoman sultan was nonetheless the badge of vassalage, and Romanians had little likelihood of winning independence in league with their suzerain. A third possibility for Romania was to do nothing, that is, to join no power or powers and to await the outcome of an anticipated war. Few Romanians favored this policy, for it meant full reliance on the powers to determine Danubian Romania's future, perhaps without reference to its aspirations. Hence Romania's goals appeared obtainable primarily in cooperation and alliance with Russia.

Russians and Romanians lacked a formal covenant after 1711. The Danubian principalities of Moldavia and Wallachia had concluded agreements with Russia during the last half of the seventeenth century for joint efforts in the name of Christianity against Islam. The defeat of a Russo-Romanian army led by Peter the Great (1682–1725) spelled disaster. Romanians had obviously disregarded the Ottoman sultan's capitulation of 1512 for Moldavia, which stipulated their support of Turkey. The Turks consequently ended the era of native princes in Danubian Romania and inaugurated rule by Phanariots. For more than a century, Greeks from the Phanar district in Constantinople purchased the crowns of Moldavia and Wallachia. The Phanariots were chiefly interested in their own enrichment and discountenanced the overthrow of a setup from which they profited. Russo-Turkish wars were henceforth fought without the aid of the Danubian principalities. Even after the Greek revolution, the fall of the Phanariot regime in 1821, and the subsequent restoration of native princes in Moldavia and Wallachia, Russia eschewed negotiating diplomatically with Danubian Romania. Instead, after the Russo-Turkish War of 1828–29, Russia exercised a protectorate of its own over the principalities from 1829 to 1856. Its failure in the Crimean War and the ensuing Moldo-Wallachian unification under the powers' auspices, however, created a new situation. No longer might Russia ignore the possibility of military opposition by other powers when invading Romania. Russia could, of course, strike the Ottoman Empire in the Caucasus as, in fact, it would; yet a campaign in that mountainous region and in Anatolia would be long and costly. Less international prestige might be garnered there than on the Danube; the logical place for Russia to attack the Ottoman Empire was therefore in Southeastern Europe. With war seemingly in the offing in early 1877, some Romanian statesmen wanted an understanding with Russia in case diplomatic measures did not keep the peace.

Romanians both feared and favored an alliance with Russia. They worried that concerting with the Russians might result in the forfeiture of territory or even of autonomy. Moreover, few Danubian Romanians wished to return to the pre–Crimean War days of a Russian protectorate. As already noted, one of Russia's humiliations following the Crimean War had been the retrocession of southern Bessarabia to Moldavia. Romanians still considered all of Bessarabia to be part of Moldavia. Danubian Romania had already demonstrated a degree of sovereignty in making commercial conventions, and many Romanians thought that a political-military treaty with one of the powers would confirm their country's political independence. Romanian statesmen were fully aware of their inability to withstand an invasion by either Russia or Turkey. Hence Romania chose to deal with the probable victor: Russia. For Danubian Romanians in 1877, everything depended on what the Russians did.

St. Petersburg's constant aim was to preserve its league with Austria-Hungary and Germany, but its leaders differed on what to do with Romania. Russia's ambassador in Constantinople, Nikolai P. Ignat'ev, deemed that Russia ought to use Romania as a pawn during the Balkan Crisis so as to bring pressure on the Ottoman Empire to make reforms.[2] The assistant minister of foreign affairs, Nikolai K. Girs, believed that Romania should assume an "attitude of abstention" with merely moral support for Balkan Christians; for him, Romania should be a refuge for Bulgarians and a purchaser of military supplies for the insurgents.[3] In 1875 Alexander II and Gorchakov wanted to maintain the status quo in the Balkans; Russian volunteers nonetheless participated, as we have seen, with the Serbs in fighting the Turks.

Romania's neutrality posed problems for Russians wishing to aid the South Slav rebels. So, despite Russia's official stance, Gorchakov advised the Danubian Romanians to "close their eyes" to border infractions and to avoid favoring Muslims over Christians.[4] After the defeat of Serbia's army at Aleksinac in 1876, about 5,000 Russian volunteers left Serbia. Russian statesmen then asked what Romania would do if Russia itself intervened militarily in the Balkan Peninsula. Romania's minister of foreign affairs, Nicolae Ionescu, replied cautiously that he could not predict Bucharest's plans.[5]

Romania appeared to have an ambivalent policy of beginning talks with Russia while sending special envoys to various West European capitals. Not all Romanians desired a deal with Russia. Carp thought that Russia sought solely to ruin Romania; he would rather see his country ally with Austria-Hungary, the Ottoman Empire, and Great Britain.[6] The vice president of the senate, Ion Ghica, went to Vienna and London, and the prime minister, Ion Brătianu, visited the Habsburg Francis Joseph in Nagyszeben (Sibiu) in Transylvania. But the main bargaining was at Livadia, the Russian emperor's vacation residence in the Crimea. Members of the Romanian delegation included Brătianu and the minister of war, Gheorghe Slăniceanu; they saw, among others, Alexander II, Gorchakov, and Ignat'ev.[7] Alexander announced, according to Brătianu, that he had already resolved on hostilities with the Ottoman Empire, and so Russia needed an agreement with Romania for the passage of its troops. Brătianu inquired, "and in case we refuse?" to which Gorchakov responded, "you will be crushed."[8] Brătianu retorted that Russia could hardly begin a campaign to free Christians from Muslims by destroying a Christian army. At the same time, nonetheless, Brătianu acknowledged that Romania's forces should be prepared to serve as Russia's advance guard.[9] Gorchakov, for his part, temporized with the remark: "If it comes to war, we shall understand one another."[10] A key concern for Romanians was their state's territorial integrity. Brătianu expressed his fear that Russia wanted to regain southern Bessarabia; to this Gorchakov rejoined cryptically, "What an idea."[11] Aleksandr I. Nelidov, a career diplomat who was at first entrusted with parleys for a Russo-Romanian convention, later recalled that Brătianu knew that Russia's emperor coveted a retrocession of southern Bessarabia.[12] The chief issue was, however, the transit of Russian soldiers through Romania, not Romania's military cooperation or its land. Gorchakov favored a military pact without political ramifications, for Russia was still unready to recognize an independent Romania.[13]

Serbia's collapse, Russia's support of the Bulgarians, and the prospect of Russia's interference in the Balkan Peninsula sharpened Russia's focus on Romania. A Russian crown council at Livadia during October 1876 discussed alternatives to war against the Ottoman Empire. Alexander II listened to appeals for moderation from Reitern, his minister of finance, and his minister of war, Dmitrii A. Miliutin. More militant declarations sprang from Gorchakov and Ignat'ev. Russia's financial instability and military unpreparedness were arguments against a conflict; working for war were Russia's frustration at Serbia's defeat and Russia's historic role as protector of Orthodox Christians. Alexander decided to negotiate first. He hoped that by participating in a conference of ambassadors in Constantinople, Russia would acquire a European mandate for its unilateral military action. Still, if the conference did not support Russia's policy—including the creation of a Bulgarian state—then Russia should mobilize for war. Such a mustering of soldiers was not, of course, a proclamation of war; the army was only to deploy on the Turkish frontier during December 1876 and be set for as "rapid as possible" a campaign. To ensure the swift movement of Russian troops, a convention was to be concluded with Romania.[14]

Although Russia and Romania did not sign a military accord at Livadia, negotiations for one commenced. Russian experts studied Romanian railroads, ferries, and national credit. A member of the Russian general staff, Vasilii G. Zoltarev, inspected Romania's military preparations and offered advice.[15] Hence the Livadia talks provided a basis for a future Russo-Romanian entente and gave some Romanians added confidence that their political aspirations would be realized. Miliutin proceeded to draft plans that envisioned Romania's military cooperation.[16]

After the Romanian delegation returned from Livadia, Carol announced to the legislature: "Our relations with foreign states are the best. . . . all the guaranteeing powers encourage us to maintain our neutral attitude. . . . now perhaps the Ottoman Empire will be disposed to recognize the justice of our demands."[17] Since the Livadia discussions had been secret, the deputies were aware only of a formal exchange of greetings. Carol, of course, knew about the projected convention with Russia, and so his remark about Romania's "neutral attitude" was downright hypocritical. The deputies responded to Carol's speech by affirming "strict neutrality" as the policy that corresponded to the "desires of the whole country" and conformed to "our national interests."[18] Ion Brătianu, for his part, worried that Romania's politics had become "most entangled."[19] Neutrality was certainly incompatible with a Russo-Romanian military alliance.

Negotiations began in utmost secrecy between Ion Brătianu and Nelidov in Bucharest, without the cognizance even of Nicolae Ionescu. Miliutin encouraged the deliberations, yet Gorchakov showed little regard for Romanian affairs.[20] Still, Ignat'ev called on Brătianu to agree on "anticipated eventualities" and to "conclude a military convention," which had already been "accepted in principle by both sides" at Livadia.[21] Brătianu doubted the propriety of dealing with Nelidov, since the latter was unauthorized to make a treaty and had what Brătianu considered to be merely a letter of introduction from Ignat'ev. Brătianu nonetheless consented to discuss a draft pact, which would be signed immediately preceding the outbreak of war.[22]

The vital problem of Bessarabia arose during these deliberations. Nelidov had been enjoined from pledging that Russia would renounce southern Bessarabia after the war. He argued that the Russo-Romanian covenant should avoid any political flavor and should cover only the Russian army's presence in Danubian Romania. He promised nevertheless that Russia would protect Romania's security "if it should be menaced by the passage of Russian troops."[23] Regarding the probable loss of southern Bessarabia, Ion Brătianu remarked: "I understand this, I had the feeling at Livadia that this is a question of honor for the emperor. . . . [But] we shall seek compensation and I shall be able to prepare our public opinion." Nelidov responded that Russia could not dispose of regions it did not possess; to this, Brătianu replied rhetorically: "And if the war is disastrous, how will you defend us?"[24] The first sketch of the compact, according to the nineteenth-century historian Alexandru D. Xenopol, stipulated that Romania's wholeness would be maintained for the "duration of the war."[25] Brătianu opposed this clause, and it was replaced by a vague assurance that Russia would safeguard the "actual integrity" of the country.[26] Throughout the negotiations, Brătianu was reluctant to commit himself or his government to an agreement that contravened Romania's neutrality. Russia, too, was loath to compromise its position vis-à-vis the other powers. Hence Russia and Romania would await the outcome of the conference of ambassadors in Constantinople and the forging of a firm deal between Russia and Austria-Hungary before proceeding with their own treaty.

At the same time, talks toward another goal took place in Constantinople between an English expatriate, Stephen B. Lakeman, and Savfet Paşa. Lakeman had served in the Turkish army during the Crimean War and was dubbed Mazar Paşa. He had married a daughter of Slăniceanu. The so-called Mazar Paşa coalition had formed during 1875 in Lakeman's house in Bucharest to plan the ouster of the conservative Romanian cabinet. Ion Brătianu was a member of this coalition, but we do not know if Brătianu or Slăniceanu asked Lakeman to speak on behalf of the country. Lakeman apparently indicated Romania's willingness to resist militarily a Russian invasion if the Ottoman Empire would admit the name "Romania" for the "United

Principalities of Moldavia and Wallachia."[27] Lakeman expressed Romania's neutral policy and mentioned the increase in the size of its army; at the same time, he warned that Romania's soldiers would capitulate to a Russian onslaught. Thus Turkish aid was required. Negotiations for Turco-Romanian cooperation were to be conducted secretly in Bucharest because Ion G. Ghica, Romania's diplomatic agent in Constantinople, was pro-Russian.[28] A Romanian newspaper leaked a story about Lakeman's presence in Constantinople and about a solid "understanding" that had been reached with Savfet and the grand vezir, Midhat Paşa. This entente included the Ottoman Empire's recognition of Romanian passports, regulation of the frontier on Danubian islands, approval of Romania's claim to make commercial treaties, and dispatch of an envoy to Bucharest to represent the sultan.[29] Whatever was considered in Constantinople, the Turkish governor of Tulcea, Ali Bey, visited Bucharest to pledge thirty battalions of Ottoman troops for Romania's defense; moreover, Turkish arms and munitions would be available to the Romanians in case of war.[30] Owing to Romania's neutral posture, Brătianu recommended that Carol see neither Nelidov nor Ali Bey.[31] Savfet Paşa, for his part, indicated that Turkey's proper line of defense was the Danube River; the Ottoman army would therefore refrain from entering Romania to stop a Russian attack.[32] The Turks evidently expected that the Romanians would militarily assist them, or at least would act as a buffer by continued neutrality. The Romanians, however, used their parleys in Constantinople and with Ali Bey to mask their intention to treat with Russia.

In general, the powers favored Turco-Romanian military collaboration. Representatives of Britain, France, and Italy argued that Romania's only ally could be the Ottoman Empire.[33] Advice from Germany and Austria-Hungary differed. Bismarck suggested that a convention for the passage of Russian troops would be more desirable than no agreement at all; still, he cautioned that a contract signed before Russia was ready would offer the Turks a pretext to strike.[34] Andrássy counseled Romania to preserve its neutrality by drawing its army away from Russia's presumed path, thereby avoiding contact with Russian forces.[35] On the one hand, he gave the impression to Romanians that a Russo-Romanian covenant might be a reason for an Austro-Hungarian march into their country;[36] but on the other hand, the Habsburg Empire would denounce an anti-Russian challenge by Romania.[37] Austria-Hungary aimed first to secure Russia's support for Habsburg pretensions in Bosnia and Hercegovina before countenancing a Russo-Romanian alliance.

Russo-Romanian negotiations went on in Bucharest while the ambassadorial conference met in Constantinople.[38] Neither Ion Brătianu nor Gorchakov was willing, of course, to finish the business as long as the ambassadors were working for a peaceful solution to the Balkan Crisis.[39] Russia's military leaders, however, impatiently insisted on a firm deal with Romania. Miliutin feared that Brătianu's neutral attitude would damage, or at least retard, the discussions. He therefore advocated an immediate accord.[40] In Kishinev in northern Bessarabia, Grand Duke Nikolai Nikolaevich and the chief of the Russian general staff, Artur A. Nepokoichitskii, also apprehended danger in delay. By a draft provision, Carol was to ratify the treaty twenty-four hours before Russia's declaration of war. Nepokoichitskii assumed Carol's hesitation at this stipulation to signal a refusal to unite militarily with Russia unless forced to do so by a Turkish invasion of Romanian territory.[41] He nonetheless anticipated the involvement of Romanian troops with the Russian army during the war and even perceived the possibility of Carol's taking supreme command over the armies of both countries.[42] Brătianu indeed asked for 50,000 Peabody guns plus a loan of 20 million francs, some of which was for military readiness.[43] Nikolai Nikolaevich was apparently more skeptical than Nepokoichitskii concerning Romania's eventual participation, and he foresaw Carol repudiating battle.[44]

The evident difference of opinion between Nikolai Nikolaevich and Nepokoichitskii owed much to the dynastic nature of Russia's aims. Alexander II sought to regain the dynasty's honor by defeating the Turks—without outside aid—and by retaking southern Bessarabia. Nikolai shared Alexander's hopes in contrast to Nepokoichitskii's more pragmatic approach. Russians nevertheless agreed on strategy in Romania. Miliutin, Gorchakov, and Alexander II concurred on the necessity of occupying the ports and former fortresses of Galați, Brăila, and Ismail.[45] This meant Russian control of the most important harbors on the Danube, of southern Bessarabia, and of the eastern parts of Moldavia and Wallachia. Nikolai explained, however, that Russia envisioned no military conquest but wished only to defend Balkan Christians. Russia would respect Romania's "independence, authority, and welfare" by means of a practical entente of a "purely military" and non-political character.[46]

Carol had another idea. He wanted a "political" act to regulate Russo-Romanian relations that would be signed on the eve of hostilities.[47] Although Nikolai Nikolaevich favored a pact, he feared that its ratification immediately before the outbreak of war would render it worthless, for the Russian army would be obliged thereby to forage for food and supplies as if in enemy territory.[48] Romania would, to be sure, relinquish its neutrality if it concluded an anti-Turkish alliance with Russia. An accord, if made in principle before-hand, would assure Russia's troops a secure passage to the Danube. But what would Romania gain by assisting Russia? Ion Brătianu asked Russia to provision his country with money, guns, horses, and torpedoes.[49] Miliutin, in effect, consented to Brătianu's demands.[50] Carol, who hoped to see Ro-mania's independence won on the field of battle, promised the Russian army a "sympathetic and fraternal reception."[51] He was indeed disappointed, though, that Russia's plans excluded Romania's military participation; Ro-manian forces were even to forgo guarding the vital railway span across the Siret River at Barboşi—the only rail link between Moldavia and Wallachia.[52] For the time being, however, Russian troops continued to mobilize in north-ern Bessarabia, and Turkish soldiers concentrated on the Danube at Silistra and Vidin; Romania strengthened its defenses at Calafat on the Danube and at the Barboşi bridge.[53] The drift toward war persisted; yet in January 1877 neither Russia nor the Ottoman Empire had decided irrevocably on conflict. Hence a Russo-Romanian convention remained on hold.

Romania's repeated declarations of neutrality stemmed from its lack-ing a political or military covenant and from its being unsure of Russia's intentions. Romania's army was nonetheless partially mustered, and the leg-islature approved funds to pay for munitions from an Austro-Hungarian firm.[54] In Russia, Romania's neutrality was understood to be merely a "necessity of the moment."[55] Nicolae Ionescu, the apostle of neutrality, wishfully sug-gested that Russia craved peace and would eschew combat.[56] He had earlier indicated that Romania would not "cooperate actively" with Russia even if the latter received a European mandate for intervention.[57] Romanian popu-lar opinion, as expressed in newspapers and brochures, backed Ionescu's stand. The opposition journal *Timpul* reiterated Austria-Hungary's advice: in case of a Russian invasion, Romania's soldiers were to withdraw, protect Romania's soil, and await the outcome. The Turcophil Ion Ghica—not to be confused with the Russophil diplomat in Constantinople, Ion G. Ghica—anonymously published in February 1877 a pamphlet, *Uă cugetare politica* (A Political Thought), in which he argued for the maintenance of Romania's neutrality. Romania was to dissociate militarily from both Russia and the Ottoman Empire and was to yield to the entry of any foreign army. Constantin Rosetti rejected this view but recognized the impossibility of Romania's stopping the passage of Russian troops.[58]

Romania retained its neutrality until Russia intervened. Russia had pretexts for action because of the collapse of the conference of ambassadors in Constantinople and the Turks' reluctance to reform the Ottoman Empire in favor of the South Slavs. Yet Russia was unable, as we noted, to move unilaterally without the Habsburg Empire's promise to forgo a counterattack. Austria-Hungary and Russia had already agreed in Reichstadt on 8 July 1876 to maintain equilibrium in the Balkan Peninsula if the insurgents were defeated, and to adjust their boundaries at Turkey's expense if the Serbs were victorious. The Serbs were indeed vanquished, and now Russia no longer sought merely to keep the status quo. Russia thus concluded with Austria-Hungary the first Budapest Convention on 15 January 1877. By this accord, the Habsburg Empire was to remain neutral in the event of war and then to take the Turkish provinces of Bosnia and Hercegovina, but not the *sancak,* or provincial subdivision, of Yenipazar between Serbia and Montenegro. Russia was to enter Bulgaria and obtain southern Bessarabia; no large South Slavic state was to be set up in the Balkans; and Russia was to stay out of Serbia. Austro-Hungarian influence was, in effect, to predominate in Serbia, while Russia was to be confined to operations in Romania and Bulgaria.

Ignat'ev visited Paris and London in search of support for Russia's designs. The Russian ambassador in London, Pëtr A. Shuvalov, also negotiated with Derby, the British minister of foreign affairs, for what was known as the London Protocol of 31 March 1877. This document, to which the other powers adhered, formally recognized the Serbo-Turkish peace of 1 March; moreover, the Ottoman Empire was to dismantle its army and to institute governmental reforms. If the Turks refused, the powers would decide what would happen next. Derby recommended that Russia and Turkey restrain themselves. Shuvalov remarked that Russia would demobilize if peace were promptly made between the Ottoman Empire and Montenegro and if the Turks would deal directly on rectifications in St. Petersburg.[59] Savfet Paşa replied that he was willing to sign a compact with Montenegro and to treat with Russia but was not prepared to disarm. Only if Russia deactivated would the Ottoman Empire follow suit.[60] The London Protocol was thus a dud. The powers still differed on what specifically should be done if the Turks failed to reform. No Turkish-Montenegrin peace came to pass then, and neither Russia nor the Ottoman Empire demobilized. A Russo-Turkish war increasingly appeared inevitable.

A second Budapest convention between Austria-Hungary and Russia, on 18 March 1877, confirmed and refined the earlier Budapest accord.

Gorchakov subsequently called for an expeditious conclusion of a Russo-Romanian military pact. Details could be worked out later and at leisure.[61] He had evidently overcome his former reluctance to talk to Romania because he was unable to gain the Western powers' approval for unilateral Russian action in Southeastern Europe. Carol and Ion Brătianu now posed conditions. Payment for supplies consumed by the Russian army was to be in gold rather than in Russian paper currency; furthermore, the agreement was to be adopted by Romania's legislature on the first day of the war.[62] Alexander II noted that the fulfillment of these prerequisites would be "difficult," for "even we ourselves do not know" when the war will begin.[63] Russia rejected remuneration in coin instead of paper; to use gold would have considerably raised the cost of the Russian march through Romania. Brătianu also requested large-caliber guns and one thousand horses in return for lumber to build pontoon bridges across the Danube River. Miliutin had optimistically thought that the projected military convention provided for these things;[64] it just needed to be signed in order to cement Russo-Romanian relations.

Romanian statesmen continued to seek Austria-Hungary's advice as contacts with Russia became increasingly intimate. Some Danubian Romanians feared, as we noted, that their involvement with Russia would lead to Romania's absorption into the Russian Empire. Andrássy, who had inked the Budapest conventions with Gorchakov, conceded the passage of the Russian army through Romania, but he opposed a Russian occupation or annexation of Romania.[65] Andrássy's posture was mendacious, as he had already approved southern Bessarabia's reverting to Russia. Moreover, his apparent assurance was valueless for Romania because Austria-Hungary's own neutrality precluded intervention. Nicolae Ionescu resigned in protest against deeds that he felt compromised Romania's neutrality; he was replaced by Ion Cîmpineanu as interim minister of foreign affairs.[66] Cîmpineanu informed Andrássy that Romania would remain neutral yet would be compelled to bow to the overwhelming might of the Russian army. He furthermore considered that Vienna should help Bucharest by sending gunboats to safeguard Danubian commerce in Brăila and Galaţi.[67] Austria-Hungary, along with the other powers, had a seat on the European Danube Commission; still, the powers lacked an understanding on protecting Danubian trade. The Habsburg Empire would therefore have transgressed its neutrality in complying with Cîmpineanu's request. Without Austro-Hungarian aid on the Danube and with the "inevitable" and "imminent" outbreak of war, Cîmpineanu recognized Romania's need to regulate the traversing of Russian troops.

He hoped, however, to avoid any alliance or cooperation with either Russia or the Ottoman Empire.[68] But as Carol observed, "theoretical neutrality" was a stand already "long since abandoned."[69]

Russia meanwhile decided irrevocably on war. A council on 11 April 1877 established a timetable for operations. The Russian army was to be fully mobilized by 15 April, war was to be declared on 24 April, and on the same day southern Bessarabia and the Caucasus were to be invaded.[70] The Ottoman Empire had earlier mustered its army along the Danube; a large concentration of Turkish forces was at Vidin—the nearest Danubian fortress to the Serbian frontier.[71] The Turks undoubtedly anticipated that the Serbs would join the fray. Romania's soldiers were nonetheless more threatening to the Turks. Cîmpineanu assured the Ottoman Empire that Romania's army was prepared merely to "tranquillize spirits" and to halt the exodus of Danubian residents whose lives had been endangered by Turkish troops across the river.[72] Romania's defensive measures against the Ottoman Empire notwithstanding, Carol rejected Russia's invitation to participate directly with the Russian forces. He followed Austria-Hungary's recommendation in announcing that he would withdraw Romania's battalions into Oltenia.[73] Carol earnestly wanted to win glory on the battlefield and, by doing so, to achieve Romania's independence. Still missing, however, was the complete support of his cabinet for military action; moreover, he did not wish a subordinate role in the Russian high command.

A crown council met in Bucharest to discuss neutrality and what to do in case of a Russo-Turkish war. The government had hardly been aloof in negotiating a military treaty with Russia, but since those dealings were secret, Romanian leaders could retain an outward posture of noninvolvement. A majority in the crown council considered that the best course was to yield to overpowering might. Ion Ghica advised that Romania should bow to a Turkish attack; if the Turks destroyed Danubian towns, however, Romania should fight back. He advocated an impartial balance vis-à-vis both Russia and Turkey. Constantin Bosianu, a prominent jurist, understood Romania's neutrality as implying free and equal transit across the country for both Russia and Turkey. Epureanu, who had headed the Mazar Paşa coalition in 1876, wavered on fence-sitting and recognized the need to agree with Russia on the passage of its army; hence Romania required an alliance. Dimitrie Ghica, a conservative party chief, saw detachment as pointless and envisioned a European mandate going to Austria-Hungary to occupy Romania in order to prevent an invasion by either Russia or the Ottoman Empire. The diplomat Alexandru Golescu proposed that Romania safeguard itself with Turkish help; otherwise, he argued, Romania would forfeit the powers' collective guarantee of its privileges. If the powers refused to protect Romania, then conventions regulating troop travel ought to be made with both Russia and Turkey. Constantin Rosetti opposed Turkish soldiers entering Romania and supported a pact with Russia that would preserve Romania's territorial integrity. Kogălniceanu feared the loss of southern Bessarabia and the creation of a large Slavic state south of the Danube after a victorious Russian campaign. He felt that Romania would be hurt by associating with Russia; instead, aid should be sought from the Habsburg Empire to block Turkish incursions. For Kogălniceanu, Romania's first concerns were to defend its borders and to maintain its neutrality.[74] Cîmpineanu, for his part, thought an accord with Russia ought to cover purely administrative matters, but not cooperation.[75]

Obviously, the diversity of opinion of those present at the council made it impossible for any decision to be reached. They were undoubtedly motivated by national interests; still, the powers—and now especially Russia—dictated Romania's stance. The strongest champion of a Russo-Romanian covenant was Ion Brătianu. He apparently won Kogălniceanu to his side, and the latter replaced Cîmpineanu as minister of foreign affairs. Although Kogălniceanu notified Romanian diplomats that his appointment ensured a "prudent policy"—that is, neutrality within the limits of practicality—he signed a military convention with the Russian representative in Bucharest, Dmitrii F. Stuart. He did so, he said, to keep Romania from becoming a Russo-Turkish battleground.[76]

Kogălniceanu and Stuart really inked two conventions in Bucharest on 4/16 April 1877—one political and the other technical. The preamble to the political pact recognized a duty "to ameliorate the conditions" of Balkan Christians. Russia was "to respect the inviolability of the territory" of Romania, "to maintain and defend the actual integrity of Romania," and "to respect the political rights" of the Romanian state as to "internal laws and existing treaties." The Russian army, in return, was to have free passage across Danubian Romania and was to remunerate Bucharest for its needs.[77] The technical deal, which had been discussed by Ion Brătianu and Nelidov, covered details of troop transit. Russia obtained thereby the use of Romania's railroads, roads, rivers, post and telegraph systems, and supplies. The rail tariff was reduced by 40 percent, and a committee representing the railway companies, led by Romania's minister of public works and assisted by a Russian military attaché, was to direct rail traffic and improve the lines. A Romanian commissioner was assigned to Russian headquarters to procure munitions and to support the setting up of camps, hospitals, ambulance services, and pharmacies. Russian soldiers were to stay out of Bucharest; the sick and wounded were to be treated in Russian hospitals established along the army's route, but not in Bucharest or other large towns so as to obviate or at least mitigate Russia's influence in Romania's urban affairs. Romania was to help in building bridges and in recovering Russian deserters. The cost of transit was to be paid in French or Romanian currency or in short-term bonds, but not in gold or silver.[78] Despite this formal agreement, however, the signatories would be at odds over what constituted Romania's territorial integrity, the price of Russia's march through the land, and the acquisition of local supplies.[79] Points of friction emerge, to be sure, from contracts involving national interests. The Russo-Romanian accords nevertheless represented a distinct gain for Danubian Romania. Romanians, as we have seen, had been unable to ally themselves with any foreign power for well over one hundred years. The entente perforce ignored the issue of Romania's military action; still, it admitted Romania's importance to Russia's war effort and acknowledged Romania's prerogative to conclude political covenants.

Romania mobilized its permanent and territorial army along with its militia and city guards after making the conventions, before the outbreak of war.[80] Romanian statesmen nonetheless reasserted their country's neutrality and warned about the undesirable consequences of a conflict. Kogălniceanu feared that Russian troops, upon entering Romania, would create a "troublesome situation" before the Romanian legislature had approved the concord.[81] Romania would thereby become a theater for military operations; hence he reaffirmed Romania's neutrality.[82] Romanians had indeed cause for concern: Savfet Paşa had withdrawn his assurance that Turkish soldiers would eschew overrunning Romania.[83] Twenty to thirty thousand Turkish irregular troops, the *başıbozuks,* were ready, Kogălniceanu thought, to invade as soon as Russia crossed Romania's frontier. Although Savfet was unaware of the Russo-Romanian compacts and so lacked a concrete reason to suspect the Romanians of duplicity, he wished to disencumber the Turkish army of its restrictions if it defeated Russia's forces. To have clung to the Danube River as the perimeter of the Ottoman Empire's defense in Europe would have been to renounce pursuit after a Turkish victory.

Turkey's grand vezir, Edhem Paşa, advised Romania that the concentration of Russian troops on the border dictated that Bucharest should take "military measures in common" with Constantinople "to assure the defense" of Romania.[84] This counsel stemmed from Romania's obligations as a vassal and was in harmony with international accords. The 1856 Treaty of Paris and the 1858 Paris convention stipulated that Romania's army was to secure the country's interior and frontier, and that army was to take "extraordinary measures of defense" in concert with the Turks "to repel all foreign aggression." The Turks, however, were to refrain from intervening militarily in Romania without the prior approval of the powers.[85] Kogălniceanu therefore felt justified in replying that a "grave measure" of security required consideration by the Romanian legislature.[86] To the powers he equivocated that Romania had no alliance with Russia, yet his country would retain its "national administration" by regulating the passage of Russian troops in such a way as to preserve Romania's ancient rights and privileges.[87] The transit of these troops would, after all, be with the "more or less tacit" consent of the powers.[88] Moreover, Romania was set to rebuff a Turkish attack.[89] Kogălniceanu saw the imperative of yielding to possible Russian demands that transcended provisions in the Russo-Romanian covenants. This was a question of power and survival. He and his colleagues wanted to choose the most propitious moment to break with the Turks, and they hoped to gain the fruits of Russian military triumph.

Danubian Romanians turned to Russia for help in financing their country's protection. Kogălniceanu thought the "alpha and omega" of Russo-Romanian relations lay in obtaining a Russian loan of five million rubles.[90] Alexander II seemingly favored such a concession, and during the campaign, Romania got most of what it sought. Even before Russia's declaration of war, however, St. Petersburg provided Romania with 300,000 silver rubles, or 919,702 lei, to avert a fiscal crisis.[91] This money came from income on monastic lands in Russia's northern Bessarabia. In a sense, then, the Orthodox Christian church paid for the Christian crusade against the Muslims. Carol announced an additional extraordinary credit of more than one million lei for general supplies and the military payroll. The chamber of deputies approved this decree.[92] This subvention was apparently based on the Russian grant. Russia was certainly interested in a solvent neighbor, which would be prepared to aid the passage of Russian troops and be equipped to perform military service if need be.

War was impending. Still, Romania was unready. After the rupture of Russo-Turkish relations, Carol requested that Russia postpone hostilities for a few days. He and his ministers hoped that during such a delay Romania's legislature could discuss and endorse the Russo-Romanian conventions. Ion Brătianu nevertheless admitted that the Russian high command was unfettered by Romania's desires. Nikolai Nikolaevich, Miliutin, and Ignat'ev decided that the campaign must indeed proceed—without satisfying Romania's constitutional obligations.[93] Russia's declaration of war, issued by Alexander II on 24 April 1877, expressed concern for Christians in Bosnia, Hercegovina, and Bulgaria.[94] Nikolai reminded Romanians that Russia came as an old friend; its forces would pass rapidly and peacefully through the land and respect the laws, customs, and property of the people.[95] To the Russian army, Nikolai proclaimed the holy cause of the "tsar-liberator" who had no goal of conquest.[96] As Russian troops crossed the frontier into southern Bessarabia, a Romanian crown council resolved to obviate prejudicing future legislative deliberations by still maintaining neutrality. Prefects of police were instructed to ignore the transit of soldiers, yet they were, along with town mayors, to represent—at Russian headquarters—the interests of those residing in occupied areas. Persons living near the Danube were advised to move themselves and their possessions to the interior of the country to avoid the dangers of a Turkish attack.[97]

Clashes of opinion occurred almost immediately between Russian and Romanian leaders. Kogălniceanu discovered a "patent contradiction" in the conventions and Nikolai Nikolaevich's proclamation. The latter document mentioned nothing about Romania's "rights," nor did it "safeguard the dignity" of the country or the prince; rather, it appealed over the government to the people.[98] To salve Romania's injured pride, Alexander II sent the governor of Moscow, Vladimir A. Dolgorukov, to Bucharest to explain Russia's actions: Russian soldiers arrived as "sincere friends " of the Bulgarians because the Ottoman Empire had refused to conciliate. Romania could "count on the traditional interest" and "constant support" of Russia.[99] Nikolai wrote Carol that restraint had been impossible; "strategic necessities" dictated that the emperor—"forced by circumstances"—declare war and begin the offensive. He undertook to keep Carol informed of Russian troop movements and suggested a joint "understanding" about operations.[100] Carol responded that he grasped the plans and promised to defend the Barboși bridge between Galați and Brăila until Russians replaced his soldiers. After that, the Romanian army would divide: part of it would protect Bucharest on the Sabar-Argeș line, and the bulk of it—about nineteen thousand men—would remain encamped in Oltenia. Carol thought that by the time Nikolai received his letter, the compacts would have been adopted by the legislature, and so he wished him the "most glorious success" in fulfilling a "grand and noble mission."[101]

Edhem Pașa demanded Romania's cooperation after Russia's declaration of war.[102] Kogălniceanu disingenuously answered that Romania's neutrality might be changed only by the legislature, which was to meet in a day or so.[103] Sultan Abdul Hamid II condemned Russia for rupturing diplomatic relations and proclaiming war. He reminded the powers of his desire for peace and called for material assistance from them and for spiritual aid from the Prophet Mohammed. His soldiers would be victorious, as God's will was to be done.[104]

Hostilities opened when Russian troops entered the Turkish province of Armenia and the Turkish principality of Romania. Savfet Paşa then reassessed the situation, yet reconfirmed his view that the Ottoman Empire would eschew attacking open towns on the left bank of the Danube River; although he could not restrain the Turkish army, no aggressive action was contemplated against Romania.[105] The Turks held strongly fortified positions at Vidin, Ruse, and Silistra on the Danube; the Danube was still the Turks' first "line of defense."[106] The Turks hoped to stop the Russians there, and they anticipated that the powers would intervene to save the Ottoman Empire from territorial loss and political collapse. Turkey and Romania were still at peace, and therefore Romanian citizens continued to enjoy civil protection wherever they lived or traveled in Turkey.

Constantinople nonetheless broke telegraph communications to Bucharest.[107] The Turks were fully within their rights in doing so according to the international telegraph convention that both sides had signed. By this pact, each signatory had the prerogative of halting dispatches that endangered the state's security.[108] The rupture of Turco-Romanian telegraphic relations indicated how little the Ottoman Empire trusted Romania, which the Turks were now writing off as a possible ally against the Russians.

A joint session of the Romanian senate and chamber of deputies convened with a speech by Carol two days after the outbreak of war. Because no one had recognized the country's neutrality, the prince pointed out, Romania must assure "at all costs and at any sacrifice" that it would avoid becoming a battlefield, that Romanians would escape being "massacred," and that their wealth and property would elude destruction. Since the powers had tacitly acquiesced to the entry of Russian troops, Carol requested that the legislature give his government the "necessary means" to "defend the rights and interests" of the land. From the moment he had arrived in Bucharest, Carol had contemplated the "revival of Romania, the fulfillment of its mission at the mouths of the Danube, and above all the preservation of its rights ab antiquo."[109] This "revival" and "mission" were vague expressions of national policy. Danubian Romanians had already experienced a cultural and political resurgence, but their calling focused on national survival and independence, not on leading Christian Slavs of Southeastern Europe against Muslim Turks. The Russo-Romanian conventions would nevertheless provide a basis for riding out immediate adversity and achieving full sovereignty.

Opposition legislators expressed many fears that Romanians had about dealing with Russians. The publicist Nicolae Blaremberg characterized the conventions as a grave diggers' program.[110] He would rather submit his country to fire and ruin than to accept Russia's sympathy and to divorce Turkey. Would the Russo-Romanian compacts nullify the powers' collective guarantee? Would Danubian Romania revert to being a Russian protectorate? Blaremberg hoped his country would heed international treaties and forgo participating militarily with Russia south of the Danube. Other legislators, such as Sturdza and Nicolae Ionescu, agreed with Blaremberg in wishing to hold fast to the powers' surety. Epureanu also objected to the pacts but thought that Russia would shy away from annexing Romania, for Austria-Hungary would block such a step.[111] Vasile Boerescu asked for a vote on non-involvement before addressing the covenants: ". . . everyone is for neutrality, all classes of society—merchants, industrialists, poor and rich landholders, everyone is for neutrality."[112] Carp argued that a ballot on neutrality at the point of 300,000 Russian bayonets would be a "stillborn child." He saw an obvious dichotomy between "strictest neutrality" and unilateral Russian pledges, which would lead to an "abyss between crown and country." And he underscored the "enormous sacrifice" that the conventions entailed, along with their lack of "material or moral utility." Romania was "neither rich enough nor happy enough" to forfeit the powers' safeguard.[113] Nevertheless, the conservative newspaper *Timpul* labeled as "unpatriotic and inappropriate" any difficulties its readers might make for the government, which had been "entrusted with the fate of the country."[114]

Cabinet members, as expected, supported the conventions. Kogălniceanu noted that these documents ensured the territorial status quo; the country's "integrity"—with its rights, customs, and frontier—would be preserved. Romania needed the pacts, he claimed, to avert a Turkish invasion.[115] Ion Brătianu reminded the legislators that the war was between Russia and the Ottoman Empire, completely excluding Romania. He had worked to maintain neutrality but had learned from the powers that this policy diverged from reality. Had he continued to assert neutrality in the face of the Russian advance, he would have become a ridiculous "Don Quixote of Turkey." Brătianu called on fellow Romanians for "devotion, prudence, and courage"; and he assured them that the accords protected Romania's political privileges, institutions, and wholeness. The engagements had, after all, been approved by Alexander II in a "solemn act."[116] Brătianu explained moreover that the government had taken emergency measures in establishing a fund to finance the mobilization of the army and in requisitioning war materials—which had indeed transgressed the constitutional prerogatives of the executive branch, but the senate voted to absolve the administration in view of the crisis.[117]

Two days after debate began on the conventions—and four days after the outbreak of hostilities—the chamber adopted them by a margin of 79 to 25. One day later, the senate approved them by a vote of 41 to 10. A few days thereafter, Carol endorsed them. Ratifications were exchanged in Bucharest a month after Russia's declaration of war and the entry of Russian troops into Romania.[118]

Austria-Hungary had been unready and disinterested in intervening militarily to prevent a Russian or a Turkish occupation of Romania. Danubian Romanians might forfeit their national aspirations in league with the suzerain Ottoman Empire, especially if the Turks were defeated by the Russians. On the other hand, Romanians might gain more in a future peace settlement by abetting rather than hindering the Russians. Perhaps the Russo-Romanian alliance would indeed end the powers' collective guarantee that Romania had enjoyed since 1856. Be that as it may, many Danubian Romanians thought that the outlook was auspicious. Romania's economic sovereignty, as manifested earlier in commercial agreements with Austria-Hungary and Russia, might now be expanded to political independence.

Notes

1. Vasile Boerescu's report on an interview with Andrássy shortly after the accord between Austria-Hungary and Russia leading to the Three Emperors' League, 13/25 June 1873, in Arhiva Vasile Boerescu, CXXVII/3, BNR, SM.

2. The Romanian diplomatic agent, Ion G. Ghica, told Carol, 7/19 December 1875, about a conversation with Ignat'ev in Constantinople; see *Aus dem Leben König Karls von Rumänien*, 2:483.

3. Emil Ghica (St Petersburg) to Ministerul Afacerilor Străine, 12/24 May 1876), in *Charles Ier, Roi de Roumanie*, 2:44.

4. Ion Cantacuzino (St. Petersburg) to Ministerul Afacerilor Străine, 16/28 August 1876, in *Documente privind istoria Romîniei: Războiul pentru independență*, vol. 1, pt. 2, 323.

5. Emil Ghica (St. Petersburg) to Ministerul Afacerilor Străine, 16/28 September 1876, and Ionescu (Bucharest) to Ghica, 19 September/1 October 1876, in *Documente privind istoria Romîniei: Războiul pentru independență*, vol. 1, pt. 2, 359, 361.

6. Carp (Iaşi) to Titu-Liviu Maiorescu, 9/21 October 1876, in Fond Petre Carp, S18(29)/XII, no. 3289, BAR, SC; Carp to Maiorescu, 11/23 November 1876, in ibid., S18(31)/XII, no. 3291.

7. Nicolae Ionescu's circular, 24 August/5 September 1876, in *Documente privind istoria Romîniei: Războiul pentru independenţă,* vol. 1, pt. 2, 331.

8. Xenopol, *Resboaele d'intre Ruşi şi Turci,* 2:329–30.

9. See Dmitrii A. Miliutin's notes (Livadia), 29 September/11 October 1876, in *Dnevnik D. A. Miliutina,* vol. 2 (1876–77), 92.

10. See Carol's notes on a conversation with Brătianu, 4/16 October 1876, in *Aus dem Leben König Karls von Rumänien,* 3:63.

11. Xenopol, *Resboaele d'intre Ruşi şi Turci,* 2:331; Brătianu's speeches in the senate, 13/25 February and 28 September/10 November 1878, in *Ion C. Brătianu: Acte şi cuvântări,* 3:192, 4:104.

12. Alexandre de Nelidow, "Souvenirs d'avant et d'après la guerre de 1877–1878," 245.

13. See Carol's notes on a conversation with Brătianu, 4/16 October 1876, in *Aus dem Leben König Karls von Rumänien,* 3:62–63.

14. See Miliutin's notes (Livadia), 4/16 October 1876, in *Dnevnik D. A. Miliutina,* 2:93–95.

15. Ignat'ev (Buyüdéré) to Ion Brătianu, 17/29 October 1876, in Fond Ion C. Brătianu LVI/1a, BNR, SM; Feodor L. Geiden (St. Petersburg) to Ignat'ev, 7/19 October 1876, in *Osvobozhdenie Bolgarii ot turetskogo iga,* vol. 1 (1875–77), 443.

16. Miliutin to Geiden, 5/17 October 1876, in *Osvobozhdenie Bolgarii ot turetskogo iga,* 1:439.

17. Carol's speech opening the Romanian legislature, 21 October/2 November 1876, in *Documente privind istoria Romîniei: Războiul pentru independenţă,* vol. 1, pt. 2, 394.

18. The chamber of deputies replied to Carol on 1/13 November 1876; see *Documente privind istoria Romîniei: Războiul pentru independenţă,* vol. 1, pt. 2, 411.

19. Brătianu (Bucharest) to Pia Brătianu (Florica), 22 October/3 November 1876, in *Din corespondenţă familiei Ion C. Brătianu,* 1:160–61.

20. See Miliutin's notes (Chetnerg), 21 October/2 November 1876, in *Dnevnik D. A. Miliutina,* 2:104.

21. Ignat'ev (Pera) to Brătianu, 5/17 November 1876, in Fond Ion C. Brătianu LVI/1a, BNR, SM.

22. Nelidow, "Souvenirs d'avant et d'après la guerre," 249.

23. Nelidow, "Souvenirs d'avant et d'après la guerre," 250.

24. Nelidow, "Souvenirs d'avant et d'après la guerre," 250–51.

25. Xenopol, *Resboaele d'intre Ruşi şi Turci,* 2:332; cf. Nelidow, "Souvenirs d'avant et d'après la guerre," 253–54.

26. Iorga, *Istoria Românilor,* 10:168.

27. Ion G. Ghica (Pera) to Nicolae Ionescu (Bucureşti), 30 October/11 November 1876, no. 463, in Fond Războiul pentru independenţă, 21:260, AMAE(R).

28. Sedes, *1875–1878 Osmanlı ordusu savaşları: 1877–1878 Osmanlı-Rus ve Roman savaşı,* 1:38.

29. *Pressa,* 29 September 1877 [1876], cited in Iorga, *Istoria Românilor,* 10:169–70.

30. Sedes, *1875–1878 Osmanlı ordusu savaşları: 1877–1878 Osmanlı-Rus ve Roman savaşı,* 1:37–38; cf. Iorga, *Istoria Românilor,* 10:170.

31. See Carol's notes, 16/28 November 1876, in *Aus dem Leben König Karls von Rumänien,* 3:76.

32. Ghica (Pera) to Ministerul Afacerilor Străine, 7/19 November 1876, in *Documente privind istoria Romîniei: Războiul pentru independenţă,* vol. 1, pt. 2, 440.

33. Ion Ghica (Paris) to Ministerul Afacerilor Străine, 20 November/2 December 1876, in *Documente privind istoria Romîniei: Războiul pentru independenţă,* vol. 1, pt. 2, 462–63.

34. Bismarck (Berlin) to Alvensleben (Bucharest), 28 December 1876, no. 19, in HAA, PS: Türkei, 24, vol. 55.

35. Andrássy to Bosizio (Bucharest), 17 December 1876, in HHS, PA—XXXVIII, Konsulate: Bukarest, Karton 211.

36. Alvensleben to Bülow (Berlin), 11 January 1877, no. 6, in HAA, PS: Türkei, 24, vol. 55.

37. Andrássy to Bosizio, 21 February 1877, in HHS, PA—XXXVIII, Konsulate: Bukarest, Karton 217.

38. See Carol's notes, 12/24 December 1876, in *Aus dem Leben König Karls von Rumänien,* 3:85; Stuart (Bucharest) to Gorchakov, 16/28 December 1876, in *Osvobozhdenie Bolgarii ot turetskogo iga,* 1:567.

39. Stuart to Gorchakov, 16/28 December 1876, in *Osvobozhdenie Bolgarii ot turetskogo iga,* 1:567; Nelidow, "Souvenirs d'avant et d'après la guerre," 253.

40. See Miliutin's notes (St. Petersburg), 16/28 November, 20 November/2 December, and 23 November/5 December 1876, in *Dnevnik D. A. Miliutina,* 2:112, 113, 114.

41. Nepokoichitskii (Kishinev) to Miliutin, 23 December 1876/4 January 1877, in *Osvobozhdenie Bolgarii ot turetskogo iga,* 1:571; see also Miliutin's notes (St. Petersburg), 14/26 December 1876, in *Dnevnik D. A. Miliutina,* 2:123.

42. See Nepokoichitskii's communiqué (Kishinev), 23 December 1876/4 January 1877, in *Documente privind istoria Romîniei: Războiul pentru independenţă,* vol. 1, pt. 2, 542–43.

43. Stuart to Girs, 6/18 December 1876, in *Rossiia i natsional'no-osvoboditel'naia bor'ba na Balkanakh,* 206.

44. Nikolai (Kishinev) to Alexander II, 26 December 1876/7 January 1877, in *Documente privind istoria Romîniei: Războiul pentru independenţă,* vol. 1, pt. 2, 548.

45. See Miliutin's notes (St. Petersburg), 2/14 January 1877, in *Dnevnik D. A. Miliutina,* 2:129.

46. Nikolai (Kishinev) to Carol, 12/24 January 1877, in *Independenţa României,* 1:27–28.

47. Carol to Nikolai Nikolaevich, 21 January/2 February 1877, in *Charles Ier, Roi de Roumanie,* 2:490–91.

48. Nikolai to Alexander II, 28 December 1876/9 January 1877, in *Documente privind istoria Romîniei: Războiul pentru independenţă,* vol. 1, pt. 2, 548.

49. Nepokoichitskii (Kishinev) to Miliutin, 7/19 and 8/20 January 1877, in *Rossiia i natsional'no-osvoboditel'naia bor'ba na Balkanakh,* 216, 217; see Miliutin's notes (St. Petersburg), 6/18 January 1877, in *Dnevnik D. A. Miliutina,* 2:132.

50. Miliutin to Nepokoichitskii, 8 January 1877, in *Rossiia i natsional'no-osvoboditel'naia bor'ba na Balkanakh,* 217.

51. Carol to Nikolai, 21 January/2 February 1877, in Fond Ion C. Brătianu, LIX/6, BNR, SM.

52. Alvensleben to Bülow, 11 January 1877, no. 6, in HAA, PS: Türkei, 24, vol. 55.

53. See a telegram (St. Petersburg), 3 December 1876, and a Romanian administrative report, 18 January 1877, in *Correspondance diplomatique roumaine sous le roi Charles Ier,* 176, 180–81.

54. Slăniceanu (Bucharest) to Nicolae Ionescu, 26 January/7 February 1877, Ionescu to Bălăceanu (Vienna), 5/17 February 1877, and Bălăceanu to Ionescu, 11/23 March 1877, in *Documente privind istoria Romîniei: Războiul pentru independenţă,* 2:43–44, 54, 78–79. Two hundred guns, 500 bayonets, and 500,000 cartridges were to come from Josef Pumerer of Passau.

55. Emil Ghica (St. Petersburg) to Ministerul Afacerilor Străine, 3/15 November 1876, in *Documente privind istoria Romîniei: Războiul pentru independenţă,* vol. 1, pt. 2, 419.

56. Ionescu to Bălăceanu, 15/27 February 1877, in *Correspondance diplomatique roumaine sous le roi Charles Ier,* 182.

57. Alvensleben to Bülow, 4 November 1876, no. 163, in HAA, PS: Türkei, 24, vol. 55.

58. Maiorescu, *Istoria contimporană a României,* 113–14; see notes by an anonymous editor, 12/24, 15/27, and 17/29 February 1877, in *Ion C. Brătianu: Discursuri, scrieri, acte şi documente,* vol. 2, pt. 2, 461, 464, 469.

59. Emil Ghica (St. Petersburg) to Ministerul Afacerilor Străine, 18/30 March 1877, in *Correspondance diplomatique roumaine sous le roi Charles Ier,* 186.

60. Savfet Paşa's circular, 28 March/9 April 1877, in *Correspondance diplomatique roumaine sous le roi Charles Ier,* 193–94.

61. See a summary of Gorchakov to Stuart, 14/29 March 1877, in *Osvobozhdenie Bolgarii ot turetskogo iga,* 1:629.

62. Stuart to Gorchakov, 18/30 March 1877, in *Osvobozhdenie Bolgarii ot turetskogo iga,* 1:623.

63. See Alexander II's marginal note on Stuart's report to Gorchakov, 18/30 March 1877, in *Osvobozhdenie Bolgarii ot turetskogo iga,* 1:623.

64. Nepokoichitskii to Miliutin, 25 March/6 April 1877, and Miliutin to Nepokoichitskii, 31 March/12 April 1877, in *Osvobozhdenie Bolgarii ot turetskogo iga,* 1:626–27, 629.

65. See notes by an anonymous editor, 20 March/1 April 1877, and Bălăceanu to Ion Brătianu, 29 March/10 April 1877, in *Ion C. Brătianu: Discursuri, scrieri, acte şi documente,* vol. 2, pt. 2, 558, 567.

66. Carol to Charles Anthony, 28 March/9 April 1877, in *Aus dem Leben König Karls von Rumänien,* 3:115.

67. Cîmpineanu (Bucharest) to Bălăceanu, 29 March/10 April 1877, in *Ion C. Brătianu: Discursuri, scrieri, acte şi documente*, vol. 2, pt. 2, 566.

68. Cîmpineanu's circular, 1/13 April 1877, in *Correspondance diplomatique roumaine sous le roi Charles Ier*, 187.

69. Carol to Charles Anthony, 28 March/9 April 1877, in *Aus dem Leben König Karls von Rumänien*, 3:112.

70. See Miliutin's notes (St. Petersburg), 30 March/11 April 1877, in *Dnevnik D. A. Miliutina*, 2:153.

71. See notes by an anonymous editor, 15/27 and 17/29 March 1877, in *Ion C. Brătianu: Discursuri, scrieri, acte şi documente*, vol. 2, pt. 2, 537, 548.

72. Cîmpineanu to Grigore Ghica (Constantinople), 2/14 April 1877, in *Corespondenţa generalului Iancu Ghica: 2 aprilie 1877–8 aprilie 1878*, 27.

73. See Carol's notes on a conversation with Nikolai Nikolaevich's adjutant, Georgii I. Bobrikov, 2/14 April 1877, in *Aus dem Leben König Karls von Rumänien*, 3:117.

74. See extracts from the crown council's proceedings, 1/13 April 1877, in *Ion C. Brătianu: Discursuri, scrieri, acte şi documente*, vol. 2, pt. 2, 569–71.

75. Cîmpineanu to Vienna [Bălăceanu], 1/13 April 1877, in *Charles Ier, Roi de Roumanie*, 2:545–46.

76. Kogălniceanu's circular, 4/16 April 1877, in *Correspondance diplomatique roumaine sous le roi Charles Ier*, 192; for the Russo-Romanian conventions, 4/16 April 1877, see *Charles Ier, Roi de Roumanie*, 2:550–58. Alexandru Cernat became minister of war, and Ion G. Ghica went on an "extraordinary mission" to report Romanian interests to Alexander II; Kogălniceanu to Gorchakov, 4/16 April 1877, in *Documente privind istoria Romîniei: Războiul pentru independenţă*, 2:108.

77. Russo-Romanian political convention, 4/16 April 1877, in *Charles Ier, Roi de Roumanie*, 2:550–51.

78. Russo-Romanian technical convention, 4/16 April 1877, in *Charles Ier, Roi de Roumanie*, 2:551–58.

79. Georgii I. Bobrikov, "V Rumynii pered voinoi 1877 g.," 292.

80. Carol's decree, 6/18 April 1877, in *Războiul pentru independenţă naţională, 1877–1878: Documente militare*, 105–6.

81. Kogălniceanu to Ion G. Ghica (Kishinev), 11/23 April 1877, in *Independenţa României*, 4:231.

82. Kogălniceanu's circular, 5/17 April 1877, in *Independenţa României*, 4:221–22.

83. Savfet Paşa to Mussurus Paşa (London), 4/16 April 1877, in *Charles Ier, Roi de Roumanie*, 2:559.

84. Edhem Paşa to Carol, 10/22 April 1877, in *Charles Ier, Roi de Roumanie*, 2:577.

85. See articles 26 and 27 of the Treaty of Paris, 30 March 1856, in *Archives diplomatiques*, vol. 6, pt. 2 (avril, mai, juin 1866), 31; see also article 8 of the Paris convention, 19 August 1858, in ibid., vol. 13, pt. 3 (juillet, août, septembre 1873), 118.

86. Kogălniceanu to Edhem Paşa, 11/23 April 1877, in *Charles Ier, Roi de Roumanie*, 2:580–81.

Chapter Seven

87. Kogălniceanu to Bălăceanu, 7/19 April 1877, in *Charles Ier, Roi de Roumanie,* 2:563–64.

88. Kogălniceanu's circular, 5/17 April 1877, in *Independenţa României,* 4:221–22.

89. Carol to Charles Anthony, 7/19 April 1877, in *Aus dem Leben König Karls von Rumänien,* 3:127.

90. Kogălniceanu to Ion G. Ghica (Czernowitz), 9/21 April 1877, in *Documente privind istoria Romîniei: Războiul pentru independenţă,* 2:155; Ghica (Kishinev) to Kogălniceanu, 10/22 April 1877, in *Corespondenţa generalului Iancu Ghica,* 33.

91. Stuart to Ion Brătianu, 7/19 April 1877, in *Charles Ier, Roi de Roumanie,* 2:563; Brătianu to the Romanian minister of finance, Gheorghe Cantacuzino, 7/19 April 1877, and a law adopted by the chamber of deputies, 14/26 April 1877, in *Documente privind istoria Romîniei: Războiul pentru independenţă,* 2:142, 228–29. The deputies accepted the funds, which came via a Bulgarian banker in Bucharest, Evlogii Georgiev.

92. Carol's decree, 8/20 April 1877, in *Documente privind istoria Romîniei: Războiul pentru independenţă,* 2:148–50.

93. See Miliutin's notes (Kishinev), 12/24 April 1877, in *Dnevnik D. A. Miliutina,* 2:155–56; see also Carol's notes, 11/23 April 1877, in *Aus dem Leben König Karls von Rumänien,* 3:130.

94. Alexander II's proclamation (Kishinev), 12/24 April 1877, in *Charles Ier, Roi de Roumanie,* 2:585–87.

95. Nikolai's declaration (Bucharest?), 12/24 April 1877, in *Rossiia i natsional'no-osvoboditel'naia bor'ba na Balkanakh,* 235–36.

96. Nikolai's announcement (Kishinev), 12/24 April 1877, in *Charles Ier, Roi de Roumanie,* 2:587–89.

97. See a decree by the council of ministers, 12/24 April 1877, in *Ion C. Brătianu: Discursuri, scrieri, acte şi documente,* vol. 2, pt. 2, 593.

98. Kogălniceanu to Ion G. Ghica, 12/24 April 1877, in *Corespondenţa generalului Iancu Ghica,* 37–38.

99. Miliutin's notes (Kishinev), 13/25 April 1877, in *Dnevnik D. A. Miliutina,* 2:158–59; Ion G. Ghica (Kishinev) to Kogălniceanu, 12/24 April 1877, in *Independenţa României,* 4:233–34; Alexander II (Kishinev) to Carol, 13/25 April 1877, in ibid., 1:59.

100. Nikolai (Kishinev) to Carol, 14/26 April 1877, in *Independenţa României,* 1:60.

101. Carol to Nikolai, 17/29 April 1877, in *Charles Ier, Roi de Roumanie,* 2:673–74.

102. Edhem Paşa to Carol, 13/25 April 1877, in *Charles Ier, Roi de Roumanie,* 2:602.

103. Kogălniceanu to Edhem Paşa, 11/23 April 1877, in *Independenţa României,* 4:230.

104. Abdul Hamid II's proclamation, 12/24 April 1877, in *Charles Ier, Roi de Roumanie,* 2:599–600.

105. Savfet Paşa's circular, 13/25 April 1877, in *Charles Ier, Roi de Roumanie,* 2:601.

106. Edhem Paşa to Abdul Kerim Paşa, 17/29 April 1877, in *Charles Ier, Roi de Roumanie*, 2:675–76.

107. Notice from the director general of post and telegraph to Kogălniceanu, 12/24 April 1877, in *Documente privind istoria Romîniei: Războiul pentru independență*, 2:215.

108. See section 5 of the telegraph treaty (Vienna), 21 July 1868, in *Collectiune de tratatele si conventiunile Romaniei*, 138.

109. Carol's speech to the legislature, 14/26 April 1877, in *Independența României*, 1:62.

110. See notes by an anonymous editor, 16/28 April 1877, in *Ion C. Brătianu: Discursuri, scrieri, acte şi documente*, vol. 2, pt. 2, 608.

111. Mikhail M. Zalyshkin, *Vneshniaia politika Rumynii i rumyno-russkie otnosheniia, 1875–1878*, 230–32; *Neue Freie Presse*, 23 April 1877.

112. See Boerescu's speech in the senate, 17/29 April 1877, in Vasile Boerescu, *Discursuri politice*, vol. 2 (1874–83), 680, 682, 685.

113. Carp's speeches in the senate, 17/29 April and 23 April/5 May 1877, in Carp, *Discursuri*, 1:129–32, 133–36.

114. For *Timpul* (26 April 1877), see Maiorescu, *Istoria contimporană a României*, 121.

115. Kogălniceanu's speech in the chamber, 16/28 April 1877, in Kogălniceanu, *Opere*, vol. 4: *Oratorie II, 1864–1878*, pt. 4, 404, 406, 410, 411–13.

116. Brătianu's speeches of 16/28 April in the chamber, and 17/29 April 1877 in the senate, in *Ion C. Brătianu: Discursuri, scrieri, acte şi documente*, vol. 2, pt. 2, 616, 619, 622.

117. Brătianu's speech in the senate, 20 April/2 May 1877, and the senate vote of 25 to 11, in *Ion C. Brătianu: Discursuri, scrieri, acte şi documente*, vol. 2, pt. 2, 601–6.

118. The chamber voted on 16/28 April, and the senate on 17/29 April 1877; Carol approved on 21 April/3 May, and Gorchakov on 24 April/6 May 1877. Ratifications were exchanged in Bucharest on 16/28 May 1877. See AMAE(R), Fond Convenții, dosar 9, 3–100.

Chapter Eight

WAR

Romania's neutrality had been severely compromised by the presence of Russian troops in the principality and by the Romanian legislature's approval of the Russo-Romanian conventions. Danubian Romanians disregarded their prior commitments to supply military assistance to the Turks against foreign invaders. Yet with their bonds to Turkey almost completely ruptured, Romanians worried about the outcome of the Russo-Turkish War. If Russia's battalions prevailed, Russian hegemony might replace benevolent Turkish suzerainty. But if Russia took a beating in Southeastern Europe, Romania might lose its autonomy. Some Romanians reckoned they could abstain from the campaigns and still attain full political sovereignty. If Romanian soldiers triumphed on the battlefield, however, the prospect of independence would be tangibly enhanced. Hence many Romanian patriots believed that their army should play an aggressive role against the Turks.

The Ottoman Empire denounced the Russo-Romanian conventions, once they were made public, and severed relations with Romania. But at first the Turks announced that they would refrain from anti-Romanian hostilities.[1] Abdul Hamid II's chief secretary, Said Paşa, calculated the strategic improbability of retaining the Danube River frontier and so decided that the Russians should be fought south of the river. If the Ottoman Empire were victorious, the Turks might traverse the Danube and press onward to the Prut River; if the Turks were repulsed, they would relinquish the Balkan Peninsula, except for the Black Sea ports of Varna and Burgas.[2] Savfet Paşa announced that Turkish forces would stay out of Romania's Danubian cities. He explained to the great powers that Romania's actions diverged from the "free will" of its people and their own government yet were a "direct consequence of foreign occupation." This untoward situation had, in effect, transferred control from local officials to the enemy, the "usurpers of legitimate authority."[3] Moreover, the Ottoman Empire would continue to protect Romanians as loyal Turkish subjects; this shield extended to Romanian shipping as well.[4] Turkish gunboats began nonetheless to bombard Romania's riparian municipalities of Brăila and Reni after they had been occupied by the Russians. Open towns—that is those lacking fortifications and troops—

were also shelled.[5] Turkey also suspended Romania's diplomatic agency in Constantinople on 3 May 1877.[6] No longer did the Ottoman Empire recognize Romania's neutrality. For Danubian Romanians, this rupture was an opportunity to proclaim independence, but they failed to seize it immediately. Romanians still wanted sufficient preparation and unity for this step. Patriotic dreams nevertheless persisted. Perhaps independence would indeed be realized on the front lines in league with Russia.

Russia held the key to Romania's aspirations. But had not the key been turned to lock out active cooperation between the Russian and Romanian armies? The military conventions were certainly silent about such a conjunction. At this point, Ion Brătianu and Kogălniceanu, along with Carol, adroitly charted the country's policy, buffeted as Romania was by contrary winds both at home and abroad. Kogălniceanu perceived the misgivings about the conflict that occupied some of the powers and some of his compatriots. He remarked obliquely that Russian troops were merely passing through his land, and that Romania would forebear militarily abetting Russia.[7] He noted besides that the sole reason for Romania's mobilization had been to safeguard the border; once Russia's soldiers arrived, Romania's army would withdraw.[8] The establishment of Russian military headquarters in Ploieşti provided Romanian statesmen a chance, though, to urge Russian leaders to reconsider Romania's participation in the war. Brătianu and Nikolai Nikolaevich inspected fortifications together at Brăila; this visit prompted faint hopes among some Danubian Romanians that they would truly partake in the campaign.[9] Such expectations were apparently dashed when Nikolai recommended that Romania's forces move into Oltenia so as "to defend the Danube River to the west of the Olt" and thereby to protect Russia's right flank.[10] Carol agreed to this after Russian contingents had secured the railroad between Bucharest and Giurgiu; it was an honor for him to aid the "glorious" Russian army.[11] The prince envisioned even more. Why should Romania cover Russia's western wing when Russia's accords with Austria-Hungary had stipulated Habsburg neutrality? Possibly the Habsburg Empire had been insincere in its promise; perchance, too, the Ottoman Empire, despite its avowal to the contrary, might invade Oltenia. Probably, however, Austria-Hungary would remain nonembroiled, and Turkey would abstain from crossing the Danube. Romanian battalions still took a defensive stance in Oltenia and awaited Russia's call for a more aggressive military role.

Romania had about 50,000 troops and 190 cannons after the mustering of its army on 6/18 April 1877. Turkey had about 186,000 soldiers, and Russia about 159,000, in Southeastern Europe at the outset of the war. The

Turks' steel Krupp cannons were much superior to the bronze ones of the Russians.[12] And the Turks had the advantage of fighting on interior lines. Danubian Romanians persistently inquired: Will we share actively with the Russians? Ion Brătianu met with Nikolai Nikolaevich and Nelidov at Kishinev to ask for an independent part for Carol in Russia's army. At this moment, Brătianu expressed his fear of an attack by the Habsburg Empire. Romania's armed forces, in any case, required a Russian subsidy so as to operate south of the Danube. Alexander II and his consultants reassured Romanians about Austria-Hungary's intentions.[13] Some Romanian statesmen knew the substance of the Reichstadt agreement, if not the details of the Budapest conventions; hence their palpable pursuit of assurances was simply a sham. More troubling for Carol and Romanian patriots was Alexander's view that Romania's help was unnecessary. Gorchakov recommended that any Romanians traversing the Danube be directed by Russians,[14] and Girs rejected Romania's military involvement "for the moment" to propitiate Russia's relations with Austria-Hungary. Still, Girs recognized that some Russian generals sought Romania's partnership on the condition it be under Russia's control.[15] Alexander's political and military advisors were undoubtedly willing to accept Romania's assistance, but they refused Carol's request for his own command. Without such authority, however, Carol reckoned Romania would forfeit the battlefield glory requisite for national emancipation.

Russo-Romanian financial interaction was as critical as military plans. Romania's economy was unstable. Building railroads and maintaining the principality's forces during the Balkan Crisis had already depleted Romania's fiscal resources. Now Danubian navigation came to a halt owing to Russian and Turkish orders. The Turks saw the Danube River as their primary line of defense; and the Russians, once they had crossed the river, prohibited the export of grain across it. The Danube was hence effectively closed to commerce, except for the previously neutralized zone on the Serbo-Romanian frontier.[16] Russia needed Romania's food supplies and endeavored to inhibit profiteering by Romanian peasants and landholders at the expense of the Russian army. Russia's interdicting of Danubian trade and its requisitioning of Romanian goods would provide Russian legions with the bulk of Romania's agricultural output. These measures had a deleterious effect on Romania's prosperity. The restricted market for Romania's commodities triggered a decline in productivity and consequent low returns for the landed gentry.

Russia sent Romania one million francs early in May 1877 to offset the cost of its troops' transit.[17] This was, however, insufficient to sustain

Romania's army. Carol had drawn monies from his civil list to call up soldiers.[18] Ion Brătianu had furthermore gained legislative approval to issue thirty million lei in paper notes guaranteed by the value of state lands. These bills had been originally issued to meet recent budget deficits, which had reached 46.5 million lei, but they were actually used to cover in part the expenditures for mobilization.[19]

This monetary maneuver involved monastic estates, which had been laicized by Cuza in 1863, and it provided the Ecumenical Orthodox patriarch Iōacheim II (1873–78) in Constantinople an opportunity to renew the church's objections to secularization.[20] Some monastic properties had been "dedicated," as we have seen, to the Holy Places in the Middle East. Before Cuza's reform, about one fifth of Danubian Romania's annual revenues were from these monasteries; much of that income went to the places the monasteries had been dedicated to.[21] Cut off from Romanian funds, Iōacheim protested bitterly, yet to no avail.

Romania's treasury notes of 1877 nevertheless lacked the respect of hard currency. Kogălniceanu thus demanded an additional five million francs from Russia to keep Romania's army in the field and to operate the railroads.[22] He reckoned that Romania's credit had been "completely compromised" by the conventions with Russia; therefore his country was unable to raise loans at home or abroad: "Our resources are completely exhausted. Our commerce is in complete stagnation because of the suspension of Danubian navigation. . . . All our cities and all the villages of the littoral have been abandoned by their inhabitants. . . . The total of our receipts is not sufficient to hold together our administration nor [is] . . . our army placed to defend advanced positions and to facilitate the entry of Russian troops."[23]

A subsidy was urgently needed. Reitern, the Russian minister of finance, was at first "very reserved" about Romania's "pretext of a financial crisis."[24] To cover Russia's costs in Romania, however, Reitern awarded the principality an extra three million francs, or 750,000 rubles; Gorchakov, in approving this step, stipulated that these funds were to be expended according to the "necessities of the situation."[25] Still, since Russia's disbursements for supplies were by letters of credit in Romanian lei, the three million francs were undoubtedly intended to meet Romania's budgetary desiderata.[26] This seems to have been more of an outright grant than a reimbursable subvention. Alexander II observed that Romania had only offered to cooperate with Russia as a pretext for extracting cash.[27] Romanian requirements were indeed great, yet Russia wanted a safe and friendly rear guard. Even had monies been withheld, Romanian patriots were nevertheless ready to endorse the Russian cause in Southeastern Europe. Russia paid Romania to secure the smooth and rapid passage of its troops to the Danube and to ensure that conditions behind the fighting would not become chaotic owing to Romania's fiscal collapse.

Russia's decision to wage war alone against the Ottoman Empire was important for Danubian Romanians as well as for other peoples in Southeastern Europe. Balkan Christians might have marched with the Russians. The Serbian statesman Jovan Marinović had visited St. Petersburg on a special mission for Prince Milan after the Serbs were defeated in 1876. This was about a month after Ion Brătianu's discussion with Russian leaders at Livadia. Marinović told about Serbia's readiness to assist Russia in crossing the Danube. Russia counted on Serbia's military support; still, a Russian envoy to Belgrade failed to persuade Ristić, Serbia's minister of foreign affairs, to take bellicose measures. Resistance to Serbia's reentry into the war was evident in the *skupština,* or parliament, and cabinet. Serbian policy had essentially become one of neutrality. Ristić favored that path, but like Romania, Serbia wanted unanimity. Its prime minister, Stevča Mihailović, and the minister of war, Sava Grujić, favored joining Russia. Milan agreed and announced that Serbia would be prepared if Russia provided funds. To this end, Gheorghe C. Catargi, a Romanian in the Serbian army, went to Kishinev after Russia's declaration of hostilities to promise Serbian solidarity. But Gorchakov, as with Romania's offer, was against Serbia's aid. Combat should be left to Russia and the Ottoman Empire. Austro-Hungarian animosity would ensue if the Serbian, Romanian, or Greek armies participated.[28] Thus Serbia was to remain neutral.

Only the Serbs of Montenegro continued to campaign against the Turks, but the Ottoman Empire finally crushed the Bosnian insurrection in August 1877. What about the prospect of a Balkan alliance against Turkey? In July 1875, Serbia had futilely proposed a secret treaty with Greece, and in 1876 a Serbian emissary, Milutin Garašanin, was in Athens. Greece was, however, unwilling to unite with Serbia. Some Greeks viewed Serbia's stance to be a reflection of Russian Pan-Slavism and dreaded the possibility of a Slavic domination of the Balkan Peninsula. To be sure, the Greeks coveted Thessaly, Epirus, and Crete; nonetheless, British diplomatic pressure against a Balkan pact, anti-Slavic fears, and the remoteness of Greece from Serbia worked against a mutual undertaking. Despite Serbia's plea, the Greek government of Konstantinos Kanaris and Kharilaos Trikoupis preserved neutrality.[29]

Serbia also appealed to Romania for help against the Ottoman Empire. Romania's neutrality, however, precluded direct cooperation between the two countries. While in Bucharest during June 1877 en route to interview Russian officials in Ploieşti, Milan undoubtedly had talks with Romanian statesmen.[30] But Kogălniceanu calculated that a military contract with a beaten Serbia would be valueless, especially because of Serbia's overtly pacifist posture.[31] No Serbo-Romanian covenant ensued. Serbo-Romanian negotiations did, however, result in a short-term commercial convention that was signed by Ristić and Kogălniceanu.[32] Serbia reentered the war in December 1877 only after obtaining a Russian subsidy equivalent to Romania's— that is, about four million francs.

Romania also considered collaborating with Greece. Was not Greece interested in obviating Russia's being the sole sponsor of Orthodox Christians in Southeastern Europe?[33] Ion Brătianu and Kogălniceanu urged a compact,[34] but none came to pass. The failure of a Greco-Romanian understanding may be attributed to some of the same factors that hindered a Greco-Serbian accord. Romania had territorial objectives in the Ottoman Empire, such as the Danube Delta and possibly Dobrogea, yet Greece had far more to win. Russia probably discouraged a Greco-Romanian pact as unnecessarily complicating the Balkan Crisis. If Greece and Romania triumphantly fought the Ottoman Empire, then Russia's program in Bulgaria might founder. National aims and political realities militated against alliances in Southeastern Europe in the 1870s, just as they had a decade earlier.

Romania continued to prepare for hostilities without Balkan allies yet with Russia's aid. The chamber of deputies, led by Constantin Rosetti, adopted a measure proroguing courts of law for the "duration of the war" and during Romania's "occupation by a foreign army." Government was henceforward by decree. The cabinet reserved the right to declare a "state of war, occupation, or siege" in any locality.[35] Carol applied this law on 3 May 1877, commencing thereby a "state of war and occupation" in many places.[36] On this date, the Ottoman Empire, as we noted, suspended Romania's diplomatic agency in Constantinople.

The trumpet of Romanian patriotism blared in the legislature. One deputy, Anastasie Stolojan, asked why the Romanian army refrained from assisting Russia. Had not the Ottoman Empire ruptured relations and bombarded Romania's ports? He therefore submitted a motion to abolish legal, political, and economic ties with Turkey. Another deputy, Petre Gradişteanu, amended this to give the ministry absolute freedom of action. Ion Ghica, the most articulate Turkophil in the chamber, opposed the project because real independence was impossible in the foreseeable future. Russia's occupation of his country precluded sovereignty. Ghica's argument was certainly logical.

The neutralist Nicolae Ionescu agreed with Ghica. He observed that Romania was financially unready, and he warned against belligerency. Kogălniceanu and Ion Brătianu replied for the regime and for militant patriots. Kogălniceanu explained that the "Young Turks" were more "fanatical" than their fathers, as could be seen in the shelling of Romanian towns. This was reason enough to end the Ottoman yoke. Furthermore, according to the Turkish ambassador in Vienna, Aleco Paşa, from the moment the Russo-Romanian conventions had been signed, the Ottoman Empire had been at war with Romania. This was Kogălniceanu's view as well. Still, Kogălniceanu was a better historian than lawyer in this instance, for it would have been illicit for the suzerain Turks to proclaim war on part of their own realm. The Turkish army might intervene to quell an insurrection, but not to wage war. The bonds of vassalage were about to break, however, and war it would be. Brătianu supported Kogălniceanu, appealing to the heroism of the people and expressing the need "to affirm and to assure the Romanian nationality before Europe."[37]

The chamber subsequently approved a resolution recognizing the disintegration of Turkish links and the existence of a "state of war" with the Ottoman Empire. It authorized the cabinet "to take all measures for the defense and assurance of the existence of the Romanian state" so that after the war Romania would have a "well-defined position . . . to fulfill its historic mission." The senate adopted an almost identical motion propounded by Dimitrie Ghica.[38] Kogălniceanu made clear to the powers that the Turks' suspending Romania's diplomatic agency in Constantinople and firing at open Romanian municipalities had been so insulting that "we are at war with Turkey"; by "patent hostility" the Ottoman Empire "broke the bonds" with Romania. Hence Romania must cease being an "impassive spectator": Romanians would "repel with force acts of aggression . . . [and] defend our soil, safeguard our institutions, and assure our political existence."[39] Kogălniceanu forebore suggesting that Romania take the offensive, but he recognized that the Turkish garrison on the Danubian island of Ada Kale had impeded navigation and consequently should be bombarded.[40] Had the cabinet accepted Kogălniceanu's proposal about Ada Kale, the neutrality of the Danubian frontier with Serbia would have been violated, thereby losing Romania's protection from invasion through Serbia.

Why did Romania declare a "state of war" yet not independence? Full sovereignty spelled the close of autonomy as guaranteed by the powers. So Romania's political leaders sought advice from those powers. However, the European cabinets generally considered that nothing could be done for the peoples of Southeastern Europe until the conclusion of Russo-Turkish hostilities. The powers refused to help. Romanians were thus on their own concerning independent statehood, which seemed to be directly linked to the war's outcome.

The legislature considered the next momentous step on 9 May 1877. In the chamber, Kogălniceanu asked, "in case of war, with relations broken, what are we? We are independent. . . . We are in a state of war with Turkey," and Romania is a "free and independent nation."[41] Ion Brătianu later remarked that because diplomacy had failed to keep the peace, no one was "sure about the consequences of this terrible convulsion in the Balkan Peninsula . . . [, and the] terrible political and social crisis" made it uncertain which side would win. He then catalogued Romania's grievances against the Ottoman Empire: villages were "bombarded, burned, and pillaged"; plains and cornfields were "devastated and burned"; sentries along the Danube were "killed and mangled in a most barbaric way"; peasants were "robbed of their plowshares and led into slavery together with their women and children, as in the days of Mohammed II." Romanians had "to save the political individuality" of their country.[42] Whatever the accuracy of Brătianu's vivid denunciation, the legislature proclaimed independence. The chamber resolved that the "war between Romania and Turkey, that the broken relations with the Porte, and that the absolute independence of Romania have received official consecration."[43] The senate acted in a similar vein; it advised the government in addition to assure that Romania's sovereignty would be "recognized and guaranteed" by the powers.[44] Not all Romanians were enthusiastic about such a move; some feared negative political consequences.[45] Most nevertheless wanted sovereignty as well as the invaluable safeguard of the powers; another Belgium or Switzerland might then emerge on the lower Danube River.

The day after the declaration of independence, 10 May 1877, was a national holiday commemorating Carol's advent in Bucharest. Calinic, the Romanian metropolitan, noted the state's new role by wishing the prince a long reign on the "throne of an independent Romania." Carol responded to several motions and to the metropolitan's toast by announcing that the "force of developments and patriotism" together with the "invincible voice of justice" affirmed the "rights of the Romanian people to an absolutely independent national life." He anticipated "the recognition of Romania as an absolutely independent state."[46] The die had been cast. Romanians were now, in their view, sovereign, and that status would be confirmed by the powers, presumably following military victories.

Independence spelled an end of the annual tribute paid to the Ottoman Empire. This final sign of vassalage, which had lasted more than three centuries, disappeared when funds allocated for it went to Romania's armed forces.[47] Moreover, ten million lei from a loan to build railways not directly connected to the war effort were diverted to purchase munitions and other military supplies.[48] The tribute of almost one million lei was therefore relatively insignificant compared to railroad monies, yet it had been of high symbolic importance for Romanians.

The powers withheld recognizing Romania's independence until after the war and the Congress of Berlin. Indeed, Andrássy would acquiesce in Romania's being invaded by either Russia or the Ottoman Empire.[49] He opposed Romania's military participation in the war but would not "veto" it; Romania should, however, abjure acquiring the right bank of the Danube River and endangering free trade on it.[50] International treaties fixed Romania's position, which could be changed only by the powers at the peace table.[51] Tisza adamantly rejected Romania's independence. He and many other Hungarians feared that a sovereign Danubian Romania would become a powerful magnet, attracting Romanians from Transylvania and the Banat and disrupting the economic and political life of the Magyar portions of the Habsburg Empire. The border was closed during the war so that Austria-Hungary's Romanians would be disentangled from Danubian Romania's army in Oltenia.[52] Kogălniceanu, dreading Habsburg animosity—Vienna's assurances of neutrality notwithstanding—remarked that Bucharest neither needed nor wanted Romanian volunteers from Transylvania.[53] Tisza noted, however, that Transylvanian Romanians from Fogaras (Făgăraş) and Nagyszeben, aiming to enroll in Romania's army, passed the frontier without passports and were welcomed joyfully at Ploieşti.[54] Andrássy called for the extradition of these volunteers.[55] Kogălniceanu replied that a mere handful of Transylvanian Romanians had arrived. His land, in any case, owed hospitality to refugees of any nationality, including Romanians, and should offer asylum and protection; still, Romania repudiated the spread of nationalistic feelings to Transylvania, the Banat, and Bukowina.[56] Tension persisted. Guerrilla contingents secretly organized in Transylvania, according to one account, seeking to destroy railroads and bridges behind Romania's army lines. A group of armed Székelys, the mountain-dwelling Magyars of eastern Transylvania, was in fact stopped by imperial authorities before entering Romania. A rumor that Hungarian military units had encamped on the eastern bank of the Cerna (Czerna) River in Romania proved to be false; a peasant had mistakenly assumed a Romanian border patrol to be a foreign army.[57] Although these reports were immaterial or frivolous, they profoundly impressed Romanian statesmen. Romania's frontier with Austria-Hungary was vulnerable because Romanian troops had concentrated on the Danube, and the home guard was ill trained and poorly equipped. The smoldering hostility of Hungary's leaders toward Romania's aspirations certainly worried Romanian officials.[58] Furthermore, many Poles formed military companies in Bukowina, threatening the Russian army from the rear.[59] The immediate Polish objective was apparently to blow up bridges throughout Romania. The ultimate goal was probably to help Turkey defeat Russia. The Polish generation of 1863 might then create a Polish state. Despite alleged conspiracies among Hungarians against Romania and among Poles against Russia, the Habsburg Empire's boundary with Romania remained essentially inviolate. Vienna scrupulously observed its neutrality, thereby frustrating Magyar and Polish activists.

The other powers concurred with Austria-Hungary that Romania's independence should be considered later in making peace.[60] Germany had a special claim. Bülow renewed the demands of German financiers: Romania's sovereignty might only be acknowledged when railroad stockholders were satisfied; that is, Romania was to pay interest on rail shares to the Strousberg-Bleichröder syndicate.[61] Italy agreed with the rest of the powers during the Balkan Crisis, but some Italians wanted territorial compensation in Southeastern Europe if the Turks were defeated. Melegari, Italy's minister of foreign affairs, seemingly envisioned Italy's occupation of Illyrian ports and the formation of an Italian protectorate in Albania.[62] Still, Italy in the 1870s was more concerned about the Habsburg Trentino and Trieste than about Ottoman Albania; military weakness and the ongoing necessity of consolidating national unity also worked against an Italian intervention in Southeastern Europe. The Ottoman Empire, of course, denounced Romania's declaration of independence. Savfet Paşa contemplated the "ruin" of the Moldo-Wallachians and warned about the "disastrous consequences" that the "grave disturbances" in Romania would have for the "equilibrium of Europe."[63] Russia was also unenthusiastic about Bucharest's proclamation and about the prospect of Romanian involvement in the campaigns. Gorchakov advised that Danubian Romania would enter the war at its "own expense," at its own "risks and perils," and under Russian military command. Any Romanian action in isolation from Russia's army was a "political impossibility"; Romania's soldiers were unnecessary, for Russia's forces were "more than sufficient" to win the war.[64] Nelidov recommended that Romania maintain its internal security and avoid imperiling Russian troops.[65]

Russia reckoned that Romania, like Serbia, lacked the economic capacity for effective armed assistance.[66] Gorchakov informed Carol that Russia waived Romania's cooperation, warranting that the powers would endorse Romania's independence after the war. As we have seen, however, Russians disagreed with one another. Russia's general staff calculated that Romania's military support would aid in bringing the war to a speedy and victorious conclusion,[67] and Russian military authorities continued to call for the collaboration of Balkan Christians against the Muslim Turks. However, Gorchakov persevered in rejecting it because the peoples of Southeastern Europe would thereby gain a tribune in peace deliberations and so might thwart Russia's ambitions.

Romania's pronouncement of independence had to be implemented to fulfill national dreams. While Russia's army occupied the land and vetoed help, Romania's sovereignty was merely a pretension. But would independence mean a better life for Danubian Romanians? The regime refrained from promising social improvements. Most of the political ideals of the governing elite—the generation of 1848, 1857, and 1866—had been achieved by Europe's guarantee of autonomy, the merger of Moldavia and Wallachia, and a foreign prince. The powers had assured Romania's de facto independence in domestic matters, and the unilateral 1877 declaration broadcast de jure independence in foreign affairs. Sovereignty had so far been denied by the powers, yet Romania's patriots hoped it would be confirmed after a triumphant war.

Romania next proposed neutralizing and demilitarizing the lower Danube River, and it ordered guns from abroad.[68] On both counts, Bucharest was frustrated. Romania already lacked fortifications on its side of the Danube, but the most the powers were willing to concede was the demilitarization of the right bank. Russia opposed a neutral Danube, as it would stymie a Russian attack on the Ottoman Empire in Europe. As to foreign arms, Romania soon discovered that the neutral Habsburg Empire blocked the shipment of weapons from factories in Austria-Hungary and Germany. Romania was therefore compelled to rely almost exclusively on military supplies from Russia.

Russia's essential logistical problem was transportation. Romania's railroads did not meet Russia's lines at convenient places; moreover, men and matériel had to be transshipped from one freight car to another in Iaşi owing to the difference between Romania's standard-gauge track and Russia's wider gauge. As we noted in Chapter Four, Poliakov consequently began in July 1877 to build a railway from Bolgrad in southern Bessarabia to Reni on the Danube. He hastily finished this work, opening it in November 1877. Poliakov also started to construct a railroad from Frăteşti, near Giurgiu, westward to the embarkation point at Zimnicea.[69] This line remained incomplete.

Russia's army crossed the Danube at Zimnicea. Carol meanwhile joined his troops at Poiana, close by Calafat on the Danube, where he awaited an opportunity to lead them in combat.[70] After the fall of the Danubian fortress of Nikopol, Russia asked Romania to garrison it and to supervise the captured Turkish soldiers. Carol was at first reluctant to do so.[71] Gorchakov, who had resisted employing the peoples of Southeastern Europe in the war effort, either was overruled by Russian military authorities or had mellowed during his sojourn in Bucharest. In any case, he now supported this maneuver and tied it to Romania's sovereignty. Gorchakov promised, "I shall be the first to call for your independence."[72] Russia's bidding was hardly what Romania needed to win glory on the battlefield; yet Carol, grasping at straws, seized it. Andrássy encouraged Romania to take this step but advised "great prudence."[73] Still, lacking both a comprehensive military agreement with Russia and the legislature's approval, about 10,000 Romanians crossed the Danube at Turnu-Măgurele and preempted Nikopol.[74]

Russia's advance southward halted at Pleven, and Nikolai Nikolaevich invited Carol "to cross the Danube" himself with Romania's army to protect Russia's western flank. Nikolai concluded that a Romanian military demonstration was "indispensable" for the further movement of Russia's army.[75] He also urged Serbia to declare independence and enter the war.[76] Serbia complied yet requested a large subsidy and a month to prepare. Romania also hedged. Carol insisted that his army needed ammunition and a bridge across the Danube; and, most important, he wanted an independent command.[77] Carol evidently played for time, being convinced that Russia would make major concessions.

While Russia's forces were before Pleven, Ion Brătianu visited Russia's military headquarters seeking financial aid. Miliutin agreed to it, for he was anxiously expecting Romania's martial assistance.[78] In addition, Nikolai Nikolaevich informed Carol that Romania's troops were "absolutely necessary" in Bulgaria. Carol was especially pleased that Russia would allow Romanian soldiers to be led by their own officers, with Carol himself at the head of the Russo-Romanian army on the western flank. Carol was now persuaded he might conduct independent operations, even without a definitive Russo-Romanian military pact.[79] Romania's prince was nominally to direct the trans-Danubian Romanian army of about 32,000 men together with about 52,000 Russians; the defending Turkish commandant, Osman Paşa, had about 32,000 men.[80] Romania's army was unquestionably necessary after Russia's second unsuccessful assault on Pleven at the end of July 1877; but Miliutin worried about the untoward consequences of putting Carol in charge. He noted that a "significant part" of Russia's army and "important strategic points" were being entrusted to someone who was "completely inexperienced in military action" and who was surrounded by "superficial, ambitious" persons desiring to fulfill a "historic role."[81]

Carol, his military counselors, and Ion Brătianu made the final decision to fight the Ottoman Empire. A large number of officers disagreed, however, about the feasibility of cooperating with Russia. Without the advice and consent of Romania's legislature, and still without a specific Russo-Romanian military understanding, Carol plus Brătianu and a few others nonetheless forced the issue. The minister of war, Alexandru Cernat, resigned his ministerial post so as to supervise Romania's army at Pleven.[82] Carol provided his troops with some reasons for a bold step. Battles were already being waged near the frontier, and if the Turks succeeded, the countryside would obviously suffer "massacre, pillage, and devastation." The army's "duty" was to rescue the homeland from the "barbarous invaders."[83] The Turks had, of course, eschewed invading Romania, but Carol was appealing to patriotic feelings rather than pleading before the bar of truth. Once across the Danube, Carol proclaimed that vigorous military participation was something Romanians "did not want [and] did not provoke." He had initially contemplated merely guarding the border against a hostile Turkish attack. Now Romania's actions were "dictated by our national and economic interests . . . [to end] the war of extermination against all Christians." Carol explained that his soldiers were in Bulgaria to hasten peace, "to establish solidly our right as a free nation . . . to strengthen the regard and belief" in Romania by the powers.[84] He left out of these announcements the personal prestige he hoped to win for himself. Carol perforce identified closely with Romania's national aspirations from the day he had arrived in the principality. A victorious campaign might indeed assure the powers' recognition of Romania's independence. The ambitions of the prince and of many patriots, then, were one and the same.

Romania's offensive centered at Grivița, a fortified outpost of the Pleven citadel. The Turks at Pleven continued to resist after Romania's entry into the fray; nevertheless, the fall of the Grivița redoubt on 30 August/ 11 September 1877 gave Romanians the battlefield glory they craved. Of the 16,000 casualties, 2,695 were Romanians.[85] Russo-Romanian forces, at

Russia's prompting, subsequently seized the Turkish stronghold of Rakhovo on the Danube. After the collapse of Pleven and the Russo-Turkish armistice at Adrianople on 23 January/4 February 1878, Romanian troops also captured the Danubian fortress of Vidin.[86]

Romanians, as we have seen, differed about their involvement south of the Danube River. Kogălniceanu anticipated that Carol, as commander of both Russian and Romanian troops, would incur the suspicion of the Habsburg Empire, whose support was deemed essential in concluding a peace settlement that would satisfy Romania. Covering for Carol's deeds, Kogălniceanu redefined Romania's policy. A prolonged war would compromise Romania's commercial life, for agricultural exports by river and sea had ceased. He therefore affirmed that Romania's only honorable course was to participate in the campaigns so as to safeguard the public wealth, to assure the country's security, and to appease the martial ardor of Romania's youth. All Orthodox Christians had, he contended, called for Romania's assistance.[87] To be sure, Greece had requested Romania's help in fighting the Ottoman Empire in 1866 and 1869; and Serbia made similar requests in 1867, 1868, and 1876. But this time, Romania had Russia's financial and military backing as well as Austria-Hungary's tacit approval. Many Romanians were then confident that the Turks would fold; thus Romania had little to lose and much to gain. Later, before a joint session of Romania's chamber and senate, Carol claimed: "On the field of battle in Bulgaria our soldiers confirmed" a Romanian independence that would be "recognized by all Europe," for the "time of vassalage was past," and Romania was a "free and independent land."[88] Carp concurred that the army had been courageous in Bulgaria, yet he reminded senators that recent military endeavors lacked the nature of a "public act" sanctioned by the nation. Crossing the Danube, he argued, had been contrary to Romania's interest; moreover, battleground successes had failed to ensure the preservation of southern Bessarabia, nor did they guarantee Romania's acquisition of the Danube Delta or Dobrogea.[89] Kogălniceanu disagreed with Carp,[90] and the latter's foresight was ignored by many of Romania's patriots, who focused primarily on war, fame, and independence.

None of the powers immediately recognized Danubian Romania's sovereignty. Despite Romania's proclamation and its victories in the field, decisions by the powers at the Congress of Berlin in 1878 were required to clarify its international status. Romania temporarily retained its nominal role as a privileged principality of the Ottoman Empire. Before independence would be sanctioned, problems had to be resolved regarding the retrocession of southern Bessarabia to Russia, the annexation of Dobrogea, the enactment of a constitutional revision in favor of the Jews, and the purchase of German shares in Romania's railroads.

For Danubian Romanians, however, the strings connecting their country to the Ottoman Empire had been snapped by their declaring independence and waging war. Many Romanians then repudiated a restoration of the old regime. Romania had indeed abandoned its protected position of autonomy confirmed by the powers, and so assumed the burden of self-defense. Peace was still to be concluded, but Romanian patriots had achieved, at least in their own eyes, their fundamental objective.

Notes

1. Bălăceanu (Vienna) to Kogălniceanu, 20 April/2 May 1877, in Fond Ion C. Brătianu, LIX/8, no. 12, BNR, SM.

2. Said Paşa's notes, 8/20 April 1877, in *Sbornik turetskikh dokumentov o poslednei voine*, 6.

3. Savfet Paşa's circular, 20 April/2 May 1877, in *Charles Ier, Roi de Roumanie*, 2:685–87.

4. Savfet Paşa's circular, 21 April/3 May 1877, in *Charles Ier, Roi de Roumanie*, 2:692.

5. See notes by an anonymous editor, 21 April/3 May and 22 April/4 May 1877, in *Ion C. Brătianu: Discursuri, scrieri, acte şi documente*, vol. 2, pt. 2, 629; Carol to Charles Anthony, 24 April/6 May 1877, in *Charles Ier, Roi de Roumanie*, 2:712.

6. Savfet Paşa to Grigore Ghica, 21 April/3 May, and Ghica to Ministerul Afacerilor Străine, 22 April/4 May 1877, in *Charles Ier, Roi de Roumanie*, 2:691–92, 696.

7. Kogălniceanu to Bălăceanu, 7/19 and 10/22 April 1877, in *Independenţa României*, 4:225, 228.

8. See Kogălniceanu's circular, 23 April/5 May 1877, in Fond Ion C. Brătianu, dosar 22, AIC, CR.

9. Carl Offerman (Bucharest) to Bleichröder (Berlin), 7 May 1877, in HAA, PS: Türkei, 24, vol. 60; Aleksandr A. Iakobson (Iaşi) to Girs (St. Petersburg), 26 April/8 May 1877, in *Osvobozhdenie Bolgarii ot turetskogo iga*, 2:55.

10. Nikolai (Kishinev) to Carol (Bucharest), 22 April/4 May 1877, in *Independenţa României*, 1:65.

11. Carol to Nikolai, 25 April/7 May 1877, in *Charles Ier, Roi de Roumanie*, 2:718–19.

12. Carol's notes, 26 April/8 May and 29 April/11 May 1877, in *Aus dem Leben König Karls von Rumänien*, 3:149. For figures on the active Russian army on 15/27 April 1877, see *Sbornik materialov po russko-turetskoi voine*, 1:138; Nicolae Ciahir, *Războiul pentru independenţa României în contextul european (1875–1878)*, 172, 175, 176, 178; Nichita Adăniloaie, *Independenţa naţională a României*, 203; *Sbornik turetskikh dokumentov o poslednei voine*, 11.

13. Nelidov (Ploieşti) to Gorchakov, 7/19 May 1877, and Alexander's II's marginal note, in *Osvobozhdenie Bolgarii ot turetskogo iga*, 2:67.

14. Ion G. Ghica (St. Petersburg) to Kogălniceanu, 9/21 May 1877, in *Corespondenţa generalului Iancu Ghica*, 74–75.

15. Ion G. Ghica (St. Petersburg) to Kogălniceanu, 10/22 May 1877, in *Corespondenţa generalului Iancu Ghica*, 75–76.

16. Ion G. Ghica (Kishinev) to Kogălniceanu, 16/28 April 1877, in *Corespondenţa generalului Iancu Ghica*, 41–42; Edhem Paşa to Abdul Kerim Paşa, 17/29 April 1877, in *Charles Ier, Roi de Roumanie*, 2:675–76. These restrictions were not lifted until November 1878; see *Aus dem Leben König Karls von Rumänien*, 4:127.

17. See Chapter Seven above. The sum was 300,000 rubles, or 919,702 lei.

18. Carol to Ion Brătianu, 20 April/2 May 1877, in *Charles Ier, Roi de Roumanie*, 2:684–85.

19. For the legislature's project of 11/23 May 1877, approved by the senate on 4/16 June by a vote of 31 to 18 and by the chamber of deputies on 7/19 June 1877 by 45 to 21 and promulgated into law on 10/22 June 1877, see *Ion C. Brătianu: Acte şi cuvântări*, 3:24–25, 308–11. These paper notes were withdrawn on 1/13 July 1880. See an anonymous editorial annotation in Carp, *Discursuri*, 1:137.

20. Iōacheim II (Constantinople) to the great powers, 18/30 November 1877, in HAA, PS: Türkei, 24, vol. 62.

21. Cf. Chapter Two above; Andreiu de Shaguna, *Istoria biserichei ortodokse răsüritene universale dela întemeierea ei pănă în zilele noastre*, 2:245–48, 250–51; Marin Popescu-Spineni, *Procesul mănăstirilor închinate: Contribuţii la istoria socială românească*, 119.

22. Kogălniceanu (Bucharest) to Ion G. Ghica, 9/21 May 1877, in Fond Ion C. Brătianu, LIX/8, no. 66, BNR, SM; Kogălniceanu to Ghica (Kishinev), 18/30 April 1877, in *Corespondenţa generalului Iancu Ghica*, 43; cf. Nelidov (Ploieşti) to Gorchakov, 7/19 May 1877, in *Osvobozhdenie Bolgarii ot turetskogo iga*, 2:67.

23. Kogălniceanu to Ion G. Ghica (St. Petersburg), 28 April/10 May 1877, in *Corespondenţa generalului Iancu Ghica*, 53–54.

24. Ion G. Ghica (St. Petersburg) to Kogălniceanu, 26 April/8 May 1877, in *Corespondenţa generalului Iancu Ghica*, 55–56.

25. Reitern (St. Petersburg) to Ion G. Ghica, 4/16 May 1877, in Fond Ion C. Brătianu, LIX/8, no. 150 bis, BNR, SM; Gorchakov to Nelidov, 14/26 May 1877, in *Osvobozhdenie Bolgarii ot turetskogo iga*, 2:77; Ion Brătianu to Kogălniceanu, 7/19 May 1877, in *Documente privind istoria României: Războiul pentru independenţă*, 2:640.

26. See an additional Russo-Romanian agreement, 16/28 June 1877, in *Documente privind istoria României: Războiul pentru independenţă*, 4:38–40.

27. Alexander II's marginal note on a letter from Nelidov (Ploieşti) to Gorchakov, 7/19 May 1877, in *Osvobozhdenie Bolgarii ot turetskogo iga*, 2:67.

28. David MacKenzie, *The Serbs and Russian Pan-Slavism, 1875–1878*, 160–62, 198–209.

29. Stavrianos, "Balkan Federation," 112–13.

30. Kogălniceanu to Alexandru Plagino, 21 May/2 June 1877, in *Documente privind istoria României: Războiul pentru independenţă*, 3:244. Milan stayed in Bucharest with his uncle Alexandru Catargi.

31. Kogălniceanu to Nicolae Calimaki-Catargi (Paris), 22 June/4 July 1877, in *Documente privind istoria României: Războiul pentru independenţă*, 4:167.

32. See the Serbo-Romanian accord signed by Ristić in Belgrade, 23 September 1877, and by Kogălniceanu in Bucharest, 3/15 October 1877, in *Documente privind istoria României: Războiul pentru independenţă*, 6:621–22.

33. Calimaki-Catargi to Ministerul Afacerilor Străine (Bucharest), 14/26 May 1877, in *Documente privind istoria României: Războiul pentru independenţă*, 3:108.

34. Evangelos Kofos, "Greek-Romanian Attempts at Collaboration on the Eve of Romania's Independence," 625–27.

35. The chamber voted 67 to 4 in favor of this resolution, 21 April/3 May 1877; see *Documente privind istoria României: Războiul pentru independenţă*, 2:332–33.

36. See Carol's decree, 29 April/11 May 1877, applied retroactively to 3 May 1877, in *Documente privind istoria României: Războiul pentru independenţă*, 2:469–70.

37. Kogălniceanu's speeches in the chamber, 29 April/11 May 1877, and in the senate, 30 April/12 May 1877, in Kogălniceanu, *Opere*, vol. 4: *Oratorie II*, pt. 4, 455, 461, 462, 467–68; Brătianu's speech in the chamber, 29 April/11 May 1877, in *Ion C. Brătianu: Discursuri, scrieri, acte şi documente*, vol. 2, pt. 2, 642–43, 655. Aleco Paşa, or Alexandru Vogoridis, was a Greco-Romanian in Turkish service. Kogălniceanu's phrase "Young Turks" refers to reform-minded, nationalistic intellectuals—also called "Young Ottomans"—who were active in the 1860s and 1870s; they were not the later "Young Turks," who held political sway in Turkey from 1908 to 1918.

38. The chamber voted on 29 April/11 May 1877, 58 to 29 with 5 abstentions, and the senate did so on 30 April/12 May 1877, 38 to 7 with 1 abstention; *Independenţa României*, 4:253–54.

39. Kogălniceanu to Ion G. Ghica, 1/13 May 1877, in *Corespondenţa generalului Iancu Ghica*, 67–68; Kogălniceanu's circular, 2/14 May 1877, in *Charles Ier, Roi de Roumanie*, 2:742–43.

40. Kogălniceanu to Bălăceanu, 6/18 May 1877, in *Documente privind istoria României: Războiul pentru independenţă*, 2:597–98.

41. Kogălniceanu's speech in the chamber, 9/21 May 1877, in Kogălniceanu, *Opere*, vol. 4: *Oratorie II*, pt. 4, 478–79.

42. Brătianu's address to Carol, 10/22 May 1877, in *Ion C. Brătianu: Acte şi cuvântări*, 3:22–23. For a list of Turkish transgressions from 25 April/7 May to 18/30 May 1877, see *Documente privind istoria României: Războiul pentru independenţă*, 3:401–2.

43. The chamber voted, 9/21 May 1877, 79 in favor with 2 abstentions; *Independenţa României*, 4:254. Nicolae Ionescu abstained; see Maiorescu, *Istoria contimporană a României*, 123.

44. The senate's vote was 32 to 0, 9/21 May 1877; *Independenţa României*, 4:255.

45. Maier, *Rumänien auf dem Weg zur Unabhängigkeitserklärung*, 465–67; Zalyshkin, *Vneshniaia politika Rymynii i rumyno-russkie otnosheniia*, 245–46.

46. Carol's speech to the president of the court of appeals, 10/22 May 1877, in *Charles Ier, Roi de Roumanie*, 2:761–62.

47. The chamber voted 68 to 0, 11/23 May 1877; see *Documente privind istoria României: Războiul pentru independenţă*, 3:49.

48. The chamber approved the measure involving the Ploiești-Predeal and Adjud-Ocna lines by a vote of 58 to 4, 3/15 May 1877; the senate concurred by 24 to 3, 5/17 May 1877; *Ion C. Brătianu: Acte și cuvântări*, 3:303–4; Alvensleben (Bucharest) to Bülow (Berlin), 31 May 1877, no. 139, in HAA, PS: Türkei, 24, vol. 60.

49. Andrássy (Vienna) to Bosizio (Bucharest), 21 February 1877, and Andrássy to Julius Zwiedinek-Südenhorst (Bucharest), 21 April 1877, in HHS, PA—XXXVIII, Konsulate: Bukarest, Karton 217.

50. Andrássy to Zwiedinek, 7 July 1877, in HHS, PA—XXXVIII, Konsulate: Bukarest, Karton 217.

51. [Tisza] (Tisza Dob) to Béla Orczy (Vienna), 11 May 1877, in HHS, PA—XXXVIII, Konsulate: Bukarest, Karton 217; Andrássy's circular, 1/13 May 1877, in *Documente privind istoria României: Războiul pentru independență*, 2:532; Bălăceanu to Kogălniceanu, 12/24 May 1877, in *Independența României*, 4:256–57.

52. Tisza (Budapest) to Andrássy (Vienna), 18/30 June 1877, in *Independența României*, vol. 2, pt. 2, 63.

53. Kogălniceanu to Bălăceanu, 3/15 June 1877, in *Independența României*, 1:129.

54. Tisza to Calice (Bucharest), 29 May/10 June 1877, and Zwiedinek to Andrássy, 31 May 1877 and 5/17 June 1877, in *Independența României*, vol. 2, pt. 2, 35, 41, 45–46.

55. Bălăceanu to Kogălniceanu, 1/13 June 1877, in *Documente privind istoria României: Războiul pentru independență*, 3:468.

56. Kogălniceanu to Bălăceanu, 13/25 June 1877, in *Documente privind istoria României: Războiul pentru independență*, 3:710.

57. Mihail Mitilineu (Bucharest) to Kogălniceanu (Huși), 12/24 September 1877, Bălăceanu to Kogălniceanu, 13/25 and 16/28 September 1877, I. Nucșoreanu (Turnu-Severin) to Kogălniceanu, 29 September/11 October 1877, Haralambie (Craiova) to Kogălniceanu, 29 September/11 October 1877, and Kogălniceanu to Bălăceanu, 29 September/11 October 1877, in *Documente privind istoria României: Războiul pentru independență*, 6:189, 206–7, 239–40, 421–22.

58. Cf. the support provided by Hungarians to Romania's war effort; see Ștefan Csucsuja, "Manifestări ale solidarității maselor populare maghiare cu războiul pentru independența României."

59. Kogălniceanu to Bălăceanu, 3/15 October 1877, and Bălăceanu to Kogălniceanu, 4/16 October 1877, in *Documente privind istoria României: Războiul pentru independență*, 6:501–2, 531.

60. Andrássy's circular, 12/24 May 1877, in *Documente privind istoria României: Războiul pentru independență*, 3:60; Bălăceanu to Kogălniceanu, 12/24 May 1877, and Bălăceanu to Kogălniceanu, 14/26 May 1877, in *Independența României*, 4:256–57, 264; Degré (Berlin) to Kogălniceanu, 15/27 May and 30 May/11 June 1877, in *Independența României*, 4:268, 283; Calimaki-Catargi to Kogălniceanu, 16/28 May 1877, in *Documente privind istoria României: Războiul pentru independență*, 3:138; Mihail Obedenaru (Rome) to Kogălniceanu, 31 May/12 June 1877, in *Independența României*, 4:287.

61. Degré to Kogălniceanu, 7/19 May 1877, in *Documente privind istoria României: Războiul pentru independență*, 2:629; Degré to Kogălniceanu, 17/29 May

1877, in *Independenţa României*, 4:269; Degré to Kogălniceanu, 27 May 1877 and 1/13 June 1877, in *Correspondance diplomatique roumaine sous le roi Charles Ier*, 209, 214–15.

62. Obedenaru to Ministerul Afacerilor Străine, 10/22 September 1877, in *Documente privind istoria României: Războiul pentru independenţă*, 6:157–58.

63. See Savfet Paşa's circular, 24 May/5 June 1877, in *Charles Ier, Roi de Roumanie*, 2:807–9.

64. Nelidov to Romania's government, 17/29 May 1877, in *Charles Ier, Roi de Roumanie*, 2:787–89.

65. Letter from Nelidov and Nikolai Nikolaevich (Ploieşti) to the Romanian government, 17/29 May 1877, in Fond Ion C. Brătianu, LIX/8, no. 182 ter., BNR, SM.

66. Miliutin's notes (Kishinev), 12/24 April 1877, in *Dnevnik D. A. Miliutina*, 2:155.

67. See notes on Carol's conversation with Gorchakov (Ploieşti), 2/14 June 1877, in *Charles Ier, Roi de Roumanie*, 2:827.

68. Kogălniceanu's circular, 22 June/4 July 1877, in *Charles Ier, Roi de Roumanie*, 2:854–56. Romania received, via Russia, 25,000 Krnka guns manufactured in Prague; Ciahir, *Războiul pentru independenţa României*, 181. Among other weapons, the Ottoman Empire had some American arms, such as 334,000 Peabody-Martini-Henry rifles; *Sbornik turestkikh dokumentov o poslednei voine*, 11; cf. a note from the chief quartermaster general, Mahmud Paşa, to the first privy chamberlain of the sultan's house, Said Paşa, 17/29 May 1877, in Sedes, *1875–1878 Osmanlı ordusu savaşları: 1877–1878 Osmanlı-Rus ve Roman savaşı*, 2:92.

69. Alvensleben to Bülow, 11 July 1877, no. 202, in HAA, PS: Türkei, 24, vol. 61; Petre S. Aurelian to Ion Brătianu, 8/20 July 1877, in *Documente privind istoria României: Războiul pentru independenţă*, 4:455; Dmitrii A. Obolenskii (Bucharest) to Kogălniceanu, 26 August/7 September 1877, and Kogălniceanu to Obolenskii, 29 August/10 September, 1877, in ibid., 5:615, 663; Alvensleben to Bülow, 28 November 1877, no. 337, in HAA, PS: Türkei, 24, vol. 62.

70. Carol's notes, 1/13 July 1877, in *Aus dem Leben König Karls von Rumänien*, 3:197.

71. Carol to Kogălniceanu, 7/19 July 1877, Ion G. Ghica (Biała) to Carol, 9/21 July 1877, and Colonel Gherghel (Tŭrnovo) to Carol, 15/27 July 1877, in *Charles Ier, Roi de Roumanie*, 2:866–68, 870–71.

72. Princess Elizabeth (Cotroceni) to Carol, 24 July 1877, in *Charles Ier, Roi de Roumanie*, 2:870.

73. Kogălniceanu (Vienna) to Carol (Poiana), 22 July/3 August 1877, in AIC, CR, dosar 7/1877.

74. Carol (Poiana) to Kogălniceanu, 13/25 July 1877, in *Documente privind istoria României: Războiul pentru independenţă*, 4:552; Kogălniceanu to Carol, 13/25 July 1877, in *Correspondance diplomatique roumaine sous le roi Charles Ier*, 227; Mansfield (Bucharest) to Derby, 29 July/10 August 1877, in *Independenţa României*, vol. 2, pt. 2, 118.

75. Nikolai (Tŭrnovo) to Carol, 19/31 July 1877, in *Charles Ier, Roi de Roumanie*, 2:880.

76. MacKenzie, *The Serbs and Russian Pan-Slavism*, 220.

77. Carol to Nikolai, 19/31 July 1877, Carol (Poiana) to Nikolai (Tŭrnovo), 22 July/3 August 1877, Ion Brătianu (Turnu Măgurele) to Carol (Şimnic), 28 July/9 August 1877, Nikolai (Gorna Studena) to Carol, 2/14 and 3/15 August 1877, and Nepokoichitskii (Gorna Studena) to Slăniceanu, 11/23 August 1877, in *Charles Ier, Roi de Roumanie,* 2:881, 887, 893, 894–98, 901. Russia sent Romania forty torpedoes.

78. Miliutin's notes, 6/18 August 1877, in *Dnevnik D. A. Miliutina,* 2:204.

79. Nikolai (Gorna Studena) to Carol, 6/18 August, Carol to Nikolai, 10/22 August, and Nikolai (Gorna Studena) to Carol (Corabia), 19/31 August 1877, in *Charles Ier, Roi de Roumanie,* 2:899, 900–901, 911.

80. Carol (Poiana) to Nikolai (Tŭrnovo), 22 July/3 August 1877, in *Independenţa României,* 1:168; *La guerre d'Orient,* section 17, 9–10; Zalyshkin, *Vneshniaia politika Rumynii,* 270; Viktor I. Vinogradov, *Russko-turetskaia voina 1877–1878 gg. i osvobozhdenie Bolgarii,* 175.

81. Miliutin's notes, 17/29 August 1877, in *Dnevnik D. A. Miliutina,* 2:208.

82. Carol's notes, 19/31 August 1877, in *Aus dem Leben König Karls von Rumänien,* 3:243.

83. Carol's declaration (Corabia), 20 August/1 September 1877, in *Documente privind istoria României: Războiul pentru independenţă,* 5:544.

84. Carol's pronouncement to the Romanians (Poradim), 27 August/8 September 1877, in *Documente privind istoria României: Războiul pentru independenţă,* 5:626–29.

85. For an eyewitness account of the fall of Pleven, see Carol (Poradim) to Bamberg, 26 November and 8/20 December 1877, in Fond Dimitrie A. Sturdza, 5:681, BAR, SC; see also Carol's notes, 1/13 September 1877, in *Aus dem Leben König Karls von Rumänien,* 3:272.

86. Adăniloaie, *Independenţa naţională a României,* 330–58; Ciahir, *Războiul pentru independenţa României,* 205–6, 209–11. Romania took Rakhovo on 9/21 November 1877, Pleven finally fell on 28 November/10 December 1877, and Vidin on 12/24 February 1878; Serbia reentered the war on 2/12 December 1877.

87. Kogălniceanu's circular, 30 August/11 September 1877, in *Documente privind istoria României: Războiul pentru independenţă,* 5:675–76.

88. Carol's speech to the legislature, 3/15 November 1877, in *Independenţa României,* 4:316–17.

89. Carp's speech in the senate, 26 November/8 December 1877, in Carp, *Discursuri,* 1:153–56.

90. Kogălniceanu's speech in the senate, 26 November/8 December 1877, in Kogălniceanu, *Opere,* vol. 4: *Oratorie II,* pt. 4, 509–11.

Chapter Nine

PEACE

Europe's great powers, as signatories of the Treaty of Paris terminating the Crimean War, were technically responsible for the Danubian Romanian lands. But they had been unable or unwilling to sustain Romania during the Balkan Crisis and War of 1877. Romanians, for their part, were militarily incapable of shielding themselves alone. Their neutrality had obviously been contravened when Russian troops traveled on their railroads and roads to invade the Ottoman Empire. Romania's targets were henceforth to secure national independence and to preserve the principality's territorial integrity. The powers' decisions, however, more than Romanian actions and appeals, were the core of peacemaking.

Great Britain endeavored during the war to prevent Russia's annexation of the Bosporus, the Dardanelles, and the Sea of Marmara. Russia sought to avert a British naval intervention at the straits yet nonetheless proposed that Britain occupy the Dardanelles. In return, Russia was to gain a fort on the Bosporus and to annex southern Bessarabia as well as Batum in the Caucasus. Austria-Hungary was to receive Bosnia and Hercegovina. Russia also planned for a large Bulgarian state, with compensation for Romania in Dobrogea.[1] Danubian Romanians reckoned with the ongoing presence of Russian soldiers in their country and so looked to Russia's leadership and supposed benevolence in concluding a satisfactory treaty with Turkey.

Ion Brătianu thought his country would benefit from the eventual peace settlement because Romanian troops had actively participated in the victory and even held fortified towns on the southern bank of the Danube River.[2] Russia decided unilaterally to represent both allies in negotiating with the Ottoman Empire. Alexander II sent a draft agreement to Berlin and Vienna for consideration and approval by other members of the Three Emperors' League. This project stipulated political independence for Romania and Serbia, Romania's transfer of southern Bessarabia—to the Chilia branch of the Danube—to Russia, and Romania's acquisition of Dobrogea and the Danube Delta.[3]

Russia barred Romania from the Russo-Turkish armistice discussions in Kazanlŭk and later in Adrianople. Instead, Nikolai Nikolaevich simply assured Carol that the "essential bases of peace" conserved "all of Romania's interests."[4] Romania's council of ministers nevertheless appointed an army officer, Eracle Arion, to announce Romania's goals at Kazanlŭk. Moreover, Arion was to sign a separate truce with the Ottoman Empire. Romania's terms were: (1) Turkey's "formal and absolute" recognition of Romania as a fully "sovereign state"; (2) Romania's continued occupation of the Danubian fortresses of Nikopol, Rakhovo, Lom, and Vidin until the signing of a definitive treaty; (3) the razing of Danubian strongholds, beginning with the one on Ada Kale Island; (4) Turkey's cession of the Danube Delta to Romania; and (5) a Turkish indemnity of one hundred million francs for Romania's wartime expenses, the reconstruction of railroads, and the repatriation of prisoners.[5] The Ottoman Empire was thereby to pay for Romania's passage from vassalage to independence.

Russia's officials received Arion at Kazanlŭk with much pomp but without seriously considering Romania's program. Nelidov, the Russian envoy, told Arion to take his case to St. Petersburg.[6] Nelidov also recounted a parallel situation at the end of the Franco-Prussian War in 1871 when Prussia dealt alone—for itself and its allies—in making peace with France.[7] Ignat'ev frankly denied Romania's participation in the parleys with the Ottoman Empire and demanded Russia's recovery of southern Bessarabia.[8] Alexander II and Gorchakov argued that Romania was merely autonomous and so was ineligible to join international deliberations. Still, Russia promised that Romania would soon be truly sovereign with an "ample indemnity" in the Danube Delta and Dobrogea in return for its loss of southern Bessarabia.[9] According to the Russo-Turkish armistice at Adrianople on 31 January 1878, Romania was indeed to be independent with "adequate territorial compensation," though without specific mention of southern Bessarabia, Dobrogea, or the delta.[10] Gorchakov aptly identified southern Bessarabia as "one of the most delicate questions."[11]

What was at issue? Bessarabia, with its predominantly Romanian-speaking inhabitants, lies between the Dnestr and Prut rivers. It had been a segment of the Roman, Byzantine, and first Bulgarian empires as well as of Kievan Rus. After the Mongol conquest in the thirteenth century, Bessarabia was part of the Romanian principality of Moldavia. The Ottoman Empire obtained suzerainty over Moldavia, including Bessarabia, by the fifteenth century. Subsequent Russo-Turkish wars involved Bessarabia as an object of exchange. During one conflagration, Russia temporarily occupied Bessarabia but returned it to Turkey according to the terms of the Küçük Kaynarca Treaty in 1774, a status reaffirmed at Iaşi in 1792 following renewed hostilities.

Another conflict ended at Bucharest in 1812 with Russia annexing Bessarabia; by a later pact at Adrianople in 1829, Russia also acquired the Danube Delta. The powers, who concluded the Crimean War at Paris in 1856, had southern Bessarabia going to Moldavia and the delta to the Ottoman Empire. The powers endeavored to secure free navigation there and so placed the lower Danube under a European commission that met in Galaţi. Southern Bessarabia then had a highly mixed population of about 150,000—embracing Romanians, Bulgarians, Ukrainians, Russians, Tatars, Germans, and others—in an area of roughly 4,000 square miles.[12] The Russo-Romanian political convention of 1877 stipulated, as we have seen, Romania's territorial integrity, yet the Russo-Turkish armistice concluded in Adrianople anticipated frontier changes. Gorchakov correctly foresaw Russia's need for the powers' support in regaining southern Bessarabia, as they had collectively determined the Bessarabian matter in 1856.

Romania's leaders knew that St. Petersburg wanted southern Bessarabia. In Ploieşti in June 1877, Gorchakov had told Ion Brătianu and Kogălniceanu about Russia's aims.[13] Miliutin likewise informed Brătianu that southern Bessarabia constituted a "painful wound" for all Russians, one the war "must heal." Brătianu replied that Russia's taking of this parcel would weaken its "moral influence."[14] Morality, however, cut two ways. Gorchakov viewed southern Bessarabia as Russia's just perquisite, something affecting its "honor and dignity."[15] He admitted that Russia had promised to protect Romania's wholeness against a Turkish attack, but he insisted that Russia had never pledged to allow this "scrap of land" to remain in Romania.[16] Carol wrote to Alexander II indicating that a border rectification would be "most delicate," something touching Romania's "national susceptibilities."[17] Gorchakov warned that Romania should voluntarily leave southern Bessarabia or have it preempted directly by force from the Ottoman Empire without reference to Romania. And in that case, Bucharest would realize no compensation in Dobrogea.[18]

The terms of the Adrianople armistice dismayed many Romanians. What had been alluded to or discussed privately was henceforth the topic of much debate. The consensus was that losing terrain was undesirable, and gaining trans-Danubian lands was worse. Romania would thereby become involved in "inextricable complications" with the Slavs of Southeastern Europe—as Sturdza, the minister of finance, cautioned—giving Russia "frequent occasions to meddle" in Romania's affairs.[19] The conservative party chief in the senate, Dimitrie Ghica, urged that southern Bessarabia be retained.[20] Ion Brătianu noted that Russian newspapers reported Romania might be indemnified with Danubian islands near Giurgiu; yet he deemed Romanians ready to make every sacrifice to preserve "untouched" their native soil.[21] Brătianu contended that the "Romanian nation would never consent either to the cession or to an exchange of its territory, even should the compensation be more advantageous."[22] According to Brătianu, neither Gorchakov nor Ignat'ev had broached the subject of southern Bessarabia at his wartime interview at Livadia; they had said they only sought to defend Romania's integrity, hence the Russo-Romanian conventions of 1877. He would rather resign as prime minister than abandon any portion of his country.[23] Kogălniceanu argued that Romania should eschew swapping southern Bessarabia for another province, for that would be "insulting . . . [and] contrary to Romania's national interests."[24] He thought Romania should militantly resist yielding southern Bessarabia; but if it must be relinquished, then Romania's winnings in Dobrogea should include the Danubian fortress of Silistra.[25] Carp perceived somewhat dimly the realities of the situation. He asserted that as geography dictated Russia's foreign policy, St. Petersburg's goal was to command important trade routes between Europe and Asia. The key to Russia's program was thus "the opening of the Dardanelles and the closing of the Danube."[26] Mastery of southern Bessarabia was, of course, irrelevant to blocking egress from the Danube, for the navigable Sulina channel was farther south in the mid-delta; however, this verity may have been only a quibble in the eyes of the land-oriented Romanians. Carol, for his part, believed Romania's military cooperation at Pleven obviated the forfeiture of southern Bessarabia;[27] in any case, "not a chamber, nor a government, nor a Romanian" would agree to retrocession.[28] After the forensics, the legislature unanimously approved a resolution rejecting the reversion of southern Bessarabia to Russia.[29]

Romania's parliamentary oratory undermined Russo-Romanian relations. Girs considered Romania's vote a "direct offense" against his emperor and an "act of hostility" toward Russia.[30] Moreover, Ion G. Ghica had antagonized Alexander II, and so Gorchakov refused to speak to him.[31] Kogălniceanu explained that the legislature was the "legal organ" of Romania empowered to express discontent with Russo-Turkish negotiations at San Stefano. Other Romanian concerns were the sequestration of railroads by the Russian army, the stagnation of commerce, the threat of typhus, the repatriation of prisoners of war, Romania's nonparticipation in the peace talks, and independence.[32] Carol complained that the powers lacked sympathy for Romania's needs; he appealed in vain to Germany for help in saving southern Bessarabia.[33] Bismarck was more interested, though, in becoming a mediator at a future international congress than in supporting Romania's claims. Austria-Hungary saw southern Bessarabia as a matter of Alexander II's personal honor, which it was.[34]

Russia regarded the Danubian fortress of Vidin as an object of exchange. During the war, Gorchakov thought Vidin and the Danube Delta, but not Dobrogea, would be adequate compensation for Romania in return for southern Bessarabia.[35] After the Adrianople armistice, Nikolai Nikolaevich reckoned the Ottoman Empire would evacuate Vidin, which was in turn to be occupied by Romania.[36] Carol agreed to retain Danubian strongholds until Turkey paid for Romania's wartime damages.[37] Kogălniceanu argued that Romanians had peacefully lived for centuries with Serbs and Bulgarians, yet the annexation of Vidin would endanger that harmony. But he would keep Vidin until the Turks paid reparations.[38] The Ottoman Empire, however, rejected any indemnity, for Romania had rebelled against the suzerain sultan, not declared war; rather, Romania must reimburse Turkey for having seized monastic lands belonging to Orthodox Christian Holy Places in the Ottoman Empire.[39]

The principal belligerents formally ignored Romania's involvement in the campaigns, and so Romania was absent from the peace table at San Stefano. Hence the only way for Bucharest to end the hostilities was in the same manner they had begun. By a decree of 16 February 1878, Carol terminated the "state of war" with the Ottoman Empire.[40]

The Russo-Turkish peace preliminaries—signed on 3 March 1878—were the work of the Russian envoys, Ignat'ev and Nelidov, and adhered to by Savfet Paşa and Turkey's ambassador to Germany, Saadulah Bey. The two powers exchanged ratifications in St. Petersburg on 17 March 1878. Thereby Romania, Serbia, and Montenegro received independence. Russia gained southern Bessarabia, the eastern Black Sea port of Batum, and the fortified towns of Ardahan and Kars in Turkish Armenia. The settlement envisioned a sizable Bulgarian state, which would be militarily occupied by Russia for two years; Russian troops had the right of passage through Romania during that time. The lower Danube River was to be demilitarized, and Ada Kale Island evacuated by the Turks. The Ottoman Empire was to cede Dobrogea, Danube Delta, and the Insula Şerpilor in the Black Sea to Russia for later transfer to Romania in return for southern Bessarabia.[41] Serbia's witnesses to the final agreement, Milojko Lešjanin and Gheorghe Catargi, called for an enlarged Serbia—with the addition of lands in Macedonia—should Austria-Hungary seize Bosnia and Hercegovina. Romania lacked observers at San Stefano, so Russia was to transmit the accord to Bucharest.[42]

Several days after the deliberations at San Stefano, Austria-Hungary invited the powers to a peace congress, which ultimately met in Berlin. The Russo-Turkish covenant had stipulated the inadmissible. To be sure, Russia had abjured demanding the straits or the Persian Gulf for itself; but Britain objected to a big Bulgaria that incorporated regions claimed by Greece, and to Russia's political preponderance in Constantinople. Southern Bessarabia and Batum became pawns vis-à-vis Bulgaria, which was Russia's satellite and Turkey's vassal. The Habsburg Empire also used the southern Bessarabia issue to push its own pretensions in Bosnia and Hercegovina. Vienna reckoned that a large Bulgaria would block the Dual Monarchy's eventual winning of a trade outlet to the Aegean Sea via the Yenipazar *sancak,* a provincial subdivision, and a railroad through Greece. Owing to the unacceptability of San Stefano provisions to the strongest naval power, Britain, and to its own most interested neighbor and accessory, Austria-Hungary, Russia had to assent to a congress.

Romania requested a vote at the Berlin Congress. Kogălniceanu offered as precedent the attendance of Belgium's delegates to the London conferences of 1830 and 1831 when it separated from the Netherlands.[43] Russia rejected Romania's suggestion, for Sardinia had not been represented in the partial forging of modern Italy at Villafranca in 1859.[44] Girs and Gorchakov advised that Romania—along with Serbia and Montenegro—was indeed to be heard at the congress, yet not to participate in making decisions. Andrássy agreed: Romanians might attend and speak only on matters affecting themselves. In any case, Romania's entry to the congress depended on a prior understanding by the powers signatory to the Treaty of Paris. France, Britain, and Germany subscribed to Andrássy's views.[45]

Romanians' patriotic fervor soared after the publication of the San Stefano terms. Carol, to be sure, counted on the powers to ensure Romania's acquiring Dobrogea in return for southern Bessarabia.[46] A rumor circulated nonetheless in Russia that Romania was mobilizing its troops to show that southern Bessarabia would not be voluntarily yielded.[47] Ion Brătianu complained that sacrificing land would infringe on Romania's "rights of autonomy, independence, and sovereignty," but he also recognized that Bessarabia had for a "long time" been under "foreign domination."[48] He nevertheless continued to appeal for support from Austria-Hungary and Germany to save southern Bessarabia.[49] This was hollow diplomacy. Alexander II at first sought to ameliorate the "actual tension" in Russo-Romanian relations.[50] The Russo-Romanian conventions of 1877, according to Gorchakov, obliged Russia to defend Romania against the Ottoman Empire, and nothing more.

If Romania refused to retrocede southern Bessarabia, Russia would forcibly take it. Alexander was reportedly losing his patience and was prepared to occupy Romania militarily and disarm its army.[51] Carol appeared adamant. He vowed that Romanian soldiers who had "fought at Pleven under the eyes of Emperor Alexander II might be crushed and slaughtered, but never disarmed."[52] Brave indeed was the rhetoric of national pride. Without the backing of the other powers, however, Romania had no chance of holding southern Bessarabia.

The San Stefano stipulation for a Russian road through Romania to Bulgaria also provoked an angry response in Bucharest. Did such a road signify an overweening Russian presence in Romania during the two years that Russia's troops would be south of the Danube River? Girs reaffirmed Russia's need for an overland route to Bulgaria.[53] The Russo-Romanian conventions of 1877 had provided for the passage of Russia's army, and so, in Miliutin's view, communications had already been regulated.[54] Gorchakov, however, anticipated yet another compact, presumably to cover the ensuing two years.[55] Girs and Gorchakov denied that Russia intended to maintain fortifications or to garrison soldiers in Romania, but Gorchakov fretted that Romania was unprepared to sustain and protect the artery.[56] Kogălniceanu protested Russia's path in Romania and insisted that Russia instead use maritime transport via Black Sea and Danubian ports.[57] He inveighed against Russia's "illegal occupation" of southern Bessarabia and rejected an additional Russo-Romanian pact.[58] Ion Brătianu worried about St. Petersburg's goals, for Russia had four times more soldiers in Bucharest than Romania.[59] Kogălniceanu described Russia's forces as being a "quasi-permanent installation"—no longer "transitory"—in Romania. Because of this peril, rumor became reality, and Romania's troops assumed a defensive posture between Piteşti, Cîmpulung, and Tîrgovişte.[60] The chamber of deputies approved four million lei for military supplies, and the army evacuated Bucharest.[61] When Russia entered Romania in 1877, Romania's legions had concentrated in Oltenia; now they were east of Oltenia, in Muntenia, near the Carpathian Mountains. The wartime allies had verily become adversaries.

The powers addressed Romania's problems before the Berlin Congress took place. Salisbury, Britain's minister of foreign affairs, proposed that Russia reduce its forces in Bulgaria and promptly pull them altogether out of Southeastern Europe.[62] He considered, moreover, that the retrocession of southern Bessarabia was indefensible by the "principles of International Law."[63] Still, this matter was merely byplay in a larger game. Russia favored an accord with Britain, for it required help at the peace table. Mutual concerns dictated the Anglo-Russian agreement of 30 May 1878, by which Russia was to receive southern Bessarabia and Batum, and Bulgaria was to be partitioned. British interests were hardly at stake in southern Bessarabia; thus, despite his "profound regret," Salisbury yielded that morsel.[64] The Habsburg Empire went farther. Andrássy opposed Russia's apparent plan to erect fortifications and to prolong its stay in Southeastern Europe.[65] He also sought assurances that a Bulgarian state would not imperil Vienna's potential southward expansion. Austria-Hungary and Britain then concluded an entente on 6 June 1878. This understanding planned for a small Bulgaria and a Habsburg occupation of Bosnia. Furthermore, Russia was to forswear Dobrogea, and its army was to withdraw from Bulgaria in six months.[66] St. Petersburg henceforth no longer claimed a military road in Romania; its trans-Danubian troops would subsequently leave by the Black Sea harbors of Varna in Bulgaria and Burgas in Eastern Rumelia.

Austria-Hungary had, of course, its own agenda, yet it jibed with Romania's. Increasingly cordial relations ensued between the two sides. Andrássy and Tisza allowed the passage of arms and munitions from Transylvania to Romania.[67] The Habsburg Empire's wartime neutrality was evidently an issue no more. Ion Brătianu took heart; his country was now militarily ready with 60,000 soldiers to defend itself.[68] Andrássy counseled patience: Romania could scarcely fight alone against Russia; in any case, he affirmed, Romania would gain Dobrogea and the Danube Delta in exchange for its loss of southern Bessarabia.[69] Carol, upon returning to Bucharest from a journey through Oltenia and Muntenia, where he inspected his troops,[70] was also convinced that Romania lacked the resources and adequate military assistance for a campaign against Russia.

Southern Bessarabia remained a paramount anxiety for Romania's patriots. How might Romanians reconcile the sacrifice of any component of their homeland with the idea of patriotism? Romanians renewed their protests. Dimitrie Ghica recommended that Romania not "sell a plot of soil or receive anything in exchange for part of our country." Ion Brătianu concurred, for "divine justice" and "human justice" should ultimately preserve Romania's perquisites.[71] Constantin Rosetti advised, though, that if southern Bessarabia were to be surrendered, Romania should be "poor and pure" by dissociating itself from the congress.[72] The cabinet nevertheless authorized Romania's delegates to the congress, Brătianu and Kogălniceanu, to sustain the "rights and interests of the nation."[73] However, the powers had already decided the fate of southern Bessarabia, and so Andrássy warned that Romania's continued resistance to reality would spell its "material or political" dependence on Russia.[74] Brătianu, who feared forfeiting Austria-Hungary's backing in other matters, reluctantly recognized the inevitable.[75] But he lamented the inadequate time to prepare his compatriots for the retrocession.[76] Carol also fully understood the powers' determination, and he noted that "the friendship of a whole people [the Russians] was worth more than a scrap of land."[77]

The powers' delegates to the Berlin congress, which met from 13 June to 13 July 1878, evaluated and then rewrote the San Stefano provisions. The powers honored accords reached before the congress. Romania's aims in Berlin were to have its sovereignty confirmed and to gain appropriate compensation for southern Bessarabia. Despite the prior Anglo-Russian agreement, Britain's prime minister, Benjamin Disraeli, Earl of Beaconsfield, initially opposed the retrocession of southern Bessarabia and joined France's minister for foreign affairs, William H. Waddington, in calling for religious freedom in Romania.[78] Britain saw southern Bessarabia as a pawn to be pushed so as to prevent Russia from controlling the Bosporus and the Dardanelles. Alexander II's instructions to his emissaries envisioned the trading of southern Bessarabia for Dobrogea; hence Gorchakov and Shuvalov insisted on this exchange.[79] Kogălniceanu and Ion Brătianu spoke before the congress on 1 July 1878. Kogălniceanu recapitulated Romania's concerns and pleaded that his homeland be kept territorially intact. He also urged that Romania be spared from serving as a military corridor during Russia's occupation of Bulgaria, that Romania acquire the Danube Delta, that Romania collect a war indemnity from the Ottoman Empire, that Romania's independence be validated, and that its neutrality be guaranteed. Brătianu told the congress of his "profound sorrow" at the likely loss of southern Bessarabia, which would destroy "all confidence in the efficacy of treaties" and paralyze Romania's "pacific development and its desire for progress."[80] France, Austria-Hungary, Italy, and even Russia—albeit somewhat reluctantly—endeavored to award Romania suitable reparations in Dobrogea.[81] The Berlin covenant would next stipulate Romania's sovereignty, which would be contingent upon the assurance of religious liberties and the retrocession of southern Bessarabia; Romania was furthermore to have Dobrogea.[82] Beaconsfield acknowledged Russia's "political ingratitude,"[83] but the powers' needs, not compassion for Romania's patriotic longings, keyed the settlement at Berlin.

News of the congress's decision about southern Bessarabia evoked a stormy response in Bucharest. Rosetti's *Romanulu* inveighed bellicosely against the powers. Kogălniceanu conceded nevertheless that Romania had no choice; it must submit to the powers' dictates and accept the "painful sacrifice imposed by circumstances."[84] In closing the legislature for the summer, Carol complained about the "difficult sacrifices" required by the powers. He nonetheless trusted that the legislators' patriotism and wisdom would ultimately demonstrate Romania's maturity and prudence, showing the powers that Romania deserved far more than it had received at Berlin.[85] He then ordered the demobilization of the army, and Romanian troops returned to Bucharest. Russia's forces subsequently moved across the Prut River, thereby evacuating Romania.[86]

Russo-Romanian negotiations about southern Bessarabia began promptly after the signing of the Treaty of Berlin. Stuart, Russia's diplomatic agent in Bucharest, proposed a Russo-Romanian commission to delimit the frontier and to transfer fiscal, administrative, and judicial business to Russian authorities.[87] This had been the procedure when Russia passed southern Bessarabia to Moldavia in 1857. Cîmpineanu, Romania's finance minister, initially indicated, however, that such a body might be a pretext for prolonging Russia's occupation and for refusing to deliver Dobrogea.[88] Kogălniceanu also opposed a commission because the Berlin accord already defined the boundary: the Prut River and the mid-channel of the Chilia, or northern branch of the Danube's outlet to the Black Sea.[89] Ion Brătianu, who feared tarnishing his political career by yielding any part of his country, preferred that southern Bessarabia be ceded without legislative action.[90] For Carol, the "loss of a province is always a severe blow for a dynasty." He trusted, however, that the "odium" of retrocession would not engulf him, reckoning that he had the right cabinet to muster popular acceptance of the Berlin stipulations.[91] Carol's message to the legislature in the autumn of 1878 clearly identified the "grievous sacrifice" in southern Bessarabia; he appealed to the legislators as "mature men, as inflexible patriots," to do their duty in implementing Europe's "painful sentence."[92] Kogălniceanu attempted to rally support by suggesting that "Bessarabia is not a question of land but of water"; Europe now relied on Romania to assure the liberty of the Danube at its Sulina mouth.[93] A committee report in the chamber acknowledged that Romania must defer to the collective will of Europe and appreciated the annexation of Dobrogea as strengthening the state.[94] After a lengthy and bitter debate, the senate and chamber approved the exchange of southern Bessarabia for Dobrogea.[95] From 13 to 18 October 1878, Russia took southern Bessarabia while Romania's officials withdrew.[96]

Peacemaking was solely in the hands of the powers at Berlin. Romania was merely a witness, not an integral participant, in its own destiny. To be sure, Danubian Romanians had declared their national independence and zealously cooperated in defeating the suzerain Ottoman Empire. The powers had nevertheless bluntly rejected Bucharest's entreaties to partake as an equal in their deliberations. The Berlin covenant understandably corresponded to the powers' interests, notably that of Russia in its annexation of southern Bessarabia, and placed conditions on recognizing Romania's sovereignty. Romania had, in addition to yielding a segment of its patrimony, to resolve other weighty matters before the powers would sanction its new international status. The powers' proposals and injunctions during and after the Congress of Berlin vexed and frustrated many Danubian Romanians. Romanians' anxieties were neither imaginary nor transitory, as they would fully discover in ensuing controversies.

Notes

1. Bălăceanu (Vienna) to Ministerul Afacerilor Străine, 21 June/3 July 1877, in *Documente privind istoria României: Războiul pentru independenţă,* 4:141–42.

2. Miliutin's notes, 4/16 November 1877, in *Dnevnik D. A. Miliutina,* 2:238–39.

3. Alexander II (Poradim) to William I, 27 November/9 December 1877, in *Osvobozhdenie Bolgarii ot turetskogo iga,* 2:341.

4. Nikolai (Kazanlŭk) to Carol (Bucharest), 29 December 1877/10 January 1878, in *Documente privind istoria României: Războiul pentru independenţă,* 8:332.

5. Kogălniceanu (Bucharest) to Arion, 2/14 January 1878, in HHS, PA—XXXVIII, Konsulate: Bukarest, Karton 223.

6. Nelidov (Shipka) to Ion Brătianu, 4/16 January 1878, and Kogălniceanu to Ion G. Ghica (St. Petersburg), 9/21 January 1878, in *Documente privind istoria României: Războiul pentru independenţă,* 8:409, 461.

7. Arion (Kazanlŭk) to Kogălniceanu, 10/22 January 1878, in *Correspondance diplomatique roumaine sous le roi Charles Ier,* 246.

8. Miliutin's notes, 3/15 January 1878, in *Dnevnik D. A. Miliutina,* 3:10.

9. Ion G. Ghica (St. Petersburg) to Kogălniceanu, 14/26 January 1878, in *Corespondenţa generalului Iancu Ghica,* 125–26; Ghica to Kogălniceanu, 14/26 January 1878, in *Independenţa României,* 4:328.

10. Protocol signed by Nikolai Nikolaevich and the Turkish minister of foreign affairs, Server Paşa (Adrianople), 19/31 January 1878, in *Recueil d'actes internationaux de l'Empire Ottoman,* 3:507; Arion (Adrianople) to Kogălniceanu, 20 January/1 February 1878, in *Independenţa României,* 4:330–31.

11. Gorchakov to Ignat'ev (Adrianople), 20 January/1 February 1878, in *Osvobozhdenie Bolgarii ot turetskogo iga,* 2:440.

12. Russian and Romanian statistical data differ on southern Bessarabia. According to Russia's governor of Bessarabia in the 1870s, Nikolai I. Shebeko, Russia lost 1,354 square miles in the late 1850s together with 127,030 residents; Pompei N. Batiushkov reckons that Russia won 3,932 square miles with 127,451 people in 1878; Batiushkov, *Bessarabiia: Istoricheskoe opisanie,* 162, 170. Romania's first

economist, Nicolae Suțu, basing his figures on a census of Moldavia in the 1860s, gives 4,088 square miles with 178,007 dwellers in southern Bessarabia; Nicolas Soutzo, *Quelques observations sur la statistique de la Roumanie.*

13. Note on a meeting between Carol and Gorchakov (Ploieşti), 2/14 June 1877, in *Charles Ier, Roi de Roumanie,* 2:827.

14. Miliutin's notes, 4/16 November 1877, in *Dnevnik D. A. Miliutina,* 2:239.

15. Ion G. Ghica (St. Petersburg) to Kogălniceanu, 14/26 and 16/28 January 1878, in *Corespondenţa generalului Iancu Ghica,* 128, 130–31.

16. Gorchakov's circular, 31 January 1878, in Nikolai P. Ignat'ev, *San Stefano: Zapiski grafa N. P. Ignat'eva,* 332–34.

17. Carol to Alexander II, 22 January/3 February 1878, in AIC, CR, dosar 14/ 1878; Kogălniceanu to Ion G. Ghica, 23 January/4 February 1878, in *Corespondenţa generalului Iancu Ghica,* 134–35; Carol to the crown prince of Prussia, Frederick William, 26 February 1878, in HAA, PS, Türkei, 24, vol. 63.

18. Ion G. Ghica (St. Petersburg) to Kogălniceanu, 25 January/6 February 1878, in *Corespondenţa generalului Iancu Ghica,* 137–38.

19. Dimitrie Sturdza (Bucharest) to Ion Ghica, 1 February 1878, in Fond Ion Ghica, XIV, 314, BAR, SC.

20. *Monitorul oficial al României,* 27 January/8 February 1878, 445; *Neue Freie Presse,* 5 February 1878.

21. See a report in *Petersburger Herald* for 2/14 March 1877, and Brătianu's speech in the senate, 3/15 March 1877, in *Ion C. Brătianu: Discursuri, scrieri, acte şi documente,* vol. 2, pt. 2, 500, 506–7.

22. Brătianu's speech in the chamber of deputies, 26 January/7 February 1878, in *Ion C. Brătianu: Acte şi cuvântări,* 3:167.

23. Brătianu's senate speech, 13/25 February 1878, in *Ion C. Brătianu: Acte şi cuvântări,* 3:191–92.

24. Kogălniceanu's senate speech, 13/25 February 1878, in Kogălniceanu, *Opere,* vol. 4: *Oratorie II,* pt. 4, 553.

25. Ion G. Ghica to Kogălniceanu, 14/26 January 1878, Kogălniceanu to Ghica, 18/30 January and 24 January/5 February 1878, in *Corespondenţa generalului Iancu Ghica,* 128, 132, 136–37.

26. Carp's senate speech, 13/25 February 1878, in Carp, *Discursuri,* 1:165.

27. Carol to Charles Anthony, 2/14 January 1878, in *Aus dem Leben König Karls von Rumänien,* 3:438–40.

28. In the senate, 26 January/7 February 1878, Brătianu quoted Carol, in *Ion C. Brătianu: Acte şi cuvântări,* 3:181.

29. For the votes in the chamber and senate, 25 January/6 February 1878, see *Ion C. Brătianu: Acte şi cuvântări,* 3:169, and Kogălniceanu, *Opere,* vol. 4: *Oratorie II,* pt. 4, 529.

30. Ion G. Ghica (St. Petersburg) to Kogălniceanu, 29 January/10 February 1878, in *Corespondenţa generalului Iancu Ghica,* 141.

31. Ferdinand von Langenau (St. Petersburg), to Andrássy (Vienna), 1/13 February 1878, no. 7F, in HHS, PA—X, Rußland, Karton 71; cf. Ghica (St. Petersburg) to Kogălniceanu, 11/23 February 1878, in *Corespondenţa generalului Iancu Ghica,* 146–47.

32. Kogălniceanu to the Ottoman Empire, 21 January/2 February 1878, in *Correspondance diplomatique roumaine sous le roi Charles Ier*, 261; Kogălniceanu to Ghica (St. Petersburg) and to the Ottoman Empire, 3/15 February 1878, in *Documente privind istoria României: Războiul pentru independenţă*, 9:223–24, 224–25; Kogălniceanu to Ghica, 7/19 February 1878, in *Corespondenţa generalului Iancu Ghica*, 145–46.

33. Carol to Frederick William, 26 February 1878, in HAA, PS, Türkei, 24, vol. 63.

34. Langenau to Andrássy, 24 January/5 February 1878, in HHS, PA—X, Rußland, Karton 70.

35. See a letter from the Russian imperial councilor, Aleksandr G. Zhomini, to military headquarters, 6 June 1877, in Mikhail A. Gazenkampf, *Moi dnevnik, 1877–78 gg.*, 38.

36. Nikolai (Adrianople) to Carol, 21 January/2 February 1878, in AIC, CR, dosar 16/1877; cf. Andrássy to Zwiedinek (Bucharest), 6 February 1878, in HHS, PA—Konsulate: Bukarest, Karton 223; see Ignat'ev's notes, 21 January 1878, in Ignat'ev, *San Stefano*, 47, 55–56; Nikolai P. Ignat'ev, *Posle San Stefano: Zapiski grafa N. P. Ignat'eva*, 86. See the Turkish-Romanian convention providing for Romania's occupation of Vidin signed by Izzet Paşa and Ştefan Fălcoianu (Vidin), 23 February 1878, in *Nouveau recueil général de traités*, vol. 3, pt. 1, 244–45.

37. Carol to Nikolai (Adrianople), 23 January/4 February 1878, in AIC, CR, dosar 16/1877.

38. Carol to Frederick William, 23 January/4 February 1878, and Carol's notes, 27 January/8 February 1878, in *Aus dem Leben König Karls von Rumänien*, 3:465, 469; Kogălniceanu's senate speech, 13/25 February 1878, in Kogălniceanu, *Opere*, vol. 4: *Oratorie II*, pt. 4, 560.

39. Ignat'ev, *San Stefano*, 206, 275; cf. Popescu-Spineni, *Procesul mănăstirilor închinate*, 119, and chapters Two and Eight above.

40. See Carol's decree, 4/16 February 1878, in *Războiul pentru independenţă naţională*, 1877–1878, 580.

41. See the treaty (San Stefano), 3 March 1878, in *Recueil d'actes internationaux de l'Empire Ottoman*, 3:509–21. Insula Şerpilor (Isle of Serpents) is a tiny—0.08-square-mile—island about thirty miles east of the principal—navigable—Sulina fork of the Danube Delta. It was uninhabited in modern times but had a lighthouse to guide ships approaching the Danube.

42. Ignat'ev (San Stefano) to Gorchakov, 25 February/9 March 1878, in *Osvobozhdenie Bolgarii ot turetskogo iga*, 2:561.

43. Kogălniceanu to Bălăceanu, 24 January/5 February 1878, in HHS, PA—XXXVIII, Konsulate: Bukarest, Karton 223.

44. Ion G. Ghica to Kogălniceanu, 11/23 February 1878, in *Corespondenţa generalului Iancu Ghica*, 148.

45. C. A. Balaşiu (Berlin) to Ministerul Afacerilor Străine, 10/22 February 1878, Ion G. Ghica to Kogălniceanu, 14/26 and 15/27 February, N. Steriadi (Vienna) to Ministerul Afacerilor Străine, 16/28 February, and Nicolae Calimaki-Catargi (Paris) to Ministerul Afacerilor Străine, 18 February/1 March 1878, in *Documente privind*

istoria României: Războiul pentru independenţă, 9:286, 321, 326, 333, 351–52; see also Ghica to Kogălniceanu, 14/26 February 1878, in *Corespondenţa generalului Iancu Ghica,* 150.

46. Carol (Bucharest) to Prince Leopold von Hohenzollern (Sigmaringen), 18 March 1878, in Fürstliches Hohenzollernsches Haus Archiv, Abteilung Hohenzollern-Sigmaringen, Rubrik 53b, Kasten XXIX, Fach 27, Faszikel no. 1 (69) (hereinafter cited HHA, HS).

47. Langenau to Andrássy, 10 March 1878, in HHS, PA—X, Rußland, Karton 71. Kogălniceanu alluded to this prospect in the chamber, 5/17 April 1878; see *Monitorul oficial al României,* 6/18 April 1878, 2276.

48. Brătianu's speeches in the senate, 4/16 April, and in the chamber, 8/20 April 1878, in *Ion C. Brătianu: Acte şi cuvântări,* 3:274, 292.

49. Brătianu traveled to Vienna and Berlin from 31 March to 15 April 1878; *Aus dem Leben König Karls von Rumänien,* 4:15.

50. Alexander II (St. Petersburg) to Carol, 28 March/9 April 1878, in AIC, CR, dosar 14/1878.

51. Ion G. Ghica to Kogălniceanu, 28 February/12 March, 1/13 March, and 20 March/1 April 1878, in *Corespondenţa generalului Iancu Ghica,* 160–61, 171–72; Kogălniceanu to Bălăceanu, 16/28 March 1878, in Fond Ion Ghica, IX, no. 104, BAR, SC; Ion G. Ghica to Kogălniceanu, 21 March/2 April 1878, in AIC, CR, dosar 26/1878.

52. Kogălniceanu to Ion G. Ghica, 21 March/2 April 1878, in *Corespondenţa generalului Iancu Ghica,* 174; cf. Carol's notes, 21 March/2 April 1878, in *Aus dem Leben König Karls von Rumänien,* 4:18.

53. Ion G. Ghica to Kogălniceanu, 29 March/10 April 1878, in *Corespondenţa generalului Iancu Ghica,* 181.

54. Langenau to Andrássy, 13 March 1878, no. 15D, in HHS, PA—X, Rußland, Karton 71.

55. Gorchakov (St. Petersburg) to Stuart (Bucharest), 9/21 April 1878, in Fond Mihail Kogălniceanu, XVIII, no. 185, BAR, SC.

56. Langenau to Andrássy, 10/22 May 1878, no. 23C, in HHS, PA—X, Rußland, Karton 71.

57. Kogălniceanu's circular, 14/26 March 1878, in *Independenţa României,* 4:345.

58. Kogălniceanu to Ion G. Ghica, 3/15 April and 7/19 April 1878, in *Corespondenţa generalului Iancu Ghica,* 193, 196; Kogălniceanu to Ion Brătianu, 5/17 April 1878, in *Ion C. Brătianu: Acte şi cuvântări,* 3:279.

59. Brătianu to Bălăceanu, 28 April/10 May 1878, in HHS, PA—XXXVIII, Konsulate: Bukarest, Karton 223.

60. Carol's notes, 20 April/2 May 1878, and Kogălniceanu to Stuart, 24 April/6 May 1878, in *Aus dem Leben König Karls von Rumänien,* 4:38, 39.

61. Carol's notes, 26 April/8 May and 29 April/11 May 1878, in *Aus dem Leben König Karls von Rumänien,* 4:40, 41; Cernat (Calafat) to Brătianu, 6/18 May 1878, in *Ion C. Brătianu: Acte şi cuvântări,* 4:11–12. Romania's troops concentrated at Piteşti, Curtea de Argeş, Tîrgovişte, and Slatina.

62. Salisbury's circular, 14 April 1878, in HHS, PA—I, Geheim Acte, Karton 23.

63. Salisbury to Loftus (St. Petersburg), 24 May 1878, in Benedict H. Sumner, *Russia and the Balkans, 1870–1880,* 645.

64. See the Anglo-Russian agreement, signed by Salisbury and Shuvalov, 30 May 1878, in Sumner, *Russia and the Balkans,* 648.

65. Andrássy to Zwiedinek, 27 March 1878, in HHS, PA—XXXVIII, Konsulate: Bukarest, Karton 223; Andrássy to Langenau, 16 May 1878, in HHS, PA—X, Rußland, Karton 70.

66. See the Anglo-Austrian agreement, signed by Elliot, the British ambassador, and Andrássy in Vienna, 6 June 1878, in William A. Gauld, "The Anglo-Austrian Agreement of 1878," 111.

67. Bălăceanu (Budapest) to Ion Brătianu, 12/24 May, Bălăceanu (Vienna) to Brătianu, 19/31 May 1878, and Constantin Rosetti (Bucharest) to Brătianu (Berlin), 7/19 June 1878, in *Ion C. Brătianu: Acte şi cuvântări,* 4:22–23, 40, 61. Romania received 16,600 Peabody rifles from Nagyszeben in Transylvania.

68. Brătianu to Bălăceanu, 3/15 June 1878, in Fond Ion C. Brătianu, XLVIII/1, BNR, SM.

69. Bălăceanu to Kogălniceanu, 7/19 June 1878, in Fond Ion C. Brătianu, XLVIII/ 2, BNR, SM; Bălăceanu to Carol, 9/21 June 1878, in AIC, CR, dosar 32/1878.

70. For Carol's trip from 29 April/11 May to 15/27 May 1878, see *Aus dem Leben König Karls von Rumänien,* 4:40–51.

71. Brătianu's speech and an excerpt of Ghica's remarks in the chamber, 25 May/6 June 1878, in *Ion C. Brătianu: Acte şi cuvântări,* 4:47, 52.

72. Rosetti to Brătianu (Berlin), 11/23 June 1878, in *Ion C. Brătianu: Acte şi cuvântări,* 4:63.

73. Journal of the council of ministers and Carol's approval, 26 May/7 June 1878, in *Ion C. Brătianu: Acte şi cuvântări,* 4:52–53.

74. Bălăceanu to Kogălniceanu, 25 June/7 July 1878, in Fond Mihail Kogălniceanu, XI, no. 48, BAR, SC; see also Bălăceanu to Dimitrie Sturdza, 23 June/5 July 1878, in Fond Dimitrie A. Sturdza, II, no. 245, BAR, SC.

75. Brătianu (Berlin) to Carol (Cotroceni), 10 June 1878, in Fond Ion C. Brătianu, XLVIII/2, BNR, SM.

76. See notes by Georg I. Bobrikov, a Russian military adviser in Berlin, June 1878, in Bobrikov, "V Rumynii pered voinoi 1877 g.," 338.

77. Carol to Charles Anthony, 8/20 June 1878, in *Aus dem Leben König Karls von Rumänien,* 4:64.

78. Congress of Berlin protocol nos. 9 and 10, 29 June and 1 July 1878, in *Recueil d'actes internationaux de l'Empire Ottoman,* 4:80–81, 88.

79. Alexander II's orders (Tsarskoe Sele), 27 May/8 June 1878, in *Osvobozhdenie Bolgarii ot turetskogo iga,* 3:126–27, 131; Congress of Berlin protocol no. 9, 29 June 1878, in *Recueil d'actes internationaux de l'Empire Ottoman,* 4:81–83.

80. Congress of Berlin protocol no. 10, 1 July 1878, in *Recueil d'actes internationaux de l'Empire Ottoman,* 4:84–87.

81. Congress of Berlin protocol no. 10, 1 July 1878, in *Recueil d'actes internationaux de l'Empire Ottoman,* 4:89–91.

82. See articles 43, 44, 45, and 46 of the Treaty of Berlin, 13 July 1878, in *Recueil d'actes internationaux de l'Empire Ottoman,* 4:189.

83. Carol's notes, 20 June/2 July 1878, in *Aus dem Leben König Karls von Rumänien,* 4:74–75.

84. Kogălniceanu's circular, 7/19 August 1878, and Kogălniceanu (Vienna) to Ion Cîmpineanu (Bucharest), 11/23 August 1878, in Fond Ion C. Brătianu, XLVIII/ 4, BNR, SM.

85. Carol's speech in the legislature, 5/17 July 1878, in *Monitorul oficial al României,* 6/18 July 1878, 3943.

86. Carol's decree on demobilization (Sinaia), 29 July/10 August 1878, effective 5/17 August 1878, in *Ion C. Brătianu: Acte şi cuvântări,* 4:359. See Cernat's announcement to some active troops (Sinaia), 30 July/12 August 1878, in Nichita Adăniloaie, "Noi documente privitoare la războiul pentru independenţă (1877–1878)," 880–81; Carol's notes, 24 April/6 May, 18/30 July, 29 July/10 August, and 13/25 August 1878, in *Aus dem Leben König Karls von Rumänien,* 4:40, 86, 92, 96. Romania's army had been absent from the capital for about 111 days.

87. Stuart to Kogălniceanu, 11/23 August 1878, no. 1174, in Fond Ion C. Brătianu, XLVIII/4, BNR, SM.

88. Cîmpineanu to Carol, 12/14 August 1878, in AIC, CR, 46/1878.

89. Kogălniceanu to Stuart, 25 August/6 September 1878, in Fond Ion C. Brătianu, XLVIII/4, BNR, SM. The Stari Stambul, or southernmost fork of the Danube's unnavigable Chilia branch, was to be the frontier.

90. Brătianu (Marienbad) to Constantin Rosetti (Bucharest), 14/26 August 1878, in Fond Ion C. Brătianu, XLVIII/4, BNR, SM.

91. Carol to Charles Anthony, 23 July/4 August 1878, in *Aus dem Leben König Karls von Rumänien,* 4:89; Carol to Leopold, 18 September 1878, in HHA, HS, Rubrik 53b, Kasten XXIX, Fach 27, Faszikel no. 1 (69).

92. Carol's speech in the legislature, 15/27 September 1878, in *Regele Carol I al României,* 2:239–40.

93. Kogălniceanu's senate speech, 28 September/10 October 1878, in *Monitorul oficiale al României,* 3/15 October 1878, 5571.

94. See the committee report in the chamber, 29 September/11 October 1878, in *Monitorul oficial al României,* 1/13 October 1878, 5545.

95. The senate, while alluding to "painful sacrifices" but not mentioning Bessarabia, approved the measure by 48 to 8 with one abstention, 28 September/10 October; the chamber did so, stipulating Bessarabia, by 83 to 27, 30 September/12 October 1878; *Monitorul oficial al României,* 3/15 and 4/16 October 1878, 5584, 5630. Among opponents were such Moldavians as Nicolae Ionescu, Dimitrie Sturdza, and Carp.

96. Kogălniceanu to George Vîrnav-Liteanu (Berlin), 29 September/11 October 1878, in Fond Ion C. Brătianu, XLVIII/6, BNR, SM; Carol's notes, 1/13 and 6/ 18 October 1878, in *Aus dem Leben König Karls von Rumänien,* 4:112, 113. See the procès-verbal fixing the Russo-Romanian boundary on the lower Danube River, signed by the Romanian senior army officers Eustaţiu Pencovici and Dimitrie Dimitrescu-Maican, and a Russian colonel, Tugenhold, 5/17 December 1878 (Bucharest), in *The Map of Europe by Treaty,* 4:2842–43.

INDEPENDENCE

Victories on the battlefield and at the peace table had still failed to win recognition of Romania's independence by Europe's great powers. Europe hedged on Romania's new standing. Bucharest was first to cede southern Bessarabia to Russia—and, as we have seen, it grudgingly did so—and to confer civil and political rights on its inhabitants without regard to their religious beliefs. It was furthermore to acquire the Danube Delta and Dobrogea, whose southern boundary was to be fixed by a European commission. In settling such affairs, the powers focused on Dobrogea's frontier and on privileges for Romania's Jews. Intermingled with these questions was Romania's foreign-owned railroad, which the powers, especially Germany, sought to have Romania purchase. Indeed, the powers withheld their formal acknowledgment of Romania's sovereignty until they were satisfied that Bucharest had acquiesced to their wishes. Danubian Romanians chafed at Europe's requirements, but they eventually complied.

Dobrogea, like Bessarabia, is primarily a Romanian-speaking territory. It had been, at one time or another, part of the Roman, Byzantine, as well as both medieval Bulgarian empires, and then was briefly in the Danubian principality of Wallachia from 1404 to 1417, before falling to Ottoman control, which lasted until 1878. The Danube Delta was traditionally within Dobrogea, except during Russia's control of the delta from 1829 to 1856. In 1878 Dobrogea's area was about 6,000 square miles, including roughly 1,000 square miles of the delta, with a Black Sea coastline of approximately 140 miles. Hence Romania gained in Dobrogea about 2,000 square miles more than it lost in southern Bessarabia. Dobrogea also had a larger population, with about 200,000 dwellers, approximately 50,000 more than southern Bessarabia. The populace of both regions was highly mixed. At the end of the 1870s, Dobrogea had Tatars and Turks—many of the latter probably evacuated along with the Ottoman army during the war—followed numerically by Romanians, Bulgarians, and Russians.[1]

The great powers at the Congress of Berlin, as we have seen, awarded Dobrogea and the Danube Delta to Romania. Some Romanian representatives worried about the prospects of a Russian takeover or a Bulgarian national rebellion in Dobrogea. Kogălniceanu contended that Europe needed a strong Romania to keep Russia away from the Danube, and that Danubian Romanians would form a stable wedge between Slavs to the north and south.[2] Ion Brătianu visualized Dobrogea as vital to free navigation on the Danube. He compared the strategic value of southern Bessarabia, which was vulnerable because of its open frontier with Russia, to Dobrogea, which was clearly separated from Russia by Europe's greatest river, its delta, and the Black Sea. Russia might indeed one day seize Dobrogea, yet by doing so it would provoke a major war. Furthermore, Bulgarian colonies in Dobrogea were smaller than those in southern Bessarabia. He therefore discounted the risk of an anti-Romanian uprising by Bulgarians in Dobrogea.[3] These arguments persuaded Romanian legislators, who voted overwhelmingly to take Dobrogea and the Danube Delta.[4] Carol then advised Romanian soldiers: "We do not enter Dobrogea as conquerors, but . . . as friends, as brothers" of the local residents. In pronouncing its annexation, Carol recalled that Dobrogea was formerly a Romanian province, and he promised equal treatment of Muslims and Christians.[5]

Russia had pledged Dobrogea, as already noted, to Romania during the 1877–78 war. Originally, Russia intended to hold Dobrogea—from a spot on the Danube River above Rasovo, about thirty-seven miles downstream from Silistra, to another one north of Mangalia on the Black Sea—before ceding it to Romania in exchange for southern Bessarabia.[6] At the Congress of Berlin, Russia yielded to Austria-Hungary's proposal to find an appropriate site near Silistra for a bridge[7] to tie Dobrogea to the Muntenian riparian town of Călăraşi. The powers then agreed on a Romanian-Bulgarian border running from a point east of Silistra to another one south of Mangalia. Details about the frontier were to be settled by a European delimitation commission.[8]

Romania wanted more of Dobrogea than the powers had awarded. Kogălniceanu pleaded for a defensible border west, not east, of the Silistra fortress. For him, Silistra was "indispensable."[9] The Habsburg Empire had promised during the war to assist Romania in gaining part of Dobrogea,[10] had spoken on Romania's behalf at the Congress of Berlin, and later continued trying to befriend Romania so as to ensure free Danubian navigation and to offset Russia's presumable aspirations in Southeastern Europe. Ignat'ev, Russia's architect of the San Stefano peace preliminaries, had indeed calculated that Dobrogea might go to Bulgaria.[11] Andrássy offered to obtain as much as possible for Romania in Dobrogea, but not Silistra.[12]

Bucharest preferred a simultaneous trade of southern Bessarabia for Dobrogea.[13] St. Petersburg, however, insisted that Romania refrain from annexing Dobrogea until its southern frontier had been set. Russia also demanded that Romania agree, prior to taking Dobrogea, to an additional military convention that would regulate the homeward passage of Russian soldiers from Bulgaria via Dobrogea and permit Russia to build military roads, piers, and wharves there.[14] After Romania had fulfilled its treaty obligation by retroceding southern Bessarabia, Kogălniceanu asserted, Romania would occupy Dobrogea except for "contested" places to be decided by the commission.[15] He nevertheless concurred in Russia's right of transit for its army through Dobrogea, besides by way of Romania itself; but he adamantly rejected a Russian military artery.[16]

From 21 October to 17 December 1878, the European boundary commission for Dobrogea worked out the delimitation of the Romanian-Bulgarian border.[17] The main issue was the site for a bridge to link commercial centers with existing highways on either side of the Danube River. The Russian commissioner, Andrei A. Bogoliubov, proposed a viaduct at the Romanian village of Dichiseni on the left bank of the Borcea (the northern branch of the Danube) about seventeen miles downstream from Silistra, or at Hîrşova about seventy-four miles downstream. Representatives of the other powers, however, reckoned that Hîrşova failed to square with the intentions of the Berlin treaty's framers, for it was too far from Silistra. They excluded Dichiseni as well because it lay in an area of canals, stagnant ponds, marshy soil, and the island of Balta, which was subject to inundation; this would have necessitated one of the most expensive pontoon-type bridges in modern times. In this area, the Dobrogean shore was uninhabited and lacked nearby roads. The commissioners selected instead a point about one-half mile downstream from the walls of Silistra, opposite Călăraşi in Romania. They next drew rather effortlessly the frontier line eastward to the south of Mangalia on the Black Sea coast. Bogoliubov criticized their plan as depriving Silistra of its adjacent fields and ignoring ethnic factors. He also contended that the commissioners' decisions must be unanimous to be binding; since such resolve was wanting, he refused to sign the commission's final act.[18]

Romania hankered for Silistra itself. Kogălniceanu had instructed his nonvoting emissary to the commission, the statesman Mihail Pherekyde, to sway the powers' commissioners. He was nevertheless seemingly content with the commission's determination, despite its having fallen short of Romania's goal.[19] Russia countered by suggesting a conference of ambassadors in Constantinople to consentaneously settle the matter.[20] The other powers deprecated Russia's recommendation and held to the commission majority's findings. Salisbury, the British minister of foreign affairs, for example, justified the commission's frontier as enabling Romania to build a trans-Danubian railroad bridge.[21]

Bucharest resolved to seize the southern Dobrogea frontier so as to enforce a quarantine after the outbreak of pestilence in Astrakhan, on the Volga River delta in Russia. This measure sought additionally to defend the border, regulate imports, and collect customs duties.[22] Russia protested and called on Romania to withdraw from the environs of Silistra because the quarantine imperiled Russian communications south of the Danube River.[23] Gorchakov repudiated Romania's maneuver and proposed that the forces of both countries retreat one and a quarter miles from the frontier, thereby creating a neutral zone. Romania might then establish sanitary and customs stations along the new line.[24] He resurrected Russia's plan for a Romanian bridge at Dichiseni, halfway between Silistra and the Dobrogean village of Rasovo; he also suggested again that the border be decided by the powers' ambassadors at Constantinople, especially because Romania had provoked an "armed conflict" with Russian soldiers.[25] Russia's Dobrogea boundary commissioner, General Feodor A. Fel'dman, urged that Russian and Romanian troops evacuate particularly the small fort of Arab-Tabia near Silistra to avoid strife.[26] Bucharest, however, ignored St. Petersburg's objections in erecting a *cordon sanitaire* against the plague. Cîmpineanu, Romania's fledgling minister of foreign affairs, clung firmly to Romania's deployment of troops but recognized the imminence of a Russo-Romanian encounter.[27] Great Britain supported Romania's stance, while Austria-Hungary cautioned against antagonizing Russia, and Germany criticized Romania for having overlooked the European nature of the problem.[28] Bucharest explained that its occupation of the border hardly constituted an "act of aggression," for Dobrogea was still jointly managed by Russian and Romanian military authorities. Moreover, the Treaty of Berlin had stipulated the razing of all fortresses on the Danube; hence Russia's claim that the strategic value of Silistra had been damaged by Romania's taking Arab-Tabia was, according to Cîmpineanu, specious.[29]

Romania's footing in southern Dobrogea was precarious, for Russian troops still south of the Danube River outnumbered its forces. A clash erupted in February 1879. Gheorghe I. Anghelescu, a Romanian general, inveighed against "regrettable" deeds committed by a Russian mounted patrol; one Romanian officer and three enlisted men had been captured and sent to Küçük Kaynarca in Bulgaria.[30] Russia's commanding general at Silistra, Viktor F.

Vinberg, deplored the incident, yet demanded the immediate evacuation of Arab-Tabia.[31] Anghelescu countered that Arab-Tabia was in Romania's hands owing to terms of the Treaty of Berlin and the European Delimitation Commission; the only way that Russia could have it was by violence, and that would tarnish Russia's "military glory."[32] After asking Ion Brătianu for instructions, Anghelescu announced that he had been ordered to decamp so as to preclude further discord.[33] Brătianu remarked, "We are in the situation of a man who stops and looks back to see if he has taken the wrong road."[34] Romania's position was indeed perilous at Arab-Tabia: Romania had merely 120 soldiers and no artillery there, versus 8 Russian battalions, 4 artillery batteries, and 2 cavalry regiments.[35]

The powers sought a solution, but Russia was intractable. Gorchakov maintained that Silistra was "inseparable from its suburbs," and so people there would be unduly exasperated at having to cross the Romanian-Bulgarian frontier to "graze their herds [and] till their fields." Furthermore, Silistra's environs were populated exclusively by Bulgarians.[36] To underscore his displeasure, Gorchakov recalled Stuart, Russia's diplomatic agent in Bucharest.[37] Andrássy moderated by recommending that a conference of ambassadors convene in Constantinople, together with a Turkish representative, to adjudicate—by majority vote—the border crisis.[38] The other powers substantially concurred with Andrássy's initiative. Russia was, however, unconvinced. Girs admitted that a plurality might settle details, yet questions of principle required unanimity.[39] Arab-Tabia evidently embodied some such still-obscure fundamental for St. Petersburg.

Russia then tried to end the impasse by suggesting that the Serbian boundary commission be authorized to define the Dobrogea line.[40] The other powers demurred. Russia warned Romania that it would defer appointing a diplomat to Bucharest until the Arab-Tabia imbroglio had been resolved; Russia further counseled Romania to reach an accord with Bulgaria whereby the two would share the expense of building a bridge.[41] Romania did not bite. Girs next propounded a technical commission consisting of engineers to survey the frontier and determine—by majority vote—a bridge site beyond Silistra's outskirts.[42] Salisbury opined that such a body would be less qualified than the original experts.[43] The powers nevertheless accepted Russia's proposal.

The technical commission met from 27 October to 11 November 1879 to set a point for a trans-Danubian bridge. Russia called for a spot, as it had in 1878, about seventeen miles downstream from Silistra.[44] The other powers, led by Austria-Hungary, reckoned again that the marshy terrain chosen by Russia would entail a costly span about seven and one-half miles long.[45] The commissioners agreed to retain the boundary drawn by the European Delimitation Commission but recommended that a sliver of land—not including Arab-Tabia—be in Bulgaria; that is, Bulgaria was to have the road from Silistra to Karaorman, eight miles away, leading toward Varna on the Black Sea.[46] Heinrich von Haymerle, Austria-Hungary's new minister of foreign affairs, accused the engineers of overstepping their mandate.[47] The other powers followed Haymerle's prompt, and so the technical commission merely reaffirmed the first commission's bridge site.[48]

Romanians were apprehensive about the future of Dobrogea. Despite the technical commission's findings, Ion Brătianu maintained Romania's historic right to Silistra itself. He recalled Ignat'ev's wartime promise for a Romanian Dobrogea extending southward along the Black Sea coast past Mangalia to Varna, and foresaw—if Bulgaria received Arab-Tabia—Romania's option of either "reconquering [sic] Silistra or running the risk of losing Dobrogea" altogether.[49] Russia continued to push for a border rectification further to the north,[50] and Austria-Hungary began to waver. Haymerle offered Bulgaria, as per the technical commission's suggestion, a segment of the Silistra-Karaorman road that protruded into Romania's envisioned share of Dobrogea.[51] Russia eventually concurred in this "practical compromise."[52] Romania's new minister of foreign affairs, Vasile Boerescu, refused to consider this suggestion because of expected opposition to such a deal in the Romanian legislature.[53] He asserted that Romania's prior withdrawal from Arab-Tabia had already promoted "grave inconveniences" affecting customs, security, and potential bridge building.[54] Ştefan Fălcoianu, a Romanian nonvoting representative to both commissions, also resisted the frontier change on "topographic, administrative, and strategic" grounds; a span near Silistra would therefore be infeasible.[55]

The fledgling autonomous principality of Bulgaria constantly proclaimed, as did Romania on its own behalf, its territorial integrity. The large Bulgaria envisioned by Russia at San Stefano was not to be. It forfeited land at Pirot to Serbia in the west, areas to a new Turkish province of Eastern Rumelia and to other regions of the Ottoman Empire in the south, and a slice of Dobrogea to Romania in the north. Bulgaria repeatedly protested that the powers sacrificed its interests at Silistra, Mangalia, and along its northern border.[56] Bulgaria's Prince Alexander I (1879–86) of Battenberg intimated, though, that he was indifferent toward Arab-Tabia, for it lacked strategic value, and he engaged to support the powers' decision.[57] Russian diplomats encouraged Haymerle to renew his proposal to yield the Silistra-Karaorman road to Bulgaria yet to retain Arab-Tabia in Romania.[58] Girs indicated that Russia would accept such a compromise if Bulgaria assented to it.[59] Bucharest then reminded the powers about the urgency of the perilous situation: brigands from Romania were raiding Bulgaria's villages, and soldiers from Bulgaria were disturbing the peace in Dobrogea.[60] Haymerle prodded Bulgaria to adhere to his frontier adjustment.[61] Alexander agreed, but only if Romania were obligated to construct the projected railway bridge.[62] Haymerle rejected this proviso.[63] Vasile Boerescu continued to oppose any modification of the boundary, whereas Ion Brătianu worried that Russia would soon unilaterally give Dobrogea to Bulgaria.[64] Bulgaria ultimately subscribed to the revamped border without reservations.[65] The powers also approved the revised line in August 1881 after Russia's quibble about the gutter of the Silistra-Karaorman roadway and lengthy footdragging by the Ottoman Empire.[66] The powers neglected, however, to notify Romania and Bulgaria of their accord until March 1883.[67] Romania and Bulgaria next formed their own boundary commission, which worked from 1884 to 1886—punctuated by minor provocations by both sides—to mark the frontier.[68]

The outcome disappointed many Romanians. They lamented the diminution of the Dobrogean frontier's strategic worth and the impracticability of a trans-Danubian bridge near Silistra.[69] Ion Brătianu accused Austria-Hungary of abandoning Romania's claims, but Vasile Boerescu nonetheless appreciated the Habsburg Empire's good offices in saving Arab-Tabia for Romania.[70]

The victorious Russo-Romanian allies had parted company after the war. Russia courted Bulgaria, although St. Petersburg's influence south of the Danube River waned after it failed to preserve the large Bulgaria envisioned in the San Stefano peace preliminaries and to gain Arab-Tabia for the new regime in Sofia. Romania's animosity toward Russia, which had been triggered by the retrocession of southern Bessarabia, intensified owing to the Russo-Romanian military confrontation in Dobrogea. This dispute, which seemed to be merely a proverbial tempest in a teapot, signified a fundamental divergence between Bucharest and St. Petersburg. The Habsburg Empire encouraged Romania in Dobrogea in order to further that rift and to turn the attention of Danubian Romanians away from the aspirations of their kith and kin in Habsburg Transylvania. Austria-Hungary's confederate, Germany, evinced indifference to the Dobrogean issue yet used it as a lever to facilitate the sale of German-owned railways to Romania. Moreover, France, Britain, and Germany focused more on the emancipation of Romania's Jews than on Dobrogea. Romania nevertheless regarded Dobrogea as being inexorably tied to its national prestige and to its future economic development on the Danube and along the Black Sea coast. No bridge of any type— for trains or carts or pedestrians—would, however, be erected close to Silistra. Romania would grant citizenship without distinction of ethnicity or religion to citizens of the Ottoman Empire residing in Dobrogea at the outset of the war, and the Romanian language was obligatory in the state schools of Dobrogea.[71] Still, the problem of integrating the disparate Dobrogean peoples into Romanian society would long occupy the government at Bucharest.

The Congress of Berlin, as we have seen, awarded southern Bessarabia to Russia and Dobrogea to Romania. Its delegates also discussed religious freedom in Southeastern Europe. Gorchakov warned that Jews constituted a "veritable scourge" for residents of Serbia, Romania, and some provinces of Russia. He subscribed, notwithstanding, to a proposal by Waddington, France's minister of foreign affairs, enunciating the "principle of religious equality." Representatives of the other great powers concurred as well, and the Ottoman Empire acquiesced. This axiom would be applied to Bulgaria, Serbia, Montenegro, and Romania.[72] As for Romania, the powers decided— in article 44 of the Treaty of Berlin—that no one might be excluded from "civil and political rights" because of "religious belief"; all of Romania's inhabitants, including foreigners, were to possess creedal freedom. The powers' recognition of Romania's independence thus hinged not only upon its retrocession of southern Bessarabia but also upon its fulfillment of the stipulation calling for religious liberty and equality.[73] The Romanian constitution of 1866 did not include the latter and so had to be amended. According to article 7 of Romania's constitutional charter, only Christian aliens might be naturalized and thereby enjoy civil and political perquisites and religious prerogatives.[74] The powers fastened on article 7 but ignored Romania's civil code of 1864, which also precluded non-Christians from Romanian citizenship.[75] They undoubtedly anticipated that a modification of the constitution would dictate subsequent legal changes.

Romania's neighbors acknowledged its sovereignty despite the Berlin agreement's injunctions. Russia had, after all, accepted Romania's de facto independence in concluding trade and military conventions with it before the 1877–78 war. Gorchakov regarded an upgrading of Russia's office in Bucharest to be "superfluous," but Girs, his chief assistant for foreign policy, persuaded Alexander II to elevate Russia's general consul in Romania to a minister resident.[76] Francis Joseph I and Andrássy sought to maintain Austria-Hungary's influence in Romania as a counterpoise to Russia's presumed territorial ambitions in Southeastern Europe.[77] Vienna's commercial covenant of 1875 with Bucharest had, moreover, presaged the Habsburg Empire's approbation of Romania's sovereignty. Vienna and Bucharest would indeed exchange plenipotentiary ministers.[78] And by the end of 1878, Romania and its former suzerain, the Ottoman Empire, had ministers resident in each other's capitals.[79]

The recently constituted Kingdom of Italy verged on endorsing Romania's independence. Italy's minister of foreign affairs, Luigi Corti, hoped his country—as a sister Latin state—would be the first power to appoint a plenipotentiary minister to Bucharest.[80] Germany, however, sharply protested Italy's intention.[81] Rome therefore modified its stance; Saverio da Fava would receive diplomatic credentials to Bucharest, yet with the proviso that Romania provide a written guarantee to solve its Jewish question. Carol refused, and Italy's recognition lapsed.[82] The powers in Western Europe would henceforth act in concert to ensure Romania's adherence to the Berlin agreement's terms concerning citizenship for its foreigners.

Carol opened the legislature, after its extraordinary session dealing with southern Bessarabia and Dobrogea, by calling upon senators and deputies to convene in "revision assemblies" so as to amend the constitution and thus end "political inequality on account of religion."[83] Romanians were deeply divided about Jewish aliens in their midst. Ion Brătianu had earlier contended that it was a "monstrous, unacceptable supposition" that Romania would "commit suicide" by naturalizing its Jews en masse. He admitted that creed should be no hindrance to citizenship, yet he would defend Romania's "economic, social, material, and political interests." He later remarked that Jews formed a "permanent danger" for the Romanian people.[84] Constantin Rosetti considered the Berlin dictate about religious parity to be a needless meddling in Romania's internal affairs. For Rosetti, Romanian Jews were nonexistent; rather, Jews in Romania were under foreign protection as international vagabonds with their own peculiar language, habits, and customs. Romania might nevertheless accept Jews as citizens if they conversed only in Romanian and adopted Romanian ways.[85] Nicolae Voinov, a senator, foretold the "emancipation of the Jews [being] dragged over the corpse of Romania."[86] Carp observed that "modern ideas are fine, but they cannot change a social situation in twenty-four hours"; such notions, if applied violently, would produce chaos.[87] As the debate raged, an anti-Jewish riot erupted in Iaşi, triggered by the presence of Christian women at a rabbi's burial. Police successfully quelled the disturbance without loss of life.[88] Still, this event augured poorly for a dispassionate settlement of the Jewish issue.

Carol calculated that a "protracted and fierce struggle" would continue in the legislature, for Jewish enfranchisement spelled "social revolution."[89]

Carol sent envoys to various European capitals to elicit, with scant effect, recognition of Romania's independence.[90] Bismarck—owing chiefly to prompting by Bleichröder, his personal banker—solicited Andrássy's aid in strictly enforcing article 44 of the Treaty of Berlin in Romania. However, Andrássy was loath to incur "odium" from exerting heavy pressure on behalf of the Jews.[91] Sturdza, Romania's minister of finance—who was in Berlin to negotiate the purchase of Bucharest's German-owned railroad—suggested revamping the constitution so that religion would not impede anyone from exercising civil and political rights; special laws would implement this plan.[92] Negative response to this proposal in Paris, London, Berlin, and Rome— where it was viewed as being too vague—led Cîmpineanu to hold the Jewish question *in suspenso:* "We can wait."[93]

Carol launched the revision assemblies of the senate and chamber by noting that Romania's article 7 paralyzed the regime. He maintained that the country never had a "spirit of intolerance" but rather had one of "hospitality [and] toleration." To be sure, its "national commerce and industry" had been endangered by an "invasion" from abroad; hence the constitution's framers introduced article 7. The powers now required Romania to "conform" to "ideas that dominate in civilized lands." He offered no specific solution but advised the representatives to shield Romania's "vital interests." Romania needed a compromise.[94]

The government, however, failed to lead. This passivity prompted the powers to search for leverage. Bismarck proposed that a conference of ambassadors convene in Constantinople to enforce article 44 of the treaty. Andrássy demurred because of his foreboding that Romania, in retaliation, would turn to Russia for protection.[95] Bismarck next suggested that the Turkish sultan's suzerainty be restored in Bucharest. The powers might then deal with the Ottoman Empire for the emancipation of Romania's Jews.[96] Salisbury contended that Romania should insert the treaty's article 44 word for word in place of the constitution's article 7. Waddington concurred, but Andrássy disagreed, as did Bucharest.[97] Russia's stand seemed ambivalent. Did Russia want to separate Moldavia from Wallachia, as a persisting rumor had it, and then place Dobrogea and Bulgaria under Russia's auspices? Or did Russia seek to guard Romania's stakes, as St. Petersburg's temporary emissary at Bucharest, Aleksandr A. Iakobson, claimed? Iakobson accused the Alliance Israélite Universelle of aiming to transform Romania into a second Palestine via Jewish immigration and Jewish real-estate purchases.[98]

The revision assemblies selected a commission of senators and deputies to draft a measure regarding Romania's Jews. Two plans ensued. The majority chose to delete article 7 from the constitution and admit indigenous Jews as denizens. The minority, supported by Ion Brătianu, offered Jews citizenship according to categories that included military veterans, graduates from Romania's schools, founders of industries, philanthropists, and creative writers in the Romanian language. Apart from these groups, native Jews, who had never been safeguarded by one of the powers, were to wait ten years before naturalization. The majority and minority agreed on one issue: Jews were not to be landowners.[99] Carol privately labeled both commission reports as "insane and perfidious."[100] Austria-Hungary opposed the restriction on landholding; Germany, France, and Great Britain at first rejected the minority's categories; Italy would accept whatever Romania decided. Bleichröder demanded that all of Romania's Jews who were not under foreign aegis be immediately emancipated.[101]

Ion Brătianu shuffled his cabinet in response to the powers' antagonism toward Romania's machinations, and released a program. It promised to ensure that creedal differences would not block "gaining and exercising political rights." The ministers nonetheless pledged to defend the country's "national and economic interests." The government sought "individual naturalization" yet also curbs on acquiring rural property.[102] It also requested, with Carol's approval, a legislative recess for a month to study the problem.[103] The assemblies adjourned to collect information as well as to dampen popular indignation and fears.[104] At their reopening, Carol expressed confidence in the representatives and restated the regime's proposal about the "principle of religious liberty and civil and political equality" conditioned by Romania's "national and economic necessities."[105]

Vasile Boerescu, who had replaced Cîmpineanu as minister of foreign affairs, solicited advice firsthand from the powers. They rebuffed this step, reckoning they had nothing further to say about the matter.[106] Boerescu suggested that Romania's autochthonous Jews might enjoy civil, but not political, prerogatives. All aliens, including Jews, were to be eligible for citizenship without religious distinction. However, Romania could hardly emancipate all at once those persons speaking foreign languages or having extrinsic customs and sentiments. Boerescu favored naturalizing Jews who were Romanian citizens and "sufficiently assimilated."[107] On his trip, Boerescu discovered that France, Britain, and Germany opposed his lists and now favored categories—which had been suggested by a minority in the assemblies' commission—while Austria-Hungary merely professed "platonic sympathy," and

Russia seemed to be unconcerned about the issue.[108] Boerescu nonetheless persisted in asking the assemblies to adopt an outline of his plan because the powers, he calculated, would ultimately accept it.[109] Still, his defiant stance elicited scant support from his colleagues in the cabinet.

The government subsequently introduced its proposal to the assemblies. Article 7 was to be revised so that religious differences would not hamper "acquiring and exercising civil and political rights." Aliens and Romania's subjects might be naturalized separately by particular laws. Only Romania's citizens might own rural property; yet Ottoman citizens in Dobrogea were to gain Romanian citizenship without restrictions on possessing rural lands. Persons born and raised in Romania who had never been protected by one of the powers might be emancipated by the assemblies. Finally, Romania's Jewish subjects, who had become "assimilated" Romanians, might be citizens, their creed notwithstanding, upon application within one year of the new article 7's implementation. Six categories—drawn up by Kogălniceanu, the interior minister, from the minority's prior agenda in the assemblies' commission—comprising 1,074 Jews, were to be emancipated forthwith: 883 war veterans, 44 academic degree holders from Romania's schools, 47 educators trained abroad, 2 philanthropists, 85 founders of commercial or industrial enterprises, and 13 contributors to Romanian literature.[110] Local Jews protested, though, for this program excluded many deserving Jews. Moreover, some individuals in the government's groups were dead, mentioned twice, non-Jews, or protected by one of the powers.[111]

This project engendered a hefty debate. The lawyer Blaremberg cautioned that the "Talmud would replace the Cross" in Romania. Carp conceded that "Jews are masters of our economic production," yet he moderately supported the regime's scheme in admitting that "liberty does not create civilization."[112] The poet Alecsandri warned about the rapid increase in the number of Romania's Jews, from very few in the census of 1859–60 to 6.59 percent in 1879. Furthermore, Romania's Jews were proportionally far more numerous than those in other states.[113] Maiorescu, a literary critic, had earlier considered that only Jews begotten in Romania and not under foreign protection might be naturalized.[114] In the assemblies, however, Maiorescu contended that the categories and lists failed to oblige Jews to manifest a desire to be citizens.[115] Oratory led to modifications in the initial design. The categories of Jews to be naturalized were sharply curtailed so as to include only army veterans of the 1877–78 war. The definitive text retained the basic guarantee of civil and political perquisites regardless of religious persuasion. Aliens had to petition the government—indicating their wealth and profession and requesting citizenship—and then wait ten years before emancipation. Some individuals who were exempt from this path were those who had established important commercial or industrial firms in the country, those with "distinguished talents," and those born in Romania and not safeguarded by one of the powers. Lastly, only Romanian citizens might procure rural property. Dropped from the final act were stipulations in the original blueprint about Ottoman citizens in Dobrogea and Romania's already absorbed subjects.[116] Vasile Boerescu appealed to the representatives' "patriotism" that they might understand their "national and economic interests" and so. "assimilate . . . slowly [and] gradually" the Jews, thereby enabling Romania to "enter the European family." After the rhetoric, the assemblies adopted the constitutional revision.[117]

The assemblies thereupon emancipated the 888 Jews who had served in the Russo-Romanian-Turkish war.[118] Ion Brătianu remarked: "We have done everything that is humanly possible; we have employed all means; we have used every argument except the cannon." Carol concurred, reflecting that the new article 7 was the best Romania could achieve.[119] He thanked the representatives for their "long and laborious" task in which they had addressed "thorny and onerous questions" with "patriotic and enlightened zeal" together with "honesty and abnegation, with tact and unanimity."[120] Boerescu explained to the powers that the revision of the constitution required a two-thirds majority vote, and such was only attainable by compromise.[121]

Boerescu next called upon the Western powers to acknowledge Romania's sovereignty.[122] France and Britain were favorably disposed yet would await Germany's concurrence.[123] Italy then asked for and received a note from Bucharest in which Romania vaguely promised its Jews the right to citizenship, their complete assimilation, and an end to restrictions on foreigners acquiring rural property.[124] Italy hence accepted Romania's autarchy. Germany withheld its recognition, however, until Romania had satisfied German investors in the railroad.

Romania had, to be sure, adopted the principle of religious equality and made a token effort to emancipate its Jews. But three powers still eschewed acclaiming Romania's independence.

Romania adhered, as we noticed, to provisions in the Treaty of Berlin in retroceding southern Bessarabia to Russia, annexing Dobrogea from the Ottoman Empire, and espousing the idea of religious equality in its constitution. The Western powers, except for Italy, refused, however, to confirm Romania's statehood until a matter, which had been neither mentioned in the covenant nor even discussed at the Congress of Berlin, had been re-solved. That was the issue of Romania's railroads. It embodied significant political and financial problems for the Bucharest government. After all, the German holders of Romania's railway stocks sought, as we have observed, to profit as much as possible from their investments.

At the outset of the 1877–78 war, Bismarck informed Russia and Ro-mania that Berlin would withhold recognizing Romania's independence until the latter had reimbursed German creditors with eleven million francs.[125] Gorchakov rejected having to pay Romania's debts, but Bucharest appar-ently used about half of the one million francs it had received from Russia to indemnify German investors in June 1877.[126] After the fall of Pleven, when the war's outcome was no longer in doubt, Bleichröder complained to Bis-marck about Romania's 300 million marks' indebtedness to 100,000 Ger-man shareholders. Germany again indicated it would repudiate a fully sovereign Romania and defer a German-Romanian trade convention until Romania had discharged its liabilities.[127]

Controversy and misunderstandings about the railroads led Romania to propose purchasing the German-owned portion of them. Bismarck wor-ried, however, about untoward consequences for German investors if Ro-mania should do so via a deal with a Russian consortium.[128] Austria-Hungary also stewed about this prospect, as Andrássy envisioned mutual advantages in firmly tying together the rail systems of the Habsburg Empire and Roma-nia.[129] Neither Russia nor Austria-Hungary would, however, become finan-cially involved in the railway sale.

Cîmpineanu, the finance minister, commenced negotiations with Ger-man investors prior to the Congress of Berlin.[130] Later, Sturdza, who replaced Cîmpineanu, offered to exchange the society of shareholders' 5-percent obli-gations for 6-percent securities, issued by the Romanian government, that would be assured by a mortgage on the railroad and be redeemable by 1923. Romania wanted the company's seat moved from Berlin to Bucharest when it had a majority of the stock.[131] Bleichröder opposed the immediate transfer of the firm's headquarters and called for a lien on income from Romania's tobacco monopoly plus an encumbrance on the lines.[132] Sturdza agreed to drop the relocation—in a projected convention—to grant a premium of 2 percent on common and 2.5 percent on priority shares to ensure a prompt conversion, and to accept mortgages on the railways and the tobacco mo-nopoly.[133] Carol complained, however, that Bleichröder stonewalled Sturdza, and contended that Romania must first resolve its Jewish question before addressing the railroad.[134] Germany itself disagreed. Bismarck told Vasile

Boerescu that Germany sought a speedy solution to the railway problem, after which it would moderate its stance on Romania's Jews and recognize Romania's independence.[135] Bleichröder and his fellow financiers in Berlin eventually approved Sturdza's initiative. The two sides concurred as well that one hundred common shares would receive sixty state bonds, while three priority shares would get two state bonds. This disparity was chiefly due to the low annual yield of the original stock, which had fallen from 5 percent in 1873 to 1 percent in 1876 and 2 percent in 1878.[136]

Topics of contention included the site of the company's seat and two mortgages—on the railroad and on Romania's tobacco monopoly. The railway itself, which had opened and was operating by 1875, was nevertheless relatively inconsequential in negotiating mortgages because Romania had already guaranteed the lines. The enterprise's headquarters, situated in Berlin, might shift to any place selected by the society's council of supervision.[137] Why did Germany resist its transfer to Bucharest? Was it leverage for protecting Germany's creditors and for emancipating Romania's Jews? Why was Romania intent on having the business's seat? Was this another symbol of Romania's independence? The tobacco monopoly was a complicated matter, too. Tobacco was a luxury commodity, being imported principally from the Ottoman Empire; Romania had fruitlessly attempted to launch and then corner its domestic cultivation and sale from 1865 to 1867. Carol next sponsored a tobacco monopoly in 1872, guided by a British consortium backed by the Bank of Roumania in London and the Pester Ungarische Kommerzial Bank in Budapest.[138] This group was to raise Romania's income; it did so by bringing in about eight million lei per annum, or 8.76 percent of Romania's revenues in 1875 and 9.89 percent in 1877. The 1877–78 war, though, wrecked havoc with this concern's profits, roughly half of which it retained, with the other half going to Romania. It suspended payments at the end of 1878, and so Romania sequestered the monopoly in the spring of 1879.[139] The current and potential earnings of this institution were quite apparent to Romania's legislators, who scorned shackling its receipts to the railroad. Also, how might Romania's sovereignty be fully secured if it lost complete control of its tobacco?

Carol privately belittled the rail purchase, for he reckoned that the state's managing and operating of the lines would be more arduous and more expensive than the company's. Moreover, he frowned on Romania's insuring the redemption by encumbering its tobacco.[140] Sturdza agreed, his prior commitment in Berlin notwithstanding, since tampering with the tobacco mortgage might imperil Romania's credit. Kogălniceanu preferred to resign as interior minister than accept the tobacco deal.[141] Bleichröder was, however, adamant: Romania's tobacco was the contract's foundation stone.[142] Prime Minister Ion Brătianu deplored Romania's economic entanglements abroad, such as the 1875 commercial convention with Austria-Hungary and foreign control of the tobacco monopoly; he nonetheless considered Sturdza's project to be financially sound.[143]

Romania's plodding pace in handling the railway question induced Germany to ask Austria-Hungary to intervene in Bucharest. Andrássy had endeavored to avoid Romania's animosity in the Jewish issue; but Haymerle, his successor at the ministry of foreign affairs, championed Germany's investors.[144] This backing was due to the Habsburg Empire's own rail interests in northern Romania and to the conclusion of an Austro-German alliance on 7 October 1879. Vasile Boerescu then urged the immediate transfer of the company's seat to Bucharest after it had been approved by the stockholders in Berlin.[145] Bleichröder's colleague, Hansemann, of the Disconto-Gesellschaft in Berlin, insisted, however, that the switch be postponed for two years, as envisioned in the terms formulated by Sturdza for exchanging certificates.[146] Germany's foreign affairs ministry—in which a former envoy to Bucharest, Joseph M. von Radowitz, was influential—supported the bankers, rejected Boerescu's plea, and tied the railway issue to Arab-Tabia in Dobrogea and Romania's independence.[147]

Ion Brătianu defended the railway convention in the chamber of deputies, describing the purchase as a "difficult and complicated" problem, yet one of "great economic, financial, and political importance." He appealed to the deputies' "patriotism" to adopt it.[148] They did so, with an amendment that the administrative headquarters be switched immediately to Bucharest.[149] Germany declared this to be a breach of good faith. Radowitz intimated that they would "show [the Romanians] what it means to make such insolent sport with a great power," and he renewed Germany's threat to withhold recognition.[150] Would the senate reverse the chamber's decision? Senators such as Alexandru Lahovari contended that the proposed acquisition was wasteful because Romania would lose its tobacco monopoly; furthermore, it would benefit only Germany's shareholders—some of whom would try to keep the company's seat in Berlin, thereby leaving Romania with merely partial ownership of the lines—and would transform Romania into Germany's vassal.[151]

Germany was inflexible. According to its justice minister, Heinrich von Friedberg, Berlin might be incapable of aiding its investors if the rail company's seat were in Bucharest.[152] Bismarck next envisioned backing

Russia in the Arab-Tabia question and solicited help from the Western powers in unraveling the imbroglio.[153] Italy had, as we noted, already opted to acknowledge Romania. France and Great Britain, however, followed Germany's lead.[154] Austria-Hungary would, too, but Haymerle recoiled at cooperating if Arab-Tabia became a divisive factor.[155] He called on Romania to abandon the troublesome amendment. If Ion Brătianu were unable or unwilling to do so, the cabinet should be reshuffled so as to reach a solution.[156] Sturdza contemplated resigning. Brătianu worried that the collapse of his ministry would endanger Carol, for a specious rumor circulated in Bucharest that financially linked the prince to the transaction.[157] Brătianu then asked Germany to declare formally that the railway's administration would transfer to Bucharest when the legislature restored and embraced the original project.[158] The bankers refused to budge. Friedberg also advised against this measure, as it was a judicial, not a diplomatic, affair.[159] Germany promised anew to accept Romania's sovereignty once the railroad deal had been consummated. Radowitz warned, however, that a continuation of the standstill would trigger a rupture of German-Romanian relations.[160]

Romania reluctantly acquiesced to pressure by the Western powers on the government and by the house of Hohenzollern on the prince.[161] The senate reconsidered its amendment to the convention. George Manu, who had commanded the artillery at Pleven in the campaign of 1877, was the regime's principal adversary in the senate. He accused Sturdza of arbitrarily juggling numerical data, claiming that Romania's "monetary advantages [would be] illusory and fantastic." The pact itself was politically, financially, and economically "disastrous" and was simply a "point of departure for new difficulties" entailing "new financial sacrifices." The rail purchase should encompass all, not a majority, of the shares to avoid an "uncertain and critical financial situation."[162] The ministers nevertheless prevailed, and the senate restored the initial blueprint.[163] Debate resumed in the chamber after the deputies returned from a Christmas recess. Blaremberg characterized the accord as "fatal for the country," and Nicolae Ionescu censured the cabinet for taking orders from Berlin. Ion Brătianu discounted his opponents' arguments, for they had failed to pinpoint "any real danger [or] any serious inconvenience" for Romania; they merely addressed "general juridical theories [and] assumptions."[164] Vasile Boerescu explained that Romania's negotiations with the society resulted in a "bilateral contract"; therefore both sides had to sanction changes to it. He identified the "hegemony of Germany, which is today the first power in Europe." Each power viewed the railways as a "kernel of discord [or a] germ of danger." Romanians sought a fresh start: "we no longer want to be anybody's vassal—not of Russia, Turkey, Germany, nor Austria; . . . we want only to emancipate the railroad, and we want as well that this economic emancipation be as real as the political one."[165] The deputies then approved the original agreement. It provided, as we have seen, for mortgages on the lines and on the tobacco monopoly, as well as for the company's seat to be in Bucharest—after Romania had more than one half of the stock and the transfer had been approved by the shareholders' assembly in Berlin.[166]

Carol congratulated the senators and deputies for having resolved "onerous and thorny international socioeconomic questions" by putting "political equality regardless of religion" into Romania's constitution, and for winning "control of its arteries of communication: the railroads."[167] The Berlin bankers phlegmatically applauded the outcome.[168] Romania would finally gain the lines two years later. The shareholders' assembly in Berlin overwhelmingly endorsed the sale.[169] Bleichröder and the Disconto-Gesellschaft eventually consented to refinance the 6-percent state bonds with 5-percent debentures, still guaranteed by mortgages on the railways and revenue from the tobacco monopoly.[170] Some dissatisfied investors had, however, launched litigation, thereby delaying the relocation of the administrative headquarters to Bucharest.[171] The legislature ultimately requested, and the stockholders acceded, to liquidate the company, with Romania assuming financial responsibility for its bonds.[172] Thus Romania had the consortium's 568 miles of railways. It then procured 39 miles through Dobrogea, from Cernavodă on the Danube River to Constanţa on the Black Sea, from a British firm in 1882; in 1889 it also sequestered, and subsequently bought, 138 miles in northern Moldavia that had been managed by an Austro-Hungarian corporation.[173]

When Romania adopted the rail convention in 1880, Bleichröder considered the door open for the powers to acknowledge Romania's independence. He deemed Romania to have started on the "way toward civilization," but it needed to go farther for its Jews.[174] France, Britain, and Germany contemplated accepting Romania's sovereignty.[175] Romania's petition, Austria-Hungary's backing, and Germany's concurrence led to an identic note being drafted by France, which was individually presented by the envoys of the Western powers on 20 February 1880 to the regime in Bucharest.[176] This note reminded Romania that it had yet to comply completely with the stipulations in the Treaty of Berlin concerning its non-Christians. The powers nevertheless appreciated Romania's assurances to do more on its aliens' behalf, and so they recognized Romania's independence and were ready to inaugurate regular diplomatic relations.[177]

Many Danubian Romanians assumed that their country's independence had been courageously earned in combat against the suzerain Turks. Romania's neighbors—the multinational Romanov, Habsburg, and Ottoman empires—agreed, for they properly assessed the vital political, economic, and military value of having a friendly state on the lower Danube River. The more distant powers—Germany, France, Britain, and Italy—endorsed humanitarian and commercial aims. Romania opted for the principle of religious equality in its constitution, although it naturalized few of its numerous Jews. A more encompassing emancipation of the Jews was to await the constitution of 1923. Romania's animosity toward, and suspicion of, its Jews persisted, and is an ongoing problem. The railroad, which the powers elided at the Congress of Berlin, was inexorably linked to the Jewish issue because one prominent Jewish financier in Berlin, in particular, endeavored mightily to ameliorate the situation of his coreligionists and to negotiate the railway sale. Germany used the Jewish predicament and Romania's claims on the Dobrogea frontier to appease its rail investors. A railway bridge at Silistra was not to be, but later one went up at Cernavodă in 1895, and another between Giurgiu and Ruse in 1954, thereby tieing Romania's communications to the Black Sea ports of Constanţa and Varna. Possession of Dobrogea and the railroads heightened Romania's national pride and partly compensated for its loss of southern Bessarabia. Indeed, the Danube Delta and Dobrogea, with its Black Sea coast, had an economic potential superior to that of southern Bessarabia. Some Romanians would be surprised when, after World War I, they regained all of Bessarabia, Bukowina, the Banat, and Transylvania, which had briefly been held by Mihail the Brave in 1600. The groundwork for a greater Romania had, however, been laid by the generation that embraced full sovereignty after the Russo-Romanian-Turkish War.

Notes

1. Russian authorities asked Romanian officials in 1877 to conduct an inventory of the Tulcea *sancak,* or the Dobrogea provincial subdivision—excluding Silistra on the Danube River and Mangalia on the Black Sea, which were in other *sancaklar.* It disclosed 227,719 residents: 31.27% Tatars, 21.61% Turks, 20.42% Romanians, 13.76% Bulgarians, 5.59% Russians, 3.07% Circassians, 1.53% Greeks, 0.76% Germans, and 2% others; see a report by A. Stoianovici, countersigned by Ştefan Fălcoianu, October 1877, in Fond Dimitrie A. Sturdza, Varia XVI, no. 180, BAR, SM. A bureaucrat at Russia's embassy in Constantinople, Vladimir A. Teplov, who set Dobrogea's populace at 165,000, lumped Bulgarians and Russians together at 31.15%, with 26.24% Tatars, 13.88% Turks, 17.27% Romanians, 4.0% Circassians,

2.85% Germans, 1.97% Greeks, and 2.64% others; see Vladimir A. Teplov, *Materialy dlia statistiki Bolgarii, Frakii i Makedonii*, 26–27, 204–5.

2. Kogălniceanu's speech in the chamber of deputies, 30 September/12 October 1878, in Kogălniceanu, *Opere*, vol. 4: *Oratorie II*, pt. 4, 628–29.

3. Brătianu's speech in the chamber, 30 September/12 October 1878, in *Monitorul oficiale al României*, 4/16 October 1878, 5627–29.

4. The senators endorsed the annexation, voting 48 to 8, on 28 September/10 October; the deputies concurred, 83 to 27, on 30 September/12 October 1878; *Monitorul oficiale al României*, 3/15 and 4/16 October 1878, 5584, 5630. By the Treaty of Berlin, Romania also acquired the Isle of Serpents (Insula Şerpilor) in the Black Sea.

5. Carol's army order and his proclamation in Brăila to the Dobrogean peoples, 14/26 November 1878, in *Regele Carol I al României*, 2:258, 259–60.

6. Articles 6 and 19 of the Russo-Turkish peace preliminaries at San Stefano, 3 March 1878, in *Recueil d'actes internationaux de l'Empire Ottoman*, 3:513, 517.

7. Congress of Berlin protocol no. 15, 8 July 1878, in *Recueil d'actes internationaux de l'Empire Ottoman*, 4:136.

8. Article 46 of the Treaty of Berlin, 13 July 1878, in *Recueil d'actes internationaux de l'Empire Ottoman*, 4:189.

9. Kogălniceanu to Bălăceanu (Vienna), 2/14 August 1878, no. 11268, Zwiedinek (Bucharest) to Andrássy (Vienna), 18 August 1878, no. 120, and Kogălniceanu to Bălăceanu, 23 October/4 November 1878, in HHS, PA—XII, Türkei Varia, Karton 256; see also Kogălniceau's circular, 7/19 August 1878, in Fond Ion C. Brătianu, XLVIII/4, BNR, SM.

10. Bălăceanu to Brătianu (Craiova), 2 July 1877, in Fond Ion C. Brătianu, AIC, CR, dosar 22.

11. Ignat'ev suggested in January 1878 that Bulgaria receive Dobrogea after financially compensating Romania for it; Ignat'ev, *San Stefano*, 327; or Bulgaria could have it if Romania failed to retrocede southern Bessarabia; see his letter to Gorchakov, 16/28 April 1878, in Ignat'ev, *Posle San Stefano*, 76.

12. Andrássy to Ernst von Mayr (St. Petersburg), 26 August 1878, in HHS, PA—XII, Türkei Varia, Karton 256.

13. Kogălniceanu's circular, 25 October 1878, no. 15385, in HHS, PA—XII, Türkei Varia, Karton 256.

14. Miliutin's notes, 13/25 October 1878, in *Dnevnik D. A. Miliutina*, 3:98; Kogălniceanu to Bălăceanu, 14 November 1878, in HHS, PA—XII, Türkei Varia, Karton 256; see also Carol's notes, 29 October/10 November 1878, in *Aus dem Leben König Karls von Rumänien*, 4:128.

15. Kogălniceanu to Vîrnav-Liteanu (Berlin), 29 September/11 October 1878, in Fond Ion C. Brătianu, XLVIII/6, BNR, SM.

16. László von Hoyos-Springenstein (Bucharest) to Andrássy, 30 October 1878, no. 143, in HHS, PA—XVIII, Rumänien Varia I, Karton 50; Kogălniceanu to Ion G. Ghica (Livadia), 13 November and 3/15 November 1878, in Fond Ion C. Brătianu, XLVIII/8, BNR, SM. A Russo-Romanian note, 13/25 November 1878, regularized the movement of Russian troops in Dobrogea; see Hoyos to Andrássy, 25 November 1878, in HHS, PA—XXXVIII, Konsulate: Bukarest, Karton 223.

17. See abstracts of the commission's thirteen protocols (Constantinople and Silistra), 21 October–17 December 1878, in *The Map of Europe by Treaty,* 4:2822–24.

18. Karl C. H. von Ripp, "Denkschrift" (Constantinople), 31 December 1878, in HHS, PA—XII, Türkei Varia, Karton 256. Ripp was Austria-Hungary's delegate on the commission, each emissary being a senior army officer. The commission decided that the village of Küçük Kaynarca would remain in Bulgaria. For the act of 17 December 1878 (Constantinople) with 4 annexes, see *The Map of Europe by Treaty,* 4:2825–41.

19. Kogălniceanu to Pherekyde, 19/31 October 1878, in Fond Ion C. Brătianu, XLVIII/6, BNR, SM; Kogălniceanu to Bălăceanu, 30 November 1878, in HHS, PA—XII, Türkei Varia, Karton 256.

20. Andrássy's circular, 2 December 1878, in HHS, PA—XII, Türkei Varia, Karton 256.

21. Salisbury to Adolf von Montgelas (London), 23 December 1878, in HHS, PA—XII, Türkei Varia, Karton 256.

22. Cîmpineanu to Ion G. Ghica and Bălăceanu, 10/22 January 1879, in HHS, PA—XII, Türkei Varia, Kartons 257, 254.

23. Miliutin's notes, 21 January/2 February and 27 January/8 February 1879, in *Dnevnik D. A. Miliutina,* 3:113, 115.

24. Gorchakov to Ion G. Ghica, 22 January/3 February 1879, Cîmpineanu to Bălăceanu, 6/18 February 1879, and Langenau (St. Petersburg) to Andrássy, 6/18 February 1879, in HHS, PA—XII, Türkei Varia, Karton 258; Miliutin's notes, 6/18 February 1879, in *Dnevnik D. A. Miliutina,* 3:118.

25. Gorchakov to Evgenii P. Novikov (Vienna), 22 January/3 February 1879, in HHS, PA—XII, Türkei Varia, Karton 258.

26. Hoyos to Andrássy, 30 January 1879, no. 44, in HHS, PA—XII, Türkei Varia, Karton 258.

27. Cîmpineanu to Bălăceanu, 31 January and 1 February 1879, in HHS, PA—XII, Türkei Varia, Karton 258.

28. Andrássy to Hoyos, 2 February 1879, Károlyi (London) to Andrássy, 3 February 1879, and Andrássy to Langenau and Hoyos, 6 February 1879, in HHS, PA—XII, Türkei Varia, Karton 258; see also a report by Vîrnav-Liteanu, mentioned in Carol's notes, 2/14 February 1879, in *Aus dem Leben König Karls von Rumänien,* 4:170.

29. Cîmpineanu to Bălăceanu, 3 February 1879, in HHS, PA—XII, Türkei Varia, Karton 258; see article 52 of the Treaty of Berlin, in *Recueil d'actes internationaux de l'Empire Ottoman,* 4:190.

30. Anghelescu (Ostrov) to Viktor F. Vinberg, 6/18 and 7/19 February 1879, in Gheorghe I. Anghelescu, *[Fruntaria Dobrogei: Chestiunea Arab-Tabiei],* nos. 1, 2.

31. Vinberg (Silistria) to Anghelescu, 7/19 February 1879, in Anghelescu, *[Fruntaria Dobrogei],* no. 3.

32. Anghelescu to Vinberg, 7/19 February 1879, in Anghelescu, *[Fruntaria Dobrogei],* no. 4.

33. Anghelescu to Ion Brătianu, n.d., no. 5, and 8/20 February 1879, no. 7, and Anghelescu to Vinberg, 8/20 February 1879, no. 6, in Anghelescu, *[Fruntaria Dobrogei];* see also Cîmpineanu to Bălăceanu, 7/19 and 21 February 1879, in HHS, PA—XII, Türkei Varia, Karton 258.

34. Hoyos to Andrássy, 19 February 1879, no. 41, in HHS, PA—XII, Türkei Varia, Karton 258.

35. Anghelescu to the minister of war, Nicolae Dabija, 13/25 February 1879, in *Anghelescu, [Fruntaria Dobrogei]*, no number.

36. Gorchakov to Novikov, 9 February 1879, in HHS, PA—XII, Türkei Varia, Karton 258.

37. Langenau to Andrássy, 14 February 1879, telegram no. 22, in HHS, PA—XII, Türkei Varia, Karton 258.

38. Andrássy to Károlyi, 14 February 1879, in HHS, PA—XII, Türkei Varia, Karton 258.

39. Girs (St. Petersburg) to Novikov, 24 March 1879, no. 1020, in HHS, PA—XII, Türkei Varia, Karton 258.

40. Girs to N. A. Fonton (Vienna), 28 July/9 August 1879, in HHS, PA—XII, Türkei Varia, Karton 258.

41. Ion G. Ghica to Ministerul Afacerilor Străine, 18/30 August 1879, no. 13, in Arhiva Mihail Kogălniceanu, LXI/5, BNR, SM; Ghica reported a conversation with Zhomini.

42. Kálnoky (St. Petersburg) to Andrássy, 11/23 August 1879, no. 37B, in HHS, PA—XII, Türkei Varia, Karton 258; Fonton to Andrássy, 28 August 1879, and Kálnoky to Andrássy, 15 September 1879, telegram no. 129, in HHS, PA—XII, Türkei Varia, Karton 257.

43. Franz Deym von Stritez (London) to Andrássy, 4 September 1879, telegram no. 69, in HHS, PA—XII, Türkei Varia, Karton 257.

44. Miliutin's notes, 25 October/6 November 1879, in *Dnevnik D. A. Miliutina*, 3:174.

45. Franz Jäger, "Exposé" (Vienna), 14 October 1879, in HHS, PA—XII, Türkei Varia, Karton 257; Jäger was Austria-Hungary's delegate to the technical commission.

46. Jäger (Călăraşi) to Heinrich von Haymerle (Vienna), 3 November 1879, in HHS, PA—XII, Türkei Varia, Karton 257.

47. Haymerle's circular, 3 November 1879, in HHS, PA—XII, Türkei Varia, Karton 257.

48. See abstracts of the commission's seven procès-verbaux (Silistra and Bucharest), 27 October–11 November 1879, in *The Map of Europe by Treaty*, 4:2939–40.

49. Hoyos to Haymerle, 11 November 1879, no. 225, in HHS, PA—XII, Türkei Varia, Karton 257.

50. Girs (Livadia) to Pavel P. Ubri (Berlin), 8/20 November 1879, in HHS, PA—XII, Türkei Varia, Karton 259.

51. Haymerle to Imre Széchényi (Berlin), 10 December 1879, in HHS, PA—XII, Türkei Varia, Karton 259.

52. Novikov to Haymerle, 28 January 1880, in HHS, PA—XII, Türkei Varia, Karton 259.

53. Hoyos to Haymerle, 14 February 1880, no. 20, in HHS, PA—XII, Türkei Varia, Karton 259.

54. Boerescu (Bucharest) to Steriadi (Vienna), 26 February 1880, telegram no. 2465, in HHS, PA—XII, Türkei Varia, Karton 259.

55. Boerescu to Bălăceanu, 2/14 March 1880, no. 3590, in HHS, PA—XII, Türkei Varia, Karton 259.

56. See Bulgaria's memorandum, 4/16 November 1879, in Fond Ion C. Brătianu, LVIII/3, BNR, SM.

57. Kálnoky to Haymerle, 18 March 1880, telegram no. 31, in HHS, PA—X, Rußland, Karton 74.

58. Széchényi to Haymerle, 20 March, 4 April, and 10 April 1880, and Haymerle to Széchényi, 31 March 1880, in HHS, PA—XII, Türkei Varia, Karton 259. Shuvalov, Russia's ambassador in London, and especially its envoy in Berlin, Pëtr A. Saburov, prompted Haymerle's initiative.

59. Kálnoky to Haymerle, 9/21 April 1880, no. 22B, in HHS, PA—XII, Türkei Varia, Karton 259.

60. Remus N. Oprean (Constanţa) to Ministerul de Interne, 12 April 1880, no. 2382, and Vasile Boerescu to Bălăceanu, 16 April 1880, in HHS, PA—XII, Türkei Varia, Karton 259.

61. Haymerle to Rudolf von Khevenhüller-Metsch (Sofia), 27 April 1880, in HHS, PA—XII, Türkei Varia, Karton 259.

62. Khevenhüller to Haymerle, 4 and 12 May 1880, in HHS, PA—XII, Türkei Varia, Karton 259.

63. Haymerle to Khevenhüller, 14 May 1880, in HHS, PA—XII, Türkei Varia, Karton 259.

64. Boerescu to Bălăceanu, 29 April 1880, and Hoyos to Haymerle, 26 May 1880, no. 64A, in HHS, PA—XII, Türkei Varia, Karton 259.

65. Khevenhüller to Haymerle, 28 May 1880, in HHS, PA—XII, Türkei Varia, Karton 259.

66. Kálnoky to Haymerle, 9 June 1880, and Constantin von Trauttenberg (St. Petersburg) to Haymerle, 18/30 June 1880, no. 41C, in HHS, PA—XII, Türkei Varia, Karton 259. See the amendments to articles 6 and 7 of the European Delimitation Commission's act of 17 December 1878 adopted by the powers between 9 August 1880 and 11 August 1881, in *The Map of Europe by Treaty*, 4:2995–96.

67. Mayr (Bucharest) to Kálnoky (Vienna), 8 November 1882, no. 104C, Dimitrie Sturdza (Bucharest) to Mayr, 11 February 1883, and Rüdiger von Biegeleben (Sofia) to Kálnoky, 10 March 1883, no. 9F, in HHS, PA—XII, Türkei Varia, Karton 255.

68. Eissenstein (Bucharest) to Ministerium des Außern, 5 September 1885, no. 56A, and V. Steinbach von Hidegkut (Sofia) to Ministerium des Außern, 8 and 22 September 1885, nos. 46B and 48D, in HHS, PA—XII, Türkei Varia, Karton 255.

69. Carol (Sinaia) to Leopold (Sigmaringen), 29 January 1880, in HHA, HS, Rubrik 53b, Kasten XXIX, Fach 27, Faszikel no. 1 (69); Hoyos to Haymerle, 20 and 22 June 1880, in HHS, PA—XII, Türkei Varia, Karton 259.

70. Hoyos to Haymerle, 14 and 31 July 1880, in HHS, PA—XII, Türkei Varia, Karton 259.

71. See articles 3, 5, 15, and 20 of the Dobrogea charter of 7 March 1880, in *Ion C. Brătianu: Acte şi cuvântări*, 5:365–67. The chambers adopted the charter by 58 to 5 with 2 abstentions, 12/24 February; the senate did so by 28 to 3, 4/16 March 1880.

72. Congress of Berlin protocol nos. 8, 10, and 17 of 28 June, 1 and 10 July 1878, in *Recueil d'actes internationaux de l'Empire Ottoman*, 4:67, 88, 157.

73. Articles 43 and 44, Treaty of Berlin, 13 July 1878, in *Recueil d'actes internationaux de l'Empire Ottoman*, 4:189.

74. Articles 5, 6, 7, and 8 of the constitution, 30 June/12 July 1866, in *Desbaterile Adunării Constituante*, 290–91.

75. Article 9 of the civil code, 26 November/8 December 1864, in *Codice Civile*, 5.

76. *Journal de St. Pétersbourg*, 16/28 August 1878.

77. Andrássy to Langenau, 2 August 1878, in HHS, PA—X, Rußland, Karton 70; Bălăceanu (Baden) to Andrássy, 9 August 1878, with Francis Joseph's marginal note, in HHS, PA—XVIII, Türkei Varia, Karton 50; Andrássy to Mayr, 4 September 1878, in HHS, PA—X, Rußland, Karton 70.

78. Carol's decree (Sinaia), 11/25 September 1878, no. 2050, in *Monitorul oficial al României*, 15/27 September 1878; Andrássy to Kogălniceanu, 6 October 1878, in HHS, PA—XVIII, Türkei Varia, Karton 50.

79. Suleiman Bey presented his Turkish credentials in Bucharest, 3/15 December 1878; see *Aus dem Leben König Karls von Rumänien*, 4:149.

80. Obedenaru (Rome) to Kogălniceanu, 15 August and 14 October 1878, in Bossy, *Politica externă a României*, 177–81.

81. Auswärtiges Amt (Berlin) to Keudell (Rome), 8 November 1878, no. 363, in HAA, PS, Türkei, 24, vol. 67.

82. Carol's notes, 30 October/11 November, and his letter to Charles Anthony, 5/17 November 1878, in *Aus dem Leben König Karls von Rumänien*, 4:128, 133; Pierre-Henri Fourier de Bâcourt (Bucharest) to Waddington (Paris), 19 November 1878, no. 35, in Ministère des Affaires Étrangères, *Documents diplomatiques français*, 2:401–2.

83. Carol's speech in the legislature, 13/27 November 1878, in *Ion C. Brătianu: Acte și cuvântări*, 4:372.

84. Brătianu's speech in the chamber, 25 February 1878, in *Ion C. Brătianu: Acte și cuvântări*, 4:241, 256; Bleichröder (Berlin) to Crémieux (Paris), 12 April 1878, in Carol Iancu, *Bleichröder et Crémieux: Le combat pour l'émancipation des Juifs en Roumanie devant le Congrès de Berlin—Correspondance inédite (1878–1880)*, 146–47.

85. *Românul*, 18/30 December 1878.

86. Hoyos to Andrássy, 13 March 1879, no. 60, in HHS, PA—XVIII, Rumänien Varia I, Karton 50.

87. Carp's senate speech, 6 December 1878, in Carp, *Discursuri*, 1:173.

88. Cîmpineanu (Bucharest) to Bălăceanu, 28 March 1879, and Hoyos to Andrássy, 3 April 1879, no. 73, in HHS, PA—XVIII, Rumänien Varia I, Karton 50.

89. Carol to Leopold, 11 March 1879, in HHA, HS, Rubrik 53b, Kasten XXIX, Fach 27, Faszikel no. 1 (69).

90. Carol to Leopold, 10 January 1879, in HHA, HS, Rubrik 53b, Kasten XXIX, Fach 27, Faszikel no. 1 (69).

91. Andrássy to Hoyos, 1 March 1879, and Hoyos to Andrássy, 6 March 1879, no. 56, in HHS, PA—XVIII, Rumänien Varia I, Karton 50.

92. Andrássy to Bosizio (Bucharest), 21 April 1879, in HHS, PA—XVIII, Rumänien Varia I, Karton 50.

93. Hoyos to Andrássy, 6 May 1879, no. 98, in HHS, PA—XVIII, Rumänien Varia I, Karton 50.

94. Carol's speech in the legislature, 22 May/3 June 1879, in *Regele Carol I al României,* 2:302–3.

95. Andrássy (Schönbrunn) to Széchényi, 23 June 1879, in HHS, PA—XVIII, Rumänien Varia I, Karton 50.

96. Andrássy to Hoyos, 30 June 1879, in HHS, PA—XVIII, Rumänien Varia I, Karton 50; Andrássy to Hoyos, 21 July/3 August 1879, in Fond Ion C. Brătianu, LVIII/1, BNR, SM.

97. Waddington to Saint-Vallier (Berlin), 29 June 1879, in *Documents diplomatiques français,* 2:528; Andrássy to Hoyos, 30 June 1879, Hoyos to Andrássy, 4 July 1879, no. 137, and Cîmpineanu to Bălăceanu, 15 July 1879, in HHS, PA—XVIII, Rumänien Varia I, Karton 50.

98. Hoyos to Andrássy, 2 July 1879, no. 132, and 9 July 1879, no. 145, in HHS, PA—XVIII, Rumänien Varia I, Karton 50.

99. Hoyos to Andrássy, 5 July 1879, no. 139, in HHS, PA—XVIII, Rumänien Varia I, Karton 50.

100. Carol to Leopold, 8 July 1879, in HHA, HS, Rubrik 53b, Kasten XXIX, Fach 27, Faszikel no. 1 (69).

101. Andrássy to Hoyos, 6 July 1879, in HHS, PA—XVIII, Rumänien Varia I, Karton 50; Radowitz (Berlin) to Reuss (Vienna), 11 July 1879, no. 502, in HHS, PA—XVIII, Rumänien Varia I, Karton 50; Salisbury to John Walsham, 28 July 1879, in *British and Foreign State Papers,* vol. 71 (1879–80), 1157–58; Haymerle (Rome) to Andrássy, 7 July 1879, telegram no. 68, in HHS, PA—XVIII, Rumänien Varia I, Karton 50; Bleichröder to the Comité Central, Alliance Israélite Universelle (Paris), 29 July 1879, in Iancu, *Bleichröder et Crémieux,* 200.

102. See the government's proposal, 11/23 July 1879, in *Ion C. Brătianu: Acte și cuvântări,* 5:312.

103. Cabinet's letter to Carol and the latter's sanction, 11/23 July 1879, in *Ion C. Brătianu: Acte și cuvântări,* 5:313–15.

104. Carol (Cotroceni) to Leopold, 8 July 1879, in HHA, HS, Rubrik 53b, Kasten XXIX, Fach 27, Faszikel no. 1 (69).

105. Carol's address (Sinaia), 11/23 August 1879, in *Regele Carol I al României,* 2:333.

106. Boerescu to Bălăceanu, 23 July 1879, in HHS, PA—XVIII, Rumänien Varia I, Karton 50; Andrássy to Hoyos, 1 August 1879, in HHS, PA—XVIII, Rumänien, Karton 13; Max von Berchem (Berlin) to Andrássy, 29 July 1879, in HHS, PA—III, Preußen, Karton 119.

107. Boerescu's circular, 13/25 July 1879, in *Independența României,* 4:568–69.

108. Boerescu (Berlin) to the cabinet, 8 August 1879, in Fond Vasile Boerescu, XXXIX/1, BNR, SM; Boerescu (St. Petersburg) to the cabinet, 1/13 August 1879, and Boerescu (Paris) to the cabinet, 21, 29, and 31 August 1879, in AIC, CR, dosar 10/1879; Bleichröder (Hamburg) to Isidore Loëb (Paris), 22 August 1879, in Iancu, *Bleichröder et Crémieux,* 210–11.

109. Boerescu (Rome) to the cabinet, 10 September 1879, in Fond Vasile Boerescu, XXXIX/1, BNR, SM; Bosizio to Andrássy, 4 September 1879, no. 184, in HHS, PA—XVIII, Rumänien Varia I, Karton 50.

110. Titu Maiorescu, *Discursuri parlamentare cu privire asupra desvoltării politice a României sub Domnia Carol I,* 2:375–76; Bosizio to Auswärtiges Amt, 24 September 1879, no. 188, in HHS, PA—XVIII, Rumänien Varia I, Karton 50.

111. Samuel Pineles (Galaţi) to Loëb (Paris), 26 September 1879, in Bibliothèque de l'Alliance Israélite Universelle, Archives Roumanie, IC 1–3 (Bucarest) (hereinafter cited BAIU, AR); Bosizio to Auswärtiges Amt, 28 September 1879, no. 190, in HHS, PA—XVIII, Rumänien Varia I, Karton 50.

112. Carp's speech in the chamber, 28 September/10 October 1879, in Carp, *Discursuri,* 1:202–3.

113. See Alecsandri's speech in the chamber, 10/22 October 1879. He erroneously set Romania's Jewish population in 1859/60 at 0.01% instead of the roughly 3% in the census report at that time; see Chapter Three above. Alecsandri cited a French economist, Alexandre Moreau de Jonnès, in putting the Jews at 3.85% in the Ottoman Empire, 1.72% in Russia, 1.67% in Austria-Hungary, 1.11% in Germany, 0.20% in Italy, 0.17% in France, and 0.01% in Great Britain; *Cestiunea Israelită înnaintea Camerilor de revisuire: Moţiunea nerevisioniştilor şi discursurile,* 160–61.

114. Bleichröder (Berlin) to Hermann Hirsch (Bucharest), 15 January 1879, in BAIU, AR, IC 1–3.

115. Maiorescu's speech, 10/22 September 1879, in Maiorescu, *Discursuri parlamentare,* 2:370–71.

116. For the new article 7, see *Desbaterile Adunărei Constituante,* 291.

117. Boerescu's speech in the chamber, 1/13 October 1879, in Vasile Boerescu, *Discursuri politice,* 2:906, 940, 986. The chamber adopted the revision on 6/18 October 1879, voting 132 to 9 with 2 abstentions, including Carp's; the senate agreed on 11/23 October 1879, balloting 56 to 2 with one abstention; Carol sanctioned the measure on 12/24 October 1879; *Ion C. Brătianu: Acte şi cuvântări,* 5:317–18.

118. The senate acted on 13/25 October, the chamber on 18/30 October, with Carol's sanction, 6/18 November 1879; Barbu B. Berceanu, "Modificarea, din 1879, a articolului 7 din Constituţie," 88.

119. Hoyos to Haymerle (Vienna), 29 October 1879, no. 214, and Bosizio to Haymerle, 8 October 1879, no. 197, in HHS, PA—XVIII, Rumänien Varia I, Karton 50.

120. Carol's speech in the legislature, 15/27 November 1879, in *Ion C. Brătianu: Acte şi cuvântări,* 5:326.

121. Boerescu's circular, 12/24 October 1879, in Fond Vasile Boerescu, XXXIX/ 1, BNR, SM. From 1866 until 1879, 227 foreigners had been naturalized; after the 888 in 1879, 57 Jews became citizens in 1880, 6 in 1881, and 7 from 1882 to 1892; see Nicolae Basilescu, *Studii sociale,* series 2: *Streinii în România,* 121; Nicolae Petrescu-Comnen, *Étude sur la condition des Israélites en Roumanie,* 67–69.

122. Boerescu to Bălăceanu, 30 October 1879, no. 15792, in HHS, PA—XVIII, Rumänien Varia I, Karton 50.

123. Beust (Paris) to Haymerle, 13 November 1879, telegram no. 142, in HHS, PA—XVIII, Rumänien Varia I, Karton 50; Salisbury to Augustus B. Paget (Rome), 8 December 1879, in *British and Foreign State Papers,* 71:1179.

124. See Romania's note-verbale (Rome), 5 December 1879, and Esarcu (Rome) to Boerescu, 16 December 1879, in Bossy, *Politica externă a României,* 204, 206–9;

Francesco Sponzilli (Rome) to Fălcoianu, 20 December 1879, in Colecția specială, 3155/156, no. 21902, BAR, SC.

125. Bismarck (Kissingen) to Bülow, 15 June 1877, and Bülow to Alvensleben (St. Petersburg), 23 June 1877, no. 128, in HAA, PS, Türkei, 104, vol. 3.

126. Alvensleben to Bülow, 15 June 1877, no. 175, and 26 June 1877, no. 179, in HAA, PS, Türkei, 104, vol. 3.

127. Bleichröder to Bismarck, 14 October 1877, Bismarck (Varzin) to Bülow, 16 October and 8 November 1877, no. 70, and Bülow to Schweinitz (St. Petersburg), 27 October 1877, no. 931, in HAA, PS, Türkei, 104, vol. 3; Bleichröder to Bismarck, 1 March 1878, and Bleichröder to Bülow, 20 February 1879, in HAA, PS, Türkei, 104, vol. 4. This debt was 370 million francs.

128. Andrássy (Budapest) to Hoyos, 1 March 1879, in HHS, PA—XVIII, Rumänien Varia I, Karton 50.

129. Hoyos to Andrássy, 20 March 1879, no. 65, and Andrássy (Vienna) to Tisza (Budapest), 7 April 1879, in HHS, PA—XVIII, Rumänien Varia I, Karton 50.

130. Alvensleben to Bülow, 18 May 1878, no. 100, in HAA, PS, Türkei, 104, vol. 3.

131. See Dimitrie Sturdza's memorandum, n.d., in HAA, PS, Türkei, 104, vol. 5.

132. Ioan Kalinderu (Berlin) to Dimitrie Sturdza, 11 July 1879, in Fond Ion C. Brătianu, LVIII/3, and Kalinderu to Ion Brătianu, 23 July 1879, in Fond Ion C. Brătianu, LVIII/4, BNR, SM.

133. Dimitrie Sturdza's memorandum, n.d., given to Bismarck, 25 July 1879, in HAA, PS, Türkei, 104, vol. 5.

134. Hoyos to Andrássy, 31 July 1879, no. 167, in HHS, PA—XVIII, Rumänien, Karton 13.

135. Bismarck to Wolfram von Rotenhan (Bucharest), 12 August 1879, no. 14, in HAA, PS, Türkei, 104, vol. 5; Vîrnav-Liteanu to Carol, 6 September 1879, in AIC, CR, 37/1879.

136. Széchényi to Andrássy, 30 September 1879, Handelspolitisch no. 96, in HHS, PA—XVIII, Rumänien Varia I, Karton 51; William A. White (Bucharest) to Salisbury, 1 November 1879, Commercial no. 31, in PRO, FO, 104/10.

137. See section 1, article 1 of *Statutes: Articles of Association of the Roumanian Railways' Share Company.*

138. Vasile Maciu, "Dezvoltarea capitalismului în Romînia între 1864 şi 1878," 473; Carol's notes, 3/15 February, 8/20 May, and 17/29 June 1872, in *Aus dem Leben König Karls von Rumänien,* 2:240, 264, 271.

139. For the 1875 state budget, see *Almanach de Gotha, 1876,* 917; for the 1877 budget, see *Documente privind istoria Romîniei: Războiul pentru independenţă,* vol. 1, pt. 1, 423; cf. Bob Dowley [Ion Ghica] (Bucharest) to James O. Morgaw (London), 4/16 April 1876, in Ion Ghica, *Opere,* 2:266; Carol's notes, 19/31 December 1877 and 28 March/9 April 1879, in *Aus dem Leben König Karls von Rumänien,* 3:417, 4:187; Ion Brătianu's speech in the chamber, 17/29 March 1879, in *Ion C. Brătianu: Acte şi cuvântări,* 4:297.

140. Bosizio to Auswärtiges Amt, 8 October 1879, no. 197, in HHS, PA—XVIII, Rumänien Varia I, Karton 50.

141. Rotenhan to Bülow, 11 September, no. 71, and 18 September 1879, no. 72, in HAA, PS, Türkei, 104, vol. 6.

142. Bleichröder to Bülow, 24 September 1879, in HAA, PS, Türkei, 104, vol. 6.

143. Brătianu to Dimitrie Sturdza (Berlin), 20 September/2 October 1879, in Fond Ion C. Brătianu, LVIII/4, BNR, SM; Hoyos to Haymerle, 12 November 1879, no. 226, in HHS, PA—XVIII, Rumänien Varia I, Karton 51.

144. Haymerle to Hoyos, 15 November 1879, in HHS, PA—XVIII, Rumänien Varia I, Karton 51; Berchem to Bismarck, 17 November 1879, no. 804, in HAA, PS, Türkei, 104, vol. 6.

145. Hoyos to Haymerle, 18 November 1879, no. 230, in HHS, PA—XVIII, Rumänien Varia I, Karton 50; Hoyos to Haymerle, 25 November 1879, no. 237, in HHS, PA—XVIII, Rumänien Varia I, Karton 51.

146. Dimitrie Sturdza to Vîrnav-Liteanu, 10/22 November 1879, no. 1493, in Fond Ion C. Brătianu, LVIII/5, BNR, SM; see article 3 of a convention signed by Sturdza and the bankers in Berlin, 2 October 1879, in Arhiva Dimitrie A. Sturdza, XIV/88, BAR, SM.

147. Vîrnav-Liteanu to Ion Brătianu, 1/13 November 1879 and 12/24 November 1879, in *Ion C. Brătianu: Acte şi cuvântări,* 5:80–81, 90; Anton von Wolkenstein (Berlin) to Haymerle, 28 November 1879, no. 42, in HHS, PA—XVIII, Rumänien Varia I, Karton 51.

148. Brătianu's speeches in the chamber, 25 November/7 December and 12/24 December 1879, in *Ion C. Brătianu: Acte şi cuvântări,* 5:103, 146.

149. The chambers voted on 28 November/10 December 1879; Rotenhan to Bismarck, 8 December 1879, no. 94, in HAA, PS, Türkei, 104, vol. 6; Rotenhan to Bismarck, 10 December 1879, no. 95, in HAA, PS, Türkei, 104, vol. 7.

150. Auswärtiges Amt to Rotenhan, 12 December 1879, no. 43, in HAA, PS, Türkei, 104, vol. 7; Széchényi to Haymerle, 10 December 1879, telegram no. 88, and letter of the same date, Handelspolitisch no. 114, in HHS, PA—XVIII, Rumänien Varia I, Karton 51.

151. Hoyos to Haymerle, 10 December 1879, no. 249, in HHS, PA—XVIII, Rumänien Varia I, Karton 51.

152. Radowitz to William I, 23 December 1879, in HAA, PS, Türkei, 104, vol. 7.

153. Auswärtiges Amt to Reuss, 12 December 1879, no. 187, in HAA, PS, Türkei, 104, vol. 7.

154. Esarcu to Vasile Boerescu, 5 December 1879, in Bossy, *Politica externă a României,* 204; Saint-Vallier to Waddington, 10 December 1879, telegram 483, and Waddington to Saint-Vallier, 11 December 1879, in *Documents diplomatiques français,* 2:597–98; Auswärtiges Amt to Georg H. zu Münster (London), 13 December 1879, no. 93, in HAA, PS, Türkei, 104, vol. 7.

155. Reuss to Bismarck, 13 December 1879, no. 519, in HAA, PS, Türkei, 104, vol. 7.

156. Haymerle to Hoyos, 13, 16, and 17 December 1879, telegrams, in HHS, PA—XVIII, Rumänien Varia I, Karton 51.

157. Hoyos to Haymerle, 18 December 1879, no. 259, in HHS, PA—XVIII, Rumänien Varia I, Karton 51.

158. Hoyos to Haymerle, 19 December 1879, no. 261, in HHS, PA—XVIII, Rumänien Varia I, Karton 51.

159. Vîrnav-Liteanu to Vasile Boerescu, 14 and 19 December 1879, in Fond Ion C. Brătianu, LVIII/6, BNR, SM; Radowitz to William I, 23 December 1879, in HAA, PS, Türkei, 104, vol. 7.

160. Vîrnav-Liteanu to Brătianu, 15 December 1879, in Fond Ion C. Brătianu, LVIII/4, and Vîrnav-Liteanu to Vasile Boerescu, 28 December 1879, in Fond Ion C. Brătianu, LVIII/6, BNR, SM.

161. White to Salisbury, 19 December 1879, no. 341, in PRO, FO, 104/8.

162. Manu's speech in the senate, 22 December 1879/3 January 1880, in George Manu, *Discursurile generalului G. Manu (1871–1906)*, 1004, 1109–10, 1111, along with a memorandum signed by Manu, Teodor Rosetti, Mavrogheni, Catargiu, and seven others.

163. The senate voted 38 to 4 with 12 abstentions, 22 December 1879/3 January 1880; Hoyos to Haymerle, 31 December 1879, no. 271, and 3 January 1880 telegram, in HHS, PA—XVIII, Rumänien Varia I, Karton 51.

164. Brătianu's speech in the chamber, 15/22 January 1880, in *Ion C. Brătianu: Acte şi cuvântări*, 5:177–78, 184.

165. Boerescu's speech in the chamber, [15/22 January 1880], in Vasile Boerescu, *Discursuri politice*, 2:1004–7, 1010, 1011, 1023–24.

166. The chamber voted 72 to 42 with 11 abstentions, 15/22 January 1880; Carol confirmed the transaction on 26 January/7 February 1880. See the convention (Berlin), 2 October 1879, concluded by Dimitrie Sturdza with the Disconto-Gesellschaft and the Samuel Bleichröder bank, in Fond Dimitrie A. Sturdza, XIV Varia/88, BAR, SM; cf. *Ion C. Brătianu: Acte şi cuvântări*, 5:334–63.

167. Carol's speech in the legislature, 12/24 April 1880, in *Ion C. Brătianu: Acte şi cuvântări*, 5:382.

168. Bleichröder to Auswärtiges Amt, 2 February 1880, in HAA, PS—Türkei, 104, vol. 9.

169. The shareholders voted 180 to 33, or 82 percent of those present, on 3 March 1880, to approbate the conversion of 54.70 percent of the invested capital; Dimitrie Sturdza (Berlin) to Ion Brătianu, 3 March 1880 telegram, in Colecţia Mihail Kogălniceanu, XI/79, BNR, SM.

170. Romania's law of 23 June/5 July 1881, and a Berlin convention, 20 July 1881, in Fond Dimitrie A. Sturdza, XIV Varia/126, BAR, SM.

171. The Council of Supervision's resolution, 18 August 1881, about the shift found confirmation by the Berlin court of appeal, 5 June 1882; Kalinderu (Berlin) to Dimitrie Sturdza, 8 June 1882, in Fond Dimitrie A. Sturdza, XIV Varia/115, BAR, SM. The major litigants had been Jacob Landau and Ludwig von Kaufmann.

172. See a Romanian law of 8/27 August 1882, a convention signed by Kalinderu for the society and Dimitrie Sturdza in Bucharest, 3/21 September 1882, and a shareholders' decision, 18/30 September 1882, in Fond Dimitrie A. Sturdza, XIV Varia/125, BAR, SM. The Banca Naţională a României became financially accountable for the lines on 10 November 1882 after an injunction from the Ilfov Tribunal de comerţ in Bucharest; see ibid.

173. See Chapter Four above. The Danube and Black Sea Railway in Dobrogea began operations in 1860; the one in northern Moldavia, built from 1869 to 1871, was run by the Kaiserliche-Königliche privilegierte Lemberg-Czernowitz-Jassy Eisenbahn Gesellschaft. See Carol's decree, 18 October 1888, and Frank Cavendish Lascelles (Bucharest) to Salisbury, 27 October 1888, no. 111, in PRO, FO, 104/17; cf. the slightly different rail lengths given in Demetru Urmă, "Un act istoric: Trecerea liniilor ferate sub o conducere unică," 116, 128–29, 132.

174. Bleichröder to Moritz von Goldschmidt (Vienna), 28 January 1880, in HHS, PA—XVIII, Rumänien Varia I, Karton 51.

175. Charles-Louis de Saulces de Freycinet (Paris) to Bâcourt, 29 January 1880, Richard B. P. Lyons, Baron Lyons (Paris) to Freycinet, 7 February 1880, and Saint-Vallier to Freycinet, 9 February 1880, in *Documents diplomatiques français,* 3:10, 15; Salisbury to White, 7 February 1880, no. 9, in PRO, FO, 104/13.

176. Haymerle to Széchényi, 2 February 1880, telegram no. 6, and Széchényi to Haymerle, 3 and 4 February 1880, telegram nos. 4 and 5, in HHS, PA—XVIII, Rumänien Varia I, Karton 51.

177. Salisbury to White, 10 and 15 February 1880, telegram nos. 11 and 15, in PRO, FO, 104/13; Bâcourt to Vasile Boerescu, 8/20 February 1880, in *Independenţa României,* 4:610–11.

Chapter Eleven

CONCLUSION

Passage along a winding road to independence transformed Romania from subservience under Ottoman suzerainty—with its autonomy guaranteed by Europe's great powers—to a stage of uncertainty. A small state surrounded by strong empires was perforce insecure. Some Romanians perceived the dangers ahead, yet most were elated at their country's new international standing and confidently expected to surmount future obstacles in achieving even more ambitious goals.

Danubian Romanians had evinced sovereignty even before the powers accepted it. The powers failed to restrain Romania from selecting a foreign prince, maltreating its Jews, and abetting Bulgarian revolutionaries. Bucharest exasperated foreign creditors when their company building Romania's railroads collapsed. Moreover, by raising its tariff Romania entered into commercial covenants with its neighbors. Neutrality during the Balkan Crisis also set Romania apart from the Ottoman Empire. Pacts with Russia at the outset of war in 1877 enabled Danubian Romanians to dodge the full costs of armed conflict. A declaration of independence and battlefield exploits filled Romanians with glorious self-esteem, especially when the Turks were defeated. The peacemaking process involved difficult issues for patriots, who confronted losing southern Bessarabia, amending their constitution, naturalizing some indigenous Jews, and purchasing the railroad. Here the powers extracted a pound of flesh; but they also awarded Dobrogea and the Danube Delta to a Romania that they would recognize in 1880 as having entered Europe's family of nations.

Romania's mode of passage was manifold. Matters were in flux in Europe, which was witnessing the formation of an Italian kingdom, a German empire, and a dual Austro-Hungarian monarchy. The powers, who were engrossed in such coeval changes, were reluctant to enforce injunctions of the Paris treaty of 1856 and convention of 1858 about Danubian Romania. They had, besides, differing views about the Ottoman Empire's role in Southeastern Europe, where the Habsburg and Romanov empires had more at stake than the Western powers. Romania's leaders utilized the powers' disunity to pursue their own objectives; in doing so, they occasionally played one power against another. Furthermore, Romanian statesmen perceived their land's need for economic development and so introduced railways and sheltered trade. They assiduously nurtured patriotic pride, which found telling expression in the legislature. Liberal and conservative politicians, as well as the prince, effectively articulated the country's purposes and goals. Orthodox Christian prelates perfunctorily blessed governmental decisions. Poets and artists depicted Romania's milieu and fervently trumpeted military feats. No preeminent personage or clique, nor any single event, even war, would be the key to success. Disagreements abounded. Major property-holders and merchants were more vocal than peasants. The absence of agrarian turbulence nevertheless reflected a fundamental social stability that allowed statesmen to stay a steady course. Romania would subsequently suffer shocks stemming from grave problems in farming, commerce, and industry, plus an ongoing struggle for the rights of minorities. In this period, Romania was, however, internally rather calm, and its leaders had the drive to achieve a national dream.

The significance of building a Romanian state was obvious to contemporaries. The protective net of the powers' assurances was indeed valuable; liberty would shatter that safety. Danubian Romanians had begun to sever their umbilical cord to the Ottoman Empire by uniting Moldavia to Wallachia and by choosing their own spokesmen within a constitutional framework. Partial freedom in internal and foreign affairs increasingly became an absolute prerogative as Romanians resolved urgent questions from 1866 to 1880. Indeed, Romania would later conclude a peacetime alliance to again ensure its being. But the quest for full sovereignty had brought Danubian Romania to maturity. Responsibility rested with many individuals who tenaciously followed a beacon of national interest that illuminated their path from vassalage to independence.

Appendix

Romania's Cabinets on the Passage to Independence

I. Lieutenant Government: Nicolae Golescu, Lascăr Catargiu, Nicolae Haralambie—11/23 February to 10/22 May 1866

>Prime minister: Ion Ghica, 11/23 February to 10/22 May 1866
>
>Interior: Dimitrie Ghica, 11/23 February to 10/22 May 1866
>
>Foreign affairs: Ion Ghica, 11/23 February to 10/22 May 1866
>
>Finance: Dimitrie A. Sturdza—interim, 11/23 February to 15/27 February 1866; Petru Mavrogheni, 16/28 February to 10/22 May 1866
>
>Justice: Ion C. Cantacuzino, 11/23 February to 10/22 May 1866
>
>Religion: Constantin A. Rosetti, 11/23 February to 10/22 May 1866
>
>War: Dimitrie Lecca, 11/23 February to 10/22 May 1866
>
>Public works: Dimitrie A. Sturdza, 11/23 February to 10/22 May 1866

II. Prince Carol, 10/22 May 1866 to 9/21 May 1881

>**1.** Prime minister, Lascăr Catargiu, 11/23 May to 14/26 July 1866
>
>>Interior: Lascăr Catargiu, 11/23 May to 14/26 July 1866
>>
>>Foreign affairs: Petru Mavrogheni, 11/23 May to 14/26 July 1866
>>
>>Finance: Ion C. Brătianu, 11/23 May to 14/26 July 1866
>>
>>Justice: Ion C. Cantacuzino, 11/23 May to 14/26 July 1866
>>
>>Religion: Constantin A. Rosetti, 11/23 May to 14/26 July 1866
>>
>>War: Ion G. Ghica, 11/23 May to 14/26 July 1866
>>
>>Public works: Dimitrie A. Sturdza, 11/23 May to 14/26 July 1866
>
>**2.** Prime minister: Ion Ghica, 15/27 July 1866 to 28 February/12 March 1867
>
>>Interior: Ion Ghica, 15/27 July 1866 to 28 February/12 March 1867
>>
>>Foreign affairs: Gheorghe Ştirbei, 15/27 July 1866 to 28 February/12 March 1867
>>
>>Finance: Petru Mavrogheni, 15/27 July 1866 to 28 February/12 March 1867
>>
>>Justice: Ion C. Cantacuzino, 15/27 July 1866 to 28 February/12 March 1867

Appendix

Religion: Constantin A. Rosetti, 15/27 July to 18/30 July 1866; Ion D. Strat, 19/31 July 1866 to 28 February/12 March 1867

War: Ion G. Ghica, 15/27 July to 5/17 August 1866;
Nicolae Haralambie, 6/18 August 1866 to 7/19 February 1867;
Tobias Gherghel, 8/20 February to 28 February/12 March 1867

Public works: Dimitrie A. Sturdza, 15/27 July 1866 to 28 February/12 March 1867

3. Prime minister: Constantin A. Krețulescu, 1/13 March to 16/28 August 1867

Interior: Ion C. Brătianu, 1/13 March to 16/28 August 1867

Foreign affairs: Ștefan Golescu 1/13 March to 16/28 August 1867

Finance: Alexandru Văsescu, 1/13 March to 16/28 August 1867

Justice: Constantin A. Krețulescu, 1/13 March to 4/16 August 1867;
Ștefan Golescu—interim, 5/17 August to 16/28 August 1867

Religion: Dumitru Brătianu, 1/13 March to 16/28 August 1867

War: Tobias Gherghel, 1/13 March to 23 May/4 June 1867;
Gheorghe Adrian, 24 May/5 June to 16/28 August 1867

Public works: Dumitru Brătianu—interim, 1/13 March to 16/28 August 1867

4. Prime minister: Ștefan Golescu, 17/29 August 1867 to 30 April/12 May 1868

Interior: Ștefan Golescu, 17/29 August to 12/24 November 1867;
Ion C. Brătianu, 13/25 November 1867 to 30 April/12 May 1868

Foreign affairs: Alexandru Teriakiu, 17/29 August to 31 October/12 November 1867; Ștefan Golescu—interim, 1/13 November to 12/24 November 1867; Ștefan Golescu, 13/25 November 1867 to 30 April/12 May 1868

Finance: Ludovic Steege, 17/29 August to 30 September/12 October 1867; Grigore Arghyropolu—interim, 1/13 October to 26 October/7 November 1867; Ion C. Brătianu, 27 October/8 November to 12/24 November 1867; Ion C. Brătianu—interim, 13/25 November 1867 to 30 April/12 May 1868

Justice: Anton I. Arion, 17/29 August to 28 August/9 September 1867; Grigore Arghyropolu, 29 August/10 September to 12/24 November 1867; Anton I. Arion, 13/25 November 1867 to 30 April/12 May 1868

Religion: Dumitru Brătianu, 17/29 August to 18/30 August 1867; Dimitrie Gusti, 19/31 August 1867 to 30 April/12 May 1868

War: Gheorghe Adrian, 17/29 August 1867 to 30 April/12 May 1868

Public works: Dumitru Brătianu, 17/29 August to 12/24 November 1867; Panait Donici, 13/25 November 1867 to 30 April/12 May 1868

5. Prime minister: Nicolae Golescu, 1/13 May to 15/27 November 1868

Interior: Ion C. Brătianu, 1/13 May to 11/23 August 1868; Anton I. Arion—interim, 12/24 August to 1/13 November 1868; Anton I. Arion, 2/14 November to 15/27 November 1868

Foreign affairs: Nicolae Golescu, 1/13 May to 15/27 November 1868

Finance: Ion C. Brătianu—interim, 1/13 May to 11/23 August 1868; Alexandru G. Golescu, 12/24 August to 15/27 November 1868

Justice: Anton I. Arion, 1/13 May to 1/13 November 1868; Constantin Eraclide, 2/14 November to 15/27 November 1868

Religion and education: Dimitrie Gusti, 1/13 May to 15/27 November 1868

War: Gheorghe Adrian, 1/13 May to 11/23 August 1868; Ion C. Brătianu—interim, 12/24 August to 15/27 November 1868

Public works: Panait Donici, 1/13 May to 15/27 November 1868

6. Prime minister: Dimitrie Ghica, 16/28 November 1868 to 1/13 February 1870

Interior: Mihail Kogălniceanu, 16/28 November 1868 to 23 January/4 February 1870; Dimitrie Ghica, 24 January/5 February to 1/13 February 1870

Foreign affairs: Dimitrie Ghica, 16/28 November 1868 to 25 August/6 September 1869; Mihail Kogălniceanu—interim, 26 August/7 September to 27 November/9 December 1869; Nicolae Calimaki-Catargi, 28 November/10 December 1869 to 1/13 February 1870

Finance: Alexandru G. Golescu, 16/28 November 1868 to 1/13 February 1870

Justice: Vasile Boerescu, 16/28 November 1868 to 20 January/1 February 1870; Dimitrie Ghica, 21 January/2 February to 23 January/4 February 1870; George G. Cantacuzino, 24 January/5 February to 1/13 February 1870

Religion and education: Alexandru Papadopol-Calimah, 16/28 November to 23 November/5 December 1868; Alexandru Crețescu, 24 November/6 December 1868 to 11/23 December 1869; George Mârzescu, 12/24 December 1869 to 1/13 February 1870

War: Alexandru Duca, 16/28 November 1868 to 13/25 June 1869; George Manu, 14/26 June 1869 to 1/13 February 1870

Public works: Dimitrie Ghica—interim, 16/28 November 1868 to 25 August/6 September 1869; Dimitrie Ghica, 26 August/7 September 1869 to 23 January/4 February 1870; Dimitrie Ghica—interim, 24 January/5 February to 1/13 February 1870

7. Prime minister: Alexandru G. Golescu, 2/14 February to 19 April/1 May
1870

> Interior: Alexandru G. Golescu, 2/14 February to 19 April/1 May 1870
>
> Foreign affairs: Alexandru G. Golescu—interim, 2/14 February to 19
> April/1 May 1870
>
> Finance: Ion A. Cantacuzino, 2/14 February to 19 April/1 May 1870
>
> Justice: Paul D. Vioreanu, 2/14 February to 19 April/1 May 1870
>
> Religion and education: George Mârzescu, 2/14 February 1870 to 19
> April/1 May 1870
>
> War: George Manu, 2/14 February to 19 April/1 May 1870
>
> Public works: Dimitrie Cozadini, 2/14 February to 19 April/1 May 1870

8. Prime minister: Manolache Costache Epureanu, 20 April/2 May to 14/26
December 1870

> Interior: Manolache Costache Epureanu, 20 April/2 May to 14/26
> December 1870
>
> Foreign affairs: Petre P. Carp, 20 April/2 May to 14/26 December 1870
>
> Finance: Constantin Grădişteanu, 20 April/2 May to 14/26
> December 1870
>
> Justice: Alexandru Lahovari, 20 April/2 May to 14/26 December 1870
>
> Religion and education: Vasile Pogor, 20 April/2 May to 22 May/3
> June 1870; Petre P. Carp—interim, 23 May/4 June to 14/26
> December 1870
>
> War: George Manu, 20 April/2 May to 14/26 December 1870
>
> Public works: George G. Cantacuzino, 20 April/2 May to 14/26
> December 1870

9. Prime minister: Ion Ghica, 15/27 December 1870 to 11/23 March 1871

> Interior: Ion Ghica, 15/27 December 1870 to 11/23 March 1871
>
> Foreign affairs: Nicolae G. Racoviţă—interim, 15/27 December to 18/
> 30 December 1870; Nicolae Calimaki-Catargi, 19/31 December
> 1870 to 11/23 March 1871
>
> Finance: Dimitrie A. Sturdza, 15/27 December 1870 to 11/23
> March 1871
>
> Justice: Dimitrie Cariagdi, 15/27 December 1870 to 11/23 March 1871
>
> Religion and education: Nicolae G. Racoviţă, 15/27 December 1870
> to 11/23 March 1871
>
> War: Eustaţiu Pencovici, 15/27 December 1870 to 11/23 March 1871
>
> Public works: Dumitru Berendei, 15/27 December 1870 to 11/23
> March 1871

10. Prime minister: Lascăr Catargiu, 12/24 March 1871 to 3/15 April 1876

Interior: Lascăr Catargiu, 12/24 March 1871 to 3/15 April 1876

Foreign affairs: Gheorghe Costa-Foru, 12/24 March 1871 to 26 April/8 May 1873; Lascăr Catargiu—interim, 27 April/9 May 1873; Vasile Boerescu, 28 April/10 May 1873 to 6/18 November 1875; Lascăr Catargiu—interim, 7/19 November 1875 to 29 January/10 February 1876; Ion Bălăceanu, 30 January/11 February 1876 to 3/15 April 1876

Finance: Petru Mavrogheni 12/24 March 1871 to 6/18 January 1875; George G. Cantacuzino, 7/19 January 1875 to 29 January/10 February 1876; Ion D. Strat, 30 January/11 February to 3/15 April 1876

Justice: Nicolae Krețulescu, 12/24 March to 7/19 June 1871; Gheorghe Costa-Foru—interim, 8/20 June 1871 to 27 October/8 November 1872; Manolache Costache Epureanu, 28 October/9 November 1872 to 30 March/11 April 1873; Christian Tell—interim, 31 March/12 April to 24 October/5 November 1873; Alexandru Lahovari, 25 October/6 November 1873 to 3/15 April 1876

Religion and education: Gheorghe Costa-Foru—interim, 12/24 March to 13/25 March 1871; Christian Tell, 14/26 March 1871 to 8/20 January 1874; Vasile Boerescu—interim, 9/21 January to 6/18 April 1874; Titu Maiorescu, 7/19 April 1874 to 29 January/10 February 1876; Petre P. Carp, 30 January/11 February to 3/15 April 1876

War: Christian Tell, 12/24 March to 13/25 March 1871; Ioan E. Florescu, 14/26 March 1871 to 3/15 April 1876

Public works: Nicolae Krețulescu—interim, 12/24 March to 7/19 June 1871; Nicolae Krețulescu, 8/20 June 1871 to 15/27 December 1873; George G. Cantacuzino, 16/28 December 1873 to 6/18 January 1875; Teodor Rosetti, 7/19 January 1875 to 30 March/11 April 1876; Alexandru Lahovari—interim, 31 March/12 April to 3/15 April 1876

11. Prime minister: Ioan E. Florescu, 4/16 April to 26 April/8 May 1876

Interior: Ioan E. Florescu—interim, 4/16 April to 26 April/8 May 1876

Foreign affairs: Dimitrie Cornea, 4/16 April to 26 April/8 May 1876

Finance: Christian Tell, 4/16 April to 26 April/8 May 1876

Justice: Paul D. Vioreanu, 4/16 April to 23 April/5 May 1876; Dimitrie Cornea—interim, 24 April/6 May to 26 April/8 May 1876

Religion and education: Alexandru Orescu, 4/16 April to 26 April/8 May 1876

War: Ioan E. Florescu, 4/16 April to 26 April/8 May 1876

Public works: Tobias Gherghel, 4/16 April to 26 April/8 May 1876

Appendix

12. Prime minister: Manolache Costache Epureanu, 27 April/9 May to 23 July/
4 August 1876

Interior: George Vernescu, 27 April/9 May to 23 July/4 August 1876

Foreign affairs: Mihail Kogălniceanu, 27 April/9 May to 23 July/4
August 1876

Finance: Ion C. Brătianu, 27 April/9 May to 23 July/4 August 1876

Justice: Mihail Pherekyde, 27 April/9 May to 23 July/4 August 1876

Religion and education: Gheorghe Chiţu, 27 April/9 May to 23 July/4
August 1876

War: Gheorghe Slăniceanu, 27 April/9 May to 23 July/4 August 1876

Public works: Manolache Costache Epureanu, 27 April/9 May to 23
July/4 August 1876

13. Prime minister: Ion C. Brătianu, 24 July/5 August 1876 to 24 November/6
December 1878

Interior: George Vernescu, 24 July/5 August 1876 to 26 January/7
February 1877; Ion C. Brătianu, 27 January/8 February 1877 to 25
May/6 June 1878; Constantin A. Rosetti, 26 May/7 June to 16/28
November 1878; Mihail Kogălniceanu—interim, 17/29 November to
24 November/6 December 1878

Foreign affairs: Nicolae Ionescu, 24 July/5 August 1876 to 24 March/5
April 1877; Ion Cîmpineanu—interim, 25 March/6 April to 2/14
April 1877; Mihail Kogălniceanu, 3/15 April 1877 to 24 November/
6 December 1878

Finance: Ion C. Brătianu, 24 July/5 August 1876 to 26 January/7
February 1877; Dimitrie A. Sturdza, 27 January/8 February to 20
February/4 March 1877; Ion C. Brătianu—interim, 21 February/5
March to 19/31 August 1877; Ion Cîmpineanu—interim, 20 August/
1 September to 22 September/4 November 1877; Ion Cîmpineanu,
23 September/5 November 1877 to 24 November/6 December 1878

Justice: Eugeniu Stătescu, 24 July/5 August 1876 to 23 January/4
February 1877; Ion Cîmpineanu, 24 January/5 February to 22
September/4 November 1877; Eugeniu Stătescu, 23 September/5
November 1877 to 24 November/6 December 1878

Religion and education: Gheorghe Chiţu, 24 July/5 August 1876 to 30
October/11 November 1878; Ion C. Brătianu—interim, 31 October/
12 November to 24 November/6 December 1878

War: Gheorghe Slăniceanu, 24 July/5 August 1876 to 1/13 April 1877;
Alexandru Cernat, 2/14 April to 19/31 August 1877; Ion C.
Brătianu—interim, 20 August/1 September 1877 to 16/28 March
1878; Alexandru Cernat, 17/29 March to 24 November/6
December 1878

Public works: Dimitrie A. Sturdza, 24 July/5 August 1876 to 4/16
January 1877; George Vernescu—interim, 5/17 January to 26
January/7 February 1877; Ioan Docan, 27 January/8 February to 20
August/1 September 1877; Petre S. Aurelian, 21 August/2
September 1877 to 25 March/6 April 1878; Ion C. Brătianu, 26
March/7 April to 24 November/6 December 1878

14. Prime minister: Ion C. Brătianu, 25 November/7 December 1878 to 10/22
July 1879

Interior: Ion C. Brătianu, 25 November/7 December 1878 to 10/22
July 1879

Foreign affairs: Ion Cîmpineanu, 25 November/7 December 1878 to 10/
22 July 1879

Finance: Dimitrie A. Sturdza, 25 November/7 December 1878 to 10/22
July 1879

Justice: Eugeniu Stătescu, 25 November/7 December 1878 to 10/22
July 1879

Religion and education: Gheorghe P. Cantilli, 25 November/7
December 1878 to 10/22 July 1879

War: Ion C. Brătianu—interim, 25 November/7 December 1878 to 7/19
January 1879; Nicolae Dabija, 8/20 January to 10/22 July 1879

Public works: Mihail Pherekyde, 25 November/7 December 1878 to 10/
22 July 1879

15. Prime minister: Ion C. Brătianu, 11/23 July 1879 to 9/21 April 1881

Interior: Mihail Kogălniceanu, 11/23 July 1879 to 16/28 April 1880;
Ion C. Brătianu—interim, 17/29 April to 14/26 July 1880; Anastasie
Stolojan—interim, 15/27 July to 19/31 July 1880; Alexandru
Teriakiu, 20 July/1 August 1880 to 9/21 April 1881

Foreign affairs: Vasile Boerescu, 11/23 July 1879 to 9/21 April 1881

Finance: Dimitrie A. Sturdza, 11/23 July 1879 to 15/27 February 1880;
Ion C. Brătianu—interim, 16/28 February to 24 February/7 March
1880; Ion Cîmpineanu, 25 February/8 March to 14/26 July 1880;
Ion C. Brătianu—interim, 15/27 July to 28 July/9 August 1880;
Ion C. Brătianu, 29 July/10 August 1880 to 9/21 April 1881

Justice: Anastasie Stolojan, 11/23 July 1879 to 28 July/9 August 1880;
Dimitrie Gianni, 29 July/10 August 1880 to 9/21 April 1881

Religion and education: Nicolae Krețulescu, 11/23 July 1879 to 21
January/2 February 1880; Vasile Boerescu—interim, 22 January/3
February to 19/31 July 1880; Vasile Conta, 20 July/1 August 1880 to
9/21 April 1881

War: Dimitrie Lecca, 11/23 July 1879 to 28 April/10 May 1880;
Gheorghe Slăniceanu, 29 April/11 May 1880 to 9/21 April 1881

Appendix

Public works: Ion C. Brătianu, 11/23 July 1879 to 23 October/4
November 1880; Nicolae Dabija, 24 October/5 November 1880 to 9/
21 April 1881

See also Mioara Tudorică and Ioana Burlacu, "Guvernele României între anii
1866–1945: Liste de miniştri," *Revista arhivelor* 32, no. 2 (1970): 429–76.

Works Cited

Unpublished

Archives du Ministère des Affaires Étrangères. Paris. (AMAE[F]). Correspondance politique (CP). Mémoires et documents.

Arhiva Ministerului Afacerilor Externe. Bucharest. (AMAE[R]). Fond Convenţii (FC).

Arhivele Statului. Bucharest. Arhiva Istorică Centrală (AIC). Casa Regală (CR). Fond Ion C. Brătianu.

Biblioteca Academiei Române. Bucharest. (BAR). Secţia de corespondenţă (SC). Arhiva Mihail Kogălniceanu. Colecţia specială. Fond Ion Bălăceanu. Fond Petre Carp. Fond Ion Ghica. Fond Mihail Kogălniceanu. Fond Dimitrie A. Sturdza.

Biblioteca Academiei Române. Bucharest. (BAR). Secţia manuscriselor (SM). Arhiva Dimitrie A. Sturdza. Dosar Dimitrie A. Sturdza. Fond Dimitrie A. Sturdza.

Biblioteca Academiei Române. Bucharest. (BAR). Arhiva Palatului (AP). Arhiva Consul Austriaci (ACA).

Biblioteca Naţională a României. Bucharest. (BNR). Secţia de corespondenţă (SC). Fond Ion C. Brătianu. Fond Mihail Kogălniceanu.

Biblioteca Naţională a României. Bucharest. (BNR). Secţia manuscriselor (SM). Arhiva Vasile Boerescu. Arhiva Mihail Kogălniceanu. Colecţia Mihail Kogălniceanu. Fond Vasile Boerescu. Fond Ion C. Brătianu. Fond Mihail Kogălniceanu. Fond Alexandru Saint-Georges.

Bibliothèque de l'Alliance Israélite Universelle. Paris. (BAIU). Archives Roumanie (AR).

Fürstliches Hohenzollernsches Haus- und Domänenarchiv: Abteilung Hohenzollern-Sigmaringen. Sigmaringen. (HHA, HS).

Hauptarchiv des Auswärtiges Amtes (Prussia; Germany). (HAA). Politischer Schriftwechsel (PS). Microfilm. University of California Library. Berkeley.

Haus- Hof- und Staatsarchiv. Vienna. (HHS). Politisches Archiv (PA). Handelspolitisches Archiv (HA). Geheim Akte.

Institutul de Istorie. Cluj-Napoca. Arhiva Vincenţiu Babeş.

Public Record Office. London. (PRO). Foreign Office (FO).

Published

Romanian words, which have undergone changes in spelling and accenting during the last two centuries, are usually given here and in footnotes in the style of the cited publication. This holds as well for cited works in other languages in the Roman alphabet; titles transliterated from Cyrillic and Greek letters conform chiefly to contemporary usage.

WORKS CITED

Acte şi documente relative la istoria renascerei Romaniei. Comp. Dimitrie A. Sturdza et al. 10 vols. in 11. Bucharest: Carol Göbl, 1889–1909.

Adăniloaie, Nichita. *Independenţa naţională a României.* Bucharest: Editura Academiei Republicii Socialiste România, 1986.

———. "Noi documente privitoare la războiul pentru independenţă (1877–1878)." *Revista de istorie* 30, no. 5 (May 1977): 861–81.

Alexandresco, Dimitrie. *Droit ancien et moderne de la Roumanie.* Louvain: J. B. Istas, 1897.

Alliance Israélite Universelle. *Bulletin.* Paris. 1861–1913. 1st ser. (1861–79); 2d ser. (1880–1904).

Almanach de Gotha: Annuaire diplomatique et statistique. Gotha: Justus Perthes, 1763–1944. Title varies.

Anghelescu, Gheorghe I. *[Fruntaria Dobrogei: Chestiunea Arab-Tabiei].* [Bucharest]: n.p., [1879]. Unpaginated; 7 letters dated 6/18 to 8/20 February 1879.

Antonescu, Corneliu. *Die rumänische Handelspolitik von 1875–1910.* Leipzig: W. Schunke, 1915.

Anul 1848 în principatele române: Acte şi documente. 6 vols. Bucharest: Carol Göbl, 1902–10.

Archives diplomatiques: Recueil de diplomatie et d'histoire. 193 vols. Paris: Amyot, 1861–1914.

Arnaudov, Mikhail. *Bŭlgarskoto knizhovno druzhestvo v Braila, 1869–1876.* Sofia: Izdatelstvo na Bŭlgarskata Akademiia na Naukite, 1966.

———. *Liuben Karavelov: Zhivot, delo, epokha, 1834–1879.* Sofia: Izdatelstvo na Bŭlgarskata Akademiia na Naukite, 1964.

Aslan, Theodor C. *Finanţele României dela Regulamentul Organic până astăzi, 1831–1905.* Bucharest: Carol Göbl, 1905.

Austria-Hungary. *Österreichische Statistik,* vol. 4: *Bericht über die Erhebung der Handelswerthe und Haupt-Ereignisse des auswärtigen Handels im Jahre 1882 in Vergleichung mit den Vorjahren,* pt. 1: *Die Statistik des auswärtigen Handels der österreichisch-ungarischen Monarchie im Jahre 1882.* Vienna: Aus der kaiserlich-königlichen Hof- und Staatsdruckerei, 1884.

"Autoritatea faptului îndeplinit executat în 1866 de cei îndreptăţiţi." Ed. Dimitrie A. Sturdza. *Analele Academiei Române,* 2d ser., *Memoriile secţiunii istorice* 34 (1911–12): 871–1024.

Băicoianu, Constantin I. *Geschichte der rumänischen Zollpolitik seit dem 14. Jahrhundert bis 1874.* Stuttgart: J. G. Cotta, 1896.

———. *Istoria politicei nóstre vamale şi comerciale de la Regulamentul Organic până în present.* Bucharest: n.p., 1904.

———. *Relaţiunile noastre comerciale cu Turcia de la 1860 până în present.* Bucharest: Eminescu, 1901.

Basilescu, Nicolae. *Studii sociale.* 2d ser., *Streinii în România.* Bucharest: Thoma Basilescu, 1903.

Batiushkov, Pompei N. *Bessarabiia: Istoricheskoe opisanie.* Ed. Mitrofan I. Gorodetskii. St. Petersburg: "Obshchestvennaia Pol'za," 1892.

Beer, Adolf. *Die österreichische Handelspolitik im neunzehnten Jahrhundert.* Vienna: Manz, 1891.

Berceanu, Barbu B. "Modificare, din 1879, a articolului 7 din Constituţie." *Studii şi materiale de istoria modernă* 6 (1979): 67–89.

Berindei, Dan. *Epoca unirii.* Bucharest: Editura Academiei Republicii Socialiste România, 1979.

Berindei, Dan, and Valerian Popovici. "Dezvoltarea economică şi socială a Principatelor în anii 1848–1864." In *Istoria Romîniei,* edited by Petre Constantinescu-Iaşi et al., 4:180–221. Bucharest: Editura Academiei Republicii Populare Romîne, 1964.

Bindreiter, Uta. *Die diplomatischen und wirtschaftlichen Beziehungen zwischen Österreich-Ungarn und Rumänien 1875–1888.* Vienna: Hermann Böhlaus, 1976.

Bismarck: Die gesammelten Werke. Ed. Hermann von Petersdorff, Friedrich Thimme, et al. 15 vols. in 19. Berlin: Otto Stollberg Verlag, 1924–35.

Bobango, Gerald J. *The Emergence of the Romanian National State.* Boulder, Colo.: East European Quarterly, 1979.

Bobrikov, Georgii I. "V Rumynii pered voinoi 1877 g." *Russkaia starina* 150 (May 1912): 290–95; 151 (September 1912): 332–42.

Boerescu, Constantin. *Discursuri politice, 1866–1891.* Bucharest: Socec, 1903.

Boerescu, Vasile. *Discursuri politice, 1859–1883.* 2 vols. Bucharest: Socec, 1910.

Boicu, Leonid. "Transporturile în Moldova între 1848 şi 1864." In *Dezvoltarea economiei Moldovei între anii 1848 şi 1864,* edited by Valerian Popovici, 429–77. Bucharest: Editura Academiei Republicii Populare Romîne, 1963.

Bossy, Raoul V. *Politica externă a României între anii 1873–1880, privită dela agenţia diplomatică din Roma.* Bucharest: Cultura Naţională, 1928.

Botez, Constantin. "Concesiunile de construcţii feroviare şi implicaţiile lor." In *Epopeea feroviară românească,* by C. Botez et al., 66–112. Bucharest: Editura Sport-Turism, 1977.

Brătianu, Dumitru. *Din arhiva lui Dumitru Brătianu: Acte şi scrisori din perioada 1840–1870.* Ed. Alexandru G. Cretzianu. 2 vols. Bucharest: Imprimeriile "Independenţa," 1933–34.

Brătianu. *Din corespondenţa familiei Ion C. Brătianu,* vol. 1 (1861–83). 2d ed. Bucharest: Imprimeriile "Independenţa," 1936. [1st ed. 1933].

———. *Ion C. Brătianu: Acte şi cuvântări.* Ed. Constantin C. Giurescu et al. Vol. 1, pt. 2 (1869–76), ed. George Marinescu and Constantin Grecescu (1935); vol. 3 (1877–78), ed. Constantin C. Giurescu (1930); vol. 4 (1878–79), ed. Nicolae Georgescu-Tistu (1932); vol. 5 (1879–80), ed. George Marinescu and Constantin Grecescu (1934). Bucharest: "Cartea Româneasca."

———. *Ion C. Brătianu: Discursuri, scrieri, acte şi documente.* Vol. 2, pts. 1, 2 (1876–77). Bucharest: Imprimeriile "Independenţa," 1912.

———. *Din scrierile şi cuvîntările lui Ion C. Brătianu, 1821–1891.* Vol. 1, pt. 1 (1848–68). Bucharest: Carol Göbl, 1903.

[Brătianu, Ion C.]. *Appel des Roumains à la Conférence.* Paris: Luxembourg, 1866.

Brezoianu, Ioan. *Vechile institutiuni alle Romaniei (1327–1866).* Bucharest: Stefan Mihălescu, 1882.

Brockhaus' Konversations-Lexikon. 14th ed. 16 vols. and 1 supplement. Leipzig: F. A. Brockhaus, 1898.

Bŭlgarska Akademiia na Naukite. *Dokumenti za bŭlgarskata istoriia.* 6 vols. Sofia: Dŭrzhavna pechatnitsa, 1931–51.

Burmov, Aleksandŭr. *Bŭlgarski revoliutsionen tsentralen komitet (1868–1876).* Sofia: Izdatelstvo Bŭlgarska Kniga, 1943.

Bush, John W. *Venetia Redeemed: Franco-Italian Relations, 1864–1866.* Syracuse, N.Y.: Syracuse University Press, 1967.

Cantemirii, Demetrii. *Descriptio antiqui et hodierni status Moldaviæ.* Edited by Alexandru Papiu-Ilarianu. Bucharest: Editura Academiei Republicii Socialiste România, 1973.

Carol. *Aus dem Leben König Karls von Rumänien: Aufzeichnungen eines Augenzeugen.* 4 vols. Stuttgart: J. G. Cotta, 1894–1900.

———. *Charles Ier, Roi de Roumanie: Chronique, actes, documents.* Ed. Démètre A. Sturdza. 3 vols. Vol. 1 (1866–75), 2 (1876–77). Bucharest: Charles Göbl, 1899–1904.

———. *Domnia regelui Carol I: Fapte-cuvântări-documente.* Ed. Dimitrie A. Sturdza. Vol. 1 (1866–76). No later volumes. Bucharest: Carol Göbl, 1906.

———. *Regele Carol I al României: Cuvântări și scrisori.* Vol. 1 (1866–77), 2 (1877–86). Bucharest: Carol Göbl, 1909.

Carp, Petre P. *Discursuri, 1866–1888.* Vol. 1. No later volumes. Bucharest: Socec, 1907.

Carte Romînească de Învățătură. Ed. Andrei Rădulescu et al. Bucharest: Editura Academiei Republicii Populare Romîne, 1961.

Cavour. *Lettere edite ed inedite di Camillo Cavour.* Ed. Luigi Chiala. 6 vols. Turin: Roux e Favale, 1883–87.

———. *La politique du comte Camillo di Cavour de 1852 à 1861: Lettres inédites avec notes.* Ed. Nicomède Bianchi. Turin: Roux & Favale, 1885.

———. *Tutti gli scritti di Camillo Cavour.* Ed. Carlo Pischedda and Guiseppe Talamo. 4 vols. Turin: Centro Studi Piemontesi, 1976–78.

Cestiunea Israelită înnaintea Camerilor de revisuire: Moțiunea nerevisioniștilor și discursurile. Bucharest: F. Göbl, 1879.

Chertan, Evgenii E. "Iz istorii russko-rumynskikh torgovykh vzaimootnoshenii v 1860–1875 godakh." *Izvestiia Akademii Nauk Moldavskoi SSR,* 1961, no. 1:18–35.

———. "Iz istorii zakliucheniia russko-rumynskoi konsul'skoi konventsii 1869 g." *Izvestiia Moldavskogo filiala Akademii Nauk SSSR,* 1961, no. 2 (80):39–54.

———. "Konventsiia o sudokhodstve po reke Prut 1866 goda." In *Tezisy dokladov vtoroi konferentsii molodykh uchënykh Moldavii,* 9–11. Kishinev: Izdatel'stvo "Shtiintsa," 1960.

———. "Russko-rumynskaia torgovaia konventsiia 1876 goda." In *Vekovaia druzhba,* 436–63. Kishinev: "Shtiintsa," 1961.

———. *Velikie derzhavy i formirovanie rumynskogo nezavisimogo gosudarstva.* Kishinev: "Shtiintsa," 1980.

———. "Velikie derzhavy i gosudarstvennyi perevorot 1866 g. v Rumynii." In *Voprosy istorii i istoriografii iugo-vostochnoi Evropy,* edited by Nikolai A. Mokhov and M. K. Sytnik, 24–58. Kishinev: "Shtiintsa," 1977.

Chiriţă, Grigore. "România în 1866: Coordinate ale politicii interne şi internaţionale." *Revista de istorie* 31, no. 12 (1978), 2197–2220.

Chuprov, Aleksandr I., and Boris F. Brandt. "Zheleznye dorogy." In *Entsiklopedicheskii slovar,* 11a (22): 778–82, 794–95. St. Petersburg: F. A. Brokgauz and I. A. Efron, 1894.

Ciahir, Nicolae. *Războiul pentru independenţa României în contextul european (1875– 1878).* Bucharest: Editura ştiinţifică şi enciclopedică, 1977.

Clark, Chester W. "Prince Gorchakov and the Black Sea Question, 1866: A Russiàn Bomb That Did Not Explode." *American Historical Review* 48, no. 1 (October 1942): 52–60.

Codice Civile. Bucharest: Imprimeria Statului, 1865.

Codicele penale şi de procedura criminale. Bucharest: Imprimeria Statului, 1866.

Codul Calimach. Ed. Andrei Rădulescu et al. Bucharest: Editura Academiei Republicii Populare Romîne, 1958.

Collectiune de tratatele si conventiunile Romaniei cu puterile straine de la annulŭ 1368 pânĕ în zilele nóstre. Comp. Mihail Mitilineu. Bucharest: Noua typographie a Laboratorilor Romăni, 1874.

Conventions de la Roumanie avec les états étrangères concernant le commerce et les marques de fabrique. Ed. Constantin Brăileanu. Bucharest: Carol Göbl, 1899.

Corivan, Nicolae. *Relaţiile diplomatice ale României de la 1859 la 1877.* Bucharest: Editura ştiinţifică şi enciclopedică, 1984.

Correspondance diplomatique roumaine sous le roi Charles Ier (1866–1880). Ed. Nicolae Iorga. Paris: Gamber, 1923.

Costin, Nicolae. "Tractaturile prin cari s'aŭ închinatŭ ţéra, de către Bogdanŭ Vv. Domnŭ alŭ Moldaviei̇̆, împĕrăţindŭ Sultan Baiazet II." In *Cronicele Romaniei seŭ Letopiseţele Moldaviei şi Valahiei,* edited by Mihail Kogălniceanu, 3:450–62. 2d ed. Bucharest: Imprimeria Naţională, 1874.

Cristea, Gheorghe. "La Guerre Franco-Allemande et le mouvement républicain de mars 1871 à Bucarest." *Revue roumaine d'histoire* 3, no. 2 (1964): 277–90.

———. "Manifestări antidinastice în perioada venirii lui Carol I în România (apriliemai 1866)." *Studii: Revistă de istorie* 20, no. 6 (1967): 1073–91.

Csucsuja, Ştefan. "Manifestări ale solidarităţii maselor populare maghiare cu războiul pentru independenţa României." *Revista de istorie* 30, no. 5 (May 1977): 811–27.

Desbaterile Adunărei Constituante din anul 1866 asupra Constituţiunei şi legei electorale din România. Ed. Alcxandru Pencovici. Bucharest: Tipografia Statului, 1883.

Diculescu, Vladimir. "Rumänien und die Frage der bulgarischen Freischaren (1866– 1868)." *Revue des études sud-est européennes* 1, nos. 3–4 (1963): 463–83.

Documente privind istoria Romîniei: Colecţia Eudoxiu de Hurmuzaki. New ser. Ed. Andrei Oţetea et al. Bucharest: Editura Academiei Republicii Populare Romîne, 1962–.

Documente privind istoria Romîniei: Răscoala din 1821. Ed. Andrei Oţetea et al. 5 vols. Bucharest: Editura Academiei Republicii Populare Romîne, 1959– 62.

Documente privind istoria Romîniei: Războiul pentru independenţă. Ed. Mihail Roller et al. 9 vols. in 10. Bucharest: Editura Academiei Republicii Populare Romîne, 1952–55. [Title varies.]

Documente privind unirea principatelor. Ed. Andrei Oţetea, vol. 3: *Corespondenţă politică (1855–1859),* ed. Cornelia C. Bodea. Bucharest: Editura Academiei Republicii Populare Romîne, 1963.

Documente privitóre la istoria Românilor. Comp. Eudoxiu de Hurmuzaki. Bucharest: Socecu & Teclu, 1876–1942. Vol. 17, *Corespondenţă diplomatică şi rapoarte consulare franceze (1825–1846).* Ed. Nerva Hodoş. Bucharest: Carol Göbl, 1913.

Dokumenti za istoriiata na bŭlgarskoto knizhovno druzhestvo v Braila, 1868–1876. Ed. Petŭr Miiatev and Georgi Dimov. Sofia: Izdatelstvo na Bŭlgarskata Akademiia na Naukite, 1958.

Eisenbahn-Jahrbuch der österreichisch-ungarischen Monarchie. New ser. Ed. Ignaz Kohn. 21 vols. Vienna: Lehmann & Wentzel, 1868–92.

Emerit, Marcel. *Madame Cornu et Napoléon III.* Paris: Les Presses modernes, 1937.

Engelhardt, Édouard. "La confédération balcanique." *Revue d'histoire diplomatique* 6 (1892): 29–55.

Ernst II von Sachsen-Coburg-Gotha. *Aus meinem Leben und aus meiner Zeit.* 3 vols. Berlin: W. Hertz, 1887–89.

France. Ministère des Affaires Étrangères. *Documents diplomatiques français (1871–1914).* 1st ser. (1871–1900). Vol. 1 (1871–75), 2 (1875–79), 3 (1880–81). Paris: Imprimerie nationale, 1927–31.

―――. *Documents diplomatiques: Negociation commerciale avec Roumanie, 1876–1885.* Paris: Imprimerie nationale, 1885.

―――. *Les origines diplomatiques de la Guerre de 1870–1871: Recueil de documents.* 29 vols. Paris: Imprimerie nationale, 1910–32.

Gane, Constantin. *P. P. Carp şi locul său în istoria politică a ţării.* 2 vols. 2d ed. Bucharest: Universul, 1936–37.

Gauld, William A. "The Anglo-Austrian Agreement of 1878." *English Historical Review* 41 (January 1926): 108–12.

Gazenkampf, Mikhail A. *Moi dnevnik, 1877–78 gg.* St. Petersburg: V. Berezovskii, 1908.

Georgescu-Buzău, Gheorghe. "Instaurarea şi organizarea regimului burghezo-moşieresc (1866)." In *Istoria Romîniei,* edited by Petre Constantinescu-Iaşi et al., 4:518–33. Bucharest: Editura Academiei Republicii Populare Romîne, 1964.

Germany. Reichsinstitut für Geschichte neuen Deutschlands. *Die auswärtige Politik Preußens: Diplomatische Aktenstücke, 1858–1871.* Ed. Christian Friese et al. Vol. 6 (1865–66), ed. Rudolf Ibbeken (1939); 8 (1866–67), ed. Herbert Michaelis (1934); 9 (1867–68), ed. Herbert Michaelis (1936); 10 (1868–69), ed. Herbert Michaelis (1939). Oldenburg: Gerhard Stalling.

Ghica, Ion. *Opere.* Ed. Ion Roman. 2 vols. Bucharest: Editura de stat pentru literatură şi artă, 1956.

Ghica, Ion G. *Corespondenţa generalului Iancu Ghica, 2 aprilie 1877–8 aprilie 1878.* Ed. Radu Rosetti. Bucharest: "Cartea Românească," 1930.

Giurescu, Constantin C. *Viaţa şi opera lui Cuza Vodă.* Bucharest: Editura ştiinţifică, 1966.

Great Britain. Foreign Office. *British and Foreign State Papers, 1812/14–1967/68.* Comp. Edward Hertslet et al. Vols. 57–71 (1866–80). London: William Ridgway, 1871–87.

———. *Correspondence respecting the Condition and Treatment of the Jews in Servia and Roumania, 1867–76.* London: Harrison, 1877.

———. *Correspondence respecting the Question of the Negotiation of Commercial Conventions by the Principalities.* London: Harrison, 1875.

———. *Further Correspondence respecting the Persecution of the Jews in Moldavia.* 3 vols. London: Harrison, 1867.

Grosul, Vladislav Ia., and Evgenii E. Chertan. *Rossiia i formirovanie rumynskogo nezavisimogo gosudarstva.* Moscow: Izdatel'stvo "Nauka," 1969.

La guerre d'Orient (1877–1878): Revue d'opérations militaires. Brussels: A. N. Lebègue, 1878.

Henry, Paul. *L'abdication du prince Cuza et l'avènement de la dynastie de Hohenzollern au trône de Roumanie: Documents diplomatiques.* Paris: Félix Alcan, 1930.

Hilke, Gerhard. "Russlands Haltung zur rumänischen Frage." *Wissenschaftliche Zeitschrift der Martin-Luther-Universität* [Halle], Gesellschafts- und sprachwissenschaftliche Reihe, 14, no. 4 (1965): 193–209.

Iancu, Carol. *Bleichröder et Crémieux: Le combat pour l'émancipation des Juifs en Roumanie devant le Congrès de Berlin—Correspondance inédite (1878–1880).* Montpellier: Université Paul Valéry, 1987.

———. *Les Juifs en Roumanie, 1866–1919: De l'exclusion à l'émancipation.* Aix-en-Provence: Éditions de l'Université de Provence, 1978.

Ignat'ev, Nikolai P. *Posle San Stefano: Zapiski grafa N. P. Ignat'eva.* Ed. Aleksandr A. Bashmakov. Petrograd [St. Petersburg]: A. S. Suvorin, 1916.

———. *San Stefano: Zapiski grafa N. P. Ignat'eva.* Ed. Aleksandr A. Bashmakov and K. A. Gubastov. Petrograd [St. Petersburg]: A. S. Suvorin, 1915.

Independenţa României: Documente. Ed. Ştefan Hurmuzache et al. 4 vols. in 5. Bucharest: Editura Academiei Republicii Socialiste România, 1977–78.

Îndreptarea Legii, 1652. Ed. Andrei Rădulescu et al. Bucharest: Editura Academiei Republicii Populare Romîne, 1962.

Ionescu, Dumitru P. "Construirea liniei ferate Iaşi-Ungheni." *Anuarul Institutului de istorie şi arheologie "A. D. Xenopol"* 23, no. 1 (1986): 283–91.

———. "Construirea liniei ferate Ploieşti-Predeal." *Revista de istorie* 39, no. 1 (January 1986): 86–95.

Iorga, Nicolae. *Istoria Românilor.* 10 vols. in 11. Bucharest: Datina Românească, 1936–39.

Istoriia Moldavskoi SSR. Ed. Lev V. Cherepnin et al. Vol. 1 (to 1917). Kishinev: "Karta Moldoveniaske," 1965.

Jakšić, Grgur, and Vojislav J. Vučković. *Spoljna politika Srbije za vlade kneza Mihaila: Prvi balkanski savez.* Belgrade: Izdaje Istorijski institut, 1963.

Jelavich, Barbara. *Russia and the Formation of the Romanian National State, 1821–1878.* Cambridge: Cambridge University Press, 1984.

Jelavich, Barbara. "Russia and Moldavian Separatism: The Demonstration of April, 1866." In *Rußland-Deutschland-Amerika: Festschrift für Fritz T. Epstein,* edited by Alexander Fischer et al., 73–87. Frankfurter historische Abhandlungen, vol. 17. Wiesbaden: Franz Steiner Verlag, 1978.

Jinga, Victor. *Principii şi orientări ale comerţului exterior al României (1859–1916).* Cluj-Napoca: Editura Dacia, 1975.

Joseph II und Katharina von Russland: Ihr Briefwechsel. Ed. Alfred von Arneth. Vienna: W. Braumüller, 1869.

Journal de St. Pétersbourg. St. Petersburg. 1825–1917.

Jovanović, Slobodan. *Druga vlada Miloša i Mihaila (1858–1868).* Belgrade: Izdavačka knjižara Gece Kona, 1923.

———. *Vlada Milana Obrenovića.* 2 vols. Belgrade: Izdavačka knjižarnica Gece Kona, 1926–27.

Karavelov, Liuben. *Sŭbrani sŭchineniia.* Ed. Tsveta Undzhieva et al. 9 vols. Sofia: Bŭlgarski pisatel, 1965–68.

Kellogg, Frederick. "The Bulgarian Revolutionary Movement in Romania, 1867–1868." In *Pŭrvi mezhdunaroden kongres po bŭlgaristika: Dokladi,* edited by Panteli Zarev et al. *Sotsialni i revoliutsionni dvizheniia v Bŭlgariia: Natsionalnoosvoboditni dvizheniia XV-XX vek,* edited by Misto Isusov et al., 1:312–24. Sofia: Bŭlgarska Akademiia na Naukite, 1982.

———. "Convenţia comercială din 1875: Un pas către independenţă?" *Studii: Revistă de istorie* 25, no. 5 (1972): 989–1003.

———. "The Structure of Romanian Nationalism." *Canadian Review of Studies in Nationalism* 11, no. 1 (1984): 21–50.

Khrestomatiia po istorii SSSR. Ed. Sergei S. Dmitriev et al. Vol. 3 (1857–94). Moscow: Gosudarstvennoe uchebno-pedagogicheskoe izdatel'stvo ministerstva prosveshcheniia RSFSR, 1948.

Kiriţescu, Costin C. *Sistemul bănesc al leului şi precursorii lui.* 2 vols. Bucharest: Editura Academiei Republicii Populare Romîne, 1964–67.

Kofos, Evangelos. "Greek-Romanian Attempts at Collaboration on the Eve of Romania's Independence." *Revue roumanie d'histoire* 16, no. 4 (October–December 1977): 619–29.

Kogălniceanu. *Mihail Kogălniceanu: Documente diplomatice.* Ed. George Macovescu. Bucharest: Editura politică, 1972.

Kogălniceanu, Mihail. *Opere.* Ed. Dan Simonescu. Vol. 4: *Oratorie II,* 1864–78. Ed. Georgeta Penelea. Pt. 1 (1864–68), pt. 2 (1868–70), pt. 3 (1870–74), pt. 4 (1874–78). Vol. 5: *Oratorie III,* 1878–91 (1984–). Ed. G. Penelea. Pt. 1 (1878–80). Bucharest: Editura Academiei Republicii Socialiste România, 1977–.

Kosev, Dimitŭr. *Kŭm istoriiata na revoliutsionnoto dvizhenie v Bŭlgariia prez 1867–1871.* Sofia: Izdatelstvo na Bŭlgarskata Akademiia na Naukite, 1958.

La Marmora, Alfonso. *Un po' più di luce sugli eventi politici e militari dell'anno 1866.* 2d ed. Florence: G. Barbèra, 1878.

Legiuirea Caragea. Ed. Andrei Rădulescu et al. Bucharest: Editura Academiei Republicii Populare Romîne, 1955.

Liluashvili, Kukuri S. *Natsional'no-osvoboditel'naia bor'ba bolgarskogo naroda protiv fanariotskogo iga i Rossiia*. Tbilisi: Izdatel'stvo Tbilisskogo universiteta, 1978.

Loeb, Isidore. *La situation des israélites en Turquie, en Serbie et en Roumanie*. Paris: J. Baer, 1877.

Loftus. *The Diplomatic Reminiscences of Lord Augustus Loftus, 1862–1879*. 2 vols. London: Cassel, 1894.

Maciu, Vasile. "Dezvoltarea capitalismului în Romînia între 1864 şi 1878." In *Istoria Romîniei*, edited by Petre Constantinescu-Iaşi et al., 4:442–81. Bucharest: Editura Academiei Republicii Populare Romîne, 1964.

MacKenzie, David. *The Serbs and Russian Pan-Slavism, 1875–1878*. Ithaca, N.Y.: Cornell University Press, 1967.

Maier, Aurel. "Drumurile şi transportul rutier." In *Geografia României*, 2:428–36. Bucharest: Editura Academiei Republicii Socialiste România, 1984.

Maier, Lothar. "Die innen- und aussenpolitischen Auseinandersetzungen um die Gründung der 'Rumänischen Eisenbahngesellschaft' 1871–1872." *Anuarul Institutului de istorie şi arheologie "A. D. Xenopol"* 23, no. 2 (1986): 491–511.

———. *Rumänien auf dem Weg zur Unabhängigkeitserklärung, 1866–1877: Schein und Wirklichkeit liberaler Verfassung und staatlicher Souveränität*. Munich: R. Oldenbourg, 1989.

Maiorescu, Titu. *Discursuri parlamentare cu privire asupra desvoltării politice a României sub Domnia Carol I*. Vols. 1 (1866–76), 2 (1876–81). Bucharest: Editura Librăriei Socecu, 1897.

———. *Istoria contimporană a României (1866–1900)*. Bucharest: Socec, 1925.

Maiorescu. *Titu Maiorescu: Critice*. Ed. Domnica Filimon-Stoicescu. 2 vols. Bucharest: Editura pentru literatură, 1967.

Manu, George. *Discursurile generalului G. Manu (1871–1906)*. Ed. Badea M. Mangâru. Bucharest: F. Göbl, 1906.

The Map of Europe by Treaty: Showing the Various Political and Territorial Changes Which Have Taken Place since the General Peace of 1814. Comp. Edward Hertslet. Vols. 3 (1864–75), 4 (1875–91). London: Butterworths, 1875, 1891.

Miclea, Ion. *Dulce Bucovina*. Bucharest: Editura Sport-Turism, 1976.

Mihordea, Vasile. *Răscoala grănicerilor de la 1866*. Bucharest: Editura Academiei Republicii Populare Romîne, 1958.

Miliutin, Dmitrii A. *Dnevnik D. A. Miliutina*. Ed. Pëtr A. Zaionchkovskii. Vols. 1 (1873–75), 2 (1876–77), 3 (1878–80). Moscow: Gosudarstvennaia Ordena Lenina Biblioteka SSSR, 1947–50.

Mosse, Werner E. *The European Powers and the German Question 1848–71, with Special Reference to England and Russia*. 1958. Reprint, New York: Octagon Books, 1969.

———. *The Rise and Fall of the Crimean System, 1855–71: The Story of a Peace Settlement*. London: Macmillan, 1963.

Napoléon III et le Prince Napoléon: Correspondance inédite. Comp. Ernest d'Hauterive. Paris: Calmann-Lévy, 1925.

Napoléon, Prince. *Discours prononcé par Son Altesse Impériale le Prince Napoléon le 15 mai 1865 pour l'inauguration du monument élevé dans la ville d'Ajaccio à Napoléon Ier et à ses frères.* Paris: E. Dentu, 1865.

Nelidow, Alexandre de. [Aleksandr I. Nelidov]. "Souveniers d'avant et d'après la guerre de 1877–1878." *Revue des deux mondes* 28 (15 July 1915): 241–77.

Netea, Vasile. "Viena." In *Reprezentanţele diplomatice ale României,* 1:155–86. Bucharest: Editura politică, 1967.

Neue Freie Presse. Vienna. 1864–1939.

Nishkov, Traian Ionesku. "Za otnoshenieto na rumŭnskata obshtestvenost kŭm bŭlgarskoto natsionalnoosvoboditelno dvizhenie prez 70-te godini na XIX v." In *Bŭlgaro-rumŭnski vruzki i otnosheniia prez vekovete: Izsledvaniia,* 1:373–404. Sofia: Izdatelstvo na Bŭlgarskata Akademiia na Naukite, 1965.

Nouveau recueil général de traités et autres actes relatifs aux rapports de droit international. Founder: Georg F. de Martens. 2d series. Ed. Charles Samwer and Jules Hopf. 35 vols. Göttingen: Librairie de Dieterich, 1876–1908.

Ollivier, Émile. *L'empire libéral: Études, récits, souvenirs.* 18 vols. Paris: Garnier Frères, 1895–1918.

Oncken, Hermann. *Die Rheinpolitik Kaiser Napoleons III von 1863 bis 1870 und der Ursprung des Krieges von 1870/71.* 3 vols. Stuttgart: Deutsche Verlags Anstalt, 1926.

Osvobozhdenie Bolgarii ot turetskogo iga: Dokumenty. Ed. Sergei A. Nikitin. 3 vols. Vol. 1 (1875–77), 2 (1877–78), 3 (1878–79). Moscow: Izdatel'stvo Akademii Nauk SSSR, 1961–67.

Păcurariu, Mircea. *Istoria bisericii ortodoxe române.* 3 vols. Bucharest: Editura Institutului biblic şi de misiune al bisericii ortodoxe române, 1980–81.

Panaitescu, Petre P. "Urcarea în scaun a principelui Carol de Hohenzollern." *Revista Fundaţiilor Regale* 6 (1 May 1939): 249–67.

Passamonti, Eugenio. "Constantino Nigra ed Alfonso Lamarmora dal 1862–1866." *Risorgimento italiana* 22 (1929): 323–468.

Petrescu-Comnen, Nicolae. *Étude sur la condition des Israélites en Roumanie.* Paris: A. Pédone, 1905.

Phōteinos, Dionysios. *Historia tēs palai Dakias, ta nyn Transilvanias, Vlachias kai Moldauias.* 3 vols. Vienna: Hiōannēs Bartholomaios Sbechios, 1818–19.

Picot. "Correspondance d'un secrétaire princier en Roumanie: Émile Picot." In *Mélanges de l'école roumaine en France,* edited by Nicolae Georgescu-Tistu, part 1, 101–215. Paris: Gamber, 1926.

Pizzala, Josef. "Der Export Österreich-Ungarns nach Rumänien." *Statistische Monatschrift* 9 (1883): 98–99.

———. "Die österreichisch-ungarische Handelsbilanz für das Jahr 1877." *Statistische Monatschrift* 5 (1879): 22–26.

Platon, Gheorghe. "Le diplomate belge Édouard Blondeel van Cuelebroeck dans les Principautés roumaines (1856–1857)." *Revue roumaine d'histoire* 16, no. 1 (January–March 1977): 43–66.

Popescu-Spineni, Marin. *Procesul mănăstirilor închinate: Contribuţii la istoria socială românească.* Bucharest: Institutul de arte grafice "Tiparul Universitar," 1936.

Posener, Solomon. *Adolphe Crémieux (1796–1880)*. 2 vols. Paris: Félix Alcan, 1933–34.

Presse. Bucharest. 1868–81.

Publicaţiunile periodice româneşti: Ziare, gazete, reviste. Ed. Nerva Hodoş et al. 3 vols. (1820–1924). Bucharest: Socec, 1913–87.

Radowitz, Joseph M. von. *Aufzeichnungen und Erinnerungen aus dem Leben des Botschafters Joseph Maria von Radowitz.* Ed. Hajo Holborn. 2 vols. 1925. Reprint, Osnabrück: Biblio-Verlag, 1967.

Războiul pentru independenţă naţională, 1877–1878: Documente militare. Ed. Dan Berindei et al. Bucharest: Editura militară, 1971.

Recueil d'actes internationaux de l'Empire Ottoman. Comp. Gabriel Noradounghian. 4 vols. Vol. 1 (1300–1789), 2 (1789–1856), 3 (1856–78), 4 (1878–1902). Paris: Librairie Cotillon, 1897–1903.

Reformele Romanilor, séu Collecţiune de toate legile şi regulamentele intrudusse in administraţiunea Romanieĭ dela 1859 ianuariŭ, pină la 1864 octomvriŭ. Ed. Ioan Brezoianu. Bucharest: Socecu, 1864.

Reglementul Organik a Prinţipatului Moldovei. Iaşi: Institutul Albinei, 1846.

Regulamentul Organik. Bucharest: n. p., 1832.

Relaţiile internaţionale ale României în documente (1368–1900). Ed. Ion Ionaşcu et al. Bucharest: Editura politică, 1971.

Riker, Thad W. *The Making of Roumania: A Study of an International Problem, 1856–1866.* London: Oxford University Press, 1931.

Romania. Ministeriu de Interne. Oficiu Central de Statistică. *Statistica din Romania— Comerciul exterior: Import şi export pe anu 1874.* Bucharest: Tipografia Statului, 1877.

Romania. Ministerul de Interne a Moldoviei. Direcţia Centrală de Statistica. *Lucrări statistice făcute în aniĭ 1859–1860,* vol. 2: *Analele statistice alle Moldav pe anu 1859 şi 60,* 29–208. Iaşi: Adolf Bermann, 1862.

Romania. Ministerul Financelor. Direcţiunea Vămilor, Timbrului şi Inregistrărei: Biuroul statisticei comerciului exterior. *Tablou general indicând comerciul României cu Terile straine in anul 1883.* Bucharest: Tipografia Statului, 1884.

Romania. *Monitorul oficiale al României.* Bucharest. 1862–1949. Title varies.

Romanulu. Bucharest. 1857–1905. Title varies.

Rossiia i natsional'no-osvoboditel'naia bor'ba na Balkanakh, 1875–1878. Ed. Aleksei L. Narochnitskii. Moscow: Izdatel'stvo "Nauka," 1978.

Russell. *The Later Correspondence of Lord John Russell, 1840–1878.* Ed. George P. Gooch. 2 vols. New York: Longmans, Green, 1925.

Russia. Ministerstvo finansov. *Obzor vneshnei torgovli Rossii po evropeiskoi i aziatskoi granitsam za 1874 god.* St. Petersburg: Tipografiia Maikova, [1875].

———. *Obzor vneshnei torgovli Rossii po evropeiskoi i aziatskoi granitsam za 1881 god.* St. Petersburg: V. Kirshbaum, 1882.

Savich, Angelaki. *Insurgenţii bulgari della 1868 sub commanda lui Hagi Dumitru şi Stefan Caradge.* Brăila: Tipographia Triangolulu, 1871.

Sbornik materialov po russko-turetskoi voine 1877–1878 gg. na Balkanskom poluostrove. 97 vols. in 111. St. Petersburg: Izdanie voenno-istoricheskoi komisii glavnogo shtaba, 1898–1911.

Sbornik turetskikh dokumentov o poslednei voine. Translated from the Turkish "Zubdetul Khakaik." Comp. Akhmed Midkhat Efendi. St. Petersburg: V. A. Poletika, 1879.

Sedes, İbrahim Halil. *1875–1878 Osmanlı ordusu savaşları: 1877–1878 Osmanlı-Rus ve Roman savaşı.* 11 vols. Istanbul: Askerî Matbaa, 1935–52.

Shaguna, Andreiu de. [Andrei Şaguna]. *Istoria biserichei ortodokse rŭsŭritene universale dela întemeierea ei pănă în zilele noastre.* 2 vols. Sibiu: Tipografia diechesan, 1860.

Sharova, Krumka. *Liuben Karavelov i bŭlgarskoto osvoboditelno dvizhenie, 1860–1867.* Sofia: Nauka i izkustvo, 1970.

Sidel'nikov, Stepan I. *Bolgarskii revoliutsionnyi tsentral'nyi komitet (1868–1872 gg.).* Kharkov: Izdatel'stvo Khar'kovskogo universiteta, 1970.

Siruni, Hagop Dj. *Domnii Români la Poarta Otomană.* Bucharest: Imprimeria Naţională, 1941.

Solcanu, Ion. "Realizări artistice." In *Petru Rareş,* edited by Leon Şimanschi, 292–318. Bucharest: Editura Academiei Republicii Socialiste România, 1978.

Soutzo, Nicolas. [Nicolae Suţu]. *Quelques observations sur la statistique de la Roumanie.* N.p: n.p., 1867.

Stan, Apostol. *Grupări şi curente politice în România între unire şi independenţă (1859–1877).* Bucharest: Editura ştiinţifică şi enciclopedică, 1979.

Statutele Uniunei Israelite din Jassi. Iaşi: Buciumul Roman, 1864.

Statutes: Articles of Association of the Roumanian Railways' Share Company. London: Office of the Council of Foreign Bondholders, 1872.

Stavrianos, Leften S. "Balkan Federation: A History of the Movement toward Balkan Unity in Modern Times." *Smith College Studies in History* 27, nos. 1–4 (October 1941–July 1942).

Stern, Fritz. *Gold and Iron: Bismarck, Bleichröder, and the Building of the German Empire.* New York: Alfred A. Knopf, 1977.

Stoianov, Zakhari. *Chetite v Bŭlgariia na Filip Totia, Khadzhi Dimitra i Stefan Karadzhata (1867–1868).* Plovdiv: Oblastva pechatnitsa, 1885.

Stoianov-Simidov, Filip. *Prochutiia Filip Totiu Voivoda.* 2 vols. Ruse: D. M. Drobniak, 1900.

Strousberg, Bethel H. *Dr. Strousberg und sein Wirken von ihm selbst geschildert.* Berlin: J. Guttentag, 1876.

Sumner, Benedict H. *Russia and the Balkans, 1870–1880.* Oxford: Clarendon Press, 1937.

Talleyrand. *Lettres inédites de Talleyrand à Napoléon, 1800–1809.* Ed. Pierre Bertrand. 2d ed. Paris: Perrin, 1889.

Teplov, Vladimir A. *Materialy dlia statistiki Bolgarii, Frakii i Makedonii.* St. Petersburg: A. Transhel, 1877.

Tractate, conventiuni şi invoiri internationale ale Romaniei actualmente in vigóre. Comp. Trandafir G. Djuvara. Bucharest: Al. Degenmann, 1888.

United States of America. House of Representatives. Executive Documents, 1866–67. 39th Congress, 2d session. Vol. 1, no. 1, pt. 2 [Diplomatic]: *Message of the President of the United States and Accompanying Documents.* Washington, D.C.: Government Printing Office, 1867.

————. Executive Documents, 1872–73. 42nd Congress, 3d session. Vol. 1, no. 1, pt. 1 [Foreign Relations]: *Papers relating to the Foreign Relations of the United States . . . with the Annual Message of the President, December 2, 1872.* Washington, D.C.: Government Printing Office, 1873.

Urmă, Demetru. "Un act istoric: Trecerea liniilor ferate sub o conducere unică." In *Epopeea feroviară românească,* by Constantin Botez et al., 113–34. Bucharest: Editura Sport-Turism, 1977.

Velichi, Constantin N. "C. A. Rosetti şi 'Comunitatea Bulgară.'" In *Omagiu lui P. Constantinescu-Iaşi,* 527–32. Bucharest: Editura Academiei Republicii Populare Romîne, 1965.

————. "Relaţiile romîno-turce în perioada februarie-iulie 1866." *Studii: Revistă de istorie* 16, no. 4 (1963): 843–65.

————. *La Roumanie et la mouvement révolutionnaire bulgare de libération nationale (1850–1878).* Bucharest: Editura Academiei Republicii Socialiste România, 1979.

Verax. [Radu D. Rosetti]. *La Roumanie et les Juifs.* Bucharest: Socecu, 1903.

Vinogradov, Viktor I. *Russko-turetskaia voina 1877–1878 gg. i osvobozhdenie Bolgarii.* Moscow: "Mysl," 1978.

Vitte, Sergei Iu. *Vospominaniia.* 3 vols. Moscow: Izdatel'stvo sotsialno-ekonomicheskoi literatury, 1960.

Din vremea renaşterii naţionale a Ţării Româneşti: Boieri Goleşti. Ed. George Fotino. 4 vols. Bucharest: Imprimeria Naţională, 1939.

Vocea nationala. Iaşi. 1866.

Xenopol, Alexandru D. *Domnia lui Cuza-Vodă.* 2 vols. Iaşi: Tipografia Editóre "Dacia," 1903.

————. *Resboaele d'intre Ruşi şi Turci şi inriurirea lor asupra ţerilor române.* 2 vols. Iaşi: H. Goldner, 1880.

Zaimov, Stoian. *Minaloto: Ocherki i spomeni iz deiatelnostta na bŭlgarskite taini revoliutsionni komiteti ot 1869–1877 god.* 3 vols. 2d ed. Plovdiv: Khr. G. Danov, 1898–99.

Zalyshkin, Mikhail M. *Vneshniaia politika Rumynii i rumyno-russkie otnosheniia, 1875–1878.* Moscow: Izdatel'stvo "Nauka," 1974.

Zane, Gheorghe. "Die österreichischen und die deutschen Wirtschaftsbeziehungen zu den rumänischen Fürstentümern, 1774–1874." *Weltwirtschaftliches Archiv* 26 (October 1927): 30–47, 262–81.

Zhechev, Nikolai. *Braila i bŭlgarskoto kulturno-natsionalno vŭzrazhdane.* Sofia: Izdatelstvo na Bŭlgarskata Akademiia na Naukite, 1970.

Index

Steege, Ludovic (1813–72), 41–42, 77
Ştirbei, Gheorghe (1832–1925), 28–29, 41, 94
Stolojan, Anastasie (1836–1901), 167
Strat, Ion D. (1836–79), 44–45
Strousberg, Bethel H., 72, 75–82, 87n. 46, 89n. 79, 90n. 90, 171
Stuart, Dmitrii F., 133n. 77, 149, 191, 202
Sturdza, Dimitrie A. (1833–1914), 13, 49–50, 76, 80, 154, 184, 197n. 95, 207, 211–14
Suczawa-Iaşi-Roman-Botoşani railway, 72
Suleiman Bey, 206, 221n. 79
Suţu, Nicolae, 193n. 12
Svoboda, 116, 122
Switzerland, 105
Szlávy, József, 94, 96

T

Talleyrand-Périgord, Charles-Maurice de, 15
Tariffs, 93, 96–98, 100. *See also* Foreign trade
Tecuci, 53
Temesvár, 85n. 14
Three Emperors, League of, 95–96, 126, 136, 182
Timok River, 124
Timpul, 145, 154
Tîrgu Ocna salt mines, 72
Tisza, Kálmán, 74, 170, 189
Totiu, Filip, 116–18, 130n. 26
Transleithania. *See* Hungary
Transylvania, 1–2, 4, 9, 22, 25, 27, 71–72, 100–101, 137, 170, 216
Transylvania-Moldavia railway, 73
Transylvania-Muntenia railway, 73–74
Treaties: Adrianople, 5, 106n. 3, 184; Belgrade, 4; Berlin, 191–92, 201–2, 205, 207, 210, 215—*see also* Congress of Berlin; Bucharest (1812), 5; Bucharest (1868), 114; Cetinje, 114, 129n. 10; Cobden-Chevallier, 94; Hünkâr İskelesi, 5;

Iaşi, 5, 183; Karlowitz, 3; Küçük Kaynarca, 5, 183; London (1878), 111n. 59; London (1880), 111n. 59; Münchengrätz, 5; Paris, 9, 17–18, 30, 51, 80, 94, 109n. 31, 117, 122, 151, 182, 187; Passarowitz, 4; San Stefano, 185–88, 190, 199, 203–4; Serbo-Romanian, 115; Voeslau, 114, 129n. 12
Trikoupis, Kharilaos, 113, 166
Tulcea, 26
Turkey: Balkan Crisis, 115, 118, 143; Bulgaria, 118; Carol I, 28–29, 39; consular jurisdiction, 39; Danube River, 153; Danubian Romania, 1–4, 18, 26–27; foreign trade, 39, 92, 96, 99; Jewish question, 54; Phanariots, 9; Russo-Turkish peace—*see* Russo-Turkish peace; Russo-Turkish war—*see* Russo-Turkish war; Serbo-Turkish war, 123–26, 128, 140–41; South Slavs, 137. *See also* Ottoman Empire
Türr, István, 36n. 79

U

Ungeny, 69
Uniate Church, 1, 3–4
United Principalities of Moldo-Wallachia, 12, 16–17, 20, 24, 27–28, 42. *See also* Moldavia; Wallachia

V

Văcărescu, Teodor (1842–1914), 76–77
Varna, 68
Venetia, 16–17, 19, 24
Vernescu, George (1830–1900), 122–24
Vidin, 175, 183, 186, 194n. 36
Vienna: battle of (1529), 3; battle of (1683), 3; convention of (1868), 73; convention of (1875), 94, 96–98, 101–3
Vîlcov, 54
Vinberg, Viktor F., 201–2
Vîrciorova, 71, 74, 123